REAL ESTATE ANALYSIS

Real Estate Analysis

RICHARD U. RATCLIFF

Professor of Land Economics
University of Wisconsin

McGRAW-HILL BOOK COMPANY, INC.

New York   Toronto   London

1961

REAL ESTATE ANALYSIS

51197

PREFACE

This book was written from a definite point of view. It is specifically designed as a basic statement for professional training and for professional service in the solution of real estate problems. Almost all real estate problems involve an investment decision—whether to buy and what to buy, whether to sell and at what price, whether to modernize or replace, whether to lend and how much to lend under what terms. Professional analysis is the evaluation of the complex factors which determine real estate productivity and value. Professional service is the guidance of the client to a sound real estate investment decision. From this point of view, therefore, we need a text which is designed to provide the understanding on which professional skill can be built and which is organized around the process of real estate investment analysis as the essence of professional service. We should become lost in the textbook which is simply a formless compendium of real estate information. The book which focuses on the real estate transaction and the legal rights of the parties has its place, as does the volume which emphasizes the operations of the real estate business. But neither one is suitable for the purposes of professional training. A general statement on the economics of land, such as my 1949 book *Urban Land Economics*, is not sufficiently pointed to the process of investment analysis.

On what logical framework, then, can one build a first book for professional training in real estate? The clue lies in the focus, already identified, on the real estate investment decision. Here, in the decision and in the investment transaction which ensues, is the critical act in the processes of urban development. This transaction is the generating force in urban growth and change; it is the determinant of land use and thus builds the urban structure. To the extent that we understand the true nature of the investment decision, we will perceive the essential character of urban growth. Because the city is an organism the productivity of every parcel is strongly affected by what is happening to other parcels. Therefore, investment analysis, in large part, is the forecasting of urban growth and change.

This book is fashioned about a hypothesis of city growth which is termed the "investment theory." Necessarily, there is much description, but it has been selected to illuminate the considerations involved in productivity analysis. There is ample recognition of the institutional factors which condition investment decisions. The book is short and designed for digestion by the beginning student in one semester. For the practitioner it will serve as a framework on which he can hang, in orderly array, the knowledge gained from experience and one in which he may find insights which give new direction to his professional efforts.

This foreword must eschew the usual bows to those persons who gave scholarly aid and comfort to the author. The book was written in the solitude of my study, and few persons other than my students and my colleague, Prof. Richard B. Andrews, have read the manuscript. Of course the contributors are legion, for there are few books which are much more than restatements of the heritage of the past. It is a matter for some uneasiness that I may have borrowed straightaway without due credit. May the victims be charitable, for the oversight is inadvertent. A well-deserved special mention has been earned by my wife, Dorothy B. Ratcliff, for skillful editorial and typing assistance.

During recent months, I have been sure that I could never face another writing chore, but I have come to recognize that this book must soon be revised. On its framework there will be new materials to be hung. And at many points, no doubt, there will be need for clarification and expansion which more classroom use will reveal and which, hopefully, will be suggested by teachers and practitioners who may read and use the present volume.

Richard U. Ratcliff

CONTENTS

I

INTRODUCTION

THE NATURE OF URBAN REAL ESTATE

In a very real sense, we urbanites live in a world of real estate—and since urbanites outnumber farmers about 9 to 1, the majority of the nation's men, women, and children are constantly exposed to the city's unique mixture of land, buildings, vegetation, vehicles, and streets. Except for the atmosphere, which nature provides and man pollutes, and the man-made movables such as furniture, clothes, and machines, our physical environment is largely real estate—the land and those things which are permanently attached to the land. The implications of this encompassment of urban man by real estate are enormous.

We are so accustomed to this world of real estate in which we live that we take it for granted. We whiz past a landscape of large, complex, and expensive structures while riding in a car on a costly pavement laid over a maze of pipes and wires without a thought of the stupendous cumulative effort which has gone into providing these essentials of modern civilization. Some $750 billion is tied up in privately owned urban real estate in this country, $570 billion representing the owners' interest and $180 billion the claims of mortgage lenders. Each year we add about $50 billion to this wealth in the form of new construction through the agency of one of the nation's largest industries which employs directly or indirectly 6 million or more workers, and which is a keystone support of the national economy.

Urban real estate is a complex commodity. In the first place, it is a manufactured product. The original gift of nature, the surface of the earth which gives support and provides space for the activities of the city dweller, is extensively modified and processed before it can be put to use for urban purposes. The land is only one of many components. It may have to be leveled off if it is hilly, or filled if it is marshy. It is no use to anyone if it is not accessible, and so we construct streets and sidewalks. That man's activities will not be flooded out when it rains or when the

1

snow melts, we put curbs and gutters along the streets and install miles of underground storm-water sewers. Tens of thousands of people could not live and work so closely packed if there were not a central source of pure water in ample supply. We therefore require a complex distribution system of pumps and buried pipes with hydrants for the fire fighters who stand off the holocausts which periodically wiped out ancient cities. And we should die like flies before the onslaught of disease but for the costly and efficient waste disposal facilities of sanitary sewer laterals, mains, interceptors, and disposal plants. In addition to these community installations, each tract or parcel of land is processed and improved in accordance with its intended use. A golf course calls for modifying the natural terrain with tees, sand traps, and putting greens. Home sites must be graded and landscaped, provided with drives and walks, and connected by pipes and wires to public services. All this is necessary so that the dwelling structure, which is to become one with the land, may be usable as a family home. Sites for factories, stores, office buildings, and courthouses require land preparation together with a wedding of the processed site and the primary structure in more or less permanent harmony. Like many another complex manufactured product, urban real estate nourishes its users with a flow of services which is the joint and indivisible product of highly diverse component parts and materials.

Long and tortuous is the process of creating or producing usable urban real estate. Much of this book is to be devoted to revealing and analyzing this process, the major participants, and the organization devoted to the procedures of land development, construction, financing and investment, marketing and managing, and finally, the exercise of public regulations and controls. We shall concern ourselves with the problems and decisions which face the individuals and agencies who participate in the various steps in this city-building sequence of creating usable and productive urban real estate.

We shall be studying a variety of problems related to this complex physical product and to the devious process of investment and production. Many of these problems relate to a unique characteristic of real estate, i.e., that it is valuable in large degree because it is the focus of a complex set of space relationships popularly called *location*. And to complicate things still further, these space relationships are constantly, if slowly, changing as the result of whole groups of economic, social, political, and technological factors.

Our commodity, real estate, is an economic good which is a physical object in a physical and social community environment. But the buying and selling of real estate is a trading in legal rights in the physical property object. Ownership is no simple concept; there are many forms and combinations of legal rights to benefits or possession of real property, and all are traded in the real estate market—fee-simple estate, tenancy in common, easements, estate for years, remainder, lien, and many more. Each set of rights has its special and particular meaning which defines the benefits and obligations of the holder and thereby sets economic value. The interpretation of these rights and the painful technicalities of transfer from one person to another—buyer to seller, landlord to tenant, mortgagor to mortgagee—are subject matter for the complex study of real estate law. In this volume, we can hope only to imbue the reader with a healthy respect for legal problems, a working knowledge of basic legal concepts and processes, and a firm determination to call in a lawyer before costly mistakes are made.

The long useful life of improved real estate, i.e., land combined with utilities and structures, makes for further complications. It is not unusual for a dwelling house to continue in use for a hundred years or more. Commercial buildings may last fifty to seventy-five years, and in other countries public buildings centuries old are still in operation. Thus decisions on real estate matters usually have a long time dimension; they call for forecasting and predicting into a far distant future which is sure to bring social and economic change of a kind which influences real estate productivity and value. For example, the large houses built for well-to-do families toward the end of the last century, with a stable in the rear; a porte-cochere; gingerbread decorations; two parlors, a library, and a dining room on the first floor; and two stories of bedrooms have seen some mighty changes during their lifetime. The three-generation families which occupied them are a rarity today. The servants needed to maintain them are unavailable, architectural tastes have been revolutionized, and the horse has been replaced by two or three cars. The neighborhood which once bore an aura of social prestige has been invaded by rooming houses, clinics, and heavy traffic; it is no longer suited to quiet family life.

CITY-BUILDING REAL ESTATE DECISIONS

Now in spite of all these complications—physical, locational, legal, temporal—individuals, business organizations, and public agencies are constantly making decisions about real estate. Each year more than 4 million families decide to purchase a home, and do so. There are countless real estate problems faced by businesses which must be resolved by decision and action. Investors and speculators are continually committing large amounts of capital on reliance of their own analytical ability and perspicacity. Public agencies of all sorts exercise all manner of administrative control over real estate or carry out legislative mandates to manipulate the real estate or mortgage markets, presumably in the public interest. It is clear enough that each individual or business has a large financial stake in

the wisdom of his real estate decisions; real estate comes in large denominations and mistakes are very costly indeed. The public bears the brunt of
the mistakes of public officials and public agencies.

Our cities are built lot by lot, parcel by parcel, through the decisions
and actions of investors and developers operating within a framework of
law and regulation, and guided and abetted by the policies and programs
of public agencies which are responsible for land use planning and the
provision of streets and public services and facilities. The public stake in
the wisdom of each one of these decisions, public and private, is high, for
in the aggregate they build a good city or a poor one. A major objective
of this book is to provide a basis of understanding of real estate problems
so that wise decisions can be made to the benefit of the individual and of
the community. Our economic system is so ordered that the individual
investor or developer prospers most who serves the community best; for
the most part, what benefits the community benefits the individual in the
long run. The temptations of short-run exploitation by individuals are
rather well inhibited by public controls such as zoning and building codes
which constrain the entrepreneur to do that which, in the long run, is
in his own best interests.

TYPICAL REAL ESTATE PROBLEMS

In order that the generalizations which have been made in the foregoing
paragraphs may come to life, it will be well to illustrate the kinds of real
estate problems which are encountered in this urban world, and which
call for decision and action. We shall see that most of the critical real
estate decisions which confront families, professional real estate operators,
bankers, and businesses are, broadly speaking, investment decisions which
call for predictions of productivity or value. Closely related are the problems of production and marketing. Investment, of course, includes the
original commitment of capital by owner and by lender, the management
of the investment to maximize productivity, and dis-investment or liquidation. Real estate decisions which face public agencies are also largely related to investment. But these are social investments, for the benefit of the
entire community, or an important segment of it, rather than for the
benefit of an individual or a corporation.

Family Real Estate Problems

From the time the young couple sets up housekeeping it is beset with
an ever-changing succession of shelter problems. The small print in the
first apartment lease raises doubts as to the rights and liabilities of a tenant
and the responsibilities of the landlord. Just the matter of picking the
right location and selecting a dwelling unit which will return the max-

imum per dollar in comfort, quiet, and satisfaction involves choices which call for knowledge of real estate productivity and its origins.

When inevitably the urge for a home of one's own becomes irresistible, the young couple, now blessed with two or three little ones, faces an awesome array of decisions. How expensive a home can we afford? What is a good location where the investment value will be best protected? How can one tell if a house is well constructed? Where do we go to shop for a home? Shall we use a broker and will his commission mean that our house will cost more? How do we tell whether $17,500 is too high a price for this home? Do we need a lawyer, an appraiser, a surveyor? How can we stretch our $2,500 down payment in order to have the home we want and need? Where and how can we secure the best mortgage financing? These points of decision are just a few examples of problems of home buying and financing. They are repeated when the family expands into another and larger home and there are the accompanying problems of selling or trading the original house.

Mortgage Lending

The mortgage lender—bank, savings and loan association, life insurance company—is a participant in almost every real estate transaction. His problem in each case is to decide how large a loan, and under what terms of repayment, would constitute a safe and profitable investment. If the property is an income property such as an apartment house, he must study its rent-producing potential and its operating costs and, in light of his forecast of trends in the local real estate market, determine how large a loan it can safely carry. The mortgage banker's evaluation of a loan to a homeowner includes important non-real estate considerations such as the income level and stability of the borrower and his credit standing, and also the probable future pattern of the market value of the collateral real estate. Should the borrower fall into hopeless default, the lender has recourse to foreclosure and the sale of the property to pay the debt. Thus he must assure himself that the sale value of the house will be sufficient at all times to cover the remaining mortgage investment.

The Real Estate Developer and Builder

The land developer and the speculative, operative, or merchant home builder sometimes operate as separate enterprises, sometimes combined into one. In any case, his financial future depends on the ability to analyze the real estate market and come out with the right decisions. The tract builder has the problem of purchasing raw land or acreage in the right location. He must design his product to supply an effective market demand in terms of size of house, price class, equipment, and architectural style. He must decide on a production volume which can be absorbed before his profits are eaten up in carrying costs on unsold inventory. He must outguess the turns in the local real estate market and foresee the effects on his sales and profits of governmental manipulations of the flow of mortgage investment funds.

Entrepreneur-Investor

The real estate investor seeks a regular return on his capital or a capital gain. In a relatively simple case, he may consider the purchase of an existing apartment building. His analysis of the investment potential of the property focuses on the development of one value figure—the amount of capital which he feels justified in investing. To make this decision, many analytical problems confront him. What will the property produce in net income and for how long? What would it cost to build a similar apartment building in a similar location? What risks and uncertainties are involved? How much of a mortgage loan can be secured, and on what terms of interest and repayment schedule? What are the probabilities of a rising or falling real estate market? What management policies will maximize net return?

The shopping-center promoter is faced with the highly complex and crucial measurement of the retail sales potential of a given site. The size and nature of the center, its buildings and parking areas, derive from this estimate. What is the trade area of the location? How many families are there, with what income, and how do they spent it? Are there now, or will there be, competing retail clusters near this site? In light of such existing and potential competition, how many dollars' worth of each kind of goods can be sold at the subject site? On this final estimate depends the size of the center, its composition, and the rental income which can be extracted from tenants. On the nature of merchant-tenants who sign up for space and the terms of their leases depends the willingness of the large insurance companies to lend the necessary capital. There are basic differences of opinion on shopping-center design, for example, as between the mall type and the strip type, but our promoter must decide on one or the other. When the project is in operation, its profitability will depend on enlightened management policies or perhaps, in part, on the promoter's ability to keep real property tax assessments at a reasonable level.

Business Real Estate

Every type of business enterprise has its real estate problems, for each one requires space and shelter, and each is either an owner of real estate or a tenant. In some lines, retailing for example, the location of the store is a prime determinant of its success or failure. Unfavorable lease terms may cause disaster. In general, it is to the advantage of both landlord and tenant to fill a given space with that type of outlet which can best exploit the location. The landlord then, must choose among tenants, and the tenant among locations.

Service activities also prosper in proportion to their convenience to clients. The noticeable trend toward outlying locations for doctors and dentists testifies to this fact. The location of industries calls for careful site selection to reduce transport costs in the procurement of materials, the distribution of the product, and the assembly of workers at the plant site. Locational decisions of the management of large-office type of activities, such as insurance companies, have led to many cases of movement to the outskirts of metropolitan areas. But not all such moves have been successful and some have been reversed because of the high turnover of female office workers. They prefer to work near the downtown shopping district where they can enjoy noontime and afterhours shopping, eat lunch at a variety of places, and be more conveniently situated for social activities. This is a locational factor which many companies underrate in making their real estate decisions.

Retail businesses are typically tenants, though there are many retailers who own their quarters. The lease terms are a problem to both landlord and tenant. The property owner needs to know the market value of his store building as a basis for reaching a rental agreement. The widespread use of the percentage lease whereby the landlord is entitled to a certain percentage of the retailer's gross sales puts landlord and tenant into a kind of partnership. The tenant arrives at an estimate of the sales potential in this location and on this basis bargains on such features as minimum rent, percentage rate, graded rentals, and length of lease. The landlord should be equally knowledgeable with respect to the locational potential if he is to strike a fair bargain. Lending institutions such as life insurance companies sometimes turn up as landlords under a scheme known as the purchase-leaseback plan of financing. For example, to raise working capital, Sears, Roebuck and Company have sold some of their store buildings to lending institutions and promptly leased them back on long-term contracts.

Public Real Estate Problems

Governmental agencies own immense areas of land. The Federal government holds title to 778 million acres valued at $72 billion. Its real estate problems are varied and extensive. The Air Force acquired 5,400 acres of land by negotiation and condemnation in southeastern Wisconsin for a bomber base which would have involved construction of a 14,000-foot runway, hangars, repair shops, sewage plants, wells and water treatment plant, drainage systems, streets, and housing and recreational facilities at a cost of many millions. When half-completed, the whole thing was called off and a new set of real estate problems was created in connection with its disposition. In postwar years, the Federal government has sold off whole cities, publicly financed and built for defense purposes, but restored to private ownership through sale. An interesting real estate problem is the claim of a certain Indian tribe for compensation for lands taken from them back in 1835. What were these thousands of acres of Wisconsin land worth in 1835?

We urbanites live most intimately with the real estate decisions of local units of government. The adoption of a master plan implemented by zoning, and an official map of future streets, highways, and public areas puts a strait jacket on city growth and structure. If it is a sound plan, everyone benefits; if unsound, individual owners suffer financial loss and the community as a whole is disorganized and inefficient. Subdivision controls and building codes are beneficial to the degree that policy decisions by city councils and administrative decisions by city officials are wise and informed. The local board of education, in selecting a site for a new elementary school, indirectly manipulates the pattern of land values in the vicinity. The local redevelopment authority, once in action, becomes a large-scale real estate developer in acquiring blighted property, clearing the land, replanning it, and marketing it for reuse by both public and private agencies. Operating as it does in the problem areas of the community, the authority faces complexities far more difficult than the typical private real estate developer.

The foregoing illustrations are real life real estate problems which call for city-building decisions. It is not hard to find many examples in our cities of unwise and shortsighted decisions by both private and public agencies. God in his infinite wisdom has given us the earth's surface, but the manner of its use has been left to human choice. And the individual and social loss because of error is measured in wasted capital resources, increased economic costs, and human discomfort; all this is multiplied by the relative permanence of the effects. Once streets are cut through and expensively improved and costly structures are sturdily built for long life, mistakes can be corrected only slowly and painfully. As a result, we find ourselves living with the real estate errors of the past for many long years after their perpetration.

INCREASING COMPLEXITY OF URBAN PROBLEMS

The dynamic urbanism of the current era of prosperity and growth multiplies real estate opportunities but magnifies and complicates the problems. We read of the "exploding metropolis" and of the enormous increase in urban population which is upon us. From the 1950 nonfarm level of 124 million we are to reach over 200 million by 1975. We are told that vast conurbations will develop as a continuous metropolis from

Boston to Washington, from Gary, Indiana, to Milwaukee, from San Diego to Los Angeles. Industries are moving to peripheral locations, shopping centers of all sizes and compositions are popping up at every strategic suburban corner. Housing tracts spread far into the countryside. And at the same time, the surge of growth forces is having effect in the central city. There are expressway systems to hasten the suburbanite to his job in the center or his wife on a shopping expedition to the downtown stores, programs to refurbish and modernize the central retail area to meet the competition of the outlying shopping center, and urban renewal projects in blighted central areas, with Federal subsidy and local aids, to replace deficit areas with new buildings and activities which will contribute to urban efficiency. Concomitantly, private nonsubsidized redevelopment of a piecemeal type is accelerating as old dwellings are replaced by towering new apartment buildings in convenient central locations.

Real estate investment decisions in this milieu are not for amateurs. The entire urban structure is in flux, the levels of values constantly shifting, the future pattern of real estate productivity uncertain and tempered by a complex of social and economic forces difficult to interpret. And deeply entangled in this mix is the hand of government in a great diversity of interventions which, though they may originate at national, state, or local levels, all have impact on each parcel of urban real estate. Today's real estate decisions require professional skill if they are to be profitable for the parties to the transaction and socially productive for the community. They must be founded on sufficient and dependable facts interpreted on the basis of an understanding of the origins of real estate values and the principles of city growth and structure.

It is not sufficient for the real estate investor to assume that growth will continue unabated in all urban areas and that property values will increase at all locations.

The home buyer is no longer safe in depending upon inflation to bail him out when he must sell upon leaving town for a new job.

The mortgage lender who relies on the ratio of the initial mortgage debt to the present market value of this property as the major test of risk is asking for trouble.

The home builder who designs his product by trial and error and produces on a hand-to-mouth basis will soon be pushed out of business.

The city planner whose head is in the clouds of noble social objectives and monumental planning can seriously damage the community, should he fail to temper his dreams with a realistic understanding of urban land economics.

And the real estate salesman and broker, yearning for professional status, cannot serve his client and his community if he is equipped only with skill in the art of salesmanship and a knowledge of the mechanics of real estate transactions. The salesman who, through ignorance, no matter how innocent, misleads either party to a real estate transaction, is a reprehensible character and a burden upon society. Certainly the appraiser, the property manager, and the real estate counselor, who are straining through their respective trade associations to convince the public of their professional competence, would be guilty of criminal misrepresentation if they were not able to evaluate the complex forces and interrelationships in the real estate market and to forecast changes in real estate productivity and value.

A FOCUS ON REAL ESTATE DECISIONS

It has been our argument that the increasing complexity of real estate problems is the product of a period of dynamic urban growth which compounds the inherently complex nature of real estate as an economic good. Real estate is of vast economic importance as individual and social capital. Upon the proper development and arrangement of our cities depend their economic efficiency and the way of life of their citizens. In large degree, the urban pattern upon which so much depends is the cumulative product of innumerable real estate decisions, public and private. It follows as the night the day, that real estate education should be preparation leading to sound real estate decisions and to the solution of complicated real estate problems. We must focus the training in this field primarily upon the problem and the decision, and secondarily on the transaction. As a practical matter, a familiarity with the mechanics of real estate transactions is useful and even essential for many persons engaged in various phases of the industry. But we have lawyers as guides through the legal maze, and bankers as experts in financing details. We urgently need counselors and trained advisers in the area which is uniquely and peculiarly real estate to evaluate the factors affecting real estate productivity and value. We need investors with a sufficient understanding of the principles of city growth and structure to assure investment decisions which will not only yield a fair return, but also contribute to an efficient community land use pattern. We can use more mortgage lenders whose understanding of the pattern of future real estate values will forestall the advance of credit to poorly conceived real estate developments. Home builders who employ scientific methods of market analysis will prosper more and better serve their customers. City planners who understand the changing patterns of land values and can find in them the clues to what people want in their cities are far more useful than the Olympic oracle who plans in accordance with his own predilections. Real estate brokers and salesmen will serve better and earn more if they are competent to give professional counsel to their clients.

ORGANIZATION OF THE BOOK

This focus on problem solving and decision making does not result in a book of problems and solutions. This is, after all, a first book in urban land economics or real estate principles. It does presume some knowledge of the world, the world of economic affairs, in particular; whether the reader's understanding of elementary economics was acquired in the classroom or in business practice is not important. Our presentation also presumes some knowledge of general business organization and methods, and of governmental powers and organization. We assume that the reader has an observational familiarity with the urban scene in its physical manifestations and some understanding of the economic and social structure of urban society.

The basic structure of this book is built on the principles of city growth. Such a framework is a natural development of our intended focus on real estate problems for almost all of them concern making, conserving, or liquidating real estate investments. And the value judgments which lead to real estate investment decisions are based on forecasts of productivity, which in turn require an evaluation of the legal, physical, and locational qualities of the property and an interpretation of real estate market conditions. The city is a physical, social, and economic organism whose anatomical form is the product of uncounted investment transactions. Because the value of real estate depends so greatly on its location, and because change at any point in the city's land use structure brings significant changes to the locational qualities at many other sites, it should be clear that an understanding of the physiology and the anatomy of cities is an essential foundation for sound urban real estate decisions.

After this introduction is a chapter on "The Urban Setting" which recounts the evolution of the city as a response to the ever-changing economic and social needs of man. In summary form, it describes the American city as we find it today—its basic economic organization, its social structure, its political form, and the geographical pattern of land utilization. On the basis of this picture of the urban areas in which real estate problems emerge and real estate decisions must be made, the reader is prepared to explore the processes of city growth which have created the city form. Understanding these principles, he can more clearly envision the origins of real estate productivity and the forces and factors which are constantly modifying the value of urban properties.

We begin the study of real estate principles with a discussion of the nature of the commodity in Chapters III to V. The purpose of this section is to introduce the reader to the physical and locational characteristics of real estate which give it economic value, and to the legal and institutional framework within which real estate transactions take place. Having identified the origins of real estate productivity and value and the institutional limitations imposed in the public interest, we proceed in Chapters VI to IX to consider the investment process by which the predictions of productivity are translated into investment decisions and transactions. Because real estate investment is so dependent upon credit, this subject calls for consideration of the agencies and processes of real estate financing. Attention is also given to the matter of managing the investment, once made, with a view to its conservation and to the maximizing of the return.

Chapters X and XI deal with real estate markets and the role they play in the investment process and the influence of market conditions on real estate values. Demand, supply, and production; the mechanics of the market and its economic functions; market indicators; and market forecasting are all subjects of discussion.

The concluding chapter, "Urban Dynamics," provides the final explanation of how individual investment decisions are translated into urban structure. It describes the dynamic environment of economic, social, technological, and political change within which real estate transactions take place and suggests some of the kinds of change which may modify real estate productivity and the pattern of urban land values in the years to come.

At the end, we have come full circle from the city as it is, through the explanation of how productivity analysis and investment decisions lead to constant modification of the urban landscape, to the city as it will be. We have portrayed the underlying processes of city growth which build our cities and create and destroy real estate values. We have offered the student a simple, logical conceptual framework, distilled from the actualities of the market, as a reference for all he may learn or hear about real estate.

Because this is a first book in real estate, we have woven into the discussion of principles an ample description of the real estate business in operation. At the appropriate points, the steps and processes involved in real estate transactions are set forth. And because of our concern that all real estate decisions be wise ones, there are constant references to typical real estate problems keyed to the presentation of relevant principles and appropriate processes. Thus the principles, we trust, will assume the aura of reality and the reader will see how they may be applied to the solution of real life problems.

II

THE URBAN SETTING

THE CITY IS MAN-MADE

Man is the only animal which exercises much control over its environment. True, birds build nests and beavers construct dams, but these are piddling accomplishments compared with moving mountains, shrinking space with jet planes, and erecting the Empire State Building. For the most part, the lower animals have either adapted to changes in environment or become extinct. Man, on the other hand, has been most ingenious and industrious in exploiting natural resources and modifying the face of the earth, not merely for survival, but for an ever-increasing standard of living. Cities are one of the products of man's ingenuity, created by him for his own purposes.

Except for scattered rural settlements, it was not until sometime between 6000 and 5000 B.C. that the first cities appeared.[1] It is significant that about this same time, between 6000 and 4000 B.C., there was a marked technological advance by man through the invention of the ox-drawn plow, the wheeled cart, metallurgy, irrigation, and the domestication of certain plants. In Egypt, India, and Mesopotamia, in combination with fertile soils, these improvements produced an agricultural surplus above the needs of the cultivators. Without this surplus, there could have been no cities; city dwellers are not food producers, but they too must eat. At best, agriculture was then a crude art and even under optimum conditions produced very little surplus. It is estimated that fifty to ninety farmers were required to maintain one city dweller. Thus there were few cities, and only small cities, by modern standards. Another limiting factor was the low level of transportation efficiency, which restricted the import of foodstuffs from other areas and which limited trade activities; and in addition, political instability and constant warfare inhibited urban expansion.

After a lull of more than 2,000 years in urban development, the Greeks

[1] Kingsley Davis, "The Origin and Growth of Urbanization in the World," *American Journal of Sociology*, vol. 60, pp. 429–437, March, 1955.

and Romans created innovations in technology and political institutions which were accompanied by the appearance and growth of strong cities such as Athens, Syracuse, Carthage, and later, Rome. This surge in urbanization occurred between 600 B.C. and A.D. 400 concomitant with the development of iron tools and weapons, alphabetic writing, improved water transportation, cheap coinage, and aggressive colonization. But only a small fraction of the then world's population lived in cities, and strong as they were, the cities were not able to stand off the onslaughts of the barbarians. Thus it was that during the Dark Ages, cities declined in size, importance, and number, and it was not until the fourteenth and fifteenth centuries that a revival began in Western Europe. This revival occurred at a time when there were technological advances in agriculture and transport, new lands being opened to development, and new trade routes being exploited. Productive efficiency was increasing through organized handicraft methods and finally, by factory methods which culminated in the Industrial Revolution.

During the last century and a half, urbanization has been proceeding at an accelerating pace. Table II-1 indicates the proportion of the world's population which live in cities.

Table II-1

Percentage of World's Population
Living in Cities

Year	Cities of 20,000 or more	Cities of 100,000 or more
1800	2.4	1.7
1850	4.3	2.3
1900	9.2	5.5
1950	20.9	13.1

SOURCE: Reprinted from Kingsley Davis, "The Origin and Growth of Urbanization in the World," *American Journal of Sociology*, vol. 60, pp. 429–437, March, 1955, by permission of the University of Chicago Press. Copyright 1955 by the University of Chicago.

In the United States, urbanization is reported in Table II-2.

It is a rather obvious point that cities are man-made and are not the gifts of nature as natural resources. But it is not so obvious that cities have developed along with civilization to perform functions necessary to man's well-being and that man, imperfectly and inexpertly, has fashioned the city to his requirements. The perspective of history shows that these requirements of man are ever-changing and that many of our urban problems result from the impact of changing needs against the physically rigid and resistant structure of the city. In the succeeding chapters of this book we will demonstrate how the city has been built and is being built—by the individual decisions of numberless investors, buyers, sellers, developers, builders, and mortgage lenders, all operating within a restraining framework of law and regulation and supplemented by public actions through government in the provision of public services and the use of land for public purposes. It is a rare thing that an entire community is planned and executed by a single agency, yet it is being done today by a private developer, Levitt, who is building a city adjacent to the Fairless steel plant near Philadelphia for a population of 50,000, and in Brazil, where a new national capital city is under construction with government planning and government funds. But this kind of comprehensive planning and integrated development is not likely soon to replace the stumbling, incremental growth of cities as the cumulative product of generations of investors and developers.

Table II-2

Nonfarm Households as a Per Cent
of All Households, United States,
1910–1959

Year	Per cent
1910	69.3
1920	72.2
1930	77.6
1940	79.7
1950	85.6
1955	88.4
1959	89.5

SOURCE: *Economic Report of the President, 1960*, U.S. Government Printing Office, Washington, 1960, table B-7, p. 89.

THE FUNCTIONAL BASIS OF CITIES [2]

The explanation of the urban organization of society will be found in the socioeconomic activities that require the concentration of people, buildings, and machines within relatively small areas. The demand for urban land arises from the need for appropriate space for the performance of these activities. When we understand why we have cities, we shall be able to determine what economic and social functions are concentrated in them and to identify the basic forces of demand for the services of urban real estate. We shall see that the particular manner in which the combination of these factors impinges upon each urban area determines its economic and social characteristics and its rate of growth.

[2] The material on the functional basis of cities, urban location, and functional variations is adapted from Richard U. Ratcliff, *Urban Land Economics*, McGraw-Hill Book Company, Inc., New York, 1949, pp. 20–41.

The process of urbanization has been complex, but the basic forces can be readily identified. In general, the change from a rural to a predominantly urban mode of living has been the accompaniment of a change from a simple handicraft economy to an advanced type of modern industrialism.[3] In a sense, cities have developed as integral parts of the productive and distributive machinery. The spatial pattern of functional areas, the street system, and the buildings that crowd the landscape, together with the people who inhabit and use them, exist as a part of the economic equipment.

Early Urban Forms

A brief view of the nature and functions of cities in the medieval era, prior to the emergence of an industrial economy, will aid in understanding the functional nature of urban organization and how it reflects the cultural characteristics of the contemporary society. Medieval cities were not unique in the supplying of a basic need which is found in even the most rudimentary forms of social groupings—the need for a place of assembly. Man, gregarious creature that he is, needs not only space to enjoy the pleasure and comfort of group contacts, but also an established place for governmental and judicial gatherings. This is true even for the simplest form of communal organization. Closely associated with these needs is the one for a central shrine for the conduct of group religious rites.[4]

Another fundamental need, at least until the development of modern methods of warfare, was a site appropriate for defense against the common enemy. From early times the city had functioned as a fortress, and among the first substantial structures to be built were protecting walls against the enemy. Thus all early city forms were enclosed, originally serving primarily as places of assembly and retreat, and not until later developing as places of permanent residence and trade.[5] But as civilization progressed and cultural institutions solidified, the functions of the places of assembly and defense were extended to include the locus of the temple and the homes of priests, magistrates, and artisans.

After the fall of the Roman Empire, the castle and the cathedral or monastery were nuclei for town formation.[6] The concentrations about the castles arose through the need for homes for the soldiers, the weapon

[3] National Resources Committee, *Our Cities*, U.S. Government Printing Office, Washington, 1937, p. 1.

[4] Henri Pirenne, *Medieval Cities: Their Origin and the Revival of Trade*, Princeton University Press, Princeton, N.J., 1925, pp. 56–57.

[5] This statement applies generally to the acropolises of the Greeks, the *oppida* of the Etruscans, the Latins, and the Gauls; the *burgen* of the Germans; the *gorods* of the Slavs; and the kraals of the South African Negroes.

[6] Adam Smith, *The Wealth of Nations*, Modern Library, Inc., New York, Book III, chap. 3, p. 373.

makers, and the other craftsmen who served the lord and his men. The castle chapel served as a parish church, and the castle walls provided refuge against the enemy. The castle was the administrative and political center of the area.[7]

The pervasive influence of religious life and ecclesiastical organization in the Middle Ages led to urbanlike developments around the numerous cathedrals and monasteries.[8] The prestige of the bishops during this period gave great importance to their places of residence; furthermore, the diocese was an important administrative unit. The town was made up of the various religious establishments; structures for the priests, the scholars and students in ecclesiastical schools; and for servitors and artisans. There were also found storehouses and granaries for the harvests of the tenant farmers of the demesne. These religious centers were often fortified. All the towns of this period served as the location for weekly markets to which the peasants of the surrounding areas brought their produce.

This discussion of the medieval town, sketchy though it has been, serves to demonstrate that the existence and the form of the town were the direct reflections of the cultural characteristics of the times. This point might be further illustrated by the transformations that occurred in Western Europe during the twelfth century. During this era, commerce and handicraft industry took their places with agriculture, and together these activities began to replace warfare and religion as the major preoccupations of society. Agricultural products were used more extensively as objects of barter or as the raw materials of manufacture. One historian comments on these changes as follows: [9]

Under the influence of trade, the old Roman cities took on new life and were repopulated, or mercantile groups formed round about the military burgs and established themselves along the sea coasts, on river banks, at confluences, at the junction points of the natural routes of communication. Each of them constituted a market which exercised an attraction, proportionate to its importance, on the surrounding country or made itself felt afar.

We have, in this period of European history, the broadening of the foundations of the present interdependent world economy reflecting a pervasive specialization of men and machines, cities and regions. In this period, there developed the strong interdependence of city and country,[10]

. . . the country attending to the provisioning of the towns, and the towns, supplying, in return, articles of commerce and manufactured goods. The physi-

---

[7] W. J. Ashley, "The Beginnings of Town Life in the Middle Ages," *Quarterly Journal of Economics*, vol. 10, p. 373, July, 1896.
[8] Pirenne, *op. cit.*, p. 66.
[9] *Ibid.*, p. 104.
[10] *Ibid.*, pp. 105–106.

cal life of the burgher depended upon the peasant, but the social life of the peasant depended upon the burgher. For the burgher revealed to him a more comfortable sort of existence, a more refined sort, and one which, in arousing his desires, multiplied his needs and raised his standard of living.

The handicraft manufacturing of the times developed with the proliferation of individual skills and the specialized production of various towns and regions. Without the concomitant development of the machinery of trade, no such specialization could have occurred. It is evident that trade and specialization were fundamental forces in the important cultural changes of the times which led to the growth of cities as integral functioning parts of the social and economic system. Because of the changes in the activities carried on in the urban areas, the form of the town changed and adapted itself to its new functions. The houses and shops of the artisans and tradesmen could no longer be contained within the walls and burst out beyond them into the surrounding countryside. The market place, as well as the castle and the cathedral, became a focus of interest and activity.

This brief historical treatment of urban functionalism has served to lead us into a more detailed consideration of the basic forces of agglomeration that have been revealed—trade and the division of labor.

Exchange as an Urbanizing Force

The familiar evidence of history, which reveals that the great cities of the ancient world were largely centers of transport and trade, strongly suggests the importance of exchange as an urbanizing force. By the term "urbanizing force" we simply mean a function that requires for its performance the geographical concentration of people and appropriate facilities. Trade and transport have long been city builders, and we must explore the reasons behind this relationship.

In the ancient world, trade was largely in the nature of an exchange of various raw materials among the territories of their extraction and, to a much lesser extent, the exchange of raw materials for manufactured and processed goods. This type of trade was based on territorial specialization in those regions of the known world which were served by transport facilities. The cities of the times were most often situated on good harbors or on inland water routes; they were the loci of docks and shipyards and the homes of captains and sailors. The merchants also found it most convenient to live at these transport nodes, as did the moneylenders who financed trading expeditions or provided working capital for the merchants. Storage facilities were required as well as inns for the traders from the hinterland. The military establishments of the times, particularly the naval bases, were located in these trading centers, and, because of their strategic position, they often served as political capitals.

It is apparent that historically cities have developed as integral parts of the machinery of exchange. Trade requires the concentration of certain facilities and of manpower. Even in its simplest form, trade involves the physical movement of goods; thus transportation and trade are inseparable. The facilities of exchange tend to concentrate at points of transshipment, at the intersections of major transport routes, and at terminal points of communication. Whether the method of transportation be ship, airplane, railroad, or camel caravan, physical facilities and manpower are required for the servicing of the transport equipment, for the unloading and loading of goods, for sorting and storing, and for the conduct of the merchants' business. In addition, there are essential auxiliary services, such as financing and insuring, which bring together still more people.

Specialization and trade are associated phenomena. In the early centuries of the civilized world, specialization was largely territorial and trade was mainly in raw materials among the areas of their origins. Another early development based on specialization was the exchange of foodstuffs for processed goods between town and country. As the handicraft economy took form and as the number of individual skills multiplied and the variety of manufactured products increased, there was a corresponding expansion of trade and a necessary increase in the concentrations of the complementary facilities of exchange.

This discussion has been a demonstration of the fundamental economic principle that specialization of productive activity creates an interdependence that necessitates the exchange of goods and services. Not only does the exchange process give rise to urban concentrations where the machinery of trade is assembled, but also to another agglomerative force. This derives from the fact that persons and groups who are interdependent on the exchange of goods and services find it most convenient to live and work near one another so that exchange may be most efficiently and expeditiously effected. Another advantage in the proximity of the various specialists is that a greater variety of goods and services becomes available for exchange. As the division of labor is extended, so must be the market in order to absorb the fruits of increased productivity; and as the market is extended, so must there be an expansion of the machinery of trade and transport at strategic locations. Thus specialization, trade, and urbanization move forward hand in hand.

Manufacturing and Urbanism

It is largely true that up to the Industrial Revolution trade was the primary urbanizing factor. In addition cities were founded at religious shrines or as memorials. Other settlements might be found at the sources of raw materials. But manufacturing and the processing of the fruits of the earth were of minor consequence in the development of urbanism.

During the Middle Ages, with the development of the guild system, cities became more important as manufacturing centers and there was an increase in local specialization of product. But it was the spread of machine methods, the vast acceleration in the division of labor that resulted, and large-scale factory production that became the primary forces leading to urban expansion after the Industrial Revolution. At the same time, with increasing production in quantity and variety of product, came correspondingly increased facilities for trade.

The development of large-scale production and progress in the division of labor have gone hand in hand. It is true that specialization of economic functions was advancing slowly before the Industrial Revolution. The moderate division of labor that had occurred came about through the improvement and complication of handicraft methods, the development or discovery of new products, and as a consequence, natural aptitudes and interests that led individuals to devote themselves exclusively to special tasks. But the rapid spread of factory methods during the last hundred years has created a high degree of technical division of labor and has heightened the occupational and territorial specialization that has been developing.[11] It has been pointed out that the Industrial Revolution was not only a matter of new machinery of production; there were also cheapening transportation costs, the use of coal as fuel, and the removal of trade barriers, freeing industries to locate where it was most economically advantageous for them to do so.[12]

It is readily observable that modern manufacturing methods involve large-scale production, which, in turn, brings together large numbers of people and vast physical facilities. It is also observable that manufacturing plants of various kinds and sizes are often found in groups.

LOCATION OF CITIES

An analysis of the factors that determine the location of cities will throw further light on the functional basis of the urban economy. Geography, of course, has had much to do with the location of industry and commerce and thus with the pattern of settlement.[13]

In the preindustrial period, when wars swept the land and life was cheap, those localities prospered which were favorable for defense. Many

[11] H. B. Dorau and A. G. Hinman, *Urban Land Economics*, The Macmillan Company, New York, 1928, p. 28.

[12] Edgar M. Hoover, *Location Theory and the Shoe and Leather Industries*, Harvard University Press, Cambridge, Mass., 1937.

[13] Alfred Marshall, *Principles of Economics*, 8th ed., St. Martin's Press, Inc., New York, 1930, Book IV, chap. 11, p. 268.

Greek colonies were located on a promontory or an island; the Etruscan cities were located on hilltops; and thus we can partially account for Athens and the Acropolis, Rome on its seven hills, Paris on an island, and London in the swamps.[14]

When trade began to assume a predominant role in society, those areas were favored which were located at breaks in transportation along the lines of communication between the sources of products and their final markets. Settlements were usually situated at the following points: [15]

1. Where oceans or other navigable bodies of water met land.
2. At "breaks" in mountain chains.
3. Where ocean and river or other navigable water bodies met or crossed.
4. At obstructions in the river requiring unloading.
5. At intersections of land trade routes.
6. At points where the type of transportation used required servicing.
7. Where the mountain met the plain.
8. Where there was access to a rich hinterland or tributary area.

As industry became important, those locations grew most rapidly which held some economic advantage for specific types of manufacturing. Such localities might possess one or more of the following attractions:

1. Raw materials of a particular type
2. Power resources that were necessary for a certain type of industry
3. Trained labor with special skills
4. Climate particularly suited to a given type of production
5. Large market for a certain type of product

Although in the majority of urban areas manufacturing and trade are the chief activities, there are many urban areas that owe their existence to other human activities. There are political capitals where the laws are made and from which they are administered; there are educational and religious centers and resort and health centers; and there are mining centers and settlements associated with other extractive processes. The point to be made here is that such special-function cities, also, are necessarily tied to locations of special natural advantages. Thus political capitals have been placed with regard to centrality in the area of jurisdiction, with the primary purpose of securing a location of optimum accessibility; recreational and health centers have been located in areas where the climate or other aspects of the geographic site contain elements that are advantageous for recreational or health purposes; and the relation of mining centers to geographical situation is almost too obvious to mention.

[14] Richard M. Hurd, *Principles of City Land Values*, The Record and Guide, New York, 1924, p. 22.
[15] *Ibid.*, pp. 22–24.

FUNCTIONAL VARIATION AMONG CITIES

There is specialization among cities as among men, although it can never be so sharply defined. In the majority of urban areas in the United States manufacturing or trade is the chief activity, but in many cases cities reflect a variety of aspects of our culture. One writer says that "all large cities are more or less multifunctional, and the classification of a city as industrial does not imply the absence of trade. There are shades of gradation between and among [types] and some cities are borderline." [16]

Weimer and Hoyt classify cities in the United States as [17]

1. Cities devoted primarily to commerce, which includes seaports, lake ports, river cities, and railroad terminals and junctions. Farming centers can also be included here.

2. Industrial cities, including those devoted chiefly to the manufacturing and processing of commodities.

3. Cities that rely chiefly on extractive activities, such as mining, lumbering, fishing, and similar types of economic activity.

4. Political cities, including all those for which the activities of a state or the Federal government provide the basic income source.

5. Recreational and health resorts, as well as cities in which retired people reside.

6. Educational and cultural centers.

Of cities devoted principally to commerce there are seaports, such as Baltimore, Boston, Galveston, San Francisco, New Orleans, and Montreal; lake ports, such as Buffalo, Duluth, and Port Huron; river cities, such as Louisville and Memphis; and railroad terminals and junctions, such as Chicago, Atlanta, and Springfield, Illinois. Of cities devoted to manufacturing there occur gradations of specialization. Some areas specialize heavily in the production of particular products, such as Detroit in automobiles, Gary in steel, or Fall River in textiles. In other cities manufacturing activities are more diversified, such as New York, Chicago, and Boston. Of the cities dependent upon extraction there are two types. One type includes cities devoted chiefly to the extractive industry itself, such as Hibbing, Minnesota, near which are located the huge open iron-ore pits. The second type are processing centers which are dependent upon particular supplies of raw materials and which might decline in population if the extractive operations ceased. Such cities include Birmingham, Alabama, and the Scranton–Wilkes-Barre, Pennsylvania, area.[18]

[16] Chauncy Harris, "A Functional Classification of Cities in the United States," *The Geographical Review*, vol. 33, p. 86, January, 1943.

[17] Arthur Weimer and Homer Hoyt, *Principles of Urban Real Estate*, The Ronald Press Company, New York, 1939, p. 31.

[18] Stanley McMichael and Robert F. Bingham, *City Growth and Values*, The Stanley McMichael Publishing Organization, Cleveland, 1923, pp. 31–32.

Many cities are dependent upon governmental activities, such as Washington, D.C., or any one of the state capitals of the United States. Recreational and health resorts include Miami Beach, because of its climate, and Hot Springs, Arkansas, because of its mineral water. Cities functioning as educational centers range from such areas as Grinnell, Iowa, where education is the primary function, to Madison, Wisconsin, where industry, governmental activities, and educational activities share importance. Other specialized cities include Army and Navy bases, such as San Antonio and Norfolk, New London and Pensacola; medical centers such as Rochester, Minnesota; and insurance centers such as Hartford, Connecticut.

Table II-3 indicates the relative importance of basic sources of employment in leading American cities.

Table II-3

Occupational Distribution in Selected Types of Cities, 1950
(by percentage)

Occupation group	Commercial		Industrial		Resort		Government
	Atlanta	Des Moines	Pitts-burgh	Birming-ham	Miami	Atlantic City	Wash-ington
Professional .	9.4	10.3	9.3	8.0	10.1	7.2	16.1
Managerial ..	9.8	10.9	7.5	9.0	14.7	12.1	8.3
Clerical	18.4	20.2	14.6	12.1	13.5	10.1	27.9
Sales	9.0	10.3	7.6	7.8	10.1	8.2	6.4
Craftsmen ...	13.2	14.2	17.3	15.7	15.1	14.6	12.0
Operatives ..	16.9	15.1	21.6	22.6	10.9	16.8	8.9
Service	15.4	10.9	9.6	14.2	19.4	21.6	14.4
Agriculture .	1.6	3.4	1.4	1.2	.7	4.4	1.2
Laborers	6.3	4.7	11.1	9.4	5.5	5.0	4.8
Total	100.0	100.0	100.0	100.0	100.0	100.0	100.0

SOURCE: U.S. Bureau of the Census, *Census of Population: 1950*, vol. II, *Characteristics of the Population*, parts 2, 9, 10, 11, 15, 30, and 38.

Adapted from Glenn H. Beyer, *Housing, A Factual Analysis*, The Macmillan Company, New York, 1958, p. 9.

It is possible to classify a few cities on the basis of a predominant basic activity, but in varying degree, almost all cities are multifunctional. The Chicago metropolitan area is an example of a high degree of diversification of function: a wide variety of commodities is produced; it is an important center of trade and transportation; and it has been increasing in importance as a financial center. Another obstacle to useful classification is that, regardless of the productive, distributive, or service activities that may constitute the chief functions of various communities, there are certain prominent secondary processes that appear in every urban community.

For example, the intracity distribution of goods and services is an activity that is common to all cities. Almost all cities serve as the distributive center for the surrounding rural territory. Some banking services are always needed, and all cities are provided with some form of transportation facilities. In every city the population engaged in the chief activities must be serviced in numerous ways. Governmental, retailing, recreational, and religious activities are universal in urban areas. Finally, certain types of manufacturing, which for various reasons are oriented toward the market, are present in all cities. Such manufacturing includes that which produces either highly perishable or breakable items, items that have a low value relative to weight, and items based on raw materials that are not weight losing. Examples of such products include bottled milk, beer, carbonated water, bakery goods, newspapers, and bricks.

A final point on classification is that, since cities reflect the activities of a people in a given state of technology, resources, and the arts, the functions of cities and therefore the bases of a functional classification will change as the civilization and technical knowledge shift and as changes occur in the use and location of natural resources.

INTERNAL ORGANIZATION OF CITIES

This brief historical and functional review of the evolution of cities has been intended to demonstrate how man has created, out of natural resources granted by nature, a complex localized environment the better to attain his social and economic ends. We have tried to make the point that the growth in the importance of cities in civilized society has gone hand in hand with technological, social, and political advance which have increased man's productivity. In turn, this increase in productivity has been bought only at the cost of higher degrees of specialization among men and locations. Specialization in productive functions is inevitably accompanied by interdependence, for shoemakers who spend all of the time making shoes cannot survive without the foodstuffs produced by farmers, and farmers must have shoes. Specialization and the exchange of goods and services can be more effective and the increased productivity which it engenders can be of a higher order if the specialists are in close proximity and the costs of communication and transportation can be minimized. Thus there is a strong economic impulse to concentrate productive activities—hence cities. And since the productive workers must eat and sleep and spend their wealth, where better than close to their places of work— hence bigger cities. And because there must be service workers in activities which minister to the needs of the productive workers—laundries, drugstores, theaters, and hospitals—still bigger cities.

The sociologist looks at cities as composed of people primarily, along with the artifacts, structures, and facilities of urban life. The social relationships among individuals and groups create a web of interrelationships which are organic and dynamic. And the political scientist might see in city life a governmental framework of institutions and regulations, and interpenetrating the populace, political organization and relationships. Although we urge the view that the underlying causation of urbanism is economic, we must not overlook other functions which are present in city life and which join with economic forces in molding the form and structure of the city.

It is the thesis of this book, to be repeated and restated at frequent intervals, that the functional basis of urbanism leads to an internal spatial organization of activities and facilities which reflects the requirements of these functions; that the spatial structure which results is basically orderly and predictable; that an understanding of the considerations which lead to decisions on how various parcels of land are to be used is essential to an understanding of city growth and structure; and finally, that because the city is an organism, with all parts interrelated, an understanding of city growth and structure is a prerequisite to wise land use decisions.

It is the purpose of this chapter to set the stage for the demonstration of the foregoing thesis. We have already shown that economic factors are largely responsible for the existence of cities and largely account for their locations. We have discussed the economic factors which lead to concentration in cities. We shall next explain the economic organization of the city in terms of the nature of the productive and distributive activities found there and their interconnections. The succeeding section will deal with the social composition and organization of the city. This discussion will be followed by a description of the political organization. Finally, we will describe the physical and land use structure of the city, for this is the end product of all city-building forces and activities. As the succeeding chapters of the book unveil the considerations which guide land use determination by individuals and institutions and the processes of the real estate market, we will build an orderly and usable theory of city growth which can serve as a guide to sound real estate decisions.

ECONOMIC ORGANIZATION

Scholars have long recognized that the economic activities and institutions in any community divide naturally into two categories variously termed primary and secondary, basic and nonbasic, or city-building and service activities. The term "city building" is perhaps the most descriptive of the first category, for these are the activities which explain the very existence of the city and which control the rate and nature of its growth. In tracing the origins of any city, it is usually easy to identify the reasons for its early existence. Perhaps it was a fur trading post or a railroad division headquarters or a mining town or a crossroads trading center in a farming region or a steel town convenient to ore and coal. Whatever this original economic activity, it channeled a flow of wealth or purchasing power into the young community in one form or another—the proceeds from trading with the Indians and fur trappers or barter with the farmers from the surrounding countryside; it might have been the returns from the sale of silver and gold torn from the mountains or from the sale of steel billets to fabricators in other cities. It was these proceeds from extraction, trade, or production which were the source of wages for the clerks and factory workers and the source of profits for the proprietors; these were the proceeds which paid for the store buildings, the factories, the machines, and the homes of the workers. These primary or basic economic activities provided the economic lifeblood to the burgeoning city through exporting raw materials or manufactured products or services in return for outside dollars.

The foregoing definition of city-building economic activity has included such items as mining, trade, and manufacture; these three account for perhaps the majority of American cities though they are rarely found in a pure form. Most cities are multifunctional to some degree, and in some cases manufacture and trade are well balanced, as in Chicago; in other cases mining and trade are mixed, as in Butte, Montana. But many cities include among their basic activities the provision of services to outside users. For example, medical and hospital activities in Rochester, Minnesota, are supported not by the residents of the city, but by patients from all over the country and even the world. Payments for these services flow into the community from beyond its borders. In Chicago business consulting services have clients from coast to coast. In political capitals governmental functions are primary since they are supported by tax monies collected throughout their jurisdictional areas. University cities gain basic support from tax sources, out-of-town student fees and expenditures for books and living expenses, or alumni gifts. Military posts live off tax-supported appropriations, and resort towns like Charlevoix, Michigan, from expenditures made by citizens of Detroit, Chicago, and St. Louis. Many of the residents of St. Petersburg, Florida, are pensioners and retired people who live off remittances from Social Security, pension or retirement funds, or from interest or dividends on investments, all of which flow in from outside.

Secondary or service activities would not exist in the absence of primary activities; they may serve the primary activity directly as in the case of parts manufacturers in Detroit which service the major automobile makers, investment bankers who assist in financing large business enterprises, or advertising agencies which aid in marketing locally manufactured products. These types of service activities are not clearly distinguishable from the primary industry. But there are secondary or service activities which also serve the population drawn into the community by the job opportunities in the primary activities. These service functions include the sale of lumber, shoes, nails, whisky, and all manner of consumer goods; the provision of professional services by doctors, music teachers, and lawyers; public services through schools, sheriffs, and waterworks; public utility services such as transportation, telephones, and the services of building contractors and plumbers.

It is apparent that many local businesses and services are mixtures of primary and secondary levels. Some of the products of a manufacturing plant, a packing plant for example, may be consumed in the same locality, and to this extent the production process fails to bring in purchasing power from the outside. On the other hand, many of the service activities which mainly benefit local residents also serve consumers from the hinterland and to this extent perform the primary function of channeling outside purchasing power into the community. For example, the local doctors serve both factory workers and farmers even as do the clothier, the banker, and the tavern keeper.

The economic relationships among the various business and service establishments are quite varied, ranging from close and direct to remote. Because our interest in the economic framework of the community lies in its impact on real estate values and land use arrangements in the city, it is an important observation that the characteristics of the economic organization of the community and real estate characteristics are causally related. In a later part of the book when the real estate market is being considered, we will deal with the analysis of the economic base of a community as the first step in the prediction and qualitative analysis of the demand for real estate. In the chapter on location (Chapter IV) we will explain how the relationships among the various business enterprises of the community have a marked influence on the pattern of land use which comprises the community structure. At this point we are attempting, with a broad brush, to depict the general classes of economic activity which are the natural denizens of the city and the nature of the interrelationships among them.

Economic relationships are largely based on buying and selling goods, information, or advice. In addition an indirect relationship may exist in the form of dependence upon common suppliers, common customers, or common labor supply. Among the basic activities there may be such relationships as exist between major producer and parts suppliers, as in the Detroit area. In a city such as Milwaukee where there are many types of metal working plants, there is a common dependence upon the local pool of skilled metal workers. Competitive relationships exist when producers make the same product and sell to a common group of customers. Another form of indirect relationship is created when manufacturers deal with common suppliers of raw materials and semiprocessed goods. A species of economic relationship is present between a manufacturer of heavy goods who employs manpower and a textile mill or electronics plant which hires the wives and daughters from the same families. Many kinds of business and financial services are closely associated with the basic or city-building enterprises—commercial and investment banks, accountants, advertising agencies, legal firms, and many others.

In a real sense the secondary or service type of economic activity is related to the basic activities in supplying essential services to those persons engaged in the primary activity. The direct relationship is between the individual or family and the service. Here again, service enterprises such as competing supermarkets may have common customers and common suppliers. They feed off a common labor pool and may provide jobs for the wives and children of workers in other service activities or in the basic industries.

The direct economic relationships which we have outlined are in each case manifested by the movement of goods, as in purchase and sale; the movement of persons as in employment relationships and service relationships of doctor to patient; and the communication of information between the parties. We shall see that the necessity for the movement of goods or travel by people, and the communication of information, where it is by word of mouth, all have strong locational effects. Indirect relationships may also influence the location of related business enterprises. A case in point would be a retail store such as a ladies' apparel outlet, which would tend to locate close to competing outlets in order to better serve the common customers.

To summarize our concern with the economic structure of the community:

1. The character of the basic activities influences the growth of the community and the number and kinds of people who will be drawn in by the job opportunities.

2. The number and kinds of people in the area will affect the number and kinds of service activities.

3. The nature of the basic and the service activities are the fundamental factors which will determine the arrangement of land uses in the community.

THE CITY AND THE PEOPLE

People are the active agents in making real estate decisions. This statement of a rather obvious truth carries the suggestion that the kinds of decisions which are made will depend upon the kinds of people who are making them. It behooves us, therefore, to give thought to the people who inhabit our cities and in whose interests, directly or indirectly, all real estate decisions are made.

New basic activities which move into a community are often initiated by persons or institutions outside its boundaries, and thus cannot be said to reflect the characteristics of the local population. Even the expansion of existing industry is the result of business considerations which have little local flavor. On the other hand, secondary, or service, activities appear directly in response to purely local considerations.

It is highly significant that cities are the primary points of consumption for more than three-quarters of this nation's population. And the decisions which mold the pattern of consumption in any city are necessarily local in origin. These consumption decisions reflect the way of life which the local inhabitants choose to pursue; they have a strong influence in determining the kinds of secondary activities and service facilities which will appear in response to consumer preferences and in determining the land use pattern of the community. For example, in an area where the age distribution is skewed toward the younger groups, there will be a strong demand for retail services catering to children's needs and for house furnishing and accessory shops serving young families which are equipping their households. Where older groups predominate, there may be a lesser demand for single-family homes and more for apartments, a lesser need for diaper service but a greater one for hospitals and nursing homes. The racial and cultural backgrounds of the populace will also influence consumption patterns and thus the nature and location of secondary facilities. Income levels are another factor of importance in expenditure patterns.

At any point in time the population characteristics of a city are the cumulative product of net in-migration (excess of in- over out-migration) and natural increase (excess of births over deaths). Historically cities have grown mainly through migration from rural areas and foreign lands. In recent years foreign migration has been reduced to a trickle by legal restriction, and increased fertility in urban areas has stepped up the net local contribution to population increase in most cities. However, few cities would grow in size were it not for the flow of new residents from outside drawn by job opportunities. Most immigrants come from farms and villages, but there is also a flow from cities of decreasing economic opportunity to areas of promising opportunity. Young people just entering the labor force, for example, tend to remain in their home towns when expanding activities are able to make room for them, but are compelled to leave to seek jobs elsewhere in the face of a static or declining absorptive capacity in the local labor market. Other factors stimulate intercity migration such as the salubrious climate of the South and West which attracts people of retirement age and is a factor in attracting younger families as well.

Urban populations are characterized by heterogeneity—the social and economic diversification of individuals and groups which is often obscured in aggregate figures. This highly diversified population shares a limited territory in the process of working and living; their contacts are physically close but tend to be socially distant.

Table II-4

Comparative Population Characteristics
Detroit, Scranton, Tampa–St. Petersburg, Washington
Standard Metropolitan Areas

Population characteristics	Detroit, Mich.	Scranton, Pa.	Tampa–St. Petersburg, Fla.	Washington, D.C.
Total population				
Number	3,016,197	257,396	409,143	1,464,089
Per cent increase 1940 to 1950	26.9	−14.6	50.4	51.3
Median age, years	30.4	32.6	34.9	30.6
Per cent 65 years old and over	5.4	8.8	12.2	5.9
Per cent nonwhite	12.0	0.3	13.9	23.4
Persons per household	3.49	3.50	3.0	3.32
Married couples, per cent without own household *	9.0	8.4	6.9	10.3
Persons 1 year old and over, per cent in same house, 1940 and 1950 *	82.6	92.3	71.9	74.9
Persons 14 to 17 years old, per cent in school *	88.6	87.1	84.9	86.2
Persons 25 years old and over, median school years completed *	10.1	8.8	10.1	12.2
Persons 14 years old and over				
Number in labor force	1,275,602	99,132	157,109	686,067
Male, per cent in labor force	83.3	72.2	70.9	81.1
Female, per cent in labor force	28.9	28.8	29.6	42.5
Civilian labor force, per cent unemployed	6.1	6.8	5.0	3.1
Families and unrelated individuals				
Median income * (dollars) ..	3,564	2,555	2,002	3,321
Per cent having incomes less than $2,000 *	20.2	36.5	49.9	26.5

* 1940 figures not available.

SOURCE: U.S. Bureau of the Census, *U.S. Census of Population: 1950*, vol. II, *Characteristics of the Population*, part 9, 1952, table 10.

A sense of the diversity within and among urban populations can be gained by comparing the differences among cities in the proportioning of component segments. Table II-4 records selected differential characteristics of the populations of four cities which are well known in respect to their basic, or primary, functions. The data quite clearly reflect these functions.

SOCIAL STRUCTURE

The land use pattern of the city reflects not only the characteristics of the men, women, and children who inhabit it, but also the social structure of interpersonal and intergroup relationships which have developed in the community. People form groups and the nature of these groups and the interactions among them have some influence on real estate decisions and thus on the value of land and the pattern of land use in the community. Human ecologists distinguish between two types of social integration which characterize the collective life of man.[19] By penetrating the obscuration of terminology which labels these forms of social organization "symbiotic" and "commensalistic," we find familiar groupings. Symbiotic groupings are organizations of persons who are functionally unlike and who are interdependent. The family represents the most common expression of the "internally differentiated and symbiotically integrated" group. The business corporation is another, where any number of persons, each with a specialized function, is associated in a common enterprise whose success is dependent upon the effective functioning of every member of the group.

Commensalistic groupings are composed of people who are more or less alike and who join together in categoric groupings because of common interests. Labor unions, churches, and garden clubs are of this kind. It is clear that any one individual may be a member of several groups and in both categories. The nature of these groupings and the participation of individuals in them are conditioned by the economic characteristics of the community and the social characteristics of the individuals.

The direct impact of the social structure of a community on real estate decisions and land use patterns lies in the requirements for specialized real estate facilities which are generated. Families need homes, and corporations need offices and factories. Where labor unions are strong, they usually acquire land and buildings to house union headquarters and activities. In cities where church membership is high, much space is required for the church buildings. A strong and organized interest in the arts results in music halls and art galleries.

The indirect impacts of social structure on land use are pervasive. The

[19] Amos H. Hawley, *Human Ecology*, The Ronald Press Company, New York, 1950, p. 209.

common ties of newly arrived migrants from Puerto Rico or the rural South draw them together in an enclave or ghetto which emphasizes their nonconformity and perpetuates racial conflicts. The effectiveness of local political organization has its impact on government for better or for worse. In different circumstances, it may lead to waste, corruption, and high taxes or to a reform movement which improves efficiency, raises the level of public services, and leads to public improvements which stimulate growth and increase property values. Again, citizen organizations such as parent-teacher associations, women's clubs, or housing and planning groups can bring about changes in local government personnel and policy which may greatly improve the urban environment. Organized neighborhood groups ardently fight for or against zoning changes which affect their homes. Businessmen organize to encourage new industries to move in or cooperate to lift the face of the central business district. Thus in general it may be said that the nature and the strength of social groupings in a community are potent factors in molding the land use pattern of the city.

POLITICAL ORGANIZATION

We have been describing the urban setting of those real estate decisions which generate the city structure. Most of our communities were founded on originating forces which were economic in nature, and have prospered as these or other economic factors have burgeoned or waned. Because cities are the habitat of people, the internal arrangement reflects the requirements and preferences of the unique collection of individuals and groups which are peculiar to the diverse occupants of the area. Cities could not exist in a state of anarchy so we must have government to keep the peace, regulate and restrict individual behavior for the good of all, and provide certain services which can best be provided through collective action. Real estate decisions and development, and thus the land use pattern of the community, are strongly influenced by the nature of the governmental organization, the public controls, and the public activities. A familiar example of control is the zoning ordinance; an even more familiar example of public activity is the school system. Because the powers of governmental units are geographically limited by the boundaries of their several jurisdictions, the pattern of political subdivisions in an urban area is an important aspect of the governmental or political structure.

The functions of local government are well understood and need only brief review here. In general, these functions fall into two categories: functions involving regulation and control, and functions related to the provision of public services. Among the control functions are the keeping of the peace, and many types of regulation which affect the use of land directly or indirectly. Zoning laws restrict the use which may be made of real estate and, among other things, the placement of the building on the lot. Subdivision regulations control the platting of raw land and may specify the improvements which the subdivider must install. Building codes set minimum standards for construction, and safety and sanitary codes regulate building and its operation in the public interest. Powers to control traffic can greatly affect real estate values when changes in traffic routings are made. The issuance of a liquor license will determine the use of a given parcel of land and may influence real estate values in the neighborhood.

Public services provided through governmental agencies are numerous and increasing. Education is the most extensive and the most expensive, with up to half of local expenditures devoted to schools in many areas. Garbage collection, snow removal, recreational facilities (parks, golf courses, and swimming beaches), fire protection, and public recording of real estate documents are a few examples. Other types of service involving large and expensive plants and equipment include sanitary sewer and water service, and in some cities, parking lots, bus service, and gas and electricity.

The central city usually has a mayor-council form of government, though the city-manager–council form is frequently encountered. Outlying and suburban communities may be incorporated towns and villages, but much of the rural-urban fringe is unincorporated and falls in the jurisdictional control of the township in most of our states. Over-all jurisdiction of the county gives this unit of government certain controls over unincorporated territory and makes it responsible for direct service or financial aid covering services such as police protection, road maintenance and repair, and recreation. Other types of public agencies are the special district and the authority. The district is an independent unit which functions to provide a special service such as sewage disposal or high school education in an area overlapping several political subdivisions. The authority may be set up within a city to carry out the provision of public housing, redevelopment projects, or the operation of a bridge or harbor facilities.

To finance the activities of this diverse group of territorially overlapping public bodies, the property tax is the main reliance. Revenue is also derived from fees and service charges, and for some of the direct services, such as bus transportation, from fares and fees. Federal and state aids for schools and highways make their contribution. Expenditures involving capital outlays such as streets and sanitary sewers are often financed by special assessment taxes charged against the properties benefited.

The state of the fiscal health of a community has an influence on growth patterns and real estate values. Honest and efficient government spells moderate debt and relatively low governmental costs. High taxes may result from dishonesty and graft, inefficiency and waste; or they may reflect a rapid growth in residential properties which do not support the public services for which they generate the need. High taxes discourage growth and may drive away commercial and industrial activities without whose tax contribution there is no hope of an over-all tax reduction. Communities which are bonded up to the debt limit usually have high taxes and, in addition, are often unable to finance the further extensions of public services which are required to provide adequate educational facilities, streets, storm-water drainage, and sanitary sewers. The prudent property developer or property buyer avoids the confines of hardpressed municipalities.

The outstanding functional defect of the governmental structure in the typical urban region is the lack of correspondence between the natural socioeconomic area of the community and the jurisdictional boundaries of the various governmental units. The economic unity of the metropolitan area and its social integration are based on interrelationships which know no political or governmental boundaries. On the other hand, political subdivisions are historically related to the original settlements which, over time, have coalesced to form the metropolitan community. The original boundaries tend to resist change and adjustment to new conditions. The separate suburban governmental units typically seek to maintain independence and even to expand their territorial jurisdiction through annexation of unincorporated areas in competition with the central city.

One of the unfortunate land use effects of this separation of the metropolitan area into a multiplicity of small political units is the lack of community-wide land use planning. In a number of states enabling legislation has been passed which permits the local units of government to join for planning purposes on a cost-sharing basis. Some metropolitan planning is practiced in a few places, but even under the most favorable circumstances the translation of the plan into reality is still optional with each participating unit, and the planning thus may be largely ineffectual.

Another result of the typical Balkanization of our metropolitan areas is a scattered and irrational pattern of expansion. Instead of an orderly outward growth tied in with the economical expansion of roads and public services, the usual community expands through a leapfrogging development at spots which are favored with available utilities, low taxes, or strong promotion. The consequence is to leave undeveloped wide-open spaces which result in longer travel distances for everybody and higher costs of essential services.

The differences among the municipalities in the adequacy of land use regulation and in the standards enforced act to contribute to disorderly and uneconomical growth patterns. For example, in some jurisdictions the minimum lot size has been set at an acre or more in order to prevent tract developments of modest homes which produce disproportionately low tax revenues in view of the heavy demands on public services, particularly schools. This type of development is thereby forced into locations which may not be favorable from a community-wide standpoint in light of the social costs which are created. Differences in building codes, subdivision regulations, and zoning restrictions all contribute to the disorganization of suburban development. The financial difficulties of many small suburbs prevent the installation of such essential public services as schools, water supply, and sewage disposal. The result is that either normal development is delayed or substandard living conditions are perpetuated.

LAND USE STRUCTURE

Our description of the urban setting, up to this point, has sketched the city as an economic organism which has evolved to perform for man certain wealth-getting and wealth-consuming functions. We have described the city in terms of the people who congregate there and the groups into which they consolidate and organize. Finally, we have outlined the political structure of the metropolis which has appeared in response to the necessities of regulation over congregative living and to the economies in the provision of various services through public facilities. It has been our thesis that the economic, social, and political characteristics of the community are the primary determinants of the myriad of individual real estate decisions which build and modify the land use structure of the city. Thus at any point in time the geographical pattern of the city is the cumulative reflection of the economic, social, and political history of the area. We must also recognize, of course, the importance of the geological and physical features of the natural landscape. Much of the balance of this book will be devoted to an explanation of how real estate decisions are made in real life and thus how each city becomes the product of its own peculiar combination of economic, social, and political features. But the present purpose is to present a generalized description of the urban landscape as a background against which later discussions of real estate productivity and value may take on added reality.

On the basis of observations covering many cities over many years, it is possible to discern a basic internal urban form which is repeated with variations from city to city. Although there is an essential order to the arrangement of land uses in our urban areas, it is at times distorted or obscured by physical features of the landscape or by accidental or irrational developments. It is also a fact that with the passage of time come technological and social changes which tend to modify the basic urban form. Although the urban structure is not static in its fundamental arrangement of functions and facilities, basic changes are slow and usually discernible only to the trained analyst.

Specialization and Functional Areas

The city has been described as a man-made mechanism to facilitate the conduct of basic economic and social functions. It is therefore a reasonable hypothesis that the internal organization of the city is related to these same activities and that the pattern in space of functional areas has order and meaning. Anyone can observe that the city is subdivided into many areas within which the land uses are similar or functionally related. The explanation of this tendency toward geographical groupings of similar and related activities or establishments begins with the effort of each owner or investor to find that combination of land use and location which will yield the optimum return. Consequently, all uses tend to be most advantageously located with respect to linked activities. The result is to create neighborhoods of similar or related land uses and to reduce the aggregate of the total community costs of friction to a minimum. This economic zoning or districting reflects not only the locational magnetism of linkage, but also the tendency of certain types of land use to seek proximity to attractive features of the natural or man-made landscape, and the tendency of all uses to avoid the proximity of incompatible uses and occupancies. We recognize the pervasive power of the public interest in forming the urban structure through planning activities, zoning, and other land use controls. But good planning and sound zoning must be in harmony with the underlying economic and social forces which give cause for the city's existence. Thus well-founded zoning through city ordinance and natural zoning as a product of the economic competition of uses will produce a city structure basically the same.

Movement and communication are the essence of cities. Our short history of urbanism emphasized that cities grew as specialization spread; and specialization gives rise to interdependence which requires communication and transportation. The city would be a dead thing indeed without the movement of persons, the transport of goods, and the interchange of information which the system of streets and expressways makes possible. The location and pattern of these arteries which carry the lifeblood of the community and their quality and efficiency have much to do with the pattern and productivity of urban real estate.

The component neighborhoods and districts of the city are arranged on the basic skeleton of the street system. Streets are not only a factor in the arrangement of land uses, but also a major user of land area, up to 25 or 30 per cent in most cities.

It is helpful to visualize the city as a variety of functional areas arranged in an orderly manner and superimposed on a framework of streets. However, the idealized form is only approached in real life, never fully realized. Neighborhoods are identifiable, but not strictly homogeneous or sharply defined. The processes of city building are essentially rational but the judgments and forecasts of men are subject to error and handicapped by lack of sufficient information. Thus investors make mistakes and the durability of structures perpetuates the errors. The constant change in the forces of urban growth brings obsolescence to some areas and, in combination with the physical aging of structures, causes blight and decline in utility. There are always transitional areas which are in process of readjustment in facilities and uses from the original functions to modified or new functions.

For purposes of analysis, neighborhoods can be grouped with respect to internal homogeneity as follows:

1. *Homogeneous Land Uses—Homogeneous Occupancies.* In many residential neighborhoods, all the homes are of the same general value level; they are similar in design, the lots are of the same size, and the inhabitants are alike in economic status and cultural background. Another example is the outlying shopping center which constitutes a neighborhood homogeneous in respect to its retail uses and attendant parking area.

2. *Homogeneous Land Uses—Diverse Occupancies.* Some older residential areas, usually centrally located, shift from the original homogeneity among occupant families to a mixture of old couples and widows, roomers, young childless couples, and a few families with children.

3. *Diverse Land Uses—Diverse Occupancies.* Where cities have developed without benefit of zoning, the original improvements may be a mixture of residential, retail, and industrial. A mixture may also be the product of transition. Close-in residential neighborhoods may deteriorate into a mélange of residences, commercial uses, and parking lots. Industrial areas often contain a combination of residential and commercial use.

These general neighborhood types suggest the further basic fact that many neighborhoods are so mixed as to be difficult to classify by function. The mixed areas are often in a transitional stage and the mixture is a fact which in itself delays the processes of land use succession. The result of the mixture is a blighted area where there is no economic incentive to replace the existing buildings.

A further aspect of the neighborhood components which make up the city is that the boundaries are not always easy to mark. The areas shade into one another and create interarea zones of transition that are a mixture of diverse uses and occupancies. On the other hand, there are often definite limits such as a major traffic artery, a railroad right of way, a river, or a line of hills. In residential districts, the practice of subdividing relatively large areas and the use of the tract-building approach have created homogeneous areas which are the product of more or less simultaneous development.

The major functional areas of the city which represent fairly clear-cut

types of land use have been measured for fifty-three central cities covering the following categories of use:

        Single-family dwellings
        Two-family dwellings
        Multifamily dwellings
        Commercial areas (retail, wholesale, financial, and office)
        Light industry
        Heavy industry
        Railroad property
        Parks and playgrounds
        Public and semipublic uses
        Streets

    Table II-5 shows the proportion of the total developed area in the fifty-
three cities which is in the various types of use.

Table II-5

Per Cent of Developed Area and City Area in
Various Land Use Categories in 53 Cities in
the United States

Land use	Area, acres	Developed area, per cent	City area, per cent
Single-family dwellings	101,291.81	31.81	17.76
Two-family dwellings	15,271.65	4.79	2.68
Multifamily dwellings	9,587.41	3.01	1.68
Commercial areas	10,576.21	3.32	1.85
Light industry	9,038.90	2.84	1.59
Heavy industry	11,451.39	3.60	2.01
Railroad property	15,475.11	4.86	2.71
Parks and playgrounds	21,475.06	6.74	3.77
Public and semipublic property	34,818.55	10.93	6.11
Streets	89,480.45	28.10	15.69
Total developed area	318,466.54	100.00	55.85
Vacant areas	171,674.83	.....	30.10
Water areas	80,127.61	.....	14.05
Total surveyed area	570,268.98	.....	100.00

SOURCE: Harland Bartholomew, *Land Uses in American Cities*, Harvard University
Press, Cambridge, Mass., 1955, table 3.

    We have described the city as composed of a set of functional areas
superimposed on the framework of the street system which provides
access and communication among functional areas and within them. Now
what is the spatial arrangement of the functional areas and what is its
explanation? There have been a number of attempts to state a generalized

description of the pattern of urban land uses. These generalizations recognize that all cities are similar in basic organization, but that there are differences in pattern because of geological factors and the nature of the primary activities which support the community.

One of the earliest descriptions of the city land use pattern was in terms of a series of concentric zones.[20] At the center is the central business zone with the retail area at the core and the wholesale and warehouse district at the outer edge. The second zone, surrounding the business district, is a zone of transition of old residences, rooming houses, slums, and scattered commercial and light industrial uses. Through this zone and the inner core are found wedges of industrial land use along the railroads and waterfront. The third zone from the center of this concentric pattern is occupied by workingmen's homes, and in the fourth circular zone are found the residences of middle-class families. A fifth ring is the commuters' zone of suburban communities where middle- and upper-income groups live. We shall see that this division of the city into concentric zones is a concept which has some value, but which is quite limited in its application to the modern community.

Homer Hoyt's sector theory is primarily a description of the pattern of residential development.[21] This generalization states that the homes of different income groups are found in separate wedge-shaped areas which are radial to the center of the city and may extend outward to the edge of settlement. The high-grade residential development begins near the center in the form of deluxe high-rent apartment areas and extends outward along the fastest travel routes or along lake or river front; in other cases, it progresses toward high ground and open country away from barriers to expansion. The low-rent and intermediate-rent sectors occupy less desirable portions of the community but exhibit the same tendency to take the form of sectors extending to the edge of development. Low-quality housing, for example, may follow the outward line of railroad and industrial property.

The multiple-nuclei concept of the city recognizes that there are a variety of centers about which growth occurs, each center representing a different urban function.[22] These functional centers include the central retail area, outlying retail areas, industrial and wholesaling centers, or outlying satellite communities.

None of these three conceptualizations of the urban structure is satis-

[20] Ernest W. Burgess, "The Growth of the City," in R. E. Park et al. (eds.), *The City*, University of Chicago Press, Chicago, 1925. See charts in Chapin and in Harris-Ullman article in *Annals*.

[21] Homer Hoyt, *The Structure and Growth of Residential Neighborhoods in American Cities*, Federal Housing Administration, 1939, p. 76.

[22] Chauncy D. Harris and Edward L. Ullman, "The Nature of Cities," *The Annals*, vol. 242, November, 1945, p. 13.

factory in itself, but in combination they are helpful in understanding the product of urban growth. The concentric-zone description reflects several growth tendencies, but none of them adequately. For example, it is true that there is a tendency for cities to have rings of growth like a tree; new areas are necessarily added on to the outside where open land is available. Thus as we move outward from the center we pass from the oldest to the newest. But we should be misled if we think of these age rings as full rings encircling the central core. Burgess did recognize that industrial zones interpenetrate one or more rings in following outward along railroad lines. The same thing is true of commercial uses which followed in ribbon form along streetcar lines, and in modern context, along major traffic arteries. Hoyt's observations that the format of residential areas of different quality levels is wedge-shaped is more realistic than the concept of an unbroken ring with homes of the same value level found generally equidistant from the center. It is true, however, that as the distance from the center increases, the homes in all of the sectors tend to be newer. The exception is when land use succession, such as the rebuilding of the close-in residential areas with new deluxe apartment buildings, takes place. In the inner portions of some of the sectors, the older dwellings filter down to a lower-income group not homogeneous with the inhabitants of the outer and newer ranges. The sector concept, while applied by Hoyt to residential development, has applications already mentioned to industrial and commercial land use; industrial districts tend to be attenuated along rail lines or waterfront, and string-street retail and commercial conformations follow radial traffic arteries.

The multiple-nuclei concept recognizes that cities are made up of concentrations of similar or related land uses in areas which we have called neighborhoods—the central business district, wholesale and light manufacturing, low-class residential, medium-class residential, heavy manufacturing, outlying business district, residential suburb, and industrial suburb. These examples of clusters or functional areas of similar or related land uses are not necessarily the products of parallel urban growth processes. For example, a satellite residential community may once have been an independent country village which has now coalesced with the central city and has become a medium-class residential neighborhood. Another similar area may have been developed recently by tract builders. This concept of the city has a further weakness in failing to portray the organic unity of the entire community.

In summary, the urban land use structure is composed of a group of more or less distinct functional neighborhoods superimposed on a framework of streets. Certain of the neighborhoods follow radial streets, rail lines, and waterways outward from the central business district. Residential areas tend to be wedge-shaped sectors extending from center to periphery.

As distance from the center decreases, the improvements tend to be older and the use and occupancy less homogeneous.

Certain modern tendencies conspire to make the foregoing generalization less and less useful as a basis for forecasting coming urban patterns. The decline of public mass transportation and the substitution of personal automobile transport is breaking down the structure of residential areas as it is described by Hoyt. The industrial worker neither depends on public transportation nor is his home necessarily near his place of employment. The executive drives to work, save in the largest metropolises, and lives where he will. This freedom of choice is leading to a greater diffusion, more mixture of neighborhoods, and less structuring of the metropolis.

Industrial development is no longer tied closely to rail lines, with the result that a greater scatter of industry characterizes recent development. Driven from central locations by the need for large acreage and by the congestion which hampers operations and employee movements, industrial plants are seeking suburban locations.

Retail conformations are changing to a lesser degree, but the change is significant. The central core of retail services remains dominant but is not growing in extent. New major suburban shopping centers are absorbing the added purchasing power of the growing metropolis. Suffering decline are the small neighborhood service centers, the older inlying retail subcenters, and the string-street retail developments.

There is nothing in these various generalizations on the urban land use pattern which conflicts with the basic hypotheses of urban growth which have been outlined. The geographical form of the city is the product of the demand for the services of real estate. Each function tends to be located where the locational productivity of the site is the highest among alternative sites not absorbed by more intensive uses. Thus the competition among alternative uses creates the ultimate urban patterns. It follows that the question of where new growth will occur is related to the type of land use, to the locational requirements of that type under current conditions, and to the strength of competition from other use types.

III

THE PHYSICAL FOUNDATIONS
OF REAL ESTATE VALUE

INTRODUCTION

Traditionally the value of land has been founded on its physical characteristics. From the dawn of man's history, land has been valuable because of its capacity to provide the essentials of life. Prehistoric man lived off the fruits of natural vegetation or the meat of beasts that roamed the forests or grazed on the plains. Even at this stage, our ancestors surely recognized that some tracts of land were more valuable than others, that fruit grew more abundantly in a favored spot or that a meal was easier to come by in certain forests or ranges which could support a heavier animal population. Certainly as the art of cultivating the land began to develop, differentials in land fertility were discovered, probably by trial and error, and it was recognized that certain lands were more easily cultivated and more productive because of better soil conditions and water supply. We can be sure that the nomadic tribes of herdsmen learned the advantages of different kinds of pasture lands at different seasons of the year. Land was not a free good of unlimited supply even at the dawn of civilization when only a handful of men roamed limitless expanses. The greater productivity of some lands made them relatively scarce and imparted a value which led to bloodshed and war incited by covetous persons and tribes.

We shall learn from our study of the economics of urban land that the origins of its value in modern times derive both from its physical characteristics and from its location within the urban landscape. The same two sources of value are responsible for the value of agricultural land, a fact recognized by such early economists as von Thunen. Truck gardening, for example, is typically found near cities and thus close to the point of consumption; rich soil suitable for such produce combined with convenience to high-density population creates a high agricultural land value in which location is a major factor. On the other hand, wheat lands are cultivated in many different areas of the country, but much productive wheat farming is carried on in such Western states as Montana, Wyoming, and Idaho at some distance from centers of processing and consumption. In this case, the value of the land derives largely from its physical characteristic of fertility; location plays a minor role. In the case of urban land, location is all important. It is true that the physical characteristics of the land, subsoil conditions, for example, influence value through affecting the costs of improving the land for urban uses, wet lands must be drained, and solid rock is costly to excavate for basements. But the location of the land, the space relationships with other urban facilities and activities, not only largely determines the use to which each parcel may be put but also does much to explain its productivity and value.

A logical starting point for our explorations of urban land economics is the nature of the commodity, urban land, and in particular, an identification of those characteristics of urban land which give it economic value, both physical and locational. Thus these early chapters will attempt to point out those features of real estate which must be evaluated before any sound business decision concerning it can be reached. We shall begin with a look at the physical features which impart value and attempt to point to the variations in these features which have value significance. One might assume, for example, that the larger the parcel of land, the more valuable; but this is by no means always true. Nor is it true that a hilltop location in all cases is worth more for residential purposes than a building lot on an open plain. We will consider not only the physical features of land which are the original gifts of nature in its geological evolution but also the man-made physical modifications to the land—the surface treatments of grading and filling, the construction of streets, the installation of underground pipes and wires, and the structural improvements which become physically and legally an indivisible part of the real estate. Urban real estate is very much a manufactured product and its physical value is the joint product of nature's gifts and man's modifications.

The locational qualities of urban land will be considered in Chapter IV. There we will define the term "location" in an economic context. We will consider what locational attributes are of economic significance and how they can be evaluated in their effects on productivity and value. This subject will lead us into a consideration of the internal arrangement of the city, the pattern of land uses, and the nature of the constant locational changes that are taking place. We will learn that location is but a thing of the instant, defined by a complex of space relationships that is in constant flux. Locational analysis and evaluation, then, call for an understanding of the growth processes of the city which bring constant change to the forces and factors of value which focus on any given site.

In Chapter V, the final chapter dealing with the characteristics of the commodity real estate, we recognize that economic factors are subject to definition, limitation, and modification by man-made institutions such as government and law. The real estate market deals not in land and buildings, but in interests or rights in the physical property. The differences in the value of these rights may be as great or greater than the differences in the value of various physical properties; because these combinations of rights are quite complex, we must study the bundles in which they typically come and appreciate how important it is to know exactly what rights and obligations are involved for each party in each real estate transaction. We must also recognize that our constitutions delegate to government certain powers which can greatly affect the value of ownership, such as the power to tax, to regulate use, and to acquire land compulsorily for public purposes. These powers are used in the public interest, but they can also limit the absolute control of the individual owner over his real estate.

LIMITED SUPPLY

It is undeniable that the total supply of land on the surface of the earth is limited and not expansible. But this is an academic matter as far as urban land is concerned. In most urban areas the opposite is the case; there is almost no limit to the supply of land for urban use. For the most part cities grow by absorbing farm lands. The ratio of urban land to total land in this country is about 1 to 110 which strongly suggests that no present shortage exists or is impending. It is well known that the area within a circle increases in geometric proportion as the distance from the center increases. Within 1 mile of the center there are 6.3 square miles of land in the circle; if you double the distance to 2 miles from the center, the area in the circle increases to a total of 25.1 square miles. With a 3-mile radius, the area is 56.5 square miles. Thus a city can expand to nine times the area with an extension of its boundaries to only three times the distance from the center. Farmers sell out to subdividers when they can get more than the land is worth in agricultural use. Thus, broadly speaking, agricultural land values set a floor to urban land values; the urban use must create a land value just higher than the farm value to induce a shift from one use to the other. Of course, urban land values may and do rise much higher than farm values. For example, fine corn land in the Middle West might bring $500 per acre. Farmers often hold out until urban pressures have inflated acreage values and might sell for $2,500 per acre. In a city of 100,000 population, the highest land values in the central business district might figure out to be $5,000 per front foot or over $2 million per acre.

As long as urban land values exceed agricultural values, farmers will sell to subdividers, and there will be no limit to the supply of land for urban expansion.

PHYSICAL FIXITY

The fact that real estate is permanently fixed on the surface of the earth has considerable economic significance which will unfold in our later discussions of location and of the real estate market. At this point, suffice it to say that this characteristic of fixity means that each parcel of land is vulnerable to environmental factors outside its borders. For example, if a packing plant moves in next to your home, you cannot very well pick up the real estate and move to a less odoriferous location. Each property is more or less helpless in the face of locational change and its value may be substantially affected. Of course the change may be for the better, and a good deal of real estate speculation consists in placing bets that beneficial changes in environmental factors, such as the opening of an expressway or the establishment of a new industry, will increase land values in the selected spot.

The immobility of real estate as a commodity prevents shifting it to a better market. A surplus of apartments to rent in one city may occur at a time when there is a shortage 50 miles away in another community. But the unfortunate landlords can sell their product, shelter, only in the market within which it is physically fixed.

INDESTRUCTIBILITY

It is true that space is indestructible and that on the surface of the earth we shall never have more nor less space. Thus the owner of the land holds title to a commodity which is eternal. But of course space may become useless and lose its economic value. Farm land may lose its fertility, and the ghost towns in the mining areas of the West stand in bleak testimony of the present worthlessness of space which at one time sold at premium prices. It should be noted that the man-made improvements to urban land are not indestructible. Streets erode, pipes rust, sidewalks deteriorate, and office buildings and houses decay. Real estate may be a long-lived commodity, but it is immutable only as space.

THREE-DIMENSIONAL SPACE

We have been referring to land, rather misleadingly, as space on the surface of the earth, and thus two-dimensional space. Because real estate includes a variety of man-made improvements to the land, particularly in urban areas, it is easy to see that more than length and width are required as dimensions to describe the physical content of a parcel's ownership. The sewer and water laterals and the foundations and basement of the structure are all underground at depths which range from a few feet in the case of a dwelling to 20 or 30 feet in a large multistory building. And the structure representing the major improvement may extend above the surface of the ground to the height of many hundreds of feet.

The three-dimensional nature of land is illustrated in Figure III-1. He who owns the surface of the earth also owns geometrically related space

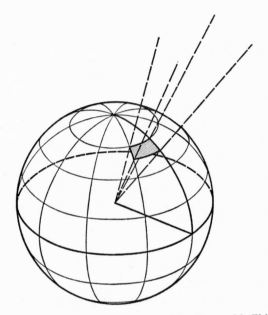

FIGURE III-1. Three-dimensional space. (Suggested by Ernest M. Fisher and Robert M. Fisher, *Urban Real Estate*, Henry Holt and Company, Inc., New York, Figure 2–1, p. 8.)

above and below the surface. For ordinary purposes of land description each parcel is defined in terms of length and width measured in a plane at and horizontal to the surface. The land ownership below the surface is contained within lines drawn through the corners of the parcel and converging at the center of the globe. Mineral rights under the surface ownership are valuable in some areas. Thus the right to mine or extract the minerals may be conveyed to one owner while the rights to use the surface area are held by another owner. In some countries, Canada for example, all mineral rights are public property while surface rights are privately controlled.

Like the subsurface, the supersurface is owned by him who owns the surface, up to a reasonable height. The term "reasonable" is variously defined, but certainly air rights extend well beyond the height of even the tallest of modern structures. Many large and valuable buildings are built on air rights, i.e., supersurface ownership together with the right to use, through ownership or lease, small parcels of the surface where piers can be set to hold up the structure. The Merchandise Mart in Chicago is a huge structure built on air rights and set on stilts above railroad tracks.

It is apparent, then, that real estate is primarily measured in three dimensions: length and width at the surface of the earth, and height from the center of the earth to a reasonable elevation above the surface. However, the third dimension does not appear in property descriptions except when some interest in sub- or supersurface rights is to be conveyed or pledged. With these exceptions real estate is physically defined only in terms of its extent and proportions on the surface plane of the earth.

LAND DESCRIPTION

When real estate is bought and sold it is essential both practically and legally to know exactly what portion of the earth's surface is to be conveyed. There have been sad cases of inaccuracies and misunderstandings on this point. It is not uncommon for a builder to construct a fine house partly on his own land and partly on the neighbor's lot. An otherwise valid deed of conveyance may be void if the identification of the real estate is uncertain. The term "legal description" is generally used to refer to an identification of the property which is sufficiently complete and exact to stand up in court. For most purposes it is not enough to refer to the real estate by street number, even in a built-up area. Such reference may identify the structure but it fails to define the area and dimensions of the land which go with it. There are three methods in common use which can provide an acceptable legal description of real estate:
1. Description by reference to the rectangular survey system
2. Description by reference to a recorded plat
3. Description by metes and bounds

Rectangular Survey System

For the most of the country, land descriptions have final reference to a basic government survey which was made by the Federal government prior to disposing of the public domain to private individuals. The survey covers all states west of the Mississippi River except Texas and all states north of the Ohio River. In addition it is used in Mississippi, Alabama, and Florida. This survey was begun pursuant to a law passed in 1785 and establishes a rectilinear system of reference lines and permanent monuments or markers to which all land description may be tied. The latitude and longitude of each monument is known so that, if necessary, every parcel of real estate could be located with reference to such known points.

The government survey established 24 north and south reference lines known as *principal meridians*, usually projected through some prominent geographical landmark. At intervals of 24 miles, north and south *guide meridians* were laid out. Because of the curvature of the earth, the north-south lines gradually converge; to adjust, every 24 miles on the north-south axis, the guide meridans were set over so that they are again just

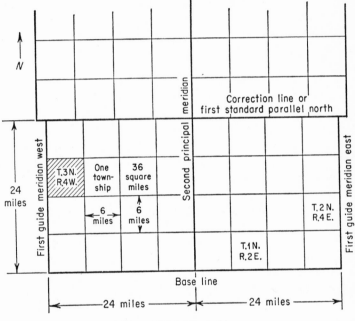

FIGURE III-2. Townships.

24 miles apart on the east-west axis. Within the guide meridians the area was further subdivided into 6-mile north-south strips (Figure III-2).

For each principal meridian, an east-west line, called the *base line*, was established, and at 24-mile intervals parallel to the base line other latitudinal *standard parallels* were drawn. Between these reference lines other lines were set every 6 miles. The result of this survey procedure was to divide all the land into townships approximately 6 miles square. The east-west rows of townships are numbered in *tiers* north of the base line. The north-south rows are numbered in *ranges* east and west of the principal meridian.

In the lower left-hand corner of the diagram, one of the townships has been labeled with its identification as commonly used in land description.

The designation "T. 3 N." means the third tier of townships north of the base line; and "R. 4 W." means the fourth range of townships west of the principal meridian. To make the description complete it is necessary to identify the principal meridian, in this case the second principal meridian.

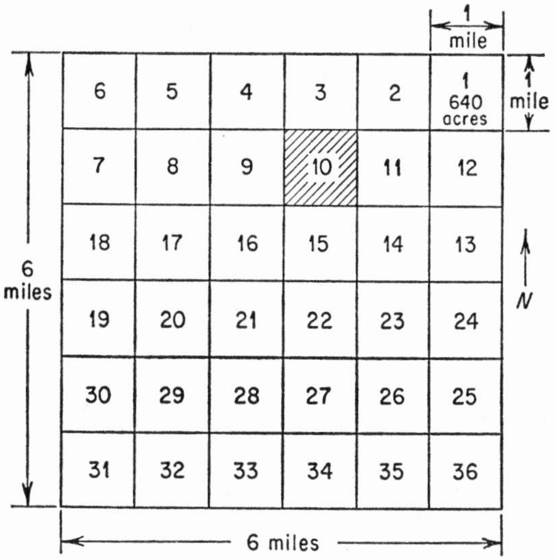

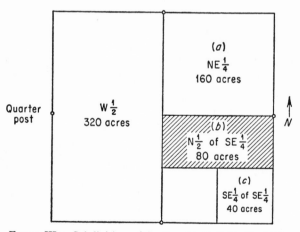

FIGURE III-3. Township T. 3 N., R. 4 W. with numbered sections.

FIGURE III-4. Subdivision of Section 10, T. 3 N., R. 4 W.

This is a sufficient indication since in all the United States there is only one second principal meridian and it is associated with its own special base line. Principal meridians are sometimes identified by number and sometimes by name, as, for example, the Mexico meridian.

Each township as established by the government survey is divided into 36 *sections,* each of which is a mile square. Figure III-3 shows how the sections are numbered for purposes of identification. Figure III-4 illustrates how a section, which contains 1 square mile or 640 acres of land, may be divided into fractional parcels and how such fractions are identified. Stakes are set at each corner of the section and at the middle of each side of the section to mark the *"quarter corners";* imaginary lines connecting the quarter corners divide the section in quarter sections of 160 acres each. As the diagram shows, the description of a fractional part of a section is simple and direct. Parcel (*a*) is the northeast quarter or NE ¼ of Section 10, T. 3 N., R. 4 W. or the second principal meridian. Parcel (*b*) is the north half of the southeast quarter or N ½, SE ¼. Parcel (*c*) is the southeast quarter of the southeast quarter or SE ¼, SE ¼. It has been a natural development that in rural areas farm ownerships usually consist of sections or fractions of sections.

Recorded Subdivision Plats

Land in urban areas is also tied to the basic government survey. When a subdivision map or plat of a group of lots is submitted for filing or recording in the public records in the county courthouse, the area which has been platted into lots must be exactly described in terms of the government survey just as rural ownerships are described. Thus the plat might cover the north half of the south-east quarter of Section 10 Town-

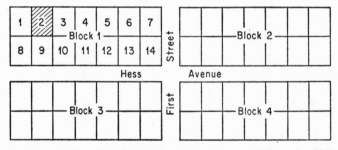

FIGURE III-5. Plat of Cherokee Subdivision, Lane County, Wisconsin. N½ of SE¼ of Section 10, T. 3 N., R. 4 W. of the second principal meridian.

ship 3 North, Range 4 West of the second principal meridian. Within this area, the subdivision plat, which has been carefully surveyed, all distances and dimensions being measured and entered on the map submitted for recording or filing, can show exactly where each lot is situated with reference to the government survey. Thus Lot 2, Block 1, Cherokee Subdivision, Lane County, Wisconsin, can be precisely located on the face of the earth by reference to the recorded map of the subdivision which, in turn, is exactly defined in terms of the government survey (Figure III-5).

Metes and Bounds

The oldest and most extensively used method for describing land throughout the world is by metes and bounds. This method requires the selection of some starting point on the boundary of the land, a point which is more or less permanently locatable, usually marked by some object called a "monument" such as an iron stake, a tree, or a rock. From this point of origin, the land is described by outlining its perimeter, moving from the point of origin in a stated compass direction for a certain distance to another natural or artificial landmark, from this corner to another monument and so on around the circumference of the land back to the point of origin. This form of description may be used anywhere but it is most common in areas not covered by the rectangular survey. In an urban area where there are many definitely established and permanent landmarks, such as public streets and recorded subdivision plats, the monuments used in a metes and bounds description can usually be artificial. For example, a building lot might be described as follows:

Beginning at a point on the north side of Johnson Street 50 feet west of the intersection of the north side of Johnson Street and the east side of Madison Avenue; thence due east parallel to the north side of Johnson Street for 75 feet; thence due north parallel to the east side of Madison Avenue for 150 feet; thence due west parallel to the north side of Johnson Street for 75 feet; thence due south parallel to the east side of Madison Avenue for 150 feet to the point of beginning.

In rural areas not under the government survey, metes and bounds descriptions may more frequently rely on natural monuments such as trees and boulders and may have reference to river beds or public roads to define parts of the boundaries. An example of such a description follows:

Beginning at a stone on the bank of Doe River, at a point where the highway from A to B crosses said river; thence 40° north of west 100 rods to a large stump; thence 10° north of west 90 rods; thence 15° west of north 80 rods to an oak tree; thence due east 150 rods to the highway; thence following the course of the highway 50 rods due north; thence 5° north of east 90 rods; thence 45° east of south 60 rods; thence 10° north of east 200 rods to the Doe River; thence following the course of the river southwesterly to the place of beginning.

PRIVATE SURVEY

Human error in land description is surprisingly common. The result of such mistakes is usually a dispute involving two parties each claiming the same land. Reasonable, though not positive, protection against controversies of this kind can be secured by the prospective buyer or mortgagee through a survey of the land before the deal is concluded. A registered surveyor, given the legal description of the real estate, proceeds to mark it out on the ground by stakes and lines. The buyer can see exactly what he is to acquire and by consultation with owners of contiguous properties may determine whether there are differences in opinion on exactly where the property lines are located. If there are differences, the buyer will want these matters cleared up before he concludes the transaction.

ECONOMIC VALUE OF SPACE

Space as such has no value; but space in the right location and combined with the right input of man-made improvements has great utility. Basically space is valuable in urban areas because it gives room for man's activities. But these activities are highly diverse and require units of space which are different in extent and proportion. The optimum unit of space is a function of the nature of the use to which it is to be put and the location of the space in the community. Locational matters are reserved for later treatment so that we will consider here only the relationships between the use of the space and its extent.

On the urban scene it is rarely true that space is valuable in direct proportion to the amount or area. Quotations of urban land values at $50 per front foot or $2.25 per square foot are misleading, for such unit prices imply that value is in direct proportion to area or to frontage on the street. For most types of improvement and use, there is a minimum lot size and units of space which are smaller are of no value whatsoever for such a use. Who would buy a home site which was 15 by 40 feet in dimensions with an area of 600 square feet? On the other hand, in a given price class of home, the space added to a lot of already adequate size will have little additional value to the owner. A lot of 12,000 to 15,000 square feet might provide most of the desired services and amenities, whereas a lot of 20,000 square feet, while adding an element of additional privacy, might call for an added load of care and maintenance which would more than offset the utilities of the additional space.

Though in some circumstances the unit value of land, dollars per square foot, tends to decline as total area rises beyond a certain point, the reverse can also be true. There are cases, for example, where combining two or more parcels into a single tract will permit a higher and more intensive use than would have been possible on one of the small parcels. The land value developed by this more intensive use means that the value of the combined lands will be greater than the sum of the values of the individual parcels. This value increment resulting from the assembly of a tract of sufficient size for a more intensive use is termed *plottage;* an example would be the plottage value created by combining two small lots, each suitable only for a single-family house, into one ownership of land large enough for an apartment building.

The economic value of land can be markedly influenced by the shape and proportions of the parcel. A residential building lot of 10,000 square feet, with dimensions of 40 by 250 feet is too narrow to allow for modern architectural standards in house design and too deep for an attractive and efficient use of the rear yard. The same area in a lot 80 by 125 feet would yield a much higher level of services to the typical American family and would command a higher price in the market.

Odd-shaped and irregular lots are difficult to develop and are often limited in the choice of uses which can be made of them. For example, a triangular lot in a business area does not lend itself to the siting of a rectangular building with the result that land is wasted, or if a triangular building is erected, the shape makes for higher costs and inefficient interior space arrangements.

Costs of land development, and thus value, are affected by the proportions of the land space. The combined costs of street grading and paving, curb and gutter, sidewalks, and sewer and water mains may be as high as $20 for every running foot. Thus a building lot with a 50-foot frontage on the street will be burdened with a development cost of $1,000 for these facilities. A 75-foot lot would carry a burden of $1,500 with no additional benefits to the lot or to its user. The user needs only a connection with the sewer and water mains and access to the sidewalk and street; the longer runs of pipe and pavement in front of the wider lot are of no intrinsic value. As a result of this characteristic of land development costs, building lots are often made narrower than they otherwise would be platted in the interests of privacy and aesthetics, particularly in the case of lots for low- and medium-priced homes.

GEOLOGICAL CHARACTERISTICS

Urban land is valuable not only as space for the activities of man but also for the physical support which it provides. The importance of the geological characteristics of agricultural land is well known—the top soil which determines its fertility, the subsoil conditions which affect drainage, and the contours of the land which influence the rate of erosion. It is also true of urban land that the natural features of the land affect productivity and value. The topography and geology of the earth's crust determine its ability to support buildings and may limit the uses to which it can be put. To a considerable extent, these natural features affect the costs of preparing and improving the land for urban uses and thus are factors in determining its value.

When an area is marshy or underlaid with bog, it may be possible to support heavy buildings only at heavy expense through the use of floating foundations or deep piling driven down until it rests on solid ground below. Wet lands can be drained, and lands subject to periodic flooding can be protected with dikes. Much of New Orleans is below the level of the Mississippi River and is kept dry by a vast system of levees and by the use of pumps to lift storm waters for deposit in the river. Such requirements add greatly to the cost of providing usable space.

Land founded on solid rock has the advantage of providing a firm base for heavy buildings, but such subsoil conditions increase costs of excavations for basements or trenches to accommodate pipes and wires. Where heavy subsoils are impervious, residential use may be precluded if individual sewage disposal fields are required in the absence of public sewer mains. Land which is rough and hilly cannot be economically used for commercial and industrial purposes, nor is it suited for economy housing because of the added costs of land preparation in the form of terraces and retaining walls. Land with forest cover may be choice for residential use or for parks, but requires costly clearing and grubbing to prepare it for industrial or commercial utilization.

Prospective developers of real estate would be well advised to study carefully the geological features of the land in which they intend to invest. Soil borings will reveal the nature of the subsoil and foretell excavation and foundation problems. The disposal of storm waters may be a costly project, and an analysis of the drainage area in which the property lies will reveal the extent of the problem. Low-lying tracts along rivers and lakes should be analyzed for evidences of flooding.

URBAN LAND AS A MANUFACTURED PRODUCT

Up to this point we have presented the value-generating attributes of land as a gift of nature—space and its geological qualities. We have pointed out some of the economic implications of these attributes and how the wary investor in real estate might go about evaluating them in their effect on land value. But virgin land is rarely usable for urban purposes; the physical changes which man makes in it, in order that it may become productive, are also sources of utility and value which must be identified and appraised. These physical changes and additions to the land in the form of streets, pipes, and structures are included in the generic term *improvements*. On the one hand, they are the source of land development costs which are usually several times the cost of the raw land; in a typical residential subdivision, the raw land or acreage may have cost the developer an average of $1,000 per lot, the streets and utilities another $1,500, and the dwelling structure $20,000. On the other hand, land would not be usable for urban purposes without this combination with improvements of various kinds.

As a result of this manufacturing process in which land is only one of the raw materials there emerges a product of great utility and value. It is an important principle to remember that the utility of urban real estate is the joint and undifferentiated product of a combination of land, labor, and materials. Attempts to assign separate values to land and building, for example, are unrealistic and futile. It is also fundamental that the costs of land improvement have no necessary relationship to the final utility and value of the real estate; its value is founded on the total services which are provided by the end product with no necessary reference to the cost of manufacture.

Land improvements fall in two broad categories: on-site and off-site. The on-site improvements include the physical changes within and upon the parcel of land representing the ownership under consideration. The off-site improvements are elsewhere, but may be as essential to the value of the land as the drives and buildings which are constructed directly on it. Nor does each parcel of urban land escape the costs of off-site improvements such as expressways and sewage disposal plants, for, through the agency of government, most of these costs are charged back in the form of direct or indirect taxation to the lands which are benefited.

Off-site Improvements

The term *improvements in common* has been applied quite aptly to the kind of physical modifications which are made for the benefit of real estate in off-site locations and where the improvements serve an entire neighborhood or community.[1] One of the first and most important of such improvements in common is the street and road system. Without access urban real estate would be valueless; the urban street system facilitates movement among all urban sites and thus serves them all. The street rights of way are publicly owned and the streets publicly maintained, but they are absolutely essential to each privately owned parcel of land in the community. Much the same can be said of the public sewage and water systems. The sewer and water mains run in ditches in the public streets and, together with the wells, sewage disposal plants, and pumping stations, serve the entire community. The disposal of storm waters is customarily handled by publicly installed facilities of gutters and storm sewers which serve large drainage areas and many private homes, stores, and factory properties.

The legal right to use the various improvements in common attaches to each parcel of real estate and has great economic significance. As long

[1] Ernest M. Fisher and Robert M. Fisher, *Urban Real Estate*, Henry Holt and Company, Inc., New York, 1954.

as each owner meets his tax obligations, he has the privilege of hooking up to the water system or running a lateral to the sewer main or connecting his property to the street with a driveway opening. Thus, effectively, his property has been improved by the availability of the public services which are outside the boundaries of his land.

The costs of such public improvements as sewer mains, streets, and sidewalks are borne by the benefited properties approximately in proportion to the benefit. As a practical matter, the formulas used by municipalities in allocating such costs among properties are necessarily crude, and they only approximate an allocation according to benefit as called for by most state laws dealing with special assessments. For example, when a water main is installed the costs are usually charged to individual properties in proportion to the number of front feet on the street in which the water pipe is installed. Thus a lot with 100 feet of frontage bears twice the burden of a lot with 50 feet on the street. It would be hard to prove that one is benefited more than the other; each has no more than the privilege of making a connection with the main to provide water service on the property.

Improvements in common are either installed by the land developer or by the appropriate unit of local government. If the land developer makes the installation—grades and surfaces the street, lays the sewer pipe in the street right of way, or installs curb and gutter or sidewalk—he includes a proportion of such costs in the price of each lot and expects to recapture his outlay for improvements out of the sales proceeds. Of course, if he does not have a salable product at his asking price, he may not get his money back, but this is true of any manufacturer who misjudges his market.

When the municipality installs the improvements, the cost is typically charged against each property in accordance with some formula which is presumed to distribute the burden in proportion to relative benefit. This special assessment tax becomes a lien on the property and must be paid like any other real estate tax except that most local governments permit it to be paid in eight or ten annual installments with interest on the unpaid balance.

Facilities for electric power, gas, and telephone service are improvements in common which usually are provided by privately owned public utility companies. Where the density of potential users is sufficient, these companies install transmission lines at their own expense and recapture the cost out of service revenues.

Not all of the costs of improvements in common are included in the price of the lot or charged against it as special assessments. In some cases the municipality meets the cost out of the general fund. Storm sewers may be financed in this way because of the great difficulty of allocating costs in accordance to benefit. Improvement costs which are financed out of the general fund increase the total of local expenditures which must be met out of general revenues largely raised from the property tax. Thus all real estate in the community is called on to share the burden ad valorem. As a result of these three different ways of financing improvements in common, it is not always possible to measure the costs of public improvements which benefit a given parcel of real estate. Some of the costs may have been absorbed by the developer and capitalized in the purchase price; other costs may have been met by advances from the local political subdivision which are being repaid through installments secured by a special assessment tax; and certain others, charged to the general fund of the municipality, are components in the annual property tax.

In analyzing the added productivity imparted to urban real estate by the availability of improvements in common at the site, both the value of the services and the burden of financial obligations to be assumed must be taken into account. The convenience and economy of public water supply and sanitary sewers are universally understood, for example, but a prospective buyer must ascertain whether they are paid for or not, before making a price offer for the land. Where there are unpaid balances from special assessments for streets, curb and gutter, sidewalks, storm sewers, sanitary sewer or water mains, the buyer assumes this obligation when he buys the real estate and should inquire at the source of official information, the local tax office, to determine exactly the amounts unpaid and the established schedule of payment.

Improvements in common which are charged against the general fund of the municipality will result in higher levels in the general property tax which may have to cover debt service obligations on public bonds issued to finance the improvement. Again, the wary real estate investor will wish to determine, before purchase, just what tax obligations he is undertaking and will adjust his price offer accordingly.

On-site Improvements

For most parcels of urban real estate the major on-site improvement is the structure. But urban sites typically require a considerable amount of additional processing before the combination of land and improvements is ready to provide its intended stream of undifferentiated services. For example, many sites require grading and leveling, in some cases calling for the removal of earth, in others for trucking it in for fill. Sloping land may need terracing, the construction of retaining walls, and special treatment for storm-water drainage. Driveways, walks, and parking areas may require surfacing. Connections with the public services call for on-site sewer laterals, water laterals, gas pipes, and electric wires. In areas not served, an individual and private sewage disposal system may be installed or a well drilled for water supply. Landscaping and planting represent another kind of land improvement which results in functional advantages, such as the provision of shade and the prevention of soil erosion, and, in addition, the aesthetic values of natural beauty and attractiveness.

For most purposes for which urban real estate is used, shelter from wind, rain, and cold is considered essential. Modern buildings perform this function and may even supply an ideal artificial climate the year round with elaborate and costly air conditioning. To the strictly physical functions may be added, in some cases, intangible services such as prestige and satisfactions which come from the occupancy of a monumental office building or a fine home.

The primary importance of the functional values of urban structures is matched by the fact that they usually represent the major improvement cost of the parcel of land which they occupy. Structures vary in purpose, size, shape, arrangement of space, materials, equipment, age, state of physical deterioration, and architectural style. Each of these qualities, and others not mentioned in this list, has its special and various effect on the productivity of the real estate. It is the purpose of the next several paragraphs to suggest how the physical attributes of the structural improvement influence the satisfactions, services, and thus the value of urban real estate. It is an important principle that the productivity of real estate has a time dimension, i.e., that it is a flow of services over time. This fact is of special importance in determining the present value of such a durable economic good as real estate. Expensive and long-lived structures typically continue in use over many years with little change in space arrangement and equipment. The difficulty of forecasting productivity under the constantly changing economic, social and technological conditions of future years suggests the need for careful and detailed analysis of the structural improvements by any prospective investor.

The value-generating characteristics of a building may be grouped for analytical purposes as follows:

1. Functional efficiency—the adaptation of the structure to the activities for which it is to be used

2. Durability—the physical qualities of the structure which determine how long it can continue to render useful services

3. Attractiveness—the aesthetic qualities of the structure

Functional Efficiency. Function is related to use, and thus the functional efficiency of the physical property is judged only in relationship to the nature of its intended utilization. Houses are tested against the demands of family living; office buildings for the conduct of certain kinds of business operations. The testing covers not only efficiency in use but also costs of operation and maintenance.

The dynamic aspect of functional efficiency is introduced by the fact that there is a continual change in social and business institutions which gives rise to continual change in the demands for the services of real estate. For example, the virtual disappearance of domestic servants has been accompanied by the need for more compact dwellings with a maximum of mechanical equipment. Present preferences for the one-story house have reduced the demand for two-story homes. Television and the do-it-yourself movement have introduced the family room into house design. In the industrial world modern technology calls for a one-level production line and a one-story plant. These many and varied changes create functional obsolescence in existing structures which were not designed for the new requirements. In light of the inevitability of change, the analyst must consider (1) the rate at which future changes are likely to take place in the nature of the activities for which the property was intended and (2) the flexibility of the physical property in accommodating to changing demands upon it. In some cases buildings can be economically modified, but in other cases the costs of modernization would be prohibitive.

For most types of use the site and its relationship to the structure is a factor in functional efficiency. Modern outdoor living calls for a yard of generous proportions. Thus a house built on too small a lot will suffer increasingly from obsolescence if this preference is to continue. The trends toward a shorter working day, a shorter work week, longer vacations, and a higher proportion of retired people in the population all suggest that the popularity of outdoor living will increase. The older shopping centers and industrial plants illustrate an unfortunate relationship of site to structures in the inadequacy of parking space. Other features of the site which may contribute to inefficiencies include its proportions, contours, elevation, and subsoil conditions. The placing of the structures on the site may deprive it of sufficient light and ventilation or may rob the occupants of privacy. Poor orientation can increase exposure to winter cold and reduce protection from the summer sun to the discomfort of the users.

The availability of public utilities and services at the site was earlier considered as a locational factor. However, site improvements are required to put these services to use. Water and sewer laterals are needed and electrical connections as well. The lack of adequate internal driveways and walks can limit the utility of the site just as lack of adequate and suitable mechanical equipment detracts from the efficiency of the structure. Changing technology and customs bring new demands for mechanical aids. Home air conditioning is relatively new, and garbage grinders were unknown only a few years ago. As built-in equipment is more widely provided in new homes, the refrigerator, the range, and perhaps the television set will become more widely accepted as a part of the real estate and an essential value base. From the standpoint of the mortgage lender, the lack of the appropriate mechanical equipment, and particularly any physical obstacles to its installation, is a danger to value stability and a source of mortgage risk.

The interior space arrangement of the structural improvements largely determines their functional efficiency. A poorly arranged home means a greater burden on the housekeeper, less convenience for the family members, and less adaptability to changing family needs. Prospective buyers are quick to recognize planning defects and resale price will suffer. The ideal structure for many kinds of business use is one which provides the greatest areas of unobstructed space so that equipment can be most effectively arranged, nonbearing partitions placed most advantageously, and subsequent modifications made most economically. Waste of space, as well as poor arrangement, is a form of inefficiency in any structure.

Some of the features of a dwelling which should be analyzed in terms of functional efficiency include:

1. Room characteristics. The size and shape of the various rooms are judged against the use for which they are intended. Cramped bedrooms or an odd-shaped living room make furniture placement difficult and comfortable use an impossibility. The placement of door and window openings and the location of wall space affect room efficiency. Room orientation—exposure to sun and view—can influence utility and comfort qualities.

2. Circulation. There should be ease of passage among the several functional areas of the house with a minimum of steps and disturbance.

3. Privacy. Certain areas for sleep, dressing, study, and socializing should be protected against intrusion and noise.

4. Storage space. Lack of different kinds of storage space in the right locations results in inconvenience, a cluttered house, and some damage to goods and chattels.

5. Kitchen efficiency. The kitchen is a production area which absorbs much of the time and energy of the housewife. Its arrangement and equipment are carefully evaluated by buyers.

Durability. The time dimension in the measurement of the services of real estate is of major importance. Thus an analysis of the physical durability of a structure is required as a basis for estimating how long it will continue to be productive. The greater the resistance to wear and deterioration, the slower will be the increase in repair and maintenance costs, the higher the quality of services which can be maintained, and the longer the economic life.

Soundness of structural design contributes to long life and value stability. Inadequate support around a stairwell or window openings in a residential structure can lead to recurring plaster cracks and floor sagging which are costly and unsightly. A sagging roof invites leaks and inadequate footings may result in uneven settling which wracks the entire structure. There are many other examples of the contributions to high repair and maintenance costs and to shortened economic life which may be made by poor structural design in foundations, exterior walls, partitions, floors, ceilings, and roofs. The same results stem from the use of equipment and materials of inadequate strength and poor quality in relationship to the functions which the materials and equipment are expected to perform. Quality of workmanship is another factor, for poor fitting of materials and careless fastening, assembly, installation, or application can seriously detract from appearance and reduce resistance to the deteriorating effects of use and of the elements.

In the evaluation of durability, a first step is the observation of the present state of wear and deterioration. The outward indications in relationship to the age of the structure and its past usage are clues to the kinds of defects which are inherent and the rate at which future deterioration may be expected to proceed. Some knowledge of structural design and building techniques is required to interpret the evidences of physical depreciation and to distinguish between wear and deterioration which is the result of basic defects, and that which is only the product of deficient care and maintenance.

Attractiveness. The visual appeal of real property is a factor in determining market value, particularly in the case of dwellings. The mortgage lender is concerned that the collateral property shall retain its market appeal over the life of the loan. Though tastes change and architectural styles come and go, continuing market acceptance is most probable when the property meets reasonable standards of simplicity, harmony among the elements, and good taste. The analyst must resist the temptation to apply his own aesthetic values when they are at variance with market-expressed preferences.

The exterior view of the property is a composition of structural design and its setting on the lot. The positioning of the main building and auxiliary structures on the site are important. The site development with its plantings, walls, walks, and drives can greatly enhance the attractiveness of the scene. Good architectural design and the tasteful use of exterior materials and colors are basic. Extreme architectural styles do not have wide acceptance among prospective buyers and therefore do not contribute to value stability.

The visual appeal of the interior of a structure is dependent on the arrangement of space, natural and artificial lighting, and interior decoration.

IV

THE LOCATIONAL BASIS
OF REAL ESTATE VALUE

INTRODUCTION

The preceding chapter on the physical origins of real estate productivity and value identified those natural qualities of land which affect its usefulness to man; also considered were the man-made modifications and improvements which convert natural space and support into the valuable commodity known as real estate. It was made clear that these physical features contribute to real estate value in varying degree and must be evaluated by the prospective investor in his analysis of the productivity of the property. But it is common knowledge that real estate is also valuable because of its locational position on the urban landscape. Thus we must study the nature of location and the characteristics of the locational qualities of real estate which influence its utility and value.

The essence of location derives from one of the elemental physical facts of life, the reality of space. We cannot conceive of existence without space; if there were no such thing, all objects and all life would have to be at one spot. If this happened to be the case real estate would have no such quality as location; all real estate would be in the same place, equally convenient to every other piece of real estate and to every human activity and establishment. But under the physical laws of the universe, each bit of matter—each atom, molecule, stone, dog, house, and man—takes up space at or near the surface of the earth. As a result no two objects can be at the same place at the same time. Necessarily, then, all people, animals, and objects are distributed in a spatial pattern. Our concern, being with real estate and cities, is to understand how this spatial pattern in cities influences the usefulness and value of particular parcels of land. Then we shall see how these spatial values, in their turn, play a part in the decisions of investors, in the development of urban land, and in the creation of a more or less orderly, consistent, and predictable spatial arrangement of urban land use.

BASIC ELEMENTS OF LOCATION

The common-sense notion of location is a useful point on which to begin our consideration of locational services and locational values. If you analyze what you mean by location of a parcel of real estate, you discover that you are thinking of places outside of and away from the site and the convenience of movement from the site to these places—the school, shopping district, church, and golf course. Or you are considering the possibility of unpleasant smells, noises, and views from a nearby industrial area. Or perhaps there comes to mind the lovely mountain view from your living-room window. Thus you are focusing your evaluation on the environment or surroundings of the site. This approach is logical and sound, for the locational services rendered the user of real estate are largely the products of space relationships between the site and other points on the urban landscape. In some cases, the user of the site places a positive value on convenience and accessibility to certain external points, as, for example, the high value placed on close proximity to an elementary school by families with small children. But the same householder will place a high value on the protection of adequate separation from an industrial or commercial district. Even in the case of the elementary school, he would prefer not to be so close as to suffer noise and confusion or to be confronted with a view of the grounds from his living-room window.

We earlier alluded to a type of positive locational value which can be enjoyed without leaving the site: the view from a high and sightly spot which is dependent upon space relationship with lake, or mountain, or peaceful valley. Another example is a favorable exposure to the prevailing summer breezes or to the warmth of the winter's sun on a southern slope. One need not travel to enjoy these benefits. In addition, there is a similar type of locational value deriving from proximity to places of prestige and fashion. In residential areas the homes of the community leaders and social lights are poles of social prestige; in the commercial district certain streets and addresses possess an aura of business prestige to which locational values attach.

In summary, then, we may identify three basic elements in the concept of location and locational returns or values:

1. Convenience: measured in the disutilities (time, cost, aggravation) of movement of persons or goods from the site to other points to which **movement is desirable or essential**

2. Favorable exposure: exposure to view, sun, and breeze, and nearness to centers of prestige and fashion

3. Unfavorable exposure: the degree of exposure to offensive influences which diminish the use-value of real estate such as unsightly views, noise, smoke, smells, and disturbance

Convenience

Convenience stands first in over-all importance among the three basic elements of location. It is a commonly recognized and easily understood quality of real estate though far from simple in many of its manifestations. We all appreciate the advantages and values of convenience of school to home, of a good lunchroom to a factory, or of a bank to a business establishment. We recognize that savings in time, effort, and cost in the movement of persons and goods is a strong locational force; and that urban activities tend to gravitate to locations which promise the maximum economy of movement to and from related activities and places. Convenience as a concept applied to a single space relationship and related to but two points in space is a simple concept, i.e., the convenience of school to home as it relates to the daily travel of a child. But convenience as a determinant in the location of a factory is quite another matter for it involves a complex of movements of people and goods to a great constellation of locations. Before we are ready to analyze these more complex locational problems, it will be necessary to consider the essential qualities of what we commonly refer to as convenience.

ESTABLISHMENT

Our concern is with the contribution which location makes to the productivity of real estate. One cannot conceive of location without thinking of a place and without reference to a particular kind of activity being conducted at that place. The location of a vacant lot can be described as a geographical phenomenon, but it has little economic significance unless evaluated in terms of a specified use of the land. Thus it will be expedient to adopt the term *establishment* as defining the basic unit of land use consisting of ". . . individuals or groups occupying recognizable places of business, residence, government, or assembly. . . ." [1] A retail store, a factory, an apartment building, and a single-family dwelling are all establishments.

But we quickly encounter a complication in the use of the notion of the establishment. The activities of most types of establishment involve a variety of functions and individuals; and the locational values for each function and individual may be quite different from the others. The differ-

[1] Robert B. Mitchell and Chester Rapkin, *Urban Traffic*, Columbia University Press, New York, 1954, p. 14.

ences in the locational preferences among the members of a family is a familiar example—father would like to be close to his job and perhaps to the golf club; mother cherishes convenience to shops and to schools; the teen-age daughter wants to live near her friends and cronies; and the baby doesn't care. For a law office, proximity to the courthouse and to business clients is valuable, but old records and case files which are infrequently used can just as well be stored in a more remote warehouse. A manufacturing enterprise may separate its business office and its production operations because of locational considerations. Thus each land use establishment is a "packet of functions" with each function probably best served in a different location.[2] The selection of an optimum location for the establishment involves a balancing of the locational pulls of the component functions, for no single location is optimum for all functions. Thus if we were looking for a good location for a wholesale sales office and warehouse, we would start with a breakdown of the activities of the business which involve the movement of persons or goods: the assembly of the goods to be stored in the warehouse; the distribution of the goods to various destinations; the journey to work of the employees and executives; and the movement of customers. Each group of movements would involve a different set of related establishments, and in each case, a different location for the wholesale house would be indicated. The selected location would be one creating the least cost in inconvenience, all movements considered.

LINKAGE

We live in a society characterized by specialization and interdependence. The economic consequences of this fact is a subject in beginning courses in economics and need not be restated here. We are directly concerned, however, with the fact that along with the specialization of function centered in the various establishments found in the urban scene there is the concomitant specialization of location, and as we have indicated in Chapter II a degree of specialization of districts or neighborhoods. The sociologists say that these interdependent establishments, each in its own special location, maintain a symbiotic, or mutually beneficial, relationship. We find significance in the relationships among the functionally specialized establishments when such a relationship results in the movement of persons or goods. This relationship is termed *linkage*, and it gives rise to certain costs created by the movements of goods or persons termed the "costs of friction." Each establishment seeks a location which will minimize these costs, and in the aggregate, establishments in a community tend, with many exceptions, to arrange themselves in an equilibrium wherein aggregate costs of friction are minimized. In a later chapter we

[2] The concept of a "packet of functions" was introduced by Robert Murray Haig.

intend to show how each establishment competes for the location which is most advantageous and how the successful bidder is that enterprise which, by reason of the savings in costs of friction, can pay the highest price. Thus each location tends to be occupied by that establishment for which it is the best suited.

Before plunging any deeper into the economics of location, it will be well to consider the nature of linkage. It is clear by now that the concept of location involves relationships or interactions between activities or persons at various points on the urban landscape. Convenience is ease of movement from point to point. We employ the term linkage to describe the relationships of locational significance which are continuing or frequently recurring between establishments. Linkage generally involves movements of persons or goods between the linked establishments, and for this reason, they tend to be near to each other. The industrial plant seeks a location convenient to a labor pool, and workers in the plant prefer to reduce the journey to work by living near the plant. The supermarket locates in the midst of a suburban residential area in order that it may be near its customers, and the housewife is influenced in selecting a home by its convenience to shopping facilities.

There are many forms of linkage which reflect various relationships among linked establishments. The travel of persons between linked establishments generally involves a round trip starting at the home base or the job (place of work) base. The objective of the trip reveals the nature of the relationship or linkage. The major trip objectives involving movement of persons might be grouped as follows:

1. To receive a service:
   A child going to school
   Visiting friends
   Going to the beauty parlor
   Going to the doctor
   A trip to the movies
   Going to a lawyer's office
   A family going to church
2. To provide a service:
   A plumber going to free a clogged drain
   A doctor on a home visit
   A salesman visiting a prospect
   A lawyer going to court
   A worker going to a factory

We must qualify the earlier statement that the movement of persons involves a round trip. A trip from the home or job base and back may include more than one intermediate stop and more than one objective. The salesman may go directly from his home to the office of a prospect, then stop for a haircut, visit another prospect, and stop in at his own office before returning home. The housewife may go downtown to have lunch with a friend, shop for a hat, see the doctor, and stop in at the bank.

The movement of goods is mainly a one-way trip. The purpose of the movement is to relocate the goods at the point of:

1. Processing, as in the transportation of raw materials or semifinished goods to a manufacturing plant.

2. Distribution, as in carrying manufactured products from factory to wholesale house or from warehouse to retailer.

3. Consumption, as in delivering articles from a department store to the home of the purchaser. The actual conveyance of the goods may be performed by either the transferor or the transferee. The department store may deliver the article, or the buyer may take it home with her after the purchase. The lumber yard may deliver a bundle of plywood to the builder on the job, or the contractor may pick it up in his own truck.

The classification of linked establishments, presented by Mitchell and Rapkin,[3] is useful in revealing the different nature of linkages encountered in real life:

1. *Dominant Use–Subordinate Use.* The subordinate use serves the dominant establishment or group of similar establishments. An example is a machine repair shop and the industrial plant or plants which it serves. In such a case the smaller operation would tend to move to the vicinity of the larger.

2. *Dominant Use–Ancillary Use.* The ancillary establishment serves the employees of the dominant use. Examples are a restaurant near a large factory or a cigar stand in an office building.

3. *Co-dominant Uses and Dominant Use–Satellite Use.* These establishments serve common customers. A large department store and an adjacent ladies' shoe store serve the same clients who come to shop in both places for shoes and to buy in one or the other. The neighboring candy store is called a satellite use because it capitalizes on the pedestrian traffic drawn into the area by the larger or dominant establishments. Stores with equal drawing power are co-dominant uses. The important feature of this form of linkage is that the linked establishments are not directly related through business contacts or transactions but are drawn together for the convenience of their common customers. Linkage of this type appears because of the characteristic of consumers to engage in comparison shopping for clothing and other types of merchandise. Competing retailers accept this practice as a given factor and locate in clusters to better serve the customer. Specialty shops patronized by comparison shoppers in the course of shopping expeditions cling as closely as possible to the shopping-goods concentrations.

[3] Mitchell and Rapkin, *op. cit.*, Chap. 7.

It may be noted parenthetically that uses which are not linked may be found in proximate locations.[4] Establishments with little or nothing in common may seek similar locations for the following reasons:

1. They may be attracted for reasons of prestige.
2. They may have similar requirements in respect to type of building or rent level.
3. They may have similar locational specifications but for entirely unconnected reasons.
4. It may be an historical accident.

Noncomplementary or nonlinked establishments may be compatible neighbors, or they may be incompatible in the sense that the activities of one interfere with the activities of the other.

TRIBUTARY AREA

In the notion of the establishment as a packet of functions there is the suggestion that each land use is the focus of its own special complex of linkages. Certainly the set of linkages which characterizes a supermarket is far different from the complex of significant space relationships focusing on the manager's home. Each type of land use differs in this respect, and within each category the set of specific linkages differs from establishment to establishment. For example, two supermarkets in the same city will have a different set of customer contacts, different employees, and different suppliers.

The tributary area of an establishment is determined by its peculiar set of linkages. We may define the tributary area of a given establishment in a given location as an irregular but roughly circular zone centering on the site and containing the establishments which are linked to it. A simple example is the tributary area of an elementary school which is a zone containing the homes of the pupils. The tributary area of a supermarket would be geographically defined by the homes of the more or less regular customers. For a home site the tributary area would be highly irregular in shape if it contained all points of contact for all members of the family. If linked to points of frequent contact, say one or more times a week, the area would be more compact though still quite irregular in shape. For purposes of locational analysis, the tributary area should include those linkages which are given consideration in the selection of a site for the establishment.

COSTS OF FRICTION

The term *friction of space* refers to the disutilities of moving persons or goods from one place to another. It is a basic physical fact that move-

[4] *Ibid.*, pp. 113, 114.

ment requires energy and time. Convenience then, is measured in the economy of time and energy.

The friction of space which separates any two points on the urban landscape is a function of several factors, some of which can be converted to a dollar-cost figure:

1. *Transportation Costs*. The direct costs of carriage can be measured in fares paid or in the operating costs of vehicles.

2. *Travel Time*. This factor is a function of the transportation facilities which are available, the street system, surfacing, traffic controls, and congestion. The time-cost depends on the value placed on the time of the persons who are traveling, or in the case of goods, the disruption of schedules, loss of business, or spoilage caused by delays.

3. *Personal Aggravations*. The discomforts of travel, the annoyances of delay and congestion, and the sense of danger are disutilities which increase the friction of space.

4. *Parking Facilities*. For most automobile trips terminal facilities are as essential to the free use of the motor vehicle as are the streets. Parking rates are a consideration.

In respect to a given linkage, the significant costs of friction are the product of the costs of each trip and the frequency of the trips. Thus in balancing the locational pulls of the various establishments to which a business enterprise is linked, infrequent and costly trips offset more frequent and less costly trips. For example, the lumber dealer balances the advantages of reducing the cost of assembling his stock of dimension lumber by locating at a railway siding where carload lots can be unloaded and stacked, against the added costs of the daily distribution of orders to local builders and users which result from the off-center location on the railroad. In the case of a retail merchant the most important trips are those of the potential customers. This consideration far outweighs the added costs of cartage and unloading of goods to stock the store in a congested district. A hosiery factory, employing a large number of women who are secondary wage earners and who must use public transportation to come to work, will locate at the center of the city at the focus of public transportation to minimize employee transport costs at the expense of higher costs in the assembly of materials and the distribution of the finished product.

Favorable Exposure

In addition to convenience as a form of locational product or income, there are advantages in locating near certain points on the urban landscape though no movement of persons or goods is involved. The returns to the user take two primary forms: prestige and aesthetic satisfactions.

For residential land use social prestige may be important. Special values attach to building sites in a neighborhood of fine houses and near the homes of community leaders. In Manhattan a Park Avenue address carries an aura of social prestige, and in every city certain neighborhoods are cherished by the socially conscious. For business use locational prestige also is a factor. Fifth Avenue implies retail elegance, and Wall Street suggests financial strength and stability. An office address in Rockefeller Center sounds a note of quality.

A location with a fine view takes on added value for residential use and for some forms of commercial use, such as a quality restaurant. The aesthetic satisfactions of an attractive outlook may derive from the beauties of nature or from a man-made vista such as the sweep of a great city.

Unfavorable Exposure

Establishments are locationally repelled by conditions or activities which are objectionable, inharmonious, or incompatible. Undesirable physical conditions are avoided such as noise, smoke, and odors. An example of an incompatible use is a church in a retail area where it is an unwelcome neighbor because it breaks the continuity of store fronts. Social incompatibility may exist among families in a neighborhood by reason of differences in cultural and economic backgrounds. Thus a favored location is one which has the protection of distance or of some physical barrier which shuts off sight and sound of the objectionable conditions.

The protection of distance against present inharmonious activities and occupancies is an important locational consideration, but a further consideration is the protection against future encroachments of objectionable uses. Such protection is found in:

1. Physical barriers such as a river or a line of hills
2. Public land use controls such as a zoning ordinance
3. Private restrictions on use contained in deeds of conveyance
4. City growth trends which shunt inharmonious uses from the vicinity of the site

LIMITATIONS ON LOCATIONAL CHOICE

The foregoing discussion has identified the nature of the locational returns which are sought by prospective users of a site. The high importance of movement of persons and goods in the conduct of the city's business is reflected in the advantage of convenience and the gravitational pull between linked establishments. For some land uses, sightly views or social or business prestige are attractions toward certain locations. For all uses there is a repulsion from the existence and threat of nearby inharmonious activities and incompatible occupancies. All of these locational forces apply to both new enterprises seeking a first site and to existing establishments now occupying less than optimum locations.

But there are limitations and restrictions on free selection and use of optimum locations by all establishments and thus on the optimum arrangement of land use in the community as a whole: [5]

1. There may be no space available at the best location.

2. The rent or price may be too high.

3. There may be zoning or deed restrictions which exclude the intended use.

4. The establishment may be anchored in its present location by an existing lease, high costs of relocation, tradition, or inertia.

DYNAMICS OF LOCATION

The concept of location is without meaning save with reference to a specific site, a particular use, a given environment, and a definite time. In our previous discussion by implication the locational services of land were presented subject to these specifications. Thus the locational pulls which we considered were as of one point in time and space and involved a particular establishment in its relationships to the then urban landscape. But all these elements are constantly changing, except of course the latitude and longitude of the site. Because of the dynamic nature of the factors of location, the evaluation of locational returns and benefits must be more than cross-sectional in time; it must take account of the probable future changes in all of the factors which influence the benefits of the site for the intended use. Possible future changes may be grouped as follows:

Changes in Linked Establishments

Any shifts in establishments which are linked with the site through the movement of persons or goods will throw the existing locational equilibrium out of balance and may reduce the aggregate of convenience enjoyed by the occupant establishment. For example, the gradual suburban shift in the locations of the homes of the members of a downtown church congregation often multiplies the aggregate friction of space to such an extent that the church plant is relocated in a more convenient spot. The relocation of a dominant establishment, such as an industrial plant, would affect the location of parts suppliers and machine repair shops which serve it.

Internal or functional changes in linked establishments which alter their activities or personnal may influence locational returns at a given site. For example, the increase in home entertainment with the advent of television has reduced the movement of persons from home to movie theater and thus reduces the value of the theater location. The extension of supermarket merchandise to include items competing with drugstores, such as

[5] *Ibid.*, p. 105.

tooth paste and cosmetics, affects drugstore locations in neighborhood shopping centers.

Changes in Nonlinked Establishments

The appearance, disappearance, or relocation of nonlinked establishments may affect a given location. In fact, any reshuffling of urban land uses disturbs the general locational equilibrium and may modify any number of significant space relationships. For example, the development of a civic center may create a barrier between sections of the central business district and interfere with important linkages. The erection of a large office building may generate pedestrian traffic which is incompatible with adjacent land uses. Changes which create vacancies may permit other establishments to move to preferred locations and touch off a general reshuffling of space relationships.

In the absence of adequate protection, inharmonious land uses, incompatible occupancies, distasteful views, and undesirable sounds and smells can invade a neighborhood to the detriment of exposed establishments. Prestige uses and occupancies which served to attract other establishments may change or depart.

Changes in Movement Channels

Modifications in public transportation facilities, routes, and fares may greatly affect the friction of space among establishments. Changes in traffic routing, street closings, new throughways, traffic controls, and parking facilities have great locational significance. The decline in the use of public transport and the rise of the private automobile as the major mode of travel have affected accessibility of sites, some favorably and some detrimentally. When streets and traffic controls are not adapted to the increasing traffic load, the result is congestion and delays in traffic flow which increase frictional costs and destroy locational values.

Changes in the Nature of the Enterprise

The locational returns to an establishment occupying a given site may increase or decrease by reason of changes in the nature of the enterprise itself. A familiar example is the change in the convenience of the location of a family's home over the normal family life cycle. A house that yields large returns in convenience to the elementary school, the playground or park, and to the homes of the children's playmates may be unfavorably located for the middle-aged parents after the children have grown and gone. In the business world the change in the methods of grocery distribution has destroyed the value of a neighborhood location for the corner grocery store and has attached locational value for the supermarket to a prominent spot on a major traffic artery.

THE PROBLEM OF LOCATIONAL ANALYSIS

This chapter has been devoted to the illumination of the factors of location which make real estate productive and valuable. These value-generating characteristics are perhaps more important and certainly more complex than the physical attributes of land or the man-made improvements which make land useful for urban purposes. Clearly, anyone who commits his capital to the purchase or development of urban real estate must rely heavily on his ability to interpret locational factors in their present and future effects upon productivity. The need for careful locational analysis of urban real estate arises in connection with many business decisions—the selection of a site for a home, a factory, a department store, a shopping center, or a filling station; the selection of an appropriate use for an available site, such as the choice of the most productive use for a vacant corner in an outlying district, or the choice of a commercial tenant by a landlord with a vacant store to rent, or the decision of the owner of an old apartment house in a declining neighborhood on whether to remodel and modernize the building; and finally, an investor's determination of the amount he would be justified in investing in an existing real estate enterprise such as an office building or apartment.

The problem of locational analysis in each of the foregoing examples is essentially the same, for it involves a given or assumed site, a given or assumed establishment, and a given urban environment. The time is the present, but locational factors are subject to constant change, and in each case the probability and nature of future changes must be estimated.

The first step in locational analysis is to determine the linkages which characterize the establishment or land use which is the existing or assumed occupant of the site. If improved real estate is involved, i.e., improved with a major structure, a study of the activity or enterprise housed by the structure will indicate the other points or establishments with which there is significant linkage. If there is a use assumed for a vacant lot or building, the same study needs to be made of the hypothetical enterprise. If the existing or assumed use is a supermarket, for example, it is clear that the most numerous linkages would be with the homes of potential customers and that other linkages with suppliers would exist. If the use were a bread bakery serving the community, linkages would exist with suppliers of flour and other ingredients, with the homes of employees, with restaurants to serve employees, and with the establishments of bread retailers, restaurants, institutions, and other bread users. Each type of establishment has its own special set of linkages.

As a second step, having identified the linkages, we must judge the relative importance of each linkage or type of linkage. We earlier suggested that the economic importance of a given linkage is a function of the cost of movement and the frequency of such movement. Costs cannot always be measured in dollar terms. For example, the risk to children crossing busy streets on the journey to school is an effective cost which leads American families to place a high value on a home location close to an elementary school. The linkages which are important to a ladies' apparel shop are with the homes of shoppers and co-dominant establishments with common customers who may be drawn to a cluster of stores for purposes of comparison shopping. The linkages important to an obstetrician are to the homes of young couples, just beginning their families, and to the hospital. A lawyer seeks convenience to the county courthouse where are kept public records of various kinds to which he frequently refers and where various judges and courts are housed, to the offices of other lawyers, and to the homes and offices of clients. For each type of establishment it is necessary to have an understanding of the nature of the activity, the function of each linkage, and the frequency of the movement in order to develop judgments on the relative importances of the various linkages which are essential or contributory in the functioning of the enterprise.

Having established for a business enterprise, a home, or some other activity the linkages which are important to its functioning, we must now locate the linked establishments in their geographic positions in the community in relationship to the site under consideration. It is then possible, in light of probable routes of travel, street patterns, and transportation facilities, to estimate the costs of friction created by each trip between the site and each linked establishment. With knowledge of the frequency of the trips, it is possible to approximate the total costs of friction for each linkage during a given period of time. All costs of friction to the establishment for all linkages represent the locational costs of doing business at that site. These costs can be quantified in dollar terms only in part in the typical problem of location analysis. However, business firms can often find more or less exact expressions for the direct costs of trucking, for commuting time of employees, and the direct costs of their transportation. The value of prompt delivery of rush orders or fast response on service calls is hard to measure, but delays in meeting the needs of customers can be costly to a business.

We have described only the first phase of locational analysis, an evaluation of the present situation. The fact that most real estate decisions are made on the basis of a long-term forecast of productivity requires that locational analysis must be extended into the future. In the discussion of the dynamics of location we identified four different kinds of change in linkages which can occur. Each change in the nature of a linkage changes the quality of the location and may change its productivity in the use under consideration. Thus a thorough study of a location calls for a study of the linked establishments in order to detect incipient change in the nature of their activities and to uncover tendencies which might result in changing their locations. For example, a location in a declining central neighborhood which is shifting into rooming-house use would not hold much future promise for a diaper service which serves families with babies. Linkages can be affected by the kind of modification in the urban structure imposed by major urban redevelopment schemes or by alterations in traffic patterns, such as the introduction of a one-way street system. The locational analyst must be sensitive to these possibilities and trends.

Another aspect of locational analysis is the evaluation of the exposure of the site to favorable and unfavorable environmental factors. The significance of each factor will depend upon the nature of the establishment on the site. Proximity to the homes of community leaders adds little to the value of an industrial site but may be of high importance in connection with residential use; a Wall Street address is of no value to a junk yard. A foundry would be an unwelcome neighbor for a retail store but not for a steel mill. Social incompatibility is less likely to develop in neighborhoods occupied by families of low income than in the districts inhabited by upper-income groups to whom social prestige is important.

In forecasting environmental change which might result in unfavorable exposure, the analyst seeks to evaluate not only the strength of the forces of change but also the protections against such change. Where there are strong barriers of a physical or legal nature, or where the basic urban growth trends are favorable, he may assume a low probability of the appearance of detrimental environmental factors.

Analyzing Residential Neighborhoods

The locational characteristics of residential areas are of major concern not only to prospective home purchasers but also to lenders in the evaluation of mortgage risk. The following neighborhood features are taken into consideration by both buyers and lenders in their efforts to appraise the strength of those locational factors which may either diminish or sustain residential property values. Attempts have been made to assign weights to the various factors, as in the FHA mortgage risk rating system, but such weights are largely matters of informed opinion which vary widely among the experts.

1. *Physical Attractiveness of the Neighborhood.* The higher the value level of the homes, the more important are the aesthetic values of an attractive area in sustaining residential property values. Architectural excellence in the surrounding homes, mature and tasteful planting of the grounds, shady streets, well-kept lawns, and well-maintained structures add a universal appeal which buyers are willing to pay for; those in the

upper-income groups are most able to pay the premium which the market usually places on such locations. The new and partially built-up area will not command the same price even though the homes be of equal architectural excellence and original cost. The difference lies in the raw appearance of vacant lots and new homes with planting only just taking hold. There is a further difference in the uncertainty concerning future building, its quality, and its occupancy. In such an area the existence of adequate zoning and protective covenants are of prime importance, but even these protections are not final guarantees which can match the assurance of quality given by the actual viewing of a built-up and mature neighborhood.

The analyst looks to both present and future. He accepts the fact that all neighborhoods lose some attractiveness as they age. The architecture becomes dated and the homes suffer from various degrees of obsolescence. The critical judgment is how fast the area will deteriorate. This rate is influenced by the original basic qualities of the architecture and construction of the homes and by the maintenance of house and yard. In turn, upkeep reflects both interest and financial ability of the owners. Thus the analyst explores the social status of the area and its resistance to decline in comparative social standing; he investigates the occupants, their age levels, family status, and financial standing as clues to the future physical attractiveness of the location.

Physical attractiveness also has real significance in the maintenance of value in commercial property. This fact is illustrated in the struggle of the central business district to retain business against the competition of shopping centers. The latter are designed to offer the shopper a comfortable and attractive environment. Downtown associations promote remodeling and rebuilding in an effort to dress up the central area and enhance its physical appeal to shoppers.

2. *Social and Economic Status of the Neighborhood.* Neighborhoods, like people, acquire reputations which condition the attitudes of prospective home buyers and influence the prices which they are willing to pay. The highest residential land values are usually found in areas inhabited by the social leaders of the community and by the highest-income groups. As a neighborhood loses social status a newer area replaces it as the pole of land value, and values in the older area suffer a decline. The clue to value change lies in the occupancy of the homes; as new generations come along there is a general decline in the social status of neighborhoods at all levels and values tend to fall. Some areas resist this change better than others because of preferential location and better protection against adverse influences. Occasionally an area will seem to renew itself through replacement families of the same social and economic status as the preceding generation of occupants. Now and then an area revives from a low estate,

such as Georgetown in Washington, D.C., which has come back from being a near slum to a fashionable neighborhood of remodeled row houses. This recovery is explained by the historical prestige of this early settlement and the convenient and close-in location. But as a rule, neighborhoods fall off over time in status and in values, and the problem of the analyst is to forecast the rate of decline.

A characteristic which imparts social attractiveness to an area is the compatibility of the resident families. The most favorable climate for social integration is a common cultural background, family composition, and economic status. Transitional areas may be less appealing to prospective purchasers though when the transition has been accomplished, value stability may be restored in the neighborhood.

3. *Transportation Facilities.* Not many years ago, the term "transportation facilities" referred to public or mass transport. In many large cities access to such facilities is still a locational factor of importance; the opportunity to commute to Manhattan or central Philadelphia via suburban trains is still a value-creating attribute of many outlying residential communities. Bus service to the Loop in Chicago supports property values in many neighborhoods. But the use of such facilities is declining as increasing proportions of the population rely on the private automobile. Thus for many areas of cities of all sizes, transportation facilities are largely the highways, arterial streets, freeways, or expressways which are convenient and available to move people from home to other linked establishments. The ease of movement, be it in public transport or on street and expressway, is value-generating in residential areas. Important considerations are the diversity and cost of available services, the quality and frequency of such service, and the time required to reach important destinations.

4. *Schools.* The importance of convenient school facilities in sustaining residential values varies according to the occupancy of the neighborhood. No feature is more important in a newly developing suburban area which typically accommodates families with young children. The parents of elementary school pupils put high value on locations within easy and safe walking distance to a school. Parents prefer to be near good high school facilities but accept the need for bus transportation to high school without much discount to the value of the home location. Residential values in the vicinity of a parochial school are strongly sustained by the demand from families of the appropriate religious faith.

There are residential areas in all cities where the school age population is small and, in consequence, school facilities are of small importance. Close-in apartment districts often contain small families, either young couples yet to start their families or older couples with children grown and gone. Many apartments are occupied by unmarried persons. In general, as neighborhoods of single-family homes begin to decline in attractiveness to young families, the school population falls off and the value-sustaining influence of convenient school facilities decreases.

5. *Churches*. Proximity to churches is of strongest value effect in residential areas where the school population is highest. Young families value such facilities to provide religious training for the children and as a community social center. Protestant families shift readily from one denomination to another so that church facilities may be adequate even though all faiths are not represented in an area.

6. *Recreational and Cultural Facilities*. Parks and playgrounds are of general value to all types of residential use. For families with small children in low-density modern suburban developments, lot sizes are sufficient to meet many of the family recreational needs. There is room for the tots to play under maternal supervision, gardening provides adult relaxation, and family picnics around the outdoor fireplace are frequent. However, the older children need larger open spaces for active play and group games such as baseball, special facilities for tennis and swimming are desirable, and picnic grounds at sightly spots give occasion for family expeditions away from home.

In congested areas parks and playgrounds have an especially high value for both children and adults. Even when the ratio of children is low, the advantages to adults in having a convenient spot to stroll in the evening and a place of escape from the confining walls of an apartment are reflected in property values.

Cultural centers such as libraries, art galleries, and museums are valuable adjuncts to residential districts, particularly where the residents are of the higher educational levels. Facilities for musical events and theatrical performances are also plus factors.

7. *Utilities and Services*. Built-up urban areas are usually provided with the full complement of public and municipal utilities and services. These include sewer, water, gas, electricity, telephone, garbage removal, fire and police protection, street lighting, street repair, street cleaning and snow removal, and drainage of storm waters. The lack of certain of these facilities and services is not considered to be a serious defect. On the other hand, certain items such as sewer, water, and electricity may be considered essential, and whatever impairs these services is of grave consequence. Thus the risk of contamination of private well water, or a deficiency in the supply of underground water would be a threat to property values in an area without public water service. Individual sewage disposal systems are satisfactory in some cases if soil conditions are favorable and if a low density of homes is maintained. But where such systems fail to operate properly, living conditions become intolerable. Inadequate facilities often lead to additional housing costs: insurance rates are higher where fire protection is insufficient; poor storm water drainage may lead to costly dam-

age; lack of police protection invites theft; and poor street maintenance creates discomfort and damage, dirt, and dust. The lower property taxes in suburban areas which usually reflect partial public services may not produce a real economy when offsetting costs are recognized.

8. *Commercial Centers.* The locational attribute of convenient shopping and service facilities for the staples of living is highly valued by American families. Thus convenience goods outlets offering foodstuffs and the general merchandise of the modern drugstore must be within easy reach. Other useful outlets include hardware and variety stores, and a laundry and dry cleaning establishment. In suburban areas it is not expected that such facilities be within walking distance of the home, but in the older and more congested residential districts, particularly apartment areas, such outlets must be within a few blocks to maintain maximum values.

The widespread development of organized shopping centers has added value to suburban locations. Many types of specialty and shopping goods have been brought to accessible locations which permit purchase without the tedious and aggravating shopping trip downtown. Proximity to a shopping center adds value to residential sites, but this factor should not be overrated. The availability of the family car for shopping means that a commercial center several miles distant is considered convenient if it can be reached without passing through congested areas. Even the trip downtown does not totally dismay the housewife on an earnest and important shopping expedition.

9. *Protection against Adverse Influences.* Among the factors of change which depress property values in residential neighborhoods, the physical aging of structures and their obsolescence in style and equipment are inexorable, though proper maintenance and modernization can modify the impact on value. Thus a neighborhood where property owners take pride in their homes will indefinitely retain most of its visual appeal and the strength of this value support lies in the character of the occupant families. Further, a general agreement among property owners to resist the invasion of inharmonious uses and occupancies can be an effective measure of protection.

The nature of the occupant families is an indicator of probability of an infiltration of incompatible residents in the area. An area in which the original families have matured, the children have left home, and the parent couples or widows are beginning to move out into smaller and more convenient quarters is open to a diversity of occupancy which leads to falling property values. As tenant occupancy increases the level of property maintenance falls off, and the social integration of the neighborhood disappears. As an offset, in areas where zoning permits, values may be sustained through increasing the intensity of use in rooming houses and by conversion of homes into a number of small apartments.

Protection against inharmonious land uses which might invade a residential area is effected through zoning and private deed restrictions, subjects which are discussed in Chapter V and elsewhere in this book. The geographical position of the neighborhood may be an effective protection if it is set off by natural barriers such as a river, a line of hills, or manmade barriers such as a railroad right of way or a major highway. In an unprotected district the degree to which land is improved and committed to a given use is a measure of the uncertainty of the nature of future development.

V

THE LEGAL DIMENSIONS
OF REAL ESTATE

INTRODUCTION

The chapters on the physical and locational attributes of real estate have laid bare the wellsprings of land value. Land is sought by users and investors to the extent that it provides space and support and that it is convenient and accessible to linked establishments. But there are other dimensional specifications of land beyond length, width, and locational space relationships. The legal content of ownership must be as meticulously measured as the physical attributes of the real estate. Property in land, or ownership, takes many forms with widely variant economic meaning. And the ownership which we take for granted is but an ephemeral aspect of the institution of property which, down through the ages, has evolved as a workable arrangement of man's devising for specifying and defending the rights of an individual in physical objects of economic value.

THE INSTITUTION OF PROPERTY [1]

In its popular connotation, the term "property" refers to land and buildings in the case of real property, and to various movable articles in the case of personal property. But the real estate market deals in rights, not directly in the land and buildings that are the property objects. For instance, in making a lease, the right of possession is exchanged for a consideration known as "rent." In an outright sale of land full ownership involving a complex of rights is the economic good that changes hands. These rights and the legal limitations that define them are constituents of the social institution of property.

Property, in the sense of ownership, has been defined as "the exclusive

---

[1] The discussion of the institution of property, feudal tenure, personalty, and fixtures is adapted from Richard U. Ratcliff, *Urban Land Economics*, McGraw-Hill Book Company, Inc., New York, 1949, pp. 6–11.

right to control an economic good." [2] Property has no significance where the property object has no economic value. Property raises a wall about ownership to exclude all others. Property cannot defend itself and cannot exist without an enforcing agency created by society.[3] Only human beings have the capacity for ownership; property would have no meaning outside the realm of human relationships, for property cannot exclude others where no others exist.

The distinction between public and private property is based upon the nature of the owner. Private property is controlled by individuals or organizations of individuals such as corporations and partnerships. Public property belongs to governmental agencies. There is another property type known as *qualified property* to cover objects that have an uncertain status, such as wild game and fish, which are the property of the state until shot or captured, and which thereupon become private property provided that the game laws of the state were not violated.[4]

Various explanations of the origins of private property have been advanced. It is sometimes explained as a natural right. In Roman law the right of property is based on occupancy or seizure. Others have contended that the individual has inherent rights in that which he produces by his own labor. The theistic conception is that property is ordained by God.[5] But none of these explanations properly takes account of the evolutionary aspects of private property. They fail to recognize the fact that property and society have evolved side by side, that property has been continually reshaped to meet the changing economic and social needs of men. Thus we arrive at the social theory of property, which explains the institution as having evolved as a medium for the promotion of the general welfare. It follows, then, that since society is dynamic, so must be the institution of property, which is subjected to constant alteration as man's notions of the general welfare shift and evolve, and as technological advance calls for new patterns of social organization.[6]

We are inclined to take for granted this basic institution of property, which has evolved with our economic organization and is an essential part of it. Down through the centuries property has been molded and fitted to the needs of the social organization, needs that are ever-changing through the broadening of knowledge, the surges of social movements, the slow changes in the social mind, and the advances of technology. In order to

---

[2] R. T. Ely, *Property and Contract in Their Relation to the Distribution of Wealth*, The Macmillan Company, New York, 1914, vol. I, pp. 101–102.

[3] H. B. Dorau and A. G. Hinman, *Urban Land Economics*, The Macmillan Company, New York, 1928, chaps. 16 and 17.

[4] R. T. Ely and G. S. Wehrwein, *Land Economics*, The Macmillan Company, New York, 1940, pp. 76–77.

[5] Ely, *op. cit.*, vol. II, chap. 22.

[6] *Ibid.*, p. 546 and chap. 6. See also Ely and Wehrwein, *op. cit.*, pp. 99–106.

clarify the evolutionary nature of the property institution it will be well to sketch its development briefly and to illustrate the point that changes in the property concept have been associated with changes in man's way of life and with advances in technology.

Primitive man in the earliest stages subsisted by the direct appropriation of the gifts of nature in the form of game, berries, and fruits. Land had no value and belonged to no one in particular, save for an ephemeral claim that existed so long as occupancy lasted but could not be maintained against a stronger man. With the development of a crude social organization, taking the form of the clan or tribe, came the tribal sanction to the evolving notion that each individual was to be protected in the ownership of that which he had captured or made. The tribal enforcement of these rights was found to be necessary to tribal unity, but recognition was not extended beyond the possessions of those persons comprising the clan. Then came the pastoral stage and with it the beginnings of the family as a primary social unit. Land became directly productive for grazing purposes, and differences in quality came to impart special value to certain tracts. Land was no longer a free good. There arose the notion of tribal rights in areas where the herds of the clan were accustomed to graze. Boundary disputes between tribes were in themselves a recognition of tribal rights in land. But land used for pasturage, as well as the land within the communal enclosure, was the common property of the tribe, and no individual could claim any portion of it as his own.

As agriculture increased in importance, the notion already accepted in the case of personal property—that a man must be protected in what he produced—came to be applied to land. At first, however, agriculture was cooperative. Then, as the family unit became more important, temporary assignments of separate plots were made to each family, at first for one season only. Later, in recognition of a kind of equity evolving from the improvement of productivity by special skill or exceptional industry, the assignments extended over a number of crop years. The next step was the development of permanent possession vested in the patriarchal or collective family. Individual hereditary property finally evolved as the patriarchal holdings began to be split up among the sons who founded new families and as the patriarchal system of family organization declined. The institution of private property has continued to evolve from this point in its history, but the changes have been less fundamental than those which have been already outlined.[7]

[7] Dorau and Hinman, *op. cit.*, pp. 262ff. See also N. L. North and D. Van Buren, *Real Estate Titles and Conveyancing*, Prentice-Hall, Inc., Englewood Cliffs, N.J., 1927, p. 2; Emile de Laveleye, *Primitive Property*, Macmillan & Co., Ltd., London, 1878, translated from the French by G. R. L. Marriott, pp. 3ff.; J. Lewinski, *The Origin of Property*, Constable & Co., Ltd., London, 1913; and P. Lafargue, *The Evolution of Property*, Charles H. Kerr and Company, Chicago, 1910.

FEUDAL TENURE

The major evolutionary shift in recent centuries in the institution of property was the disappearance of the feudal system of holding. In the manorial-feudal era through which the European nations passed, the ownership of all land was vested in the king. Lords of various ranks under the king were granted rights in large tracts in return for obligations and services, which usually included the provision of men and arms for the royal army. Peasants and serfs under the lords were granted limited rights in land in return for rents and services. From this system there gradually emerged our modern form of free proprietorship as the required services were converted into money rents and continuing obligations were extinguished by lump-sum payments.[8]

REALTY, PERSONALTY, AND FIXTURES

Property rights imply law, for law must define property and provide the vehicle of enforcement by society. It is by this means that possession resolves into property. It will be recalled that property in personal objects developed earlier than private ownership in land. In both cases the basic concept of ownership was the same and probably arose for the same reasons. In the case of personal objects there was the notion that it was mutually advantageous for all men to join in protecting the ownership of each individual in the things that he produced. In the case of land it came to be recognized that an individual could add value to land by his efforts in grading and working the soil, draining it, or adding fertilizer, thus creating an equity to be protected by group action. Although the underlying ideas of property are similar for both personal and real property, the rules of law that have grown up about them differ in material respects. The reasons for these differences are found in the special physical and economic characteristics of the property objects. For example, land is fixed and cannot be moved or concealed, whereas most items of personal property are transportable and small enough to be hidden from sight. Again, the units of land ordinarily dealt in are of relatively great value as compared with units of personal property. In fact, in early times most wealth was in the form of landed property. Another factor in the development of special rules for real property is found in the origins of English common law under the feudal system of land tenure, wherein land was held from an overlord, whereas personal property was free of such claims.

The basic differences in the rules of law governing real property (realty) and personal property (personalty) give importance to a careful

[8] Ely and Wehrwein, *op. cit.*, p. 8.

distinction between these two classes of property. A few examples of the legal effect of these differences are in point: [9]

1. In general, the transfer of title in real estate is by a written instrument, whereas the ownership of personalty may usually be transferred by delivery.

2. Estates of curtesy and dower apply to realty but not to personalty.

3. The rules governing the disposition of property upon the death of the owner differ substantially as between personalty and realty.

4. Creditors usually cannot levy upon realty until personalty has been exhausted.

5. The laws of the state in which realty is located govern the interests in it, whereas personalty is controlled by the laws of the state in which the owner is domiciled.

For most purposes, realty (real estate) refers to land, buildings, and those objects which are permanently and definitely affixed thereto. All things not realty are personalty. On the border line between these two classes of property are found fixtures, articles that have the primary characteristics of personalty but which have become so much a part of the land that they have assumed the characteristics of realty. Frequent disputes arise in connection with the sale of real estate concerning whether or not certain items are rightfully a part of the property. Items that can be identified as fixtures go with the land even if not specifically mentioned in the contract or deed. For example, in the sale of a house, the question may arise as to whether or not the window shades, the refrigerator, or the awnings go with the house. Similar questions often arise between landlord and tenant, mortgagee and owner, and mortgagee and holder of a chattel mortgage.

While no inclusive rule can be stated as a basis for defining fixtures, it is generally true that the method of attachment to the land and building, the use to which the attachment is put, and the intention of the parties are the controlling considerations. As between mortgagor and mortgagee, articles are generally assumed to be a part of the property unless it was clearly not the intent of the owner. The law favors the tenant in his right to remove at the end of his lease the fixtures that he has installed such as counters, shelves, and electrical appliances, but where he has made permanent improvements the removal of which would injure the property, he may not dismantle them.[10] Most of the disputes that arise in real estate transactions because of the difficulty of defining fixtures may be avoided by an adequate statement in the written instrument, contract, deed, mortgage, or lease, covering the intent of the parties with respect to every item not indisputably an integral part of the property.

[9] North and Van Buren, *op. cit.*, p. 27.
[10] W. J. Grange, *Real Estate*, The Ronald Press Company, New York, 1937, pp. 303, 304.

FORMS OF OWNERSHIP

Ownership has been frequently described as a bundle of rights. In the present state of its development the institution of private property does not permit an individual absolute and unlimited rights in land. His rights may be exclusive of other individuals, but, as we have seen, society has reserved certain rights, such as taxation and eminent domain, and exercises a control over the right of use. Thus the bundle of rights in the hands of an owner has been reduced as the concept of social obligation has expanded.

Ownership of real estate is not a simple concept, for ownership may take a number of forms. The rights comprising the complete bundle that makes up full ownership may be subdivided and the single rights or smaller groups of rights may be conveyed to other persons. Ownership may be enjoyed in the present or the future; and it may be that the privileges are shared among two or more persons under a number of possible arrangements. In general, ownership may be said to consist of the right of use, the right of exclusion, and the right of disposition. The right of use and the right of exclusion are the bases of the right to possession, something allied to, but distinct from, ownership and the attribute of ownership that is the foundation of its value. We think of complete ownership as inclusive of all rights except those reserved by the state. The subdivisions of ownership composed of single rights or groups of rights are known as *estates*.[11] All the legal implications of these many forms of ownership are too complicated to be considered here; the reader is referred to one of the standard works on real estate law. We shall limit our consideration to the more common forms of estates.

Freehold and Leasehold

There are two broad classes of ownership interests or estates which a person may have in land: (1) freehold and (2) leasehold.

To own a freehold estate is to have legal title to the land and the exclusive right to its possession. A freehold estate is uncertain of duration for it is subject to voluntary conveyance by deed or transfer through inheritance at any time or in the case of the life estate, it terminates at the unpredictable time of death of some specified person. There are two classes of freehold estate: (1) fee simple, which may be (*a*) absolute or (*b*) qualified; and (2) life estate, (*a*) the conventional form, or (*b*) legal life estates which are created by the operation of law and include dower, curtesy, and homestead rights.[12]

[11] *Ibid.*, p. 5.
[12] Gerald O. Dykstra and Lillian G. Dykstra, *The Business Law of Real Estate*, The Macmillan Company, New York, 1956, pp. 82–83.

Leasehold estates convey the right of use but not legal title. They are characterized by the certainty of their duration. They include: (1) estate for years, (2) tenancy from year to year, (3) tenancy at will, and (4) tenancy at sufferance. Each of these estates endures for so long as the parties determine or agree that it shall exist.

Fee-simple Estate

The highest type of estate in land, the complete private bundle of rights, is known as the fee-simple or fee-simple–absolute estate. This estate is immune from the control of other persons and is unlimited in duration, disposition, and descendability. This form of ownership, as all forms, is subject to the powers of the state to tax, to condemn, and to regulate in the public interest under the police power.

A qualified fee-simple estate is one which was granted on condition that it revert to the grantor upon a subsequent occurrence, for example, that it is to be no longer used for the purpose for which the grant was made. A school site given to the township may revert to the grantor when it ceases to be used for the specified purpose of the conveyance.

Conventional Life Estate

This form of life estate is created by an owner in fee simple by deed or will to exist only for the lifetime of a specified person, either the beneficiary or life tenant or some other person; at the death of the specified person, the ownership passes to another designated person known as the *remainderman*. An example is the case of A who conveys to his wife a life estate in land which he owns in fee simple with the provision that at her death, the property shall pass to C, their son. C is the remainderman and will own the land in fee simple. If A did not specify a remainderman, the land would revert to him or his estate at his wife's death.

Legal Life Estate

Dower and curtesy were originally common-law estates but are now covered by statutes in the majority of states. Special rules prevail in the various states. These rights do not exist in community property states.

Dower is the life estate to which a widow is entitled. It usually is a one-third interest in the land owned by her husband in fee simple during their marriage. If such land had been sold and if she joined in the conveyance, her dower right in that property was extinguished. If she did not join in conveyance, she retains a life estate in the land sold by her husband. By statute some states have abolished dower but usually provide for widows' rights to a part of the land held in fee simple; other statutes limit the dower interest to land owned at the time of the husband's death. A widow's dower interest is superior to creditors' claims against the husband.

Curtesy was a common-law right of a husband to a life estate in all land owned by his wife during their marriage if a child had been born to the union. Curtesy has been abolished in a majority of the states and some states give the husband rights which are the same as the dower of the wife.

Community property is a statutory estate which is a substitute for dower and curtesy in some states. Under the law all property acquired by either husband or wife during marriage, except by gift, devise, or descent, is held by both as equal owners. Each spouse may dispose of his half share by will, or should he die intestate, in most community property states, his half share descends to his heirs.

Homestead is a statutory protection which exempts an owner-occupied home from forced sale to satisfy the debts of the head of the family. The exemption has an upper limit in value or area of land. Homestead rights are not superior to unpaid taxes, special assessments, a purchase money mortgage, or a mortgage which was on the property when it became a homestead.[13]

Leasehold Estates

A leasehold estate is created by a contract, express or implied, which is also a conveyance. This arrangement provides that the lessee shall enter into possession and use of property owned by the lessor for a certain period of time and that the lessee shall compensate the lessor with an agreed or reasonable payment in rent or services. Only the right of possession and use is conveyed, and at the end of the time these rights revert to the lessor or landlord. The fee-simple rights of the lessor are not disturbed by the lease except to the extent of the conveyance of possession to the lessee. The owner of the fee-simple estate may sell or convey an interest in the property during the lease, but the grantee takes the property subject to the lease and thereby assumes the rights and duties of the original landlord.

Estate for Years. This form of leasehold estate is one of the more common and familiar forms. It is created by express agreement between the parties with a specified date of beginning and a certain or determinable end. The term "years" is misleading for a lease for any fixed period of time is included in this category.

Tenancy from Year to Year. The period may be from month to month, week to week, or day to day. This arrangement creates a "periodic tenancy" which automatically renews itself until terminated by sufficient notice from one of the parties to the other.

Tenancy at Will. This form of holding may be created by agreement or may arise by implication under the law. Some states have effectively abolished this form of tenancy. A tenant at will is in lawful possession with the consent of the landlord but the tenancy is indefinite as to term

[13] *Ibid.,* p. 105.

and may be ended at any time by either party. A tenancy at will is created, for example, when at the end of the lease term a tenant holds over with the consent of the landlord without a renewal or definite extension of the lease.

Tenancy at Sufferance. This tenancy involves only bare possession by a tenant who, having once occupied the property by agreement with the landlord, continues in possession wrongfully without the express consent of the landlord and in the absence of the landlord's exercise of his rights of repossession.

CONCURRENT OWNERSHIP

Ownership which vests in a single person is described in law as an *estate in severalty*. Where the same rights in land are shared by two or more persons, these persons are said to be co-owners or co-tenants. The common forms of co-tenancy are joint tenancy, tenancy by the entirety, and tenancy in common.

Joint tenancy must be created by a written instrument, usually a deed, which explicitly denotes the intention of creating this kind of tenancy. Each joint tenant receives the same estate or interest and each is considered to own the whole property subject to the interests of the other joint tenants. Perhaps the most significant feature of joint tenancy is the right of survivorship; at the death of one of the joint tenants his rights instantly vest in the surviving joint tenants, and his heirs have no claim to his interest nor can his creditors attach it. During his life, a joint tenant may convey his interest to another, but in so doing he destroys the right of survivorship, and the grantee will be a tenant in common.

Tenancy by the entirety is a form of joint tenancy in some states which can exist only between husband and wife with respect to property acquired jointly after marriage. It differs from joint tenancy in that neither spouse can disturb the right of survivorship by conveying his interest to another party.

Tenancy in common exists when the co-owners hold separate, undivided shares in the property which each co-owner may sell, pledge, or pass on to his heirs. This form of co-tenancy is preferred by the courts and is presumed to be intended unless the evidence to the contrary is specific and unequivocal.

FUTURE INTERESTS

Estates in land, freehold or leasehold, are either present interests known as *estates in possession* or future interests known as *estates in expectancy*. Present rights may be enjoyed now but the holders of future interests must await some day or some occurrence before exercising the control over the property to which their rights entitle them. Future interests fall into three groups—reversions, remainders, and executory interests.

Reversions are rights which remain in one who conveys an interest in land to another which is for a lesser period than the duration of the grantor's interest. Thus A may convey to B a life estate in property which A owns in fee simple. B enjoys a present interest as long as he lives, and A retains a reversionary future interest which restores possession and control of the property to him upon B's death. A lessee may sublease for a period shorter than the remaining period of the basic lease; he thereby retains a reversionary future interest which permits him to possess and enjoy the property during the time between the end of the sublease and the end of the basic lease.

A remainder is a future interest which is transferred at the same time as a present interest is conveyed. For example, A may will his house to his widow for her life, with his son to have the property at her death. Technically, the will conveys a life estate to the widow and to the son, the fee ownership subject to the life estate. The son's position is that of a remainderman.

An executory interest is a future interest which converts to a present interest upon the passage of a specified time or upon some event other than the expiration of another estate. A conveys property to B to become owner at the end of three years. B holds an executory interest during the three-year period.

INCORPOREAL RIGHTS

There are a group of rights which are not forms of ownership or estates in land; they are in the nature of privileges of use of the property of another. Such privileges are somewhat of a limitation on the free use of his land by the owner and thus constitute a part of the definition of his ownership.

An easement is the most common form of this category of interests in land. It is a nonrevocable right to use the land owned by another, which land is known as the *servient land*. A familiar form of easement is a right of way granted by an owner. In one form, an easement appurtenant, the right is for the benefit of other land known as the *dominant estate*, and attaches to the dominant estate even when it is conveyed to a new owner. The right of way granted to a neighboring property owner to give access to his land may be of this nature.

An easement in gross runs for the benefit of an individual and does not depend on his ownership of other land. There is no dominant estate, but the right is distinguishable from a license because it is not revocable. An example is the permission given by an owner to a power company to maintain its lines across his land.

Easements are created by express grant in writing, most commonly in a conveyance by deed; they may also be created by will or by written contract. An easement may be implied. When an owner sells a portion of his land which is entirely surrounded by other land which he owns, an easement for access to the isolated parcel is implied. Finally, an easement may be created by prescription where the use of the land for access, for example, has continued uninterrupted for a sufficient length of time, twenty-one years in some states, openly and with knowledge and acquiescence of the owner, hostile and under claim of right.[14] A short cut across A's land which has been openly used by persons occupying an adjoining property for the required period with A's knowledge and with no objection from him may create an easement by prescription.

A license gives authority to do certain acts on the licensor's land, but the fact that the right is revocable at the will of the servient owner distinguishes it from an easement. For example, the purchase of a ticket for a football game entitles the holder to enter the stadium for the purpose of viewing the game.

LIENS

A lien is a right held by a creditor to secure payment of a debt out of the debtor's property. A lien is thus in the nature of a financial interest in real estate which is enforced only if the debt which it secures is not paid. The most familiar form is the mortgage lien which is the right conveyed by the mortgagor to the mortgagee to secure repayment of the sum borrowed. When the debt is repaid the lien is extinguished; if the debt is not repaid according to the terms of the mortgage note, the lien may be enforced and the property sold to pay the debt. Other forms of lien include the tax lien which may be enforced by a public body in case of nonpayment of the property tax, and the mechanic's lien which is used to secure payment for labor services and materials employed in construction and repair of buildings. Finally, any debt or liability which is defaulted may be the basis for a judgment lien on the real estate of the debtor following prescribed court procedures. Liens of any kind may be a serious limitation on the economic value of real estate. To evaluate their importance it is necessary to know the priority of the several claims against the property. Some aspects of this matter will be covered in later discussions of mortgages and mechanic's liens.

[14] *Ibid.*, p. 527.

TITLE

We have now presented and defined the most frequently encountered forms, subdivisions, and degrees of ownership of real estate. Considering full ownership (ownership in fee simple) to represent the complete bundle of rights which an individual may hold, we have seen how the necessities of business and the diversity of individual situations have led to splitting these rights into all manner of subbundles. For example, present and future interests may be held separately; two or more individuals may simultaneously share present ownership or a lender may hold rights which he is permitted to exercise only when the debt is in default. It is these rights and combinations of rights which are the commodity traded in the real estate market. True, the land and the buildings are the tangible property objects and generate the services which are the basis of real estate value. But individuals must establish their right to enjoy in full or to share the benefits flowing from the physical property. Thus it is the legal property consisting of rights in real estate which is conveyed in a real estate transaction. In modern society these rights are the creatures of an elaborate system of law which defines the diverse forms of ownership, writes the rules for adjudicating disputes, and protects each individual in his separate ownership, under the definitions and rules, with the full force of the courts and the government.

In order for an owner to evaluate his real estate holdings, he must establish the exact nature of his rights. And so that his rights or title may be merchantable, i.e., acceptable as a commodity to be traded in the real estate market, his claim to these rights must be unchallenged. Whether his ownership is in fee simple or some lesser estate, he must have clear unclouded title, or the cloud must be identified so that it may be evaluated. For practical purposes the term *title* means ownership. We must recognize, however, that there are many forms of ownership, and that any one of these forms by reason of a claim to a share in its benefits on the part of other persons may depart from the pure form as defined by law and may thus be less valuable. An easement, an unsatisfied lien, or the outstanding dower right of a widow may modify ownership and reduce its value.

The possession of an item of personal property is commonly accepted as evidence of ownership with little legal verification required. But to establish the ownership of real estate, possession is far from conclusive evidence, for the occupant may be a trespasser, a tenant holding under one of many arrangements, or an owner possessing one of several possible estates. However, possession of the premises is generally counted as constructive notice that the occupant has rights of some kind.

There exists a system for establishing or confirming the rights of individuals in real estate and for adjudicating disputes over ownership. Basically the scheme involves the presentation of evidence that the rights of the owner have come down to him from the original grant or patent from the government of the United States to an individual through an unbroken chain of proper transfers. Any valid claims which might be presented by other persons as a result of liens, unsatisfied interests of any other kind, or improper transfers will constitute a cloud or defect on the title. In the end the courts evaluate the evidence and establish the exact nature of the ownership if the question is raised.

Statute of Frauds

With the exception of short-term leases and contracts, all real estate contracts and conveyances must be in writing to be legally enforceable. State statutes are fairly uniform in requiring a written instrument except where the duration of the conveyance or contract is less than one year. As a result of this law, the validity of a claim to an interest in real estate, with few exceptions, must be supported by a written document. This requirement discourages the concealment of interests and forestalls fraud and perjury which might succeed if oral agreements were acceptable as evidences of ownership.

Public Records

In each state provision has been made for the public recording of documents affecting real estate ownership. Usually in each county, a public office known as the county recorder, register of deeds, or county clerk is responsible for accepting and filing an exact copy of each document submitted to him. Such documents must meet certain statutory requirements as to content and form; if they comply the officer makes an exact copy, usually by photostating, and files it as a public record open to the inspection of any citizen. The law does not compel the recording of real estate documents, but a recorded document may have priority over an unrecorded instrument in the establishing of competing claims. Thus the exact time of the recording may be important since the document first recorded has priority. As a result of these rules most documents are submitted for recording within minutes after they have been signed by the parties to the transaction. To illustrate the importance of the time element, we may observe that if A mortgages his property to secure a loan from B and B fails to record the mortgage, then C, a subsequent buyer from A with no knowledge of the mortgage lien, is secure in his ownership as against B, who may seek to foreclose the mortgage to satisfy the debt. This is true even if B records the mortgage within seconds after C has recorded the deed by which title is conveyed to him.

Chain of Title

The requirement of written instruments in combination with the existence of a system of public records make it possible to inspect copies of all documents affecting the ownership of a parcel of real estate dating from the original conveyance from the government down to the present day. Thus one may trace the chain of title, link by link, through successive ownerships and may identify each interest in the property as it is created by conveyance or contract and as it is extinguished. From the exact copy of each document which is on record, an expert can determine the validity of the instrument and its true effect.

An abstract of title, or abstract, is a list in abbreviated form of all the recorded actions affecting the title to a given parcel of real estate. All documents are listed chronologically and each document is listed by type, date, and names of the parties. Included in such a listing are deeds of various kinds, mortgages, mortgage releases, mechanic's liens, and all other documents which may represent a claim against the property. Abstracts are prepared by specialized commercial organizations for a fee. They are usually known as "title companies," and they usually maintain a full duplicate set of all instruments which are recorded in the public office.

The prudent purchaser of real property seeks to assure himself that the seller possesses clear and unclouded title, i.e., that there exist no outstanding claims against the property which may be asserted after he takes title and which may reduce the value of his holding. Two courses of action are open to him: (1) he may have his own lawyer examine the chain of title to determine whether any defects exist, or (2) he may protect himself against potential claims by means of title insurance. Examples of the kinds of defects in title which may rise to plague the purchaser include errors in property description so that only a part of the property is conveyed, failure of a wife to sign a deed, thus leaving unsatisfied her dower interest, or failure to show the satisfaction of a mortgage or mechanic's lien. A study of the abstract will reveal such defects as these, but there are other defects which are not apparent from the record. Forgeries, failure to include all the heirs to an estate, and mistaken identities create the kinds of hazards which all property buyers face and against which title insurance is the usual protection.

Many types of title defect can be corrected with little difficulty or cost. A deed of correction can cure an error in description; the holder of some outstanding interest may agree to sign a release of his claim with or without compensation, depending on the nature of the claim. In some states, statutes of limitation bar adverse claims against real property after the expiration of a given period. In all states, resort may be had to the courts in a "suit to quiet title" in which, following a hearing of all claims, the court rules on their validity and the public record is made clear and final.

Title Examination

Title examination, or title search, requires a specialized skill and should be performed by a trained lawyer. He usually relies upon the abstract of title in his study of the chain of title to discover clouds or defects. When his search is complete he renders an opinion of title which identifies any defects and expresses his judgment on the significance of such defects. For example, some technical error in a document far back in the chain of title may represent no real impediment; on the other hand, the attorney may judge title to be not merchantable until a certain outstanding interest or claim has been satisfied and released.

In many cases it is the custom to require the seller of property to provide the prospective buyer with an abstract of title which contains all entries up to the present date. The buyer's attorney examines the abstract and advises his client whether or not the seller can convey clear title and specifically what defects, if any, must be removed. The examination of title by title insurance companies precedes insurance as a test of insurability just as a physical examination precedes life insurance.

Title Insurance

Title insurance, in return for a premium paid by the insured, will indemnify the insured who might be owner, tenant, or mortgage lender for loss up to the amount stated in the policy. Such loss may arise from existing title defects, liens, and encumbrances. However, the title insurance may, by exception in the policy, fail to provide protection with respect to certain title defects uncovered by the title examination and not cured by the owner. The use of title insurance is spreading among property buyers who wish to shift to the insurance company the risk that after acquisition some valid claim may have to be paid. Mortgage lenders also seek insurance protection against claims which might diminish the value of the property which secures the debt. Tenants, holding under a commercial lease, wish to be assured of uncontested possession of the land before making investments in improvements to the building such as a new store front, or in the case of a long-term lease, before building a new structure which is to be written off during the lease term.

Title Registration

In nineteen states, statutes provide for a system of title registration, known as the *Torrens system.* The basic scheme involves initial public registration of title through legal proceedings by which clear title is conclusively established in the owner. Future conveyances are by certificate from a public officer and the grantee is forever protected against claims arising out of past transactions or interests. The use of the title registration system is voluntary, and in most of the states where it is available its use is limited. The high initial cost of registering title may in part account for the failure of the plan to spread more rapidly.

CONVEYANCE OF TITLE

The transfer or conveyance of ownership of real estate is one of the most common of legal procedures. But because of the high value of the property object and the complicated types of interests in land which may exist, the forms and procedures required by law to assure the validity of a conveyance are formal and complicated. Our discussion of conveyancing will first consider the alienation of freehold estates (fee-simple and life estates). The procedures of conveyance differ with the various circumstances which give rise to the transfer of ownership; transfer may be a result of public grant, descent and will, adverse possession, condemnation, foreclosure, and the most common of all, private grant.

Public Grant

Under the various land laws passed by the Congress to provide for the disposal of the original public domain, grants were made under certain conditions to states, local public agencies, and private corporations and individuals. The document used to convey ownership from the government to the grantee is known as a "patent." Subsequent transfers by the grantee and his successors in ownership must conform to the laws of the state in which the land is situated.

Land owned by units of government at all levels, outside of the public domain or other lands covered by special legislation, are conveyed in the same manner as transfers between private owners except for limitations on the warranty of title contained in the deed.

Descent and Will

Upon the death of a real estate owner the disposition of his real property is governed by his will, and in the absence of a will, by the laws of the state on inheritance. The devisees under a will are granted title after the validation of the will by a court proceeding known as "probate." The conveyance of title is by deed signed by the executor of the will without warranty of title.

The real property of one who dies intestate, or without will, passes to the heirs automatically and instantly upon the decedent's death in accordance with the laws of descent. In most states the interests of a surviving spouse are satisfied with a dower or curtesy claim on the real estate or a distributive share of the total estate as specified by statute. Real estate passes to the children, if any; otherwise to the parents or surviving parent of the decedent. The laws of each state must be examined to determine the exact order of claims under various possible circumstances.

Adverse Possession

Under certain conditions title may automatically pass to one who has gone into possession of land and remained continuously in possession for the period of years required by law. Title passes involuntarily and without action on the part of the title holder whose name appears in the public record. No documents are signed and recorded yet the holder of the land has good title to the property which he can defend against the world. In order to establish title by adverse possession certain legal requirements must be met:

1. Possession must be "actual" for all to see, though the claimant need not live on the land. Fencing or farming the land is sufficient.

2. Possession must be "hostile" in the sense that it indicates a denial of the owner's title.

3. Possession must be "notorious" so that the real owner will be aware of the hostile occupancy.

4. Possession must be unbroken and "continuous."

5. Possession must be "exclusive" and can permit no sharing of possession with the true owner or any other.

6. Possession must continue unbroken for the period required by state statute, five to forty years in most states.

Condemnation

A public body or quasi-public corporation such as a public utility may acquire title to land by the exercise of the constitutional power of eminent domain, where the land is needed for a proper public purpose. A court proceeding is required to determine a just compensation and to vest title in the public body.

Foreclosure

The termination of legal proceedings to foreclose a lien may result in the conveyance of title to a new owner. Tax liens, mechanic's liens, and mortgage liens permit real property to be sold to pay a claim. When the procedural requirements to wipe out the interests of the owner have been met the property is sold, and a public officer executes a deed without full warranty of title.

Private Grant

The ordinary sale of real estate results in transfer of ownership by private grant. The gift of land to an individual, or the dedication or gift of land by an individual to a public agency for park purposes, for example, is also accomplished by private grant. The conveyance of title is by means of a document known as a *deed* or *indenture*. The deed is not a contract for it involves no promises, does not require the signature of the grantee or receiver of title, and is valid without a consideration. Basically the deed is simply a written statement of the action by which the grantor conveys title to the grantee. At times, conditions in the form of deed restrictions are added which are contractual in nature.

In order that valid title may be conveyed the deed must meet certain legal requirements, though it does not have to take a prescribed form. The requirements which are common to most state statutes are:

1. The transfer of a freehold estate must be evidenced in writing.

2. The grantor and grantee must be clearly and exactly named, the grantor's marital status must be indicated, and he must be legally competent to act.

3. The deed must contain specific and sufficient words of conveyance, such as "grants and conveys to the party of the second part and assigns forever."

4. The property conveyed must be described so that it can be exactly identified.

5. Deeds must be signed by the grantor as it appears on the deed. In some states the signature must be acknowledged or notarized, and some statutes call for witnesses.

6. Delivery of the deed by the grantor and acceptance by the grantee is required.

7. Though a deed may be valid without mention of a consideration, it is customary to state a nominal consideration, such as "one dollar and other good and valuable considerations."

Covenants of Title

To assure the grantee that the deed conveys good and unencumbered title, it may contain certain warranties and guarantees. Deeds are classified by the nature of the warranties:

1. Warranty deeds usually contain assertion that the grantor has good title to the land, that there are no encumbrances except as stated in the deed, and that the grantee and his successor will not be evicted or disturbed by someone with superior title or a valid lien. The grantor undertakes to defend the grantee against claims outstanding at the time of the conveyance, and in case the grantee suffers loss he may collect damages from the grantor.

2. A special warranty deed creates a liability only if the grantee is disturbed by a claim which results from some act of the grantor.

3. A quitclaim deed includes no guarantees by the grantor and conveys to the grantee only such rights, if any, as are possessed by the grantor with

no agreement for indemnification if loss should arise from existing clouds or defects of title.

4. Officer's deeds are used following some official legal proceedings; they are used to convey tax titles or to transfer ownership to a purchaser at a public mortgage foreclosure sale. The deed is signed by the appropriate public officer and contains no warranties.

Recording

A deed is usually valid as between the parties even when not recorded by the county register of deeds or other proper official. However, unless recorded, the conveyance is void as against a subsequent buyer who has no notice that the document exists. Loss of the original deed is of no consequence.

Leases

In common parlance a lease is an arrangement which conveys the right of possession without transferring ownership. Legally a lease conveys a leasehold estate from lessor to lessee; such an estate terminates at the end of a period of time as specified in the lease, and the landlord resumes possession of the property. A lease also is a contract in which the tenant or lessee agrees to pay rent. It is common to include other covenants or undertakings on the part of both landlord and tenant. A lease for less than one year may be verbal, but if the term is for more than one year, most states require a written lease.

The recording of leases is not required in most states. Possession of the property is sufficient notice to the world of the rights of the tenant.

Contracts to Convey Title

This section will consider certain real estate contracts which relate to transfer of ownership but which do not of themselves convey title.

Purchase and Sale. Real estate transactions of sale are usually formalized in a written contract of purchase and sale before the sale is consummated by actual conveyance of title. This practice is a practical necessity. After the parties have reached a meeting of the minds and are ready to commit themselves, some time is required to prepare the documents of conveyance and for the buyer to assure himself of good title either by examination of the abstract of title or by securing a title insurance policy. In either case time is required to bring the abstract up to date and to examine the chain of title. The sale may be on condition that the buyer can secure financing, and time is required for him to make the arrangements with a lender. The trouble and expense of the foregoing preparatory steps would not be justified unless both the buyer and seller were bound by the terms of the contract.

The contract should contain a positive identification of buyer and seller; an exact and inclusive description of the property to be sold including items of personal property; the price and terms of sale; a condition that the seller must convey good and merchantable title; a specification of the form of deed to be given; the dates for closing the transaction, conveying title, and giving possession of the property; and the signatures of all persons on whom the contract is intended to be binding. Remedies for breach are often listed in the contract.

Option. An option is an agreement designed to fit a situation in which the owner is willing to sell but the prospective buyer is not ready to make up his mind. In order that the buyer may be protected until he does reach a decision, the owner, for a consideration, signs a contract which commits him to sell to the person specified as optionee if the latter chooses to exercise his option within a given period of time. The optionee makes no agreement except to pay a sum of money as consideration for the option. He has no interest in the land but only the right to buy at a fixed price if he chooses. If he exercises his option it ripens into a contract of purchase and sale; if he fails to exercise the option before its expiration he has no further rights.

Escrow. This arrangement is employed widely in the closing of real estate deals. An agreement is drawn up between the parties to the transaction and a disinterested escrow agent which authorizes the agent to deliver the signed deed to the buyer when certain conditions are met. These conditions must be consistent with the purchase and sale agreement; the conditions usually include payment of the purchase price and the showing of clear title to which the buyer may succeed. The escrow agreement is irrevocable.

LIMITATIONS ON OWNERSHIP

We have seen that real estate takes physical form which can be described in three dimensions and in terms of geological characteristics, including the improvements on the land. This physical form is the property object. The property rights in the property object are quite complex and may be subdivided in a variety of combinations—to be enjoyed in the present or the future, to be shared among two or more persons, or to provide for limited use. We shall see that society, in the form of government, has reserved certain rights which limit the ownership of individuals. There are three groups of social or governmental rights which are founded on specific or implied powers of government as set forth in our constitutions—police power, eminent domain, and taxation.

In addition to the constitutional limitations on private ownership, an individual grantor may limit the future use and development of land by restrictive covenants added to the instrument of conveyance.

Police Power

Our constitutions contain a general provision known as *police power* which in its application to real estate permits the state, and by delegation, local governments, to control the development and utilization of real estate so that it may be consonant with the general welfare of the community. The courts from time to time are called on to interpret and define "general welfare" when some citizen stands up against the further invasion of his private property rights. Before the first part of this century the courts supported legislation, as in the public interest, which prohibited the use of land to create a public nuisance or to endanger health and safety. But with time an expanded interpretation of the general welfare has led to the approval of more positive regulation of property which limits its use in the interests of the sound economic and social development of the community. Building methods and materials are controlled through building, safety, and sanitary codes or ordinances, and the control of land use is exercised through zoning, subdividing, and planning regulations. Recent legal sanction has been given to public regulation of the aesthetic qualities of structures. Owners subject to police power controls are not compensated for losses in income and value which derive from restrictions deemed by the courts to be for the general welfare or in the interests of public health, safety, or morals.

Eminent Domain

Eminent domain is the constitutional power reserved by the state to acquire private property for public purposes. It is used at all levels of government to secure land for public buildings, parks, streets, and other public uses. The power of eminent domain has been delegated by the states to public utilities, such as railroads and electric companies, where the services provided are deemed to be of broad public benefit.

Real estate is expropriated from reluctant owners through a court action known as "condemnation proceedings." The rights taken may be full ownership or some lesser right such as an easement. Just compensation must be paid to the owner in the amount of the current market value of the rights of which he has been deprived. Both the question of whether the intended use of the land is a proper public purpose and the amount of the compensation are matters of judicial determination. Thus the expanding interpretation by the courts of the proper limits of governmental activity has pushed back the boundaries of private ownership by admitting new kinds of public activities to the benefits of eminent domain.

Taxation

The power to tax real estate to meet governmental costs has been reserved by the states and delegated to such political subdivisions as counties, villages, cities, and school and sanitary districts. By limiting the financial benefits of ownership, taxation is an important restriction on private property up to virtual confiscation of private property in cases where taxes absorb all profits. In a few jurisdictions the real estate tax has been an instrument of public policy to influence the use of land by levying a heavy tax on vacant land in order to hasten its improvement.

Deed Restrictions and Reservations

Another form of limitation on the ownership of land is the privately originated restrictive provision which may be contained in the deed which conveys title to a new owner. For example, the grantor may wish to prevent the use of the property for other than residential purposes; or a subdivider may seek to maintain a high quality of development by restricting construction of homes to a certain minimum in size or cost. The restrictive provisions may appear in the deed, or they may be recorded along with a new subdivision plat with all lots sold subject to the recorded restrictions.

There is an important distinction between restrictions which are conditions and restrictions which are covenants. The violation of a condition results in the reversion of the land to the grantor or his heirs. A covenant only exacts a promise to use the land in accordance with the provisions of the deed; violation may be enjoined by court action. Deed restrictions run with land and are perpetual unless the wording includes a time limit. Under some conditions courts will refuse to enforce a restrictive covenant, for example, when a substantial and permanent change in the character of the neighborhood defeats the objective intended to be achieved. Failure to enforce a restriction and general acquiescence to violations by nearby property owners may sometimes be considered by the courts as abandonment of the restrictions.

Reservations are another form of limitation to ownership which may be imposed by a grant or through provisions in the deed. The purpose is to retain some right or privilege for the benefit of the grantor. The grantor may wish to reserve an easement, or some right to perform certain acts on the property.

VI

EQUITY INVESTMENT

INTRODUCTION

In the last three chapters we have dealt with the origins of real estate productivity and value and its definition in legal rights and benefits. In pursuit of our thesis that cities are built as a result of individual investment decisions, we will describe the processes of investment in the next two chapters. Chapter VI will deal with the entrepreneurial calculations of the investor, i.e., the method of converting his expectations of productivity into an investment decision. But in the typical case the owner-investor or equity investor supplies only part of the required capital; thus Chapter VII will discuss real estate credit sources and mechanisms as well as the considerations which condition the decisions of the creditor-investor.

Qualifying our thesis on city growth, we must recognize that every instance of real estate investment does not constitute growth or change nor does it result in new capital formation. The sale of an apartment house or a dwelling to a different investor merely involves the liquidation of the investment of the original owner and the substitution of capital supplied by the buyer. No discernible change occurs in the urban landscape. On the other hand, a significant modification of the urban structure may occur without a change in ownership or the infusion of additional capital; for example, an incompatible use moving into a storeroom in the midst of a women's shopping district can diminish the attractiveness of the district and reduce values of adjacent properties. City-building investment by which cities grow involves the improving of vacant land or the redevelopment of an existing structure through modernization or conversion to a new use. Such investment is new capital formation and represents a net addition to those capital goods in the form of improved real estate which make up the city.

Types of Investor

Our discussions of the investment process will give recognition to four general types of real estate investor. We may distinguish three types of equity investor on the basis of primary motivation:

1. *Investor for Use.* This investor, the buyer of a home for his family or a store building for his merchandising establishment, expects to occupy and use the property for his own purposes and hopes to gain certain advantages over the alternative of renting space.

2. *Investor for Regular Return.* Most investors in apartment buildings or other income properties anticipate a regular and predictable return on their capital; they invest for the "long pull," though no doubt a speculative gain would be welcome.

3. *Investor for Capital Gain.* Any kind of real estate may be the object of investment in expectation of resale at a profit. During the waiting period the investor may well hope that the property will produce enough at least to cover carrying costs, but he may be willing to advance such outlays if the expected capital gain is sufficiently large.

These three types of investor supply equity capital and represent the generating force of real estate activity. With few exceptions they are joined in the investment by the fourth type of investor, the supplier of credit or loan capital:

4. *Creditor-Investor.* In most cases this is the mortgage lender who advances loan capital secured by a mortgage lien on property owned or purchased by one of the other three types of investor. The lender anticipates a regular interest return on the outstanding debt and the recapture of the capital on a contractual schedule.

In this chapter we shall be concerned with the first three types, the equity investors, and with the processes by which they arrive at their respective investment decisions. Actually each one evaluates the same set of attributes of real estate but uses a somewhat different set of weights in arriving at a conclusion. The same may be said of the creditor-investor, to be discussed in Chapter VII, for he is equally concerned with the same set of productivity characteristics though he weights them differently to reflect his special investment objectives.

Equity Investment

Our description of the procedures of investment analysis on the part of those who commit equity capital to real estate will be both idealized and realistic. Certainly not all investors employ the same approach; some are wise and some are foolish; some take time to seek out all the facts, others rush in, enticed by rosy rumor; some employ refined calculations, others rough out an answer on the back of an envelope; some invest out of ample capital which can cushion a possible loss; others risk their pitiful all and face financial disaster if their judgment is faulty. It would be impossible, therefore, to outline an investment approach which is universally followed by the great diversity of persons and businesses who own real estate. Instead, we shall set forth what we believe to be the sound approach, that which is most likely to produce wise real estate investment decisions. It reflects the analytical procedures used by most of the successful investors in one form or another; it expresses in explicit form the processes which some of them instinctively employ, and which others short-cut without departing far from the basic principles involved.

Real estate investment analysis is best illustrated by examples of properties which produce a dollar income from rents. Thus much of the discussion will revolve around this type of property. However, there will be consideration of investment problems related to properties, such as homes and churches, which yield the dollar equivalent in services and amenities. In fact, all of Chapter VIII will be devoted to the special problems of home investment.

The plan of this chapter will present the subject of equity investment as follows:

1. *Productivity Analysis.* The first step in investment analysis is to forecast the income which the property can be expected to produce.

2. *Analysis of Business Risk.* The next step is to evaluate the probability that the prediction of productivity actually will be realized.

3. *Analysis of Financial Risk.* The risk inherent in the equity return is a function of the margin of safety above fixed charges and the stability of expected earnings.

4. *Investment Value Estimate.* The justified investment value of the property can be calculated after the investor determines upon an acceptable rate of return, or yield, on the equity investment, all things considered.

PRODUCTIVITY ANALYSIS

Nature of Productivity

The benefits of real estate investment, and thus real estate value, derive from those qualities of the real estate which enable it to create excess returns over the amount invested. It follows that the primary purpose of investment is the enjoyment of the benefits over and above the return of capital. There would be no advantage to the investor unless he could recapture the capital which he invests and something more, either interest return or profit. The investor must rely on the inherent productivity of the real estate enterprise to restore his original capital and to produce this incremental interest or profit. It is true that a few investors are concerned only with the preservation of their capital and therefore seek riskless depositories for their funds without thought of interest return. But for the most part, investors choose among alternative investments on the basis of the expected interest return or profit; of course, no investment would receive consideration unless a recapture of the original investment were anticipated.

The return to the real estate investor may take the form of dollar returns from income property or services directly enjoyed by the investor-user such as a homeowner. For income property, productivity is measured by the market rent which tenants are willing to pay for the services of the real estate less the running costs of making the services available. In the case of the investor-user, the direct return can be measured by the market rent equivalent of the services which he enjoys less costs of operation. Sometimes it is useful to measure productivity as a capital value rather than as a stream of income or services. The capital value used for this purpose is usually the market value. This value represents the present or capitalized value of future returns as established by transactions in the real estate market.

Productivity is the capacity to provide a flow of services. From time to time the volume and quality of this flow will change and its market value will vary. At some time the flow may terminate. It is clear, therefore, that any measurement or expression of productivity must have a time dimension. Forecasts of productivity must be in terms of both amount and duration.

Origins of Productivity

In the earlier chapters on the physical and locational origins of real estate value the sources of productivity were revealed. The specific attributes which create value were identified as the characteristics which must be evaluated in measuring current productivity and predicting the future level and pattern of productivity.

In addition to the property and the location the local real estate market is a factor to be considered. It is a function of the real estate market to translate productivity into a dollar expression, both rental value and capital value. Thus the rental value of an apartment at any point in time is determined by the concurrent market forces of demand and supply of rental units. At another time, under different market conditions and prospects, the same apartment will have a different rental value though the services provided are unchanged. Both rental value and capital value, though basically functions of productivity, are dollar expressions which vary with changes in market balances, in market prospects, and in the institutional framework within which the market operates. For this reason forecasts of productivity require knowledge of underlying real estate market trends.

Measuring Current Productivity

The essence of productivity analysis is the forecast of future returns. But the take-off point for such a forecast is the present productivity of the property. For an existing property, the actual figures for income and expense are usually available. For a prospective new development, estimates must be made on the basis of the current performance of similar properties.

The measure of current productivity is the most important datum in the entire investment analysis. First, it is a fact, not a guess. For a going concern, it represents actual behavior; and for a prospective development, the actual behavior of similar properties provides a dependable basis of estimate. A second point is that present and near-future income figures are mathematically the most important in the final estimate of investment value. The present value of near-future returns is greater than the present value of equal returns more remotely realized.

In the case of income properties, productivity is expressed as *net income before depreciation* for investment analysis purposes. The first step is to determine the potential gross revenue with all space occupied at current market rentals. This figure is reduced to *effective gross revenue* by deductions for vacancy and collection losses. *Operating expenses* include the costs of materials and labor required to maintain the level of the services which are provided to occupants, administrative and management expenses, taxes and insurance, and reserves for the replacement of items of relatively short life. The balance after deducting *operating expenses* is *net income before depreciation*.

Gross Income

Gross income to the owner of an apartment or office building is a familiar concept for it consists of rents in hand from the tenant occupants. Rent is the price received for the use and occupancy of the premises for a given period of time. The time dimension is important, for it is significant that the services of real estate may not be consumed in advance and may not be stored for future consumption; they perish with the passing of time and are not recoverable. Thus the landlord must sell his entire stock of space each day or the opportunity is forever lost.

Forecasting the productivity of an income property is first a matter of rental rates and occupancy percentages. Note that the investor who buys income property is acquiring a stream of income which endures as long as the space is salable. Thus his expectations of income take the form of a forecast of gross income which may rise or fall but which will continue over the years of productive life remaining in the property. Rental forecasts are made in terms of market price, i.e., market-determined rents. It cannot be overemphasized that real estate revenue is based on the willingness and ability of the users (tenants) to pay for the services, and in a competitive market they will not pay more than they have to. No matter what rent schedule is set by the landlord, no matter what rents he needs to get in order to yield a satisfactory return on his investment, his actual revenue is determined by demand and supply conditions in the rental market. Thus rental forecasts start with an estimate of the rental return under present market conditions and in light of present competition and extend over the remaining productive life of the property, taking into account changing market and competitive conditions. For the early years such a forecast can be made with reasonable accuracy; except for a new property, the history of actual rent returns in the recent past may be used as a basis for extrapolation. Current market conditions can be analyzed and short-term changes foreseen and evaluated. But beyond a few years prediction of rental returns, the analyst must resort to generalized predictions in the nature of trends in a statistical sense.

Rental forecasts are made in terms of current dollars. It is reasonably assumed that as general price levels change, so will rents, capital costs, and operating expenses change accordingly and thus that the net position of the investor will remain constant.

Rental forecasts are in terms of effective gross revenue, i.e., the dollars actually received from tenants. This amount can also be defined as the potential revenue with all space rented less loss from vacancy and bad debts (uncollectible rents). "Normal" apartment vacancy is said to be 4 to 5 per cent; in its rental housing program, the Federal Housing Administration (FHA) assumes a 5 per cent vacancy as a constant deduction from potential gross revenue. The concept of normal vacancy is that some percentage of vacancy, say 5 per cent, represents a long-term balance of demand and supply in the market about which vacancy rates fluctuate in response to short-term market changes. This normal level of vacancy is assumed to account for the time between occupancies when the accommodations are being redecorated as well as to provide prospective tenants with a reasonable selection among rental units available for occupancy. Normal vacancy in this sense varies among communities in accordance with economic stability and local customs such as the use of year leases. Tenant turnover is lower in a stable market where jobs are secure and migration rates are low. The practice of using leases results in lower rates of turnover than where month-to-month tenancy predominates. Normal or typical vacancy rates also vary among types of rental property and among similar properties where management policies differ.

To some degree vacancy can be controlled by manipulating rents; other things being equal, a reduction in rents should result in a reduced vacancy loss.

Operating Expenses

We have mentioned operating expenses; here again is a familiar term but one which has a special connotation in real estate investment analysis in so far as a depreciation charge is concerned. For our purposes, operating expenses are those costs incurred in maintaining the productivity of the original real estate enterprise. Thus we exclude depreciation but include periodic charges to set up a reserve for the replacement of items of equipment, such as refrigerators, stoves, heating plant, and air conditioners, and structural parts such as the roof surfacing which must be replaced one or more times during the economic life of the structure. A typical operating statement includes the items set forth in Table VI-1.

Table VI-1

Operating Statement

Apartment property

Rental value (100% occupied)	$29,959	
Less vacancy and collection losses	898	
Effective Gross Income		$29,061
Operating expenses		
Janitor's salary	900	
Fuel	2,295	
Water	285	
Electricity	670	
Decorating and painting	909	
Repairs	1,712	
Ash removal	50	
Exterminating	175	
Advertising	47	
Janitor's supplies	250	
Miscellaneous (inspection, etc.)	150	
Management	1,400	
		8,843
Net before other expenses		$20,218
Other expenses		
Reserve for replacements	890	
Fixed charges		
Real estate taxes	5,735	
Insurance	1,150	
Total other expenses		7,775
Net income before depreciation		$12,443

As the building ages there is a tendency for operating costs to rise, but as a practical matter, the rise is so slow that few analysts take it into account. However, in the estimates for an older building, all large and unusual repairs and replacements which are likely to be required in the next few years should be taken into account. Furthermore, because property taxes are a heavy burden, and in view of the persistent and substantial increase in this burden, the analyst may be justified in reflecting a continued tax increase in his net figure.

The figure which measures the true productivity of the property and which the prospective investor converts into a capital value is the net income or the expected actual cash revenue less operating expenses required to maintain optimum productivity.

For purposes of investment analysis, depreciation is not included as an expense. The reason is that depreciation is not a cash outlay; neither is it akin in function to the operating expenses which are required to maintain the flow of services provided by the property. From the standpoint of business management, the treatment of depreciation is a matter of financial policy, for it does not affect productivity. From the standpoint of the investor, who is primarily interested in the amount of the net product and its duration, depreciation policy will be adapted to his own special investment objectives and his tax position. Note that income taxes are not included among expenses for purposes of productivity analysis since the tax amounts would reflect the special circumstances of the investor rather than the productive characteristics of the real estate.

Nonincome Properties

The productivity of properties which are owner-occupied cannot be measured in dollars actually received from occupants. If the owner-occupied property is one which is typically commercially operated such as an office building, rents from similar properties will provide a basis for estimating imputed income which then can be analyzed as if it were actual dollar income received. In the case of an owner-occupied home, the imputed income approach has limited application, and it is more customary to move directly to a capitalized expression of productivity in the form of the current market value. In the hypothetical perfect market situation, the current sales prices of similar homes would represent the market expression of the present value of future services, i.e., net productivity capitalized. In many actual market situations sales prices are useful and dependable indicators for investment purposes.

In the case of a church or other property types where sales are infrequent and properties not readily comparable, resort must be made to a cost approach. The assumption is made that the cost of the church (new) represents an expression of future productivity. As the property ages, the present value of future services falls somewhat in proportion to the passage of time. Crude as these assumptions may be, they provide the investor with a useful basis for decision making.

Predicting the Future Pattern of Productivity

Investments are made in real estate because of future benefits expected. The central problem of the investor then, is to forecast these future benefits before making the decision to invest. This forecast is the most basic and significant judgment which is made in the whole realm of real estate activity. It largely determines the nature of land development, its timing, and the very structure of our urban areas. It is at this point of decision that the professional skill of the trained and experienced real estate analyst is urgently required. In market terminology the problem is to forecast changes in "value," but the term which we have been using, "productivity," more precisely connotes the value-creating attributes of the real estate. The productivity of the property is expressed in the services it provides to users, in the net income which it produces for its owner, or in its capital value as measured in the real estate market by what price it will bring.

We have earlier identified three groups of factors which influence the pattern of productivity in level and duration: (1) the structure and other improvements to the land, (2) the location, and (3) the local real estate market. The investment analyst must examine each one of these three sets of conditioning factors and arrive at a judgment of the extent to which it may induce changes in basic and dollar productivity and in the timing of such changes. Starting with the measure of current productivity, he must create a forecast which expresses in the prediction the composite effect of all the significant factors and which represents the most probable level at each point of time up to the end of the productive life of the property.

The forecast of productivity cannot be in the nature of a precise and exact measurement. Current revenues and expenses can be measured with some certainty and will provide the take-off point. But beyond a few years into the future, and except where revenues are assured by a well-secured lease or contract, the figures can only represent a central tendency. Or, using another statistical concept, long-range predictions of productivity may be expressed as a secular trend. It is recognized that there will be cyclical fluctuations above and below this trend value, and that short-term influences will create temporary aberrations. But the assumption is that these upward and downward movements will offset one another and that the trend line will reflect a kind of average experience which is the product of the underlying, long-range influences (Figure VI-1). There will be fluctuations in general business conditions which will affect the local real estate market and there will be short-run market imbalances of local origin. But over the years, these changes will average out if the trend values are properly selected. The forecast is made in dollars of current purchasing power under the assumption that future changes in the general price level will affect revenues and costs proportionately over the long run and will affect real estate in the same degree as the rest of the economy.

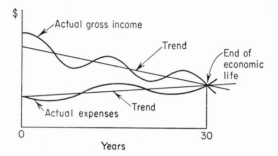

FIGURE VI-1. Prediction pattern—gross income and expenses.

The ideal productivity forecast would be built up from separate forecasts of income and expenses for each month or year during the economic life of the property. This method is rarely used in practice except for periods covered by existing leases. Instead, the predictions usually take

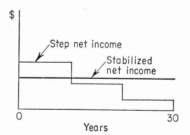

FIGURE VI-2. Prediction pattern—net income before depreciation.

one of the following forms and are expressed in terms of net income before depreciation:

1. Stabilized income: a constant annual net income over the full economic life of the property as a kind of average experience (Figure VI-2).

2. Step pattern: net income which is constant for a period and then shifts to a new level, higher or lower, for another period, and so on. There may be any number of steps during the economic life (Figure VI-2).

Except in the case of vacant land, productivity forecasts terminate at that point of time when, in the opinion of the analyst, the costs of operation will equal revenues. This equivalence marks the end of the economic life, for it is then no longer profitable to continue the enterprise. Economic life may end before this point is reached if some new and more profitable use justifies the replacement of the original enterprise. Such replacement is economical when the value of the original real estate enterprise is less than the value of the new enterprise minus the cost of the new land improvement.

ANALYSIS OF BUSINESS RISK

Any investor must depend upon the inherent productivity of the enterprise to generate a return. Productivity analysis results in a forecast which is the analyst's best estimate of the *most probable* level and pattern of such return. But the investor recognizes that there are varying degrees of risk that the expected returns will not be realized in actuality. His final investment decision will be greatly influenced by his evaluation of the degree of this risk. In sporting parlance, he must judge the odds against realizing the prediction.

The creditor-investor, a mortgagee with an apartment house as collateral, for example, is concerned primarily with the chance that revenues available for debt service will be sufficient at all times during the life of the mortgage contract to meet the mortgage payments. Since the lender cannot share in profits, he has small direct interest in the probability that revenues will produce large speculative returns except that in such case, he will benefit by a wider margin of protection against loss.

Owner-investors who seek a regular and safe return, or who are owner-users, are most concerned that returns do not fall below the expected level. Speculative investors may be willing to risk falling below this point in return for the possibility of large gains.

Another application of the analysis of business risk is in the process of converting the productivity prediction into a capital value for the investment. The selection of a capitalization rate is an important step in this procedure. The rate is largely a function of risk; a safe and sure return will justify a low capitalization rate, an uncertain return will call for a higher rate.

Risk as Uncertainty of Prediction

We must not confuse risk with fluctuation. It is quite possible to conceive of a low-risk investment with returns which fluctuate widely and frequently. If these fluctuations are certain and predictable the investor can base his calculations on a sure thing, even though the return be not constant and regular. The problem in business risk analysis is not the level or pattern of the prediction, but how sure and certain is the prediction.

The concept of risk as uncertainty of prediction justifies further explanation. Let us assume that investors in general are willing to accept a 4 per cent return on United States government bonds. In normal times this security is riskless for all practical purposes; the investor is certain of receiving interest precisely on the due date and of receiving full repayment of principal on maturity. At the time of investment prediction is certain. Compare this situation with a proposed investment in the common stock of a company manufacturing military aircraft. There may be a record over several years of a regular $3 dividend and a backlog of orders which indicate that current earnings can be maintained for four years. But changes in world conditions could lead either to cancellation of orders under a disarmament pact or to increased orders in the face of new international tensions. Rapid technological advances might make current aircraft models obsolete and result in discontinuance of their manufacture. On the other hand, the research department might produce an advanced design which would keep the company in the lead. Thus short-term forecasts of a year or so in the case of the aircraft company can be made with reasonable certainty, but predictions for more remote periods become progressively more uncertain.

In considering the aircraft manufacturer, the investor seeks a prediction of the most probable outcome, i.e., the most likely earnings experience. He must then judge the probability of the realization of the most probable earnings. If he is armed with a full array of verifiable facts, dependable inside information, and a strong consensus among informed persons, the probability will be high and the risk of prediction will be low. He can invest with a high probability of realizing his expectations and with a small probability of being either too conservative or too optimistic. But if the investor is poorly informed through lack of available information, if he can secure only hearsay evidence, and if informed opinions are diverse, the probability of the realization of the prediction will be smaller and the probability of a higher or lower actuality will be larger.

It should be clear that uncertainty increases with the remoteness of the prediction in time. The usefulness of past records as a basis for prediction diminishes rapidly as the point of prediction extends farther into the future. Trends may change direction and new forces may appear which are less and less predictable as one looks farther ahead in time. As a result higher risk rates are justified in evaluating predictions in the far, rather than the near, future.

We have outlined the factors which the analyst considers in predicting real estate productivity—the physical property, the location, and the market. He gathers what facts he can in these categories, seeks informed opinions, and finally combines it all into a judgment of his own. To evaluate business risk he must evaluate the sources of his information, its completeness and dependability as the basis of prediction, the understanding and objectivity of those persons who express opinions, and his own competence to consolidate a combination of facts and guesses into a specific forecast running over many years. If his facts are complete and accurate and his understanding adequate, his predictions may be dependable and can be used with confidence. If facts are few, of questionable origin, and the investment situation fraught with incommensurables and uncertainties, his prediction must be used with caution and with the realization that the actual returns may be quite different. Thus, the certainty of prediction is but the reflection of the adequacy of the basis of prediction. Business risk, in turn, is an expression of the degree of certainty of the prediction of productivity.

We have explained that the objective of the analyst is to predict the most probable future productivity. Statistically speaking this term does not imply that at any point in time the chances are equal that the actual figure will fall an equal amount above or below the prediction. At one time, perhaps in the early life of a resort hotel in a newly developing recreational area, the chance of a large drop below expected levels is much greater than the chance of a large rise above the forecast. Later, as the area grows to a point of stability, the chance of a large drop is much less than the chance of a substantial increment above the most probable productivity. Thus among different properties, and at different times for any given property, there may be great differences in the pattern of probabilities above and below the prediction. The decision of the investor will be influenced by the comparative chances of large and small differences above and below the predicted level of productivity at various times during the life of the investment property.

FINANCIAL RISK ANALYSIS

An investor in real estate, no matter with what diligence and skill he examines all the factors, must assume some degree of risk that the services or revenues from the property will not meet expectations. We have defined this business risk as the uncertainty of the prediction of productivity. The employment of borrowed capital, which is well-nigh universal in real estate investment, adds new elements of risk for the owner-investor which he must evaluate before arriving at an investment decision. Where debt financing is involved, the investor measures his risk in part by relating the obligations created by the debt contract to the productivity characteristics of the property. The extra risks to the owner which are created by debt financing are known as "financial risks"; they are additional

to the underlying business risks which reflect the productivity characteristics of the property without reference to financing arrangements.

Financing Pattern

In the real estate investment situation involving a mortgage debt, the
mortgage contract establishes the amount of the debt, the repayment
schedule, the interest rate, and the term of the loan. This financing pattern
may be varied in any or all of its terms, but investment analysis must
start with the assumption of a given pattern. Should the investment prove
unacceptable to an investor under the original financing pattern, the modification of one or more of the contract terms may bring it within the
range of acceptability.

The relationships between the elements of the financing pattern and the
productivity and value of the property are significant through the entire
term of the mortgage contract. Certainly the more favorable the initial
relationships, the lower the financial risk, other things being equal; but the
fact remains that the contract is usually long term, and the dangers of
loss exist throughout its life. It is the pattern of relationships over time,
therefore, which is the basis for the judgment of the degree of financial
risk.

Financial risk is proportionate to the margin of safety between the net
operating income (after operating expenses but before depreciation) and
the contract mortgage payments or debt service. Where expected cyclical
fluctuations are wide or where business risk is high, this margin of safety
should be wide in order to avoid the danger of default on the mortgage
and the possible loss of his equity by the owner. Where there is no
debt the significant relationship for the owner to evaluate is that between
operating income and operating expenses; in order that the property be
productive, outlays for operation, taxes, and management must be made.
The higher the ratio of variable to fixed expenses, the more favorable the
risk situation. In the case of an owner-occupied home with a mortgage
debt, the owner should estimate the rental value of the house in its relationship to operating costs and debt service. If default is threatened the
owner might rent the property for enough to carry the financial obligations until he can get back on his feet. This rental possibility which is
open to the borrower is a protection for the lender; in addition, should
the lender acquire the house through foreclosure, the rental return may
cover operating costs and interest on the frozen capital until the house
can be sold.

Owner's Financial Capacity and Financial Obligations

In the case of income properties the owner's circumstances are secondary, for the property is expected to carry the burden of operating

expenses and debt service. Furthermore, in many cases the property owner is a corporation created for the sole purpose of holding title with no other assets or sources of income. However, should the productivity of the enterprise drop to the danger point, the personal income and assets of the persons holding equity interests are a possible defense against default to which the lender gives some weight. From the standpoint of an individual owner, his personal financial capacity to carry the property through temporary periods of financial stringency reduces the over-all financial risk of his equity investment.

Owner-occupied home properties are financed with direct reliance on the income and assets of the borrower to meet all financial obligations. The first line of defense against default by a homeowner is his income available for housing after deducting prior obligations. Thus, the greater the margin of safety between this income and the debt service obligations set by the mortgage pattern, the lower the financial risk. The greater the other assets of the borrower which might be called upon to meet the debt obligations in case of necessity, the lower the financial risk.

Liquidity

The ease and speed with which an investment can be converted into cash are important qualities from the investor's standpoint. This is generally termed liquidity. Actually there are two processes by which cash can be secured by an equity investor:

1. Borrowing on his interest in the property. The owner-investor pledges his equity interest, for example, as security for a second mortgage loan.

2. Sale of his equity or investment.

The investor may want cash quickly to meet a personal emergency. He may wish to take advantage of a better investment opportunity. He may be faced with a decline in the productivity of the property and difficulty in meeting operating costs and debt service. For these or other reasons the lack of liquidity in any investment is a disadvantage and adds to financial risk. Thus each investment opportunity must be viewed in light of the marketability of the property and the facilities for borrowing on the investment as collateral.

COSTS OF FINANCIAL MANAGEMENT

The costs of making and servicing the investment reduce the net yield to the investor. Such costs are in part a reflection of a particular financial plan.

First, the investor must consider the initial costs of acquiring the investment. Investors may face costs of field investigation, survey, title examination, appraisals, attorney's fees, recording fees, commissions, and accounting costs. The owner-investor must meet initial costs in selecting the investment and negotiating the deal for its acquisition. There are some continuing costs of financial management, and there may be additional expenses in connection with refinancing. The investor must look ahead to expenses such as sales commissions and legal costs when he liquidates the investment. The administrative costs of managing the property are not included among the costs of financial management here; they are covered in operating costs.

INVESTMENT VALUE ESTIMATE

All real estate investors, regardless of objective and motivation, must finally face up to the problem of how much to invest in the property under consideration. At some price all real estate investments are attractive to someone. Each prospective investor must determine how much the property is worth to him; among investors this figure will vary considerably. The practical matter is to decide upon an upper limit to the capital investment which he feels is justified by his evaluation of the productivity of the property. Each one of the three basic types of investor must make such a determination before he enters the market to bid on the property. Of course he will buy the property for less if he can, but he must have a figure in mind which represents his top offer. Each investor also faces this same problem when the time comes to sell and thus to liquidate his investment. In this case he must develop a bottom price though he will, of course, try for more.

The upper limit of the investor's bid for a property is termed the "investment value." It is the value to him based on his own estimates of productivity and his own judgment on their worth to him. It reflects his judgment of the risk to his capital and necessarily reflects his individual tastes, financial situation, and tax position. This chapter has already outlined the process of productivity and risk analysis with productivity a function of the physical improvements, the location, and the local real estate market and with risk a reflection of the quality of productivity and the proposed financing arrangements. We have pointed out the necessity for predicting net income before depreciation, evaluating business and financial risk and for taking into account the liquidity of the property, the financial strength of the owner, and the costs of financial management. We now turn to the final step in the investment process—the determination of the amount of capital which may be justifiably committed to the investment, all things considered.

We shall soon see that the investment decision calls for the determination of not one value figure, but several. Five such value figures will be described along with an indication of how investors of various types employ these figures in arriving at the final investment decision. The five value figures to be discussed are:

1. Cost of replacement—new: the outlay which would be required to buy land and construct improvements which would constitute a practical alternative to the proposed investment.

2. Market price: the figure at which the property would probably sell in the market under present conditions.

3. Alternatives for market price: (a) cost of replacement—new less depreciation: the cost figure as determined in 1 above with adjustments for defects which would reduce the market price of the subject property below that obtainable for a new alternative property; (b) capitalized value of income: the present worth of future returns capitalized at a rate representative of actual transactions in the market.

4. Investment value: the present worth to the investor of the future returns capitalized at a rate acceptable to him in light of his evaluation of the investment characteristics of the property.

We propose now to discuss each of these value figures to show how it is derived and to show how each of the investor types employs it in arriving at his final investment decision.

Cost of Replacement—New

In the case of a prospective investment in an existing property, an upper limit to the investor's price offer will be set by the cost of replacement—new of the property. This cost is the sum of the purchase price of a comparable site plus the construction costs of a comparable building and other improvements where such new property is a real and practicable alternative to the purchase of the existing property. Ordinarily no investor would be justified in committing an amount larger than this cost of replacement—new, provided that the hypothetical property represents an alternative which is real. If for one reason or another he would not seriously consider buying land and building a similar structure, then this approach is of no value as an aid in reaching an investment decision. If a new building is a practical alternative, then the cost of such a property sets an upper limit to his offer on the existing real estate.

In the case where the existing property under consideration as an investment is old and obsolete, this test of the upper limit of investment value should not be forced into inappropriate and illogical use. Clearly, no one would actually set out to build new an outdated and obsolete structure, yet investments in such structures are made every day. When the existing and the hypothetical properties are far apart in the quality of the services which they would provide, there is little practical value in estimating the cost of the new one.

All types of real estate investor may be interested in cost new as an upper limit to their investment value estimates. Investor-users often face the practical alternative of buying or building. In appraisal for purposes of mortgage risk analysis the FHA has long used this value figure as the upper limit of value for loan purposes. Investors for regular return or for capital gain would not be justified in paying more than replacement cost. However, there may be certain circumstances when, in real life, exceptions are made, and an investor exceeds this upper limit:

1. An investor-user in immediate need of shelter for his family or his business activities may pay more than cost of replacement rather than face the wait during the construction process.

2. The location of the existing property may be unique and non-reproducible.

3. The advantage of assuming favorable mortgage financing, such as a low interest-bearing loan, may justify a premium price.

Market Price

No investor will wittingly pay more for a given property than the price he would have to pay for another existing comparable property. To establish this upper limit he will carefully explore the market offerings of properties which are like, or nearly like, the one under consideration. He will analyze asking prices and actual sales prices of similar properties and will arrive at an estimate of market value defined as the "most probable price" which the property would bring on the market within a reasonable time. The evidence on what other people are willing to pay for similar properties is also useful as a test of his own judgment of the investment value of the property which he contemplates acquiring.

A study of market prices in all their aspects is a valuable part of real estate investment analysis for all types of investors. Not only is such knowledge useful in setting an upper limit to investment value, but it is also an aid in the bargaining process. The investor will be in a better bargaining position if he knows what alternatives face the seller, in particular, what is the most probable price which the seller can hope to get for his property in the market. An analysis of the difference between asking prices and actual transaction prices for the same properties and information on the length of time on the market before sale will indicate whether the market is slow or active and will suggest the possibilities of beating down the price.

But the investor is concerned not only with current market value but also with the future pattern of value. Though he be acquiring the property for his own present use, he is not unmindful of the probability that at some future and indeterminate date he may wish to dispose of his investment. As a homeowner he may need a larger house, or his employment may require a move to another city. The institutional owner-user may require larger and more modern quarters, a better location, or may wish to move the home office to another city. Thus the future pattern of value is important in the practical terms of what price could be secured on liquidation of the investment.

No precise forecasts of the future market value pattern are possible. As a first step, the investor will analyze current market conditions to judge whether present values tend to be above or below the long-term trend. If either be the case, he will estimate how long before values will return to this measure of normal or central tendency and what the value of the property will be at that time. Following this point in time, his value prediction for the property will be the product of his judgment of the relative strengths of favorable and unfavorable factors affecting the deterioration and obsolescence of the structure and the value of the location. He will examine the factors of productivity which were considered in our discussion of the evaluation of productivity, for in the absence of data on actual market transactions, productivity analysis is the only basis for judging the most probable liquidation price. Though the forecast of future values can be only in general and approximate terms, it is useful in comparing properties and is valuable in providing for the investor some notion of how he will fare should liquidation become necessary.

For the investor for capital gain, the pattern of future market prices is the primary basis of his investment decision. Only when he expects to sell for more than the purchase price does he invest. Thus he must forecast future liquidation prices in order to decide how much he would be justified in investing now. For a somewhat different reason the creditor-investor is more interested in future market prices than in the present price. If foreclosure is necessary it will take place at a future time; thus the liquidation value of the collateral property at that time is the significant figure. We shall see in Chapter VII that a forecast of the pattern of future market prices is useful in setting the amortization schedule of the loan. Finally, the pattern of future values is an indicator of the liquidity of the investment and thus of use to all investors in their analysis of investment risk.

Alternatives for Market Price

For some kinds of property under certain market conditions data on actual sales of comparable properties are not available. When the market is inactive there may be only a few sales transactions with none of comparable character. Or for special purpose properties, there may exist no similar ones in the market. Under such circumstances the analyst must resort to an alternative approach to the estimate of the most probable market price. In effect, he must put himself in the place of a prospective buyer and develop a value figure which he believes such a buyer would evolve. There are two approaches to the estimate of probable market price in the absence of adequate data on actual price behavior:

1. Cost of replacement—new less depreciation
2. Capitalized value of income—market determined

Even when some current market evidence is available these substitute values provide a check, and where wide deviations occur, this fact may indicate that market data are undependable.

Cost Approach. To illustrate the cost approach to estimating market value, let us assume a factory building in a small community. It is probably a unique structure in the town, and there would be no market evidence of its value based on transactions involving similar properties. As a substitute approach, the analyst starts with the premise that such a building newly constructed would have a value equivalent to its cost. Thus the most probable market price *new* would be the sum of the cost of erecting the structure plus the present value of the site. But because the structure is thirty years old, it is presumed to be worth less than the cost new. This discount in value below cost new is generally termed "depreciation." Where market transactions are available for analysis the amount of depreciation can be established by actual market reactions in the form of prices paid for similar older properties. In the absence of market data the probable market discount for age and obsolescence can be approximated by combining (1) an estimate of repair costs required to restore the building to new condition, (2) modernization costs to bring efficiency up to the level of a newly constructed counterpart, and (3) that fraction of the estimated cost of reproduction new of the basic structure which is the ratio of expired economic life to total economic life. The basic structure is that portion of the building which is not subject to repair and modernization and which is presumed to depreciate in proportion to the passage of time up to the end of economic life. To illustrate: an examination of the subject building leads to an estimate of forty years of *remaining* useful life. This type of building is judged to have a typical *total* useful life of sixty years. For this purpose, the total loss in the estimated investment of, say $100,000, which would be required to construct the basic structure is spread evenly over its life at a constant rate of 1.67 per cent per year. Thus it is presumed that each year $1,667 of the original value is lost. Since the building has forty years of useful life remaining, forty-sixtieths, or two-thirds, of the original $100,000 will remain, or $33,333 will have been lost. This calculation suggests that a prospective buyer will reduce his purchase offer by $33,333 below cost new by reason of the fact that there remain only two-thirds the number of years of useful life which would be expected of a new building. In addition, as suggested earlier, he will further reduce his offer by the amount of the expenditures required to bring the property up to a level of efficiency equal to a new building. To repeat, this final value figure of cost new less depreciation is useful only to estimate what would be the most probable market price; the calculation reproduces in a generalized way the process by which a buyer would arrive at the price which he would be willing to pay. For the investor, therefore, in the absence of an active market for this type of property, this approach provides an estimate of probable market price and helps to set an upper limit to his original price offer. It produces a value figure beyond which no competing buyer is likely to go. The formula can also be used in predicting the future pattern of liquidation value.

Income Approach. Another device which is sometimes useful in the absence of information on actual market transactions of similar properties is the capitalization of income. For income properties of a type or size which are not often traded it is a reasonable assumption that, if they were to be sold, the price would be a function of net income productivity. Specifically, the most probable market price would be the present value of estimated future net income capitalized at a rate representing the interest return required by investors in the market on this type of investment. The steps are (1) estimate future pattern of net income before depreciation, (2) estimate reversion or liquidation value at end of economic life, (3) select capitalization rate, (4) determine present value of net income, and (5) add present value of reversion. This calculation will be described in detail in the next section of this chapter. In the case of a home the capitalization of rental value may yield a useful approximation of market value. The gross income multiplier to be described later can be employed for this purpose.

Capitalized Value of Income

The reader who is unfamiliar with the fundamentals of the mathematics of finance—present value, capitalization, amortization—is referred to the Appendix at the end of this chapter. Here he will find a simple and sufficient explanation of the arithmetic of capitalization.

The present value of the expected returns from a real estate investment is a value figure which is the basic consideration for all types of investors. No investor expects to invest more than the present worth of the future benefits to be derived from the ownership of the property. In the case of the investor for use, who receives benefits in the form of services rather than dollars, no precise calculation is possible. The homeowner invests because of the amenities and satisfactions of the way of life which ownership makes possible. Yet the price he pays for the house represents in a very real sense his dollar evaluation of these future benefits. And if one assumes that the rental value of the house is an approximate measure of the benefits, it is possible to capitalize this imputed income to arrive at a present value figure. But this kind of investment calculation is most useful and most appropriate when applied to income properties which produce a stream of dollar returns, the receipt of which is the true investment objective. It is useful for all investors when the absence of sufficient market information on actual sales forces reliance on substitute evidence. It is particularly appropriate for the investor for regular return, for it provides him with a direct answer to the question of how much capital he is justified in committing in light of expected income productivity.

Because of the wide use of debt financing, the usual investor for income is an equity investor, i.e., he invests out of his own capital only that amount which represents the difference between the total investment value of the property and the amount of borrowed capital. All his investment calculations, therefore, are focused on his own dollar contribution and the prospective investment return on the equity. He is concerned with the basic productivity of the enterprise only as it affects the final net return per dollar of his own investment. We shall see how the equity return is a function not only of productivity, but also of the amount and terms of the mortgage. Thus real estate investment analysis must take into account the effect of debt financing, and when borrowed funds are used, the capitalization process is applied to that net income which is a return on the equity interest after the debt service obligations have been met.

Trading on the Equity. In most instances of debt financing of real estate investments, the effect of the use of borrowed funds is to increase the rate of return on the equity investment above the rate of return which would have been earned on the owner's capital if he had used no borrowed funds. To illustrate the principle with an example of another form of investment, let us assume that a $10,000 bond pays $600 per year, or 6 per cent. If an investor finances the purchase of this bond by borrowing $5,000 at 4 per cent interest and adding $5,000 of his own capital, he will earn a return on his own capital contribution of 8 per cent ($600 interest return from the bond less $200 to pay interest on the borrowed capital leaves a $400 return on his $5,000 or 8 per cent). Note that if he borrowed at a higher rate, say 7 per cent, than the rate of return on the full amount of capital invested in the bond, the return on his own investment would be reduced to 5 per cent. It is a general principle, then, that the advantage of debt financing in terms of a higher rate of return on equity capital occurs only when the interest on the borrowed funds is less than the over-all return on the total investment—equity plus borrowed funds. It is therefore clear why differences in mortgage interest rates will affect the investment value of real estate.

One of the attractive features of real estate investment is the advantage of *leverage*, or trading on the equity, whereby the use of debt financing with its fixed dollar obligations permits the equity interest to enjoy all the benefits of inflationary or fortuitous increases in productivity and capital value. The total of such benefits accrues to the equity holder though he may have provided but a small fraction of the original capital. In the following example, if net income should double, the equity return in cash increases threefold:

Item	Before increase	After increase
Net income	$10,000 per year	$20,000
Debt service	5,000	5,000
Return to equity	$ 5,000	$15,000

The effect on the capital value of the equity and debt may be illustrated by assuming that the market value of the property increases by 10 per cent:

Item	Before increase	After increase	Per cent increase
Total value	$100,000	$110,000	10
Debt	80,000	80,000	0
Equity	$ 20,000	$ 30,000	50

The lower the ratio of equity to total value, the greater the effect of leverage. In the foregoing example, if debt were $90,000 and equity $10,000, the 10 per cent increase in the total value of the property would result in a 100 per cent increase in the value of the equity. The investor should recognize that leverage works both ways and that with a small equity, a small decline in productivity can wipe out the equity return and endanger the equity investment.

Investment Calculation

To illustrate the nature of the owner or equity holder's interest, let us assume he purchases a property for $100,000; he borrows $60,000 and puts in $40,000 of his own capital. The productive life of the property is estimated at forty years. The mortgage is to be amortized over twenty years. As the property ages, deteriorates, and obsolesces, it will become less and less valuable until at the end of its forty years of productive life, there will be nothing left of value save the land which we may assume to be worth $10,000 at that time. The investor will not invest unless he believes that out of the net earnings of the real estate, the following financial objectives can be accomplished:

1. Meet the debt service and thereby repay the borrowed capital

2. Return to the investor out of earnings $30,000 of his $40,000 equity investment, the remaining $10,000 being in the residual land

3. Reward the investor at an attractive rate of return on the $40,000 equity capital which was tied up in the property

Once the investor has decided what rate of return on the equity would be necessary to induce him to invest in a given real estate enterprise, he can readily calculate how much he would be justified in paying for the equity. Note that we must assume a debt of a given amount and the terms under which it has been borrowed or might be obtained from a lender.

The calculations on page 127, based on another set of assumptions, illustrate the principle that the present value of the net income before depreciation after deducting the debt service payments under the mortgage contract, plus the present value of the land reversion, plus the amount of the borrowed capital (mortgage debt) equals the total investment value of the property. The prospective investor therefore would be justified in investing equity funds up to the difference between this total value and the amount of the borrowed funds.

This calculation leads the investor to the conclusion that he could afford to pay a total price of $104,510 for the property, to be made up of a mortgage loan of $38,610 and an equity investment of $65,900. Under the assumptions the revenues from the property will be sufficient to amortize the mortgage, return to the investor his contribution of $65,900 (in part in the form of the residual land), and yield a 10 per cent return on the outstanding balances of his investment at all times.

It is to be expected that the investor-owner will require a higher rate of return on his investment than will the mortgage lender (investor-creditor). The lender has first claim on net earnings and a prior lien on the collateral property to protect against loss; thus his investment is safer than that of the equity owner. Of course, the investor-owner may enjoy a capital gain if property values rise, while the mortgage lender can only recapture his capital if the contract terms are met but might suffer loss if the productivity of the property should substantially decline. An investor-user, such as the houseowner, is not faced directly with the problem of valuing the equity. He generally considers the total price of the property and arrives at a judgment on what figure he considers a total justified investment value. The initial equity, then, is simply the difference between this total value figure and the amount which he can borrow; this difference measures the amount of capital which he must contribute out of his own funds.

Determining Land Value. On occasion an investor contemplates the creation of a new enterprise by new construction. He can readily estimate the cost of the improvements but must determine how much he can afford

Assumptions (See Figure VI-3)

Annual net income before depreciation $11,000
Economic life .... 20 years
Land value in 20 years (reversion) $20,000
Return on equity required by the investor 10%
Mortgage debt at 5% interest amortized in 10 years $38,610
Annual payment on interest and principal 5,000

Present value of equity return
  First 10 years
    Return to equity after debt service, $11,000 less $5,000 .... $ 6,000
    Present value factor (10%) 6,145
                                                                    ──────
                                                                    $36,870

  Last 10 years
    Return to equity $11,000
    Present value factor (10%) 6,145
                                                                    ──────
    Value 10 years removed $67,595

    Present value, $67,595 × factor 0.3855 .... $26,058

Present value of land residual (20 years removed), $20,000 × factor
    0.1486 .... $ 2,972

Total present value of equity
  Value of equity return
    First 10 years $36,870
    Second 10 years 26,058
    Value of land residual 2,972
                                                                    ──────
    Total equity $65,900

Mortgage loan 38,610

Total investment value $104,510

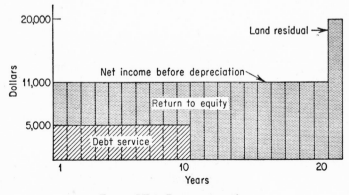

FIGURE VI-3. Return to equity.

to pay for the land. This is a simple matter once he has determined the total investment value for the entire enterprise as a going concern. By deducting the cost of improvements, he arrives at a balance which is the maximum amount he would be justified in paying for the land. For example:

Total justified investment value of property $113,000
Cost of constructing the building 80,000

Justified investment value of land .... $ 33,000

Short Cuts. The foregoing procedures for estimating investment value on the basis of expected income are recommended as bringing to bear on the matter all of the significant factors and treating the estimates mathematically in the most realistic manner. However, it is recognized that many investors use short-cut calculations in making their decisions, and some of them make no calculations at all. The two simplified calculations which are most frequently encountered are (1) the conversion of income estimates into a capital value by the use of market-determined ratios or multipliers, and (2) the capitalization of income by the straight-line depreciation—straight capitalization method.

The *gross income multiplier* is the most familiar of the ratios used to convert rental income into capital value. It is frequently used by appraisers to make a first approximation of the value of a dwelling or small rental property. The monthly rental value is multiplied by a factor which is a market-established ratio of monthly rent to capital value for similar properties. The validity of this calculation depends on the reliability of the ratio and thus on the quantity and quality of the information from which it is derived. A variation of the gross income multiplier is the ratio of annual gross income to value expressed as a per cent of value.

The straight-line depreciation—straight capitalization method starts with an estimate of the stabilized net income before depreciation, say $5,000 per year. In the case of an existing property the building-residual formula is used. The remaining economic life of the building is estimated, and the annual depreciation rate is thus determined on a straight-line basis. If economic life is twenty-five years the rate would be 4 per cent. The value of the land is determined by market comparison, and a land return at the selected capitalization rate is calculated. If the land value is $10,000 and the rate is 6 per cent, the land return would be $600. This amount is deducted from the annual net income to determine the building return, in this case, $5,000 less 600 or $4,400. If the capitalization rate on this building return portion of the income is 7 per cent there is added the depreciation rate of 4 per cent, making a total rate of 11 per cent. The building return of $4,400 capitalized at 11 per cent yields a value of $40,000 plus $10,000 for the land, or a total property value of $50,000.

In the case of a recently completed or proposed real estate enterprise it is assumed that the value of the structural improvements is equivalent to their cost of construction, and the land residual formula is employed. Thus if the building cost were $40,000 and if the estimated economic life were twenty-five years and if the capitalization were 7 per cent, the building return would be 11 per cent of $40,000 or $4,400 per year, an amount which would recapture the investment in the building in twenty-five years on a straight-line basis and yield 7 per cent on the full investment each year. The balance of the net income, or $600 per year, is the land return which, capitalized at 6 per cent, indicates a land value of $10,000 and a total property value of $50,000. This method is said to produce a conservative answer. This results from an excessive loading for depreciation because the method allows no credit for accumulated interest on the capital recaptured during the life of the building. It may be pointed out that there is no inherent virtue in a conservative estimate. A realistic estimate is much to be preferred, for it expresses the most likely outcome and permits the investor to make whatever adjustments he may wish in his final decision with a surer understanding of how it relates to the most probable result.

Capitalization of Alternative Rent. Prospective investor-users are usually confronted with the alternative of renting or buying. Though alternative properties may not be identical, the comparison, with adjustments for differences in quality, does provide the basis for setting an upper limit to the investment. If a home buyer can rent the kind of house he needs for $125 per month, he can calculate the amount which he would be justified in paying for a similar home of his own on a strictly dollar basis. If an institution can rent satisfactory office space for $4.00 per square foot, it can determine an upper limit to the investment in a new building for its own use. And if the cost of the new building exceeds this limit, the institutional investor will have a measure of how much will have to be charged against the prestige and other intangible values of a home-office building.

The method for converting the rental value of a single-family dwelling to a capital value involves the use of a gross income multiplier. On the basis of wide observation of rentals and sales the experienced analyst knows that the most probable sales price of a house of a given quality is, for example, about 100 times monthly income. For another city, price class, age group, or location the gross income multiplier may be 90 or 110. If the rent is $125 per month, $12,500 (100 times $125) is the price which the investor should not exceed for a home offering services equivalent to that which he can rent for $125 per month. The wise investor will test this conclusion by an analysis of houses currently offered in the market.

The institutional investor considering a home office can capitalize the rent which he would have to pay for equivalent space in order to set an upper limit. Assume a case in which 100,000 square feet are required. A building of about this size can be rented for $50,000 per year net, i.e., with the tenant required to pay taxes and to maintain the building. If $50,000 per year were used to finance a new building rather than to be expended for renting an existing structure, how much could be invested in land and structure?

1. The first step is to estimate the cost of acquiring a suitable site. A study of the market might reveal that $40,000 could buy the necessary land. Since this component is permanent, the usual assumption is that it will maintain its original value indefinitely. Thus only interest needs to be charged against this nondepreciating portion of the investment, say at 5 per cent:

Total available per year	$50,000
Interest on $40,000 at 5%	2,000
Balance	$48,000

2. If we assume a new building will have an economic life of fifty years we want to know how much of a capital investment in such a building can be amortized, at say 5½ per cent, during its useful life. This capital sum is the present value of an annuity of $48,000 at 5½ per cent for fifty years:

$$\$48,000 \times \text{factor } 16.5 = \$792,000$$

3. The total capital investment which the rental allocation of $50,000 per year will carry is the sum of:

Land	$ 40,000
Building	792,000
Total	$832,000

If $832,000 will provide quarters equivalent in quality to the space which can be rented at a net annual figure of $50,000, then the institution will be neither better nor worse off financially whether it rents or builds. Nonfinancial considerations which might swing the decision one way or another include the need for prompt occupancy, the diversion of energies in planning and supervising new construction, the prestige and advertising value of a new building, and the luxuries of newer equipment and modern planning.

Alteration and Demolition

Just as was the investor's decision to commit capital to the original development of land, the decision to invest in alteration, modernization, or replacement is based upon balancing the returns against the capital costs. An income property will not be remodeled unless the present value of the net income and reversion *after* the alteration is greater than the present value of the net income and reversion *before* the alteration *plus* the cost of the modernization. An example is given in the following table.

Item	Before modernization	After modernization
1. Net annual income before depreciation	$ 5,000	$ 6,000
2. Estimated duration of income	10 years	15 years
3. Present value of net income (5% capitalization rate)	$38,610	$62,280
4. Reversion	50,000	50,000
5. Present value of reversion (5%)	30,595	24,050
Total (3 + 5)	69,205	86,330

$$\begin{array}{r} \$86,330 \\ -69,205 \\ \hline \end{array}$$

Justified investment in modernization $17,125

If a 5 per cent return on capital is acceptable to the investor a modernization cost of $17,125 would be justified in the sense that this sum would be retired out of income, and in addition, 5 per cent would be earned on all unretired balances. If more than this amount were spent on modernization without a corresponding increase in net income the alteration would not be justified; the investor would have a greater return by doing nothing to the property.

Note that this calculation of alternatives takes no account of the past financial history of the property, neither the amount of capital which the owner has already invested nor the level and duration of past earnings. Only the future counts and the investor-owner will act in that manner which is most advantageous to him from now on. In the foregoing example the property is worth $69,205 based on future earnings; it is worth $86,330 if modernized (regardless of the cost of modernization) because of increased earnings and longer economic life. Thus modernization is advantageous to the owner if the cost is less than the difference in value.

The same principles obtain in the case of demolition. The end of the useful life of a structure comes when the owner will be better off demolishing it than continuing its operation. For example, assume that the annual operating expenses are:

Property taxes	
On land	$ 300
On building	700
Other operating expenses	500
Total	$1,500

If the building were to be removed taxes on the land would continue at $300, all earnings would cease, and the owner would lose $300 per year. It will be advantageous to continue to operate the building as long as the gross earnings cover the $500 of operating expenses other than taxes, plus something more than the taxes of $700 on the building, or a total of more than $1,200. If gross earnings are just $1,200 it is a matter of financial indifference whether the building is removed or not; the owner will lose $300 per year in either case. If gross earnings are $1,300 his loss will be $200 per year instead of $300 with the building demolished. If gross earnings are $1,100 he can cut his loss from $400 to $300 by tearing down the structure.

Succession. There are many cases where an improvement reaches the end of economic life long before net income declines to the vanishing point. For example, we see older residences making way for apartment buildings, and residential rental properties in mid-life are replaced by commercial developments. This process is known as "land use succession." Investors' decisions in such cases are made on the basis that the land value developed by the new use is greater than the previous value of the original property, land, and building. The entrepreneurial calculation and the logic are precisely the same as in our example of modernization. The redevelopment is justified if the present value of the new enterprise less the capital cost of the new improvement is greater than the present value of the existing property in original form. For example, assume the existing enterprise shows a total value of $50,000 based on future net income up to the end of economic life in fifteen years. The analysis of a potential new development on the same site after clearance shows that the new enterprise would have a total value of $150,000; the cost of the new improvement is estimated at $80,000. Thus the indicated land value under the new use is $150,000 less $80,000, or $70,000. Since $70,000 is more than the $50,000 value of the existing property, the owner's advantage lies in removing the old building and redeveloping the site. The economic life of the original improvement ends when the replacement takes place.

Final Investment Decision

Prudent investors of all kinds attempt to make objective and factual analyses of the investment characteristics of properties under consideration. But it is inevitable that personal biases and individual circumstances play a part in their final investment decisions. In these days of highly progressive income taxes the present tax bracket in which the investor falls is a primary consideration in many cases. For example, investors in the upper brackets are attracted by opportunities to take their investment returns in the form of capital gains. Thus their investment calculations may include the use of accelerated depreciation as permitted under the income tax laws with the result that net taxable income will be minimized, and, in effect, the income tax will be paid when the property is sold in the form of a capital gains tax at a much lower rate. For an investor with a modest personal income this advantage would be less, and the advantage of receiving current income would be greater.

The investor-user, such as the home buyer or the financial institution acquiring a home-office building, is motivated both by financial values and by intangibles. The investor-user intends to be frugal and economical, but at the same time he is influenced in the investment decision by sentiment and considerations of prestige. The investment is not usually made on a purely dollars-and-cents basis. The home is purchased as a family haven and a proper environment for growing children. The home-office building must be a symbol of pride and accomplishment and is expected to radiate an aura of strength and stability to the outside world.

The objective of the investor for capital gain is to buy at a price which will assure him a profit upon resale; he usually expects to meet the carrying costs out of the revenues produced by the property. He is sometimes willing to forego a regular return on his equity contribution in anticipation of a capital gain but he is reluctant to continue to pay out cash from his own pocket while awaiting the opportune time to liquidate. Some investors make a business of buying up old properties, investing additional sums in modernization, and selling at a profit. But investors in general seek properties which will carry themselves during the waiting period, for if market conditions continue unfavorable for any length of time, the carrying costs will soon eat up the potential profits.

The primary estimate which the investor for capital gain must make in arriving at a justified investment value is the future pattern of market or liquidation values for the property. He starts with the present market value and adjusts this figure, if necessary, to the underlying trend value. Then on the basis of productivity analysis, considering all factors which will affect future utility and thus future liquidation value, he forecasts future value trends. It is also at this time that he considers the reliability of his forecasts and the probability that his expectations will be realized.

A second calculation involves the ability of the property to carry itself during the ripening period. The usual operating expenses must be met in order that it may continue to be productive—taxes, insurance, management, and maintenance. In addition, if there is a mortgage on the property interest and principal payments must be met in accordance with the contract.

With these two estimates at hand the investor must determine how much he is justified in paying for the property in light of a composite of considerations of profit potential, risk, and carrying ability.

Dis-investment

The seller of real estate, as well as the buyer, must make an investment decision. The seller's determination of an asking price realistically should start with the same kind of analysis which is to be expected of a typical buyer-prospect in arriving at an offering price. The productivity of the property should be evaluated. Then, based on the assumed financial position of a typical buyer and the terms of financing which he could expect to secure under current money market conditions, a calculation is made of investment value which reproduces the financial analysis prospective investors will make and which develops a prediction of the price which they are likely to be willing to pay. This figure is a more realistic and useful basis for price establishment and negotiation than the usually inflated notions of the seller-owner in the absence of a realistic analysis from the viewpoint of the investor-buyer.

THE APPRAISAL OF REAL ESTATE

Real estate appraisal is commonly viewed as the process of establishing value. The narrow view, which we do not share, is that for each piece of real estate there is but one value. The contrary view is that if the appraiser is to serve his client well he must develop whatever value figure, or figures, are appropriate and useful in connection with the decision or transaction in prospect. In the pages of this chapter we have demonstrated that the several investor-types may require various value figures in arriving at a final decision—cost of reproduction, cost less depreciation, most probable market price, and capitalized income. We have shown how certain of these value figures, cost and market price, may be used to set an upper limit to the investor's price offer. Other value figures, cost less depreciation and capitalized income, are used as necessary substitutes for, or verification of, current market transaction data when such data are unavailable or inadequate. Value as capitalized income is directly useful to the investor when income properties are involved.

In the case of an award for the taking of property by condemnation the value figure to be arrived at is defined by law as a hypothetical transaction price which would be arrived at under idealized conditions which rarely, if ever, exist. Tax laws guiding the assessors of real property set forth other special purpose definitions of the value figure to be used as a tax base. The mortgage lender seeks an estimate of the most probable liquidation value. Fire losses are settled on the basis of values related to costs of reproduction and depreciation.

The foregoing examples are sufficient to demonstrate that for each real estate transaction certain value figures are appropriate. The appraisal process then, is that process which develops the value figure or figures which are relevant. Neither the definition of the value figures required nor the decision on the final transaction price are functions of the appraiser.

Consistent with this viewpoint, our discussion of real estate investment analysis has included general instructions for developing the value figures which are most frequently the concern of appraisers, sometimes under names which vary from those used here:

    I. Cost of replacement—new
    II. Cost of replacement—new less depreciation
    III. Most probable market price
        A. By market comparison
        B. By substitute approaches
           1. Cost new less depreciation
           2. Capitalization of income
    IV. Capitalized value of income

There is one important difference between real estate appraisal and real estate investment analysis which has application to the capitalization of income. The rate of capitalization which the investor employs is that which represents his own individual evaluation of risk and liquidity and his personal financial circumstances. On the other hand, in the absence of instructions to the contrary, the appraiser must attempt to interpret general market reactions to the risk characteristics of the investment and select a capitalization rate which represents actual behavior of investors in general in transactions relating to properties comparable to the property under appraisal.

APPENDIX

ARITHMETIC OF CAPITALIZATION

In the investment value calculation, two steps are employed which should be familiar to anyone acquainted with the elements of the mathematics of finance. For those to whom this is new or forgotten ground, the following brief explanation will be sufficient, if not to guarantee understanding, at least to demonstrate the process.

Basic Estimates

These estimates or judgments are required at the outset of a problem of investment value calculation:

1. On the basis of the existing or assumed development and site, fore-

cast all future revenues and expenses up to the time when expenses will exceed revenues and the end of productive life will have been reached.

EXAMPLE: Let us take the simplest example in order to illustrate the principle without complications. A new store building is being leased by A to B for $5,000 per year for fifty years. It may be assumed that at the end of fifty years, the building will be old and obsolete and ready for demolition and replacement. The landlord A is to pay the taxes of $900 per year and maintain the shell of the structure, which is estimated to cost $100 per year. Thus the net income to A will be $4,000 per year for fifty years.

2. Forecast the reversion, i.e., the value of the vacant land at the end of the productive life of the building.

EXAMPLE: In our example, the problem is to estimate the value of the land in fifty years when the lease has expired, and the original building is ready for demolition. We shall see that this estimated value will have very little influence on our final figure because of its remoteness in time. It is a common practice among appraisers to assume that present land values will be maintained indefinitely. Thus if the estimated present value of the land is $25,000, a value of $25,000 might be assigned to the land reversion with a possible adjustment to cover the cost of demolishing the old building.

3. Select capitalization rates for capitalizing income and determining the present value of the reversion.

EXAMPLE: If the tenant in our example is an excellent credit risk and the property is well located and well built, the degree of probability that the rent will be regularly paid is high and the investment risk low. Thus a low capitalization rate, perhaps 5 per cent, is appropriate. The same rate might be used for treating the reversion.

Having made the judgments required in the three foregoing steps, we can apply the arithmetic of capitalization. For those unfamiliar with the basic concepts of capitalization and present value that are a part of the mathematics of finance, the following explanations may be helpful.

Determining the Present Value of an Annuity

The capitalization of the forecast of net revenue is a matter of calculating today's lump sum value of a long series of periodic incomes. Or we may call it the present worth of an annuity, for in the calculation we treat the net income which the property produces as if it were annual payments arising from an annuity contract.

In common-sense language we might say that we seek to calculate how many dollars an investor would be justified in paying today for the privilege of receiving a regular payment of so much per year for a specified number of years. Of course, the investor would expect to get all his money back during this period and to receive a reasonable interest return on his outstanding investment, i.e., the unrestored portion of the investment from year to year.

The amortized mortgage is a familiar arrangement in which an investor, the banker, makes precisely the calculation which we are discussing. Actually he makes the calculation in reverse order, but the relationships are the same. Should you wish to borrow $10,000 and the banker wants 5 per cent interest, he can tell you exactly what regular payment you must make (usually monthly but it can be annual) for how long a time in order to repay the $10,000 and yield 5 per cent interest to him on the outstanding debt. In this example, your monthly payment would be $66 if he gives you twenty years to pay, and the interest rate is 5 per cent. Reversing this same relationship, should you tell the banker that you can pay $66 per month for twenty years, he would calculate that at 5 per cent interest he could lend you $10,000. In twenty years he would have all of his $10,000 repaid, and in the meantime, he would be receiving 5 per cent on the outstanding balance at all times. In other words, the present worth or investment value of a contract to pay $66 per month for twenty years is $10,000 assuming a 5 per cent interest or capitalization rate. Technically it is a matter of financial indifference whether he has $10,000 in hand or lends you the $10,000 with a contract to receive $66 per month for twenty years.

In our real estate valuation problem we estimate the level and duration of net income (parallel to the monthly payment on the mortgage), and we seek to calculate the present worth of that income (the original amount of the mortgage).

Note carefully that the calculation provides for the full restoration of the amount invested, and thus it accomplishes the same purpose and objective as a charge for depreciation as an expense item. Clearly, when this method is used, it would be a duplication to include depreciation as an expense; thus we always use net income before depreciation as the basic material of valuation.

Determining the Present Value of a Single Future Payment

The problem here is to calculate the value today of the right to own the land (the reversion) at the end of the productive life of the existing improvements. An estimate is made of the value of the land at that future date but that value must be discounted at a selected discount rate to give us the value of that future asset as of today. The arithmetic of the calculation (assuming a future land value of $25,000 in fifty years and a 5 per cent discount rate) is to determine an amount which, if invested today at 5 per cent and allowed to accumulate at compound interest for fifty years, would produce a total of $25,000 at the end of the fifty-year

Table VI-2
Present Worth of One Dollar per Annum
(equal annual amounts payable at end of year)

Years	Capitalization rate									
	3%	4%	5%	6%	7%	8%	9%	10%	11%	12%
1	0.971	0.961	0.952	0.943	0.935	0.926	0.917	0.909	0.901	0.893
2	1.913	1.886	1.859	1.833	1.808	1.783	1.759	1.736	1.713	1.690
3	2.829	2.775	2.723	2.673	2.624	2.577	2.531	2.487	2.444	2.402
4	3.717	3.630	3.546	3.465	3.387	3.312	3.240	3.170	3.102	3.037
5	4.580	4.452	4.329	4.212	4.100	3.993	3.890	3.791	3.696	3.605
6	5.417	5.242	5.076	4.917	4.766	4.623	4.486	4.355	4.231	4.111
7	6.230	6.002	5.786	5.582	5.389	5.206	5.033	4.868	4.712	4.564
8	7.020	6.733	6.463	6.210	5.971	5.747	5.535	5.335	5.146	4.968
9	7.786	7.435	7.108	6.802	6.515	6.247	5.995	5.759	5.537	5.328
10	8.530	8.111	7.722	7.360	7.024	6.710	6.418	6.145	5.889	5.650
15	11.938	11.118	10.380	9.712	9.108	8.559	8.061	7.606	7.191	6.811
20	14.877	13.590	12.462	11.470	10.594	9.818	9.128	8.514	7.963	7.469
25	17.413	15.622	14.094	12.783	11.654	10.675	9.823	9.077	8.422	7.843
30	19.600	17.292	15.372	13.765	12.409	11.258	10.274	9.427	8.694	8.055
35	21.487	18.665	16.374	14.498	12.948	11.655	10.567	9.644	8.855	8.176
40	23.115	19.793	17.159	15.046	13.332	11.925	10.757	9.779	8.951	8.244
50	25.730	21.482	18.256	15.762	13.801	12.233	10.962	9.915	9.042	8.305
75	29.702	23.680	19.485	16.456	14.196	12.461	11.094	9.992	9.087	8.332
100	31.599	24.505	19.848	16.617	14.269	12.494	11.109	9.999	9.091	8.333

Table VI-3
Present Worth of One Dollar

Capitalization rate

Years	3%	4%	5%	6%	7%	8%	9%	10%	11%	12%
1	0.9709	0.9615	0.9524	0.9434	0.9346	0.9259	0.9174	0.9091	0.9009	0.8929
2	.9426	.9246	.9070	.8900	.8734	.8573	.8417	.8264	.8116	.7972
3	.9151	.8890	.8638	.8396	.8163	.7938	.7722	.7513	.7312	.7118
4	.8885	.8548	.8227	.7921	.7629	.7350	.7084	.6830	.6587	.6355
5	.8626	.8219	.7835	.7473	.7130	.6806	.6499	.6209	.5935	.5674
6	.8375	.7903	.7462	.7050	.6663	.6302	.5963	.5645	.5346	.5066
7	.8131	.7599	.7107	.6651	.6227	.5835	.5470	.5132	.4816	.4523
8	.7894	.7307	.6768	.6274	.5820	.5403	.5019	4665	.4339	.4039
9	.7664	.7026	.6446	.5919	.5439	.5002	.4604	.4241	.3909	.3606
10	.7441	.6756	.6139	.5584	.5083	.4632	.4224	.3855	.3522	.3220
15	.6419	.5553	.4810	.4173	.3624	.3152	.2745	.2394	.2090	.1827
20	.5537	.4564	.3769	.3118	.2584	.2145	.1784	.1486	.1240	.1037
25	.4776	.3751	.2953	.2330	.1842	.1460	.1160	.0923	.0736	.0588
30	.4120	.3083	.2314	.1741	.1314	.0994	.0754	.0573	.0437	.0334
35	.3554	.2534	.1813	.1301	.0937	.0676	.0490	.0356	.0259	.0189
40	.3066	.2083	.1420	.0972	.0668	.0460	.0318	.0221	.0154	.0107
50	.2281	.1407	.0872	.0543	.0339	.0213	.0134	.0085	.0054	.0035
75	.1089	.0528	.0258	.0126	.0063	.0031	.0016	.0008	.00040	.00020
100	.0520	.0198	.0076	.0029	.0012	.0005	.0002	.0001	.00003	.00001

period. For such a long period, the present value of $25,000 at a 5 per cent discount rate is surprisingly small, $2,180. At a 6 per cent rate the amount would be $1,358.

A familiar form of investment which illustrates these mathematical relationships is the United States government savings bond. If you invest $75 today you will receive a lump sum payment of $100 just eight years and eleven months from now. The discount rate works out to be 3¼ per cent. The $75 is allowed to accumulate at compound interest; the accumulation of principal and interest is just $100 in eight years eleven months. Or expressed in reverse, the present worth of $100 to be received eight years eleven months from now is $75 if the discount rate is 3¼ per cent, just as the present value of the reversion, $25,000, to be received fifty years from now is $2,180 if the discount rate is 5 per cent. Thus it is a matter of financial indifference to an investor whether he has $2,180 in cash today or the promise of a lump sum of $25,000 to be paid fifty years from now (assuming a 5 per cent interest or discount rate).

Determining the Investment Value

Now let us apply the foregoing principles to the matter of determining the investment value of the property described earlier. Net revenues before depreciation are $4,000 per year for fifty years. The land reversionary value is estimated at $25,000. We select a 5 per cent rate for capitalizing income and discounting the reversion.

The first step is to calculate the present value of the stream of income of $4,000 per year. By reference to a mathematical table labeled "Present Worth of One Dollar per Annum" which can be found in appraisal manuals and textbooks on the mathematics of finance, we choose the appropriate factor for fifty years at 5 per cent. (An abbreviated form of this table is presented in Table VI-2.) This factor is 18.256, and it means that the present worth of $1 per annum for fifty years is $18.256. Since we have $4,000 per annum, the present value will be 4,000 × $18.256, or $73,024.

By reference to a table entitled "Present Worth of One Dollar," we select the appropriate factor of 0.0872 (see Table VI-3). This means that at the 5 per cent rate, the present worth of $1 to be received in fifty years is $0.0872. Thus the present worth of the $25,000 reversion is 25,000 × $0.0872, or $2,180.

The sum of the present value of the net income and the reversion, $75,204 ($73,024 + $2,180), represents the value of the real estate enterprise, land and building, as a going concern. If the improvements are in existence this is the final and complete answer, for there is no point in placing separate values on land and building which are permanently wedded and which produce a joint income. But if the income estimates are based on a hypothetical building yet unbuilt on vacant land a further calculation may be made to determine a justified value for the vacant land. Assume that the proposed building will cost $50,000 to erect. Since the total value of the going enterprise, land and building, is calculated at $75,204, an investor would be justified in paying for the land an amount up to the difference between $75,204 and $50,000, or $25,204. This figure will represent the land value under the proposed use program and cost and revenue assumptions. If this use is the optimum, or highest and best, use, then the derived land value is the highest which can be extracted and is said to be its "value."

VII

REAL ESTATE CREDIT

FUNCTIONS OF CREDIT

It rarely happens that a new real estate enterprise is created or that real property changes hands without the use of borrowed funds. Some 75 per cent of all home purchases involve debt financing, and over 50 per cent of all homes, new and old, are encumbered with debt. Almost all commercial properties require credit when built and are bought and sold only with the aid of credit arrangements. The home-building industry is dependent upon the availability of mortgage money which serves as production credit to finance construction operations; to dispose of the home builder's product, mortgage credit for the home buyer is equally essential.

In the case of the home buyer, the use of borrowed capital is usually a necessity because the price tag on the house is high in relationship to his financial resources. Credit has the effect of multiplying his purchasing power; by combining a small down payment with a large debt, he can acquire a dwelling many times as valuable as his own capital would purchase. Credit advances the time when he can begin to enjoy the comforts of a home; he would have a long wait until his savings would permit an all-cash purchase. In effect, then, credit is an advance of future savings or purchasing power; it substitutes for capital yet to be accumulated.

But the extensive use of credit includes other purposes than the multiplying of the limited savings of home buyers. Many an investor in income-producing properties such as an apartment building finds it financially advantageous to borrow a part of the required capital though his own funds might be sufficient. Some of the reasons other than lack of capital which lead to borrowing are:

1. To diversify investments and reduce over-all risk, it may be advisable to commit only a part of his funds to any one enterprise.

2. There may be other investment opportunities for a portion of his capital where a higher return can be secured.

3. He expects interest rates to rise in the future.

4. He can borrow at an interest rate lower than the expected productivity of the enterprise. Thus, the greater the debt, the higher will be the rate of return of his own invested capital. This effect is called leverage, or trading on the equity, and is explained more fully in Chapter VI.

5. He anticipates an inflationary rise in the general price level and in the returns on real estate. Thus he hopes to pay off the debt in cheaper dollars.

6. A merchandising or manufacturing concern may prefer to use available funds in the business rather than to invest it in land and buildings.

For these and other possible reasons, the capital to create or acquire ownership of a real estate enterprise or a home is usually provided in part by the owner and in part by a lender who is generally in the business of extending credit on real estate security. Both owner and lender, as suppliers of capital, are investors. The owner's contribution is called "equity capital," while the lender's capital is in the form of a "fixed value" investment from his standpoint and a "debt" from the standpoint of the owner-borrower.

The sources of capital and the factors which influence its flow into real estate are quite different as between equity funds and borrowed capital. The motivations and objectives of owner-investors are quite diverse; they include various combinations of the following: investment for use, expectation of a regular return, expectation of a capital gain, and a hedge against inflation.

The primary objectives of the lender-investor are more limited and more specific:

1. To receive a regular and predictable return on capital in accordance with the contract

2. To recapture the capital through scheduled repayment

It is customary for the owner-investor to arrange for the retirement of the debt on the property during its productive life. This has the effect of substituting the owner's capital for the borrowed dollars. In the case of an income property, the real estate enterprise itself produces a flow of revenue out of which debt service payments may be made. On the other hand, credit advanced to a home buyer must be repaid out of his personal income; thus, the home mortgage lender is dependent on the earnings and assets of the individual borrower for the payment of interest and the amortization of the debt.

Preceding investment both owner and lender undertake some form of investment analysis on which to base their decision on the quality of the investment opportunity, i.e., the probability of realizing their investment objectives. The process of investment analysis should involve the same set of factors for both types of investor. Though the home buyer invests primarily for use, he should make a comparative analysis of alternative home investment opportunities in the market and should evaluate the value stability of his prospective purchase in view of the possibility that he may sell his house at some future time. Both owner-investor and lender are concerned with the business risk of the enterprise, i.e., the level and stability of its productivity or return in relationship to the total of invested capital. Both owner and lender must evaluate the financial risk created by the proposed arrangements for borrowing capital. High percentage loans and high fixed financial charges make the owner vulnerable to fluctuations in the real estate market and to economic instability which may reduce the income of the borrower from other sources and depreciate his other assets. In addition, both owner-investor and lender are concerned with the present market value of the property and with its value stability. Though the processes of investment analysis cover the same set of factors whether the analysis is for the owner-investor or the lender, the weighting of the factors will be different and will be adapted to the relevant investment objectives.

At this point in our study of real estate it is necessary that we describe the contractual and legal machinery which society has developed over the centuries for joining the capital contributions of owner-investor and lender in real estate enterprises so that each may attain his special investment objectives, and in case of financial distress the interests of each may be equitably protected. This chapter will deal primarily with the subject of debt financing and largely with the mortgage. This familiar device is by far the most frequently employed arrangement for securing real estate credit. We will first explore the legal specifications of the mortgage and two other common financing devices, the land contract and the lease. We will then look to the sources of real estate credit. The primary types of lending institutions will be described with respect to the sources of the capital which they dispense as loans and the mortgage lending policies which they have evolved as a reflection of their financial functions. The FHA and VA programs of mortgage insurance and guarantee are to be presented as important conditioning factors in the mortgage market which influence the volume and direction of the flow of credit and the terms of lending. The process of mortgage risk analysis will be outlined. The development of a secondary mortgage market will be traced from its beginnings in the Federal Home Loan Bank System through the recent changes in the functions of the Federal National Mortgage Association. The differential nature of local mortgage markets will be described. Finally, the basic money market forces and the institutional factors of government policy will be considered in their effect on the flow of mortgage money, interest rates, and lending terms.

Table VII-1

Mortgage Debt Outstanding, by Type of Property and of Financing, 1939–1959
(billions of dollars)

End of period	All properties	Nonfarm properties							Farm properties
		Total	1- to 4-family houses					Multifamily and commercial properties	
			Total	Government underwritten			Conventional		
				Total	FHA insured	VA guaranteed			
1939	35.5	28.9	16.3	1.8	1.8	...	14.5	12.5	6.6
1940	36.5	30.0	17.4	2.3	2.3	...	15.1	12.6	6.5
1941	37.6	31.2	18.4	3.0	3.0	...	15.4	12.9	6.4
1942	36.7	30.8	18.2	3.7	3.7	...	14.5	12.5	6.0
1943	35.3	29.9	17.8	4.1	4.1	...	13.7	12.1	5.4
1944	34.7	29.7	17.9	4.2	4.2	...	13.7	11.8	4.9
1945	35.5	30.8	18.6	4.3	4.1	0.2	14.3	12.2	4.8
1946	41.8	36.9	23.0	6.1	3.7	2.4	16.9	13.8	4.9
1947	48.9	43.9	28.2	9.3	3.8	5.5	18.9	15.7	5.1
1948	56.2	50.9	33.3	12.5	5.3	7.2	20.8	17.8	5.3
1949	62.7	57.1	37.6	15.0	6.9	8.1	22.6	19.5	5.6
1950	72.8	66.9	45.2	18.9	8.6	10.3	26.3	21.6	6.1
1951	82.3	75.6	51.7	22.9	9.7	13.2	28.8	23.9	6.7
1952	91.4	84.2	58.5	25.4	10.8	14.6	33.1	25.7	7.3
1953	101.3	93.6	66.1	28.1	12.0	16.1	38.0	27.5	7.8
1954	113.7	105.4	75.7	32.1	12.8	19.3	43.6	29.7	8.3
1955	129.9	120.9	88.2	38.9	14.3	24.6	49.3	32.6	9.1
1956	144.5	134.8	99.0	43.9	15.5	28.4	55.1	35.6	9.9
1957	156.6	146.1	107.6	47.2	16.5	30.7	60.4	38.5	10.5
1958	171.9	160.7	117.7	50.1	19.7	30.4	67.6	43.0	11.2
1959	191.2	178.9	131.0	54.0	23.9	30.1	77.0	47.9	12.3

SOURCE: *Economic Report of the President*, 1960, Government Printing Office, Washington, 1960, table D-46, p. 209.

145

THE MORTGAGE

The evolution of the mortgage has a fascinating history, and modern mortgage law is intriguingly complicated. But for most purposes it is sufficient to know that a mortgage combines a contract to repay a debt and a pledge of real estate as security for repayment. These two elements may be incorporated in a single instrument, or they may be separate documents. In seventeen states,[1] the common-law theory prevails to the effect that title to the land is conveyed from the mortgagor (borrower) to the mortgagee (lender); this conveyance is defeated, or in effect, reversed when the debt is paid. In thirty-one states, the lien theory is held to the effect that a mortgage conveys no interest in land but only creates a lien on the land in favor of the mortgagee as security for the debt.[2] This lien can be exercised only if the mortgagor defaults.

Any interest in real estate which can be conveyed to another may be mortgaged. The common first mortgage is the pledge of fee title, but other interests are frequently used as security for a loan. For example, a lessee may mortgage his leasehold interest; or the owner of land already mortgaged may encumber his remaining equity through a junior mortgage. It is well to remember that the mortgagee can acquire by foreclosure no interest greater than that which his mortgagor has pledged.

The conventional form of the mortgage is a written instrument much like a deed, but it includes a provision voiding the conveyance upon payment of the debt. In some states a *trust deed in the nature of mortgage* is common. Under this arrangement, the owner conveys the land to a trustee to secure the debt due a third party. If the debt is paid the conveyance is void, but if it is defaulted the trustee is empowered to sell the land to pay the debt.

An absolute deed with no provision for voiding the conveyance upon payment of a debt will be construed by the courts as a mortgage if, in fact, the grantor is in debt to the grantee, and there exists a side agreement, oral or written, for reconveyance when the debt is paid. A deed with an option to repurchase is an equitable mortgage if intended to serve as security for a loan.

A mortgage must be in writing, and because the law has historically viewed it as a conveyance of land, it must meet the requirements of a valid deed. The consideration for the conveyance is the debt, either in

---

[1] Alabama, Arkansas, Connecticut, Illinois, Maine, Maryland, Massachusetts, Mississippi, New Hamsphire, New Jersey, North Carolina, Ohio, Pennsylvania, Rhode Island, Tennessee, Vermont, West Virginia.

[2] The practical differences lie largely in speedier and lower-cost foreclosure in the title-theory states and in more favorable rights to possession upon default.

existence, to be created when the mortgage is executed, or to be created in the future under agreement between the parties. Ordinarily the mortgage secures a promissory note executed when the mortgage is made; this note may be separate and related by reference in the mortgage, or the note may be incorporated in the mortgage instrument.

The conditions stated in the mortgage and the note include the *defeasance clause* which voids the deed when payment is made, the amount of the debt, the rate of interest to be paid, the schedule of payments of interest and principal, the final due date, provision for prepayment if desired, prohibition against commitment of waste (abuse and mismanagement of the property) by the mortgagor, and a requirement that the mortgagor is to pay all taxes and assessments and must keep the structures insured in favor of the mortgagee. If any of these express conditions is violated a default exists, and the mortgagee may proceed to foreclose his mortgage lien.

Under no circumstances is the lien of a mortgagee superior to tax liens and assessments for public improvements. To assure priority over mechanic's liens, though state laws differ, a mortgagee may have to record the mortgage before a contract for improvement of the property has been let, before any work has begun, and before any mechanic's liens have been filed.

A mortgage may be placed on land which is already under lease, but the mortgage is subject to the lease, i.e., the mortgagee cannot disturb the tenant before the lease expires so long as he pays his rent. A foreclosure sale must be subject to the lease. The mortgagee has no right to the rents reserved under the lease if the mortgage is in good standing.

A mortgagor may lease land which he has already mortgaged, but the lease is subject to the mortgage. Thus foreclosure of the mortgage terminates the lease and extinguishes both the lessee's rights of possession and his obligation to pay rent.

The existence of a mortgage lien does not bar the mortgagor from the sale of the property. In the eyes of the law, he will be selling his equity of redemption, i.e., his right to pay the debt and regain unencumbered title. In common parlance, he is said to convey his title subject to the mortgage. The grantee incurs no responsibility for payment of the debt unless there is sufficient evidence of his intention to assume the mortgage. If the purchaser agrees to assume the mortgage, he will pay to the seller only the difference between the agreed sale price and the unpaid balance of the debt which he assumes. The seller, as original mortgagor, is not relieved of his obligation to pay the debt secured by the mortgage, and the mortgagee now has two parties to look to for payment. The buyer becomes the primary obligor with the seller liable if the buyer fails to pay. Should the seller have to pay the debt, he has a claim against the buyer for the amount paid. If the mortgagee is willing to release the seller from his obligation under the mortgage and to accept the buyer in his place, the buyer then stands alone as responsible for paying the debt.

A mortgagee may transfer or assign his interest in the obligation and mortgage without securing the consent of the mortgagor. The mortgagor's position remains unchanged in burdens and obligations though he will have a different creditor.

Though there be but a single mortgage instrument in each lending transaction, there may be more than one lender. The usual method of splitting up the investment is to establish a form of trust on the basis of which mortgage bonds or certificates of beneficial interest are issued in various denominations to fit the needs of the investors. The trustee collects the mortgage payments and disburses them in accordance with the trust agreement. In case of default, he forecloses for the collective benefit of the participating investors.

REMEDIES UNDER THE MORTGAGE

In case of default upon the mortgagor's obligations, the most common remedy is foreclosure and sale. Occasionally, there is resort to a suit at law on the note without recourse to the mortgaged property. State laws differ widely in the procedural aspects of foreclosure; four methods of foreclosure are extant (1) judicial sale, (2) exercise of power of sale, (3) entry and possession, and (4) strict foreclosure. Each method has the effect of cutting off the mortgagor's equitable right of redemption and making an absolute and unconditional conveyance of title either to the mortgagee or to a purchaser, depending on the method employed. In each case, the mortgagee either secures title to the pledged property or compensation from the proceeds of the sale up to the amount due.

Judicial Sale

This is a court action which serves to enforce the mortgage lien; the property is sold under judicial process to satisfy the debt, all of the mortgagor's interest is terminated, and title is passed to the purchaser at the foreclosure sale. However, in some states the mortgagor has a statutory right to redeem the property from the sale by paying over the purchase price to the buyer.

The action begins with a suit in a court of equity by the mortgagee against the mortgagor and all parties at interest. After an opportunity for a hearing the court issues a decree or judgment of foreclosure which establishes the exact amount due and directs the property to be sold at public sale by the court officer after a certain time allowed by statute for repayment. Failure to pay within this period wipes out the equity of redemption, and the property is sold to meet the debt. Some states provide a statutory period for redemption after the foreclosure sale. The proceeds from the foreclosure sale are applied first to unpaid taxes, then to the amount due the mortgagee covering the unpaid debt, accumulated interest, taxes and insurance he may have advanced, and the costs of the foreclosure proceedings. Other unsatisfied liens, such as a second mortgage, are next paid off, and any balance goes to the mortgagor.

When the foreclosure sale fails to produce enough to pay off the mortgagor, in some states the equity court may enter a deficiency decree covering the balance due. Some states have abolished the deficiency judgment on purchase money mortgages, and some have abolished it altogether. In other states the amount of the judgment is limited to the difference between the amount due and the fair market value of the property. The purpose of this limitation is to prevent the unjust enrichment of the mortgagee at the expense of the mortgagor when, as could often happen, the mortgagee is the only bidder and bids in the property at a nominal figure.

Power of Sale

If state law permits, the mortgagor may agree, usually as part of the mortgage instrument, that in case of default the mortgagee has the power to sell the land for the debt after specified notice and without resort to a court proceeding. This is the same power which is given in a trust deed in the nature of a mortgage, the authority to sell resting in the trustee.

Entry and Possession

In four New England states,[3] default entitles the mortgagee to enter the premises peacefully, after due notice, and to retain possession for a specified period in order to terminate the mortgagor's right of redemption and secure unconditional title. Where a court proceeding is necessary to effect possession of the property the process is called "foreclosure by writ of entry."

Strict Foreclosure

This method, now rarely used because of its harshness, involves a court procedure parallel to that in foreclosure by judicial sale with the important exception that there is no public sale. Instead, after a specified time for redemption the mortgagor's rights are extinguished, and the mortgagee becomes absolute owner.

[3] Maine, Massachusetts, New Hampshire, and Rhode Island.

JUNIOR MORTGAGES

When the owner-investor needs more money than he can raise on a first mortgage, he may resort to a second or third mortgage. In form and effect, the mortgages are similar except for the priority of the rights of the mortgagees. In case of default on a junior mortgage, the mortgagee may foreclose, but this procedure may in no way disturb the rights under prior liens. A second mortgagee may choose to make payments on the first mortgage to forestall its foreclosure, but he acquires no additional rights in the property by so doing. The proceeds of sale upon foreclosure of any mortgage, regardless of priority, go first to meet the claims of the mortgagee instituting the proceedings, and any balance is paid to the subordinate mortgagees in order of the priority of their claims. The sale of the property will be subject to all senior liens, i.e., they will be undisturbed.

INSTALLMENT LAND CONTRACT

In order to finance the sale of his property, an owner (vendor) may be willing to accept payment of the purchase price in installments with only a small initial payment. Either a purchase money mortgage or an installment land contract may be used. The most significant difference is that in the case of the purchase money mortgage, title is immediately conveyed to the buyer (vendee) and the vendor takes back a mortgage to secure the unpaid balance of the purchase price. Under the land contract, the vendor retains legal title until the last installment has been paid. In each case, the vendee typically occupies the property and pays taxes and maintenance costs.

The legal instrument used for installment sales under land contract is called *contract for deed*, as well as land contract. In form it differs little from the purchase and sale agreement used to bind parties to a real estate transaction until papers are drawn and arrangements are made for the closing of the deal and the conveyance of title. The basic difference is the time interval between the signing of the contract and the conveyance of title and the schedule of the payment of the purchase price. In both cases title is not conveyed until payment has been made, but in the installment land contract the payments may be spread over many years.

In the sale of subdivision lots the land contract is frequently employed. Builders are thus able to acquire an inventory of building sites for future operations with only a minimum amount of capital tied up in land. Individuals who buy lots as sites for future homes can secure the lot of their choice with a modest down payment. From the standpoint of the subdivider, land contract sales shift the carrying costs of taxes and interest to the buyer, and there may be a tax advantage in spreading the payments over several years. Buyers who intend to build on the lots have a strong motivation to complete the payments since they must have title to the property in order to mortgage it for the funds usually required for construction.

Land contracts are used in the sale of improved property when the market is slow or when the property is hard to sell for some other reason, such as poor location or a deteriorated structure. If the seller is sufficiently eager to dispose of the property, he may offer it on land contract with a very small down payment, or none at all. In the absence of an agreement to the contrary he may mortgage the property which he has sold, for he is still its owner of record.

For the protection of the vendee, the land contract often incorporates a provision which permits the buyer, when he has paid off a substantial amount on the purchase price, to raise the balance by mortgaging the property, paying up the debt, and receiving title to the property. Or, with a substantial retirement of the debt having been made, the vendor may agree to take back a purchase money mortgage for the balance and to convey title to the vendee.

Though a land contract does not convey legal title to the vendee, the arrangement does create a beneficial ownership or equitable title. In case of default by the vendee, court action is required to wipe out this interest and restore clear title to the vendor. A common procedure upon default is forfeiture as provided under one of the terms of the contract. In this case the vendee forfeits as liquidated damages all the payments which he has made, and the vendor may regain possession of the property. Another remedy open to the vendor is suit for the specific performance of the contract, a proceeding which forecloses his vendor's lien and closely parallels foreclosure and sale under a mortgage. The vendor may secure a deficiency judgment against the vendee in case the proceeds of the sale are insufficient to meet the unpaid debt. Other remedies open to the vendor are suit for damages and suit for the payments due under the contract. Strict foreclosure is a remedy in some states. In case of default, the position of a vendor under land contract is generally more favorable than that of a mortgagee. The remedies bring quicker action with less expense. Conversely, a vendee has less protection than a mortgagor.

LONG-TERM LEASE

The long-term lease of land for a building site is a financing device which enables the entrepreneur to borrow the land directly in return for the payment of rent as an alternative to borrowing money to be used to purchase the land. The land is returned to the lender (owner) at the end of the lease period, but the period is usually long enough for the lessee to recapture out of earnings the capital which he may invest in buildings and improvements. The lease may provide for the landlord to compensate the tenant for the remaining value of the building at the end of the lease.

The lessee frequently mortgages his leasehold interest (estate) in order to finance the improvement of the land. In a simple case, an investor may lease a vacant lot for purposes of operating a parking lot for ten years at $1,000 per year. The net income after operating expenses but before rental payment is $1,500. The value of the leasehold estate is a function of the excess productivity above the ground rent or $500 per year. A leasehold mortgage is a pledge of this right to the excess productivity. Thus as security for the loan, the mortgagee relies on the earning capacity of the property over and above the ground rent. Note that a leasehold mortgage is a junior lien in view of the fact that the ground rent is a first claim on earnings, and if the rent is not paid the lease is forfeit, and possession of the land is resumed by the owner.

There is an erroneous impression among the uninitiated that by leasing the land for a real estate development, the required equity investment can be reduced by the value of the land since no capital is required for its purchase. For example, take a building to cost $100,000 to be built on land worth $20,000. The usual circumstances of borrowing as much as possible on leasehold mortgage security are assumed. Ordinarily, a two-thirds first mortgage secured by the fee would be available from the usual institutional lenders, a life insurance company, for example. To the mortgage proceeds of $80,000 (two-thirds of $120,000) would be added an equity investment of $40,000. Now assume that the land is acquired by lease and that the value of the leasehold estate is equivalent to the value of the building, or $100,000. Since the leasehold mortgage is a second lien, behind the ground rent, lenders will not be quite so liberal as in the case of a first lien on the same property. Thus a 60 per cent loan might be secured at the most, or $60,000, leaving the equity requirements of $40,000 the same as when title to the land is secured by the investor. FHA regulations provide that in the case of a leasehold mortgage, a value for the entire project be first established as if it were held in fee simple. Then the capitalized value of the ground rent is deducted from the value of the entire project to establish the figure to which the debt to value limitations apply.

SOURCES OF REAL ESTATE CREDIT

The primary source of all investment capital is the savings of individuals and corporations. The volume of savings is influenced by such basic factors as the economic health of the nation, and by the prospects for stable business conditions and a stable price level. Greater saving is encouraged by higher interest rates.

There are diverse demands for capital which are constantly made upon this pool of investment funds. The funds tend to flow to that type of investment which provides the most attractive return in relationship to safety and liquidity. The direction of this flow is also affected by prospects for prosperity, stability, or depression, and by the probable impacts on the various forms of investment. Except under extreme conditions, such as in the Depression of the middle thirties, a substantial share of the investment pool, about one-third of the net flow of capital and equity funds, finds its way into real estate mortgages.

Table VII-2

Savings in Selected Media
1955–1959
(in billions of dollars)

Medium	Year				
	1955	1956	1957	1958	1959
Savings associations	32.2	37.1	41.9	48.0	54.7
Mutual savings banks	28.1	30.0	31.7	34.0	35.0
Commercial banks	46.3	48.5	53.7	60.0	62.7
Credit unions	2.4	2.9	3.4	3.9	4.5
Mutual funds	9.0	10.3	9.9	14.8	17.5
U.S. savings bonds	50.2	50.1	48.2	47.7	45.8
Postal savings	2.0	1.7	1.4	1.2	1.0
Total	170.2	180.6	190.2	209.6	221.2

SOURCE: *Fact Book* '60, United Savings and Loan League, Chicago, Ill., p. 121. Data from Federal Home Loan Bank Board and National Association of Investment Companies.

Governmental fiscal policies can strongly affect the supply of credit in general as well as the flow of credit into real estate lending. Regulatory agencies of government and various governmental programs of intervention in the mortgage market may have great influence. Because of the pervasive influence of government in the mortgage market, we must understand the legislation in force, its intent and effect, and the agencies which have been created. Primary among these programs are those of the Federal Housing Administration (FHA), the Veterans Administration (VA), the Federal Home Loan Bank (FHLB) System, and the Federal National Mortgage Association (FNMA).

Before exploring the Federal programs we will examine the primary lenders—the institutions and individuals who are the front line mortgagees.

These agencies either employ investment capital assembled from local savers, or they are the channels for importing mortgage money into the locality. A later discussion on local mortgage markets will show how communities may differ markedly in the relative importance of the various primary lenders. Table VII-3 shows the national distribution of mortgages on one- to four-family homes made and held in 1959, by type of lender.

Table VII-3

Mortgages Made and Held in 1959 on 1- to 4-Family Properties
by Type of Lender

(in billions of dollars)

Type of lender	Mortgages held		Mortgages made	
	Amount	Per cent	Amount	Per cent
All types	$131.1	100.0	$32.235	100.0
Savings and loan associations ..	49.7	37.9	13.094	40.7
Life insurance companies	23.6	18.0	1.523	4.7
Commercial banks	19.2	14.7	5.832	18.1
Mutual savings banks	16.9	12.8	1.780	5.5
Federal agencies	6.1	4.7	6.060	18.8
Other lenders	15.6	11.9	6.060	
Individuals and others	15.6		3.946	12.2

SOURCE: Home Loan Bank Board.

Savings and Loan Associations

These local thrift institutions are the lineal descendants of cooperative associations in which the members were both the savers and the borrowers. Today they operate like savings banks with depository and lending functions separated; the savers and borrowers are different people, and savers have become "shareholders" and receive "dividends" on their deposits in lieu of interest. They may withdraw with due notice, though in practice withdrawal is usually permitted on demand. In recent years the assets of savings and loan associations have grown enormously, in part reflecting the general increase in all savings, and partly because of aggressive merchandising, promotional activities, and attractive dividend rates.

State regulatory bodies supervise the 4,400 state-chartered associations. The 1,800 federally chartered associations are regulated by the Federal Home Loan Bank Board which also may examine the associations, state and Federal, whose depositors are insured by the Federal Savings and Loan Insurance Corporation. Institutions which are members of the FHLB System, to be described later, must conform to certain standards prescribed by the FHLB Board.

Savings and loan associations are specialists in local mortgage investment. They are limited by law to mortgages and government securities, though federally chartered institutions may buy land contracts. In 1959 84 per cent of savings and loan assets were in mortgages on homes and 7 per cent in governments. In general, these institutions make loans which are more liberal in loan-value ratio and in term than is usually available elsewhere without government insurance. Depending on state law and regulation,

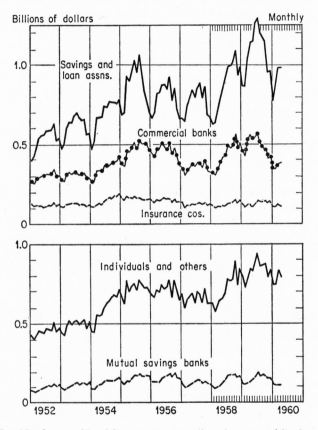

FIGURE VII-1. Nonfarm residential mortgage recordings by type of lender, 1952–1960.

loans may be up to 70 and 80 per cent of value and for terms of twenty to twenty-five years. Recent legislation in New York permits loans up to 90 per cent of value under certain conditions and federally chartered institutions may make 90 per cent loans. Interest rates tend to be higher on savings and loan advances than on loans from other sources where terms are less liberal.

Savings and loan associations depend primarily on local savings to provide investment funds. However, members of the FHLB System, now aggregating over 70 per cent of all associations and 97 per cent of all association assets, may resort to borrowing from their district FHL Board to secure additional loanable funds. Like other institutional lenders, they may sell government-insured mortgages to the FNMA or in the private secondary mortgage market to secure more free investment capital. This rarely occurs because mortgages are made as permanent investments and are generally left undisturbed in the association's portfolio. Short-term needs may be met by borrowing from commercial banks.

Because of the high dividend rates paid to attract savings, the associations must earn relatively high returns on mortgage loans. As a result, their portfolios include higher-risk loans on small and modest homes, on older properties, and on houses in new areas not fully established. Construction financing is welcomed because of favorable interest rates and additional earnings from extra fees.

As a rule these local thrift associations have not favored FHA mortgage insurance. During 1959 only 14 per cent of all FHA mortgages were originated by this type of lender. But they accounted for 22 per cent of all VA-guaranteed loans.

Mutual Savings Banks

These mutual thrift institutions are found mainly in the New England states and in New York State, where several such banks have grown to enormous size. They depend almost entirely on local sources of investment funds though they are eligible for membership in the FHLB System. Like savings and loan associations, these institutions are nonprofit, and the depositors receive dividends rather than interest. While closely regulated, they are less restricted as to investments than savings and loan associations. However, 64 per cent of their assets are in mortgages; the larger banks are interested in large loans on apartment developments and commercial properties. Some 18 per cent of aggregate assets are in United States government bonds and 15 per cent in other assets mainly corporate and municipal bonds. Some jurisdictions permit them to invest outside the state boundaries.

Traditionally, loan terms have been conservative among mutual savings banks; they were slow to participate in the FHA program and to employ high-percentage, long-term mortgage contracts. However, in recent years they have become competitive and are an important source of real estate credit in the areas in which they operate.

Commercial Banks

Although only a relatively small proportion of total assets of banks are invested in mortgages, they are one of the most important sources because of their vast aggregate resources. In 1959 they made 18 per cent of all new home mortgages and held 14 per cent. They also make loans on multifamily structures and commercial properties. By law, regulation, and banking tradition, banks restrict mortgage investment to a conservative proportion of total assets, usually to something less than total time deposits. State banks have somewhat more latitude than do national banks which are limited to 60 per cent of their time deposits or the total of capital stock and surplus. All banks may make FHA and VA loans up to the limit of eligibility for government guarantee, but national banks are restricted on conventional loans to two-thirds of value if amortized and to a twenty-year term. Nonamortized loans must be no more than 50 per cent of value and are due in five years. To secure additional loanable funds banks may sell government-guaranteed loans in the secondary mortgage market. The sources of loanable funds are savings accounts, on which the interest paid is low relative to that paid by specialized savings institutions and checking accounts on which no interest is paid. As a result bank rates on mortgages tend to reflect the lower costs of loan funds.

Reflecting the importance of liquidity in commercial bank operation, short-term construction loans are a common form of investment. Trust funds held by banks and trust companies are a source of conservative mortgage loans.

Life Insurance Companies

These huge financial institutions supply a substantial share of real estate credit. In 1959 they made 5 per cent of all home loans and held 18 per cent. They are the most important source of large loans on multifamily and commercial properties. Mortgages represent 34 per cent of their assets. About one-quarter of the nonfarm nonresidential mortgages are on commercial property. FHA and VA loans have been made in large quantity by life insurance companies and have been extensively purchased in the secondary mortgage market. Conventional loans are made on terms somewhat less liberal in loan-value ratio and maturity than by savings and loan associations but somewhat more liberal than banks. Many life companies show a preference for quality loans on the more expensive homes. Loans are made over a wide geographical area in the case of the large companies, often the entire country. The loans are placed by employees in branch offices or by loan correspondents who are brokers or agents and who receive a commission on loans placed.

The proportion of its funds which a life insurance company makes available for real estate loans is largely a matter of its current investment policy. This policy reflects yields on alternative investments, considerations of portfolio diversification, and the importance of keeping investment channels open. It also reflects expectations concerning business conditions and interest rates. Life insurance companies may join the FHLB System, but few have done so.

Mortgage Companies

The essential characteristic of mortgage companies is that they originate mortgages not for their own portfolios, but for other financial institutions with funds seeking investment. The predominant operation involves the

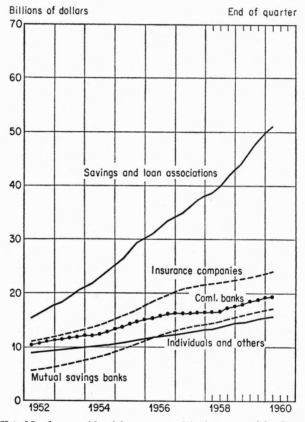

Billions of dollars   End of quarter

Savings and loan associations

Insurance companies

Coml. banks

Individuals and others

Mutual savings banks

1952   1954   1956   1958   1960

FIGURE VII-2. Nonfarm residential mortgage debt by type of lender, 1952–1960.

making of mortgages in reliance upon prior commitments from other institutions for the purchase of the mortgages. Thus the mortgage company needs only a relatively small amount of capital which it turns over frequently in the course of making and selling mortgage securities. In some cases, loans are made without advance commitments to purchase when the mortgage company believes the loan to be salable. When necessary, mortgage companies secure short-term credit from commercial banks to provide additional working capital. In addition to making and selling mortgages, the mortgage company may serve as a loan correspondent for one or more life insurance companies and may act as a loan broker.

Table VII-4

Home Mortgage Lending
by Type of Loan
1940–1958

(in thousands of dollars)

Year	All lenders			Nonfarm mortgage recordings of $20,000 or less
	Conventional	VA	FHA	
1940	$ 3,269,284	......	$ 762,084	$ 4,031,368
1941	3,821,190	......	910,770	4,731,960
1942	2,969,342	......	973,271	3,942,613
1943	3,098,304	......	763,097	3,861,401
1944	3,898,568	......	707,363	4,605,931
1945	4,983,334	$ 192,240	474,245	5,649,819
1946	7,864,912	2,302,307	421,949	10,589,168
1947	7,547,836	3,286,166	894,675	11,728,677
1948	7,885,104	1,880,967	2,116,043	11,882,114
1949	8,194,568	1,423,591	2,209,842	11,828,001
1950	10,613,520	3,073,309	2,492,367	16,179,196
1951	10,862,454	3,614,480	1,928,433	16,405,367
1952	13,354,295	2,721,075	1,942,307	18,017,677
1953	14,394,685	3,064,096	2,288,627	19,747,408
1954	16,774,579	4,257,200	1,942,074	22,973,853
1955	18,242,846	7,156,567 *	3,084,766	28,484,179
1956	18,581,449	5,868,352	2,638,186	27,087,987
1957	18,232,084	3,760,857	2,251,201	24,244,142
1958	20,971,333	1,864,949	4,551,356	27,387,638
1959	23,430,992 *	2,786,753	6,016,800 *	32,234,545 *

* All-time high.

Note: FHA-insured mortgages were first made in 1934; VA-guaranteed mortgages, in 1944.

SOURCES: Federal Home Loan Bank Board; Federal Housing Administration; Veterans Administration.

Mortgage companies have grown rapidly during the postwar building boom. They deal almost entirely in FHA and VA mortgages though there are exceptions, particularly in commercial and industrial loans. Their customers are largely insurance companies and mutual savings banks.

Chief sources of revenue for the mortgage companies are fees in connection with the sale of loans and servicing fees. When loans are sold to out-of-town buyers, it is customary for the mortgage company to service the loan during its life and receive a fee of one-half of 1 per cent on the declining balance. The accumulation of this kind of business over the years produces a substantial flow of revenue. Mortgage companies typically engage in related real estate activities such as real estate brokerage, appraising, casualty insurance, leasing, and property management.

Individuals and Other Institutions

Pension and welfare funds are becoming an important source of real estate credit. Some mortgage loans are made by casualty insurance companies, by credit unions, and out of endowment funds of eleemosynary institutions. Among Federal agencies there is limited direct lending by VA, and in the past, mortgage loans were made by the Reconstruction Finance Corporation (RFC) and Home Owners' Loan Corporation (HOLC), both of which are now liquidated. Some states have loan funds for veterans.

Noninstitutional lenders account for a large proportion of real estate credit. In 1959 individuals and other institutions together made 31 per cent of all new home mortgages (12 per cent by individuals) and held 13 per cent. This credit is supplied partly by direct lending to borrowers located by advertising or through real estate brokers. These direct loans are generally conservative in relation to the value of the property and for terms not exceeding ten years.

Individuals also acquire mortgages by purchases from such originating institutions as mortgage companies and banks. Investors of a more speculative turn may lend on the security of second mortgages or may purchase junior mortgages and land contracts, usually at a discount.

A large, but undeterminable, share of the credit advanced by individuals consists of purchase money mortgages or installment land contracts created from equities of sellers who take back mortgages as part payment or sell under land contract.

FEDERAL HOUSING ADMINISTRATION

Since its establishment in 1934, the initials FHA have become well known to the real estate industry and to home buyers and owners. Basically, the FHA is an insurance company set up to offer to mortgage lending institutions protection against financial loss on mortgages on residential structures. The original legislation was passed in a time of severe economic depression when plummeting values had destroyed confidence in real estate as mortgage security and when the mortgage market was frozen into almost total inactivity. To loosen up mortgage money and to promote recovery by stimulating house building, the Federal government undertook through the FHA insurance scheme to assume the risk of mortgage lending and to interpose the credit of the United States of America between the lender and financial loss. It is to be emphasized that FHA lends no money but only acts as insurer against the loss of funds advanced to borrowers by approved mortgagee institutions. The loss is

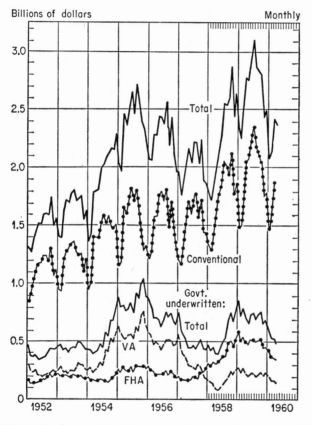

FIGURE VII-3. Nonfarm residential mortgage loans made by type, 1952–1960.

paid in FHA government-guaranteed debentures. The debentures cover loss of capital and taxes paid by the lender, unpaid interest, and certain foreclosure costs. Extra attorney's fees and reasonable cost of repair may be recovered if the proceeds from the foreclosure sale are sufficient. In some cases the FHA acquires the defaulted mortgage before foreclosure by payment of debentures in the amount of the outstanding principal and interest.

The FHA mortgage insurance plan, like any sound insurance scheme, calls for a premium, usually one-half of 1 per cent on the outstanding balance of the loan, which the borrower pays into a reserve fund, and which is in addition to the required interest payment. As insurer, the FHA carefully evaluates the mortgage risk and rejects cases which do not meet minimum standards.

The maximum interest rates on FHA-insured loans are set by FHA regulation up to a statutory limit of 6 per cent. The administration is ever reluctant to increase the rate with the result that when general interest rates are rising, FHA-insured mortgages become relatively less attractive investments until an adjustment is made. FHA financing was used on over one-quarter of all housing starts in 1958 and accounted for 17 per cent of total mortgage lending.

Commercial banks, mutual savings banks, and life insurance companies are the chief holders of FHA-insured mortgages. Savings and loan associations prefer the higher yield of conventional loans in order that they may pay dividends at a rate which will attract savings. Mortgage companies originated 38 per cent of all FHA-insured loans in 1958 with commercial banks next in order with 28 per cent.

The advantages of the FHA plan to lending institutions are:

1. Safety of principle with possible loss limited to certain out-of-pocket foreclosure expenses usually not exceeding $200 to $300

2. Fair rate of interest in light of government insurance protection

3. Liquidity and marketability because of the standardization of the instrument and the uniform protection of FHA insurance

4. Less chance of delinquency by reason of careful FHA methods of mortgage risk analysis, elimination of junior liens, and minimum standards and inspections on new construction

5. Improved competitive position since higher loan-to-value ratios and longer terms can be offered when the mortgage is FHA-insured

There are features of the FHA plan which lead some lenders to use it sparingly:

1. Increased paper work and delays in processing applications

2. Initial appraisal fee, inspection fees, and other costs

3. Alleged resistance to innovation in design, materials, and construction methods

4. Greater yield to the institution on conventional loans of higher quality where FHA insurance protection is not needed

There are important advantages to the borrowers under the FHA plan:

1. The home buyer can purchase with a low down payment.

2. The long term of the loan, moderate interest rate, and elimination of junior financing reduce monthly payments to a manageable level.

3. Total financing costs are minimized by eliminating refinancing.

4. FHA mortgage risk rating procedures and inspections prevent the home buyer from overbuying or from purchasing a home which will be a poor investment.

5. Monthly level payments including interest, principal, taxes, and insurance help to equalize the burden of housing costs.

The major portion of FHA activity has been the insuring of mortgages on one- to four-family dwellings under Section 203 of the basic law. But the agency has other mortgage insurance functions of importance which are modified and supplemented from time to time by the Congress in its use of FHA as an instrumentality of governmental policy. These functions are summarized as follows:

Title I—Modernization and Repair. The initial recovery functions of FHA at the time of its organization in 1934 included the encouragement of modernization and repair through easy credit as well as the stimulation of new construction. Title I provides for the insurance of unsecured loans made for the purposes of repair, conversion, modernization, and rehabilitation. This title has been expanded to cover mortgages on new small homes located in outlying areas and failing fully to meet the usual FHA minimum structural and locational standards.

Section 207—Rental Housing. This function involves the insurance of mortgages on multifamily rental structures.

Section 213—Cooperative Housing. Liberal credit for families of middle income is encouraged by the insurance of mortgages on cooperative housing projects.

Section 220 and 221—Urban Renewal. These sections are to aid in the financing of housing in areas cleared under urban renewal projects and to assist in the rehousing of families displaced by such projects.

Title VII—Yield Insurance. This provision is for the guarantee of a minimum yield on rental housing projects constructed by institutional investors which invest the full capital requirements without resort to mortgage financing. No project has yet been built to take advantage of yield insurance.

Section 231—Housing for the Elderly. Easy credit for the provision of housing for our senior citizens is encouraged through mortgage insurance and direct loan provisions.

Miscellaneous. FHA legislation includes special treatment for home purchasers who are now in the Armed Forces as well as mortgage insurance on rental housing projects serving military personnel. There is a special section covering housing in Alaska and for the victims of disasters such as fire and flood. Now defunct are provisions to encourage housing in defense areas and to stimulate the prefabrication industry.

VETERANS ADMINISTRATION MORTGAGE
GUARANTEE PROGRAM

The Servicemen's Readjustment Act of 1944 was to assist veterans of World War II (Korean veterans were later included) in adjusting to civilian life. In particular, the loan-guarantee provisions were to permit

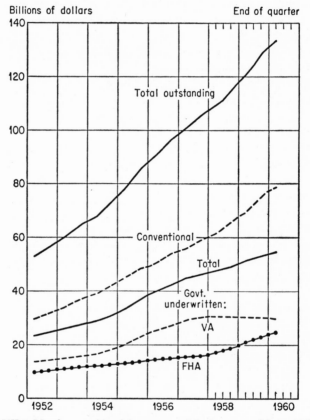

FIGURE VII-4. Nonfarm residential mortgage debt by type of loan, 1952–1960.

them to borrow on easy terms the capital which, but for the demands of military service, they might have been able to save toward home purchase, construction or repair, purchase of a farm or farm equipment, or the purchase of business property. There is no upper limit on the amount of the loan involved, but the VA will not guarantee more than a stated amount—$4,000 for farm and business realty loans and for home loans, $7,500 or 60 per cent of the loan, whichever is smaller. Thus a substantial proportion of VA-guaranteed home loans have covered 100 per cent of the value of the property. Loan terms may run to thirty years. Many lenders do not choose to make VA-guaranteed loans up to the permissible limits.

The VA guarantee is not insurance; no premium is collected, no reserve fund set up. The guarantee covers principal, interest, advances for taxes, assessments and insurance premiums, necessary repairs, and foreclosure costs. Losses are paid in cash. The fact that the guarantee may cover only a portion of the loan—for example, 60 per cent for home loans—is of little significance since there are almost no cases where the loss exceeds the guaranteed amount. From the lender's standpoint the VA protection is virtually complete, and the provisions for paying losses are more favorable than under FHA mortgage insurance.

In addition to the virtues of liberal credit and easy terms of repayment there are other advantages to the borrower. He may prepay without penalty or if he wishes to sell the property, he finds the VA financing to be an attractive feature to nonveteran buyers who assume the mortgage. For the veteran's protection the VA will guarantee no loan on property which is purchased for more than "reasonable value" as set by VA appraisers.

The maximum interest rate on VA-guaranteed loans is established by law and therefore difficult to change. In 1953 it was raised to 4½ per cent and later to 4¾ per cent and then to 5¼ from the original 4 per cent but has continued to lag behind market rates. This lag has greatly reduced the funds available for VA lending and has led to discounting VA mortgages. Because VA money is not always available to veterans in all localities, particularly in rural areas and small towns, the VA has been provided with a limited fund for direct loans where no other mortgage money can be found.

In 1958 VA financing was used on nearly 10 per cent of all private housing units started and accounted for nearly 15 per cent of the dollar

Table VII-5

VA-Guaranteed Home Loans Originated,
by Type of Lender, 1958

Type of lender	Percentage distribution
All types	100
Mortgage companies	48
Savings and loan associations	24
Mutual savings banks	16
Commercial banks	9
Life insurance companies	2
Others	1

SOURCE: Veterans Administration.

volume of all mortgage lending. All types of lending institutions have participated freely in the VA loan program and VA-guaranteed mortgages have been traded extensively in the secondary mortgage market. Out of some 17 million eligible veterans, fewer than 5 million have benefited. Though the eligibility of World War II veterans expired in 1960, it appears likely that some form of veteran's preference in the form of favorable credit terms will continue for some time.

Table VII-5 shows the distribution of VA-guaranteed home mortgages made in 1958 by type of lender.

PRIVATE MORTGAGE INSURANCE

In 1956 a Milwaukee organization, the Mortgage Guaranty Insurance Corporation (MGIC), inaugurated a mortgage insurance operation as a private venture. The plan is similar to FHA in providing protection to the lender in return for a fee or premium. It differs in that the insurance covers only the top 20 per cent of the loan, i.e., any loss in excess of 20 per cent of the unpaid balance of the mortgage, unpaid interest and taxes, and foreclosure costs must be borne by the mortgagee. Loans up to 90 per cent of the value of the property may be insured at a premium cost substantially lower than the FHA rate. The plan is particularly attractive to savings and loan associations because there is no limitation on interest rates; these institutions can secure protection on high ratio loans without sacrificing yield as is the case when the FHA interest rate limitation must be observed. Almost all of the insurance written during the first four years has been with this type of lender. Other advantages of MGIC insurance are prompt processing of applications and payment of claims in cash.

FINANCING PATTERNS

Now that we have described the various devices employed in real estate finance, it may be well to show how they are adapted to the needs of investors in actual market transactions. Much the same financial machinery is used by all real estate investors regardless of their investment objectives. However, the terms under which credit is advanced and the liberality of the advance is influenced by the purposes of the investor, his financial position, and the characteristics of the collateral property.

Home Financing

The most common credit instrument in home financing is the mortgage, and the most frequent financing pattern is a combination of an equity contribution and a mortgage debt. But the terms of the loan are subject to wide variations which are the joint product of the borrower's financial circumstances and the lender's attitude and policy. The elements which make up the basic home financing pattern are:

1. Amount of equity investment
2. Amount of borrowed capital secured by the mortgage
3. Interest rate
4. Amortization or repayment schedule

The amount of the loan, the interest rate, and the repayment schedule are stated in the mortgage note and are called the "terms" of the mortgage. The payments called for, either interest alone or interest and principal retirement, are referred to as "debt service." The repayment schedule takes one of three forms:

1. *Straight Loan*. Interest only is paid for a stated time period, and then the full amount of the loan becomes due and payable.

2. *Partial Amortization*. The schedule calls for periodic interest and principal payments until a certain portion of the debt is retired at which time the balance of the debt becomes due. The final payment of this balance is known as the "balloon payment."

3. *Complete Amortization*. The schedule requires periodic interest and principal payments until the debt is fully repaid. The debt service payments may be in equal amounts or may call for equal principal repayments with each interest payment determined by the then unpaid debt.

By varying any one of the terms of the mortgage, different levels and time patterns of debt service payments will result:

1. The higher the initial equity investment, the lower the debt burden. To reduce the debt from $10,000 to $5,000 will reduce the level monthly payment from $84.39 to $42.20 on a fully amortized fifteen-year, 6 per cent loan.

2. The lower the interest rate, the lower the burden. To reduce the interest rate from 6 per cent to 5 per cent will reduce the level monthly payment from $84.39 to $79.08 on a fully amortized fifteen-year loan of $10,000.

3. No amortization creates a lower burden than full or partial amortization. Interest alone at 6 per cent on a $10,000 loan would be $50 per month compared with a level monthly payment of $84.39 on a fifteen-year fully amortized loan at 6 per cent interest.

4. Partial amortization during the term of the loan creates a lower burden than full amortization. On a $10,000 loan to be paid down to $5,000 in fifteen years at 6 per cent interest, the level monthly payment would be $67.20 compared with $84.39 if fully amortized over the same term.

5. The longer the term of an amortized loan, the lower the burden. The level monthly payment on a full amortized $10,000 loan at 6 per cent is $84.39 at a fifteen-year term and $71.65 at a twenty-year term.

6. The level-payment plan maintains a constant burden over the full term of the loan. The proportion of each payment going to debt retirement increases over the term of the loan as the proportion going to interest decreases.

7. The constant-principal payment with variable interest payment reduces the burden with each payment. As the debt is reduced by each payment, the interest portion of the burden is progressively reduced.

Home buyers with limited liquid assets for a down payment may require additional credit to bridge the gap between the purchase price and the proceeds of the first mortgage loan. Assume that a home buyer planning to purchase a $20,000 house can secure a 70 per cent conventional loan from a savings and loan association. A 70 per cent loan, or $14,000, at 5½ per cent interest and a fifteen-year term requires monthly payments of $114.40. If the buyer can raise $3,000 in cash, he will require a second mortgage loan of $3,000 which will substantially increase the total debt service, for junior mortgages usually call for high interest rates and rapid repayment of principal. Assume that our buyer will have to pay 7 per cent interest on the second mortgage with repayment on a five-year schedule. The level payments will be $59.41. Added to the payment on the first mortgage, the total monthly debt service will be $173.81.

On occasion, the seller of the property will take back a purchase money junior mortgage as part payment. Or he may sell on an installment land contract with a modest down payment and monthly payments of principal and interest. Such contract often provides that when the unpaid balance is reduced to a point where refinancing is practicable, the buyer is to place a mortgage on the property and, with the proceeds, pay off the seller. Or the seller may agree that when the unpaid balance is reduced to a stated amount, he will convey title to the vendee and take back a mortgage to secure the balance due. If the property is already mortgaged, the vendee may make payments until the vendor's equity has been extinguished and then assume the mortgage.

High percentage long-term first mortgage financing such as has been made possible by the FHA and VA programs often eliminates the need for junior financing and results in a lesser debt service than when a combination of first and second mortgage is used. For example, in the foregoing case in which total monthly payments on the first and second mortgages are $173.81, a single twenty-five-year $17,000 FHA-insured mortgage (5¼ per cent interest plus ½ per cent mortgage insurance premium) would require a payment of $106.95.

Financing Income Property

The basic patterns of home financing are found repeated in the extension of credit on apartment and business properties. First, second, and third mortgages are employed. When a first mortgage secures a very large debt, such as on an office building or shopping center, it may be split for participation by two or more lenders. In the New York area a large mortgage may be the basis of a bond issue to permit small investors to participate.

Commercial property is sometimes financed through a combination of lease and mortgage. The investor-developer leases the site on a long-term lease, perhaps for ninety-nine years. To raise money for constructing a building he pledges the leasehold estate. When the building is finished the lease is secured by a valuable income-producing structure, and the leasehold mortgage is secured by the income of the property after paying the ground rent as explained in an earlier section.

The sale-leaseback plan has had much currency in recent years. It has been particularly attractive to retail chains who are expanding and need as working capital the funds which are tied up in the store buildings which they have built or purchased. The plan is also widely used for other types of commercial and industrial property and in connection with new construction as well as improved properties. This financing scheme calls for the lending institution to become actual owner of the collateral property through purchase for cash from the original owner-occupant. The original owner thus secures liquid capital, as he would from the proceeds of a mortgage. He continues to occupy and use the property under a long lease from the new owner-lender. The rental reserved under the lease is sufficient to amortize the purchase price paid for the property. At the end of the lease, the original owner usually has the option to renew the lease at a very low rent or to repurchase the property at an agreed price.

CONSTRUCTION FINANCING

Home builders, in the manufacture of houses, require production credit to supplement their own working capital in the financing of work in process. Relative to the financial resources of the ordinary operative builder, a very large amount of capital must be tied up in land, materials, and partly finished structures awaiting completion and sale. Some of the working capital needs are met in the form of book credit from suppliers and subcontractors, but the major portion must be borrowed either on unsecured notes or on mortgage loans with the land and houses under construction as security.

Construction mortgages may have a short term, two to six months to cover the time required for completion. In this case, the mortgage is made in reliance upon retirement out of the proceeds of a permanent mortgage to be placed on the property when finished or in anticipation of its sale with the construction loan to be retired from the receipts. In other cases, the construction mortgage is also the permanent mortgage which has a long term and which will be assumed by the ultimate buyer of the home. Unless a buyer has been found before the house is started, the builder is the original mortgagor and continues to be responsible for the mortgage payments until the mortgage is assumed by the buyer.

Construction advances on mortgage security are paid out to builders in installments as the work progresses on the structure. The lender takes precautions to assure that the dollars advanced are actually translated into materials and equipment in place in the particular structure which stands as security, and that at all times, the portion of the loan not yet advanced is sufficient to complete the building if the builder should default, and the lender should find himself with a partly finished building on his hands.

Builders on contract rely on the credit of the owner to supplement working capital. In this case the owner is the original mortgagor. The lending institution usually requires that the owner hold the building site free and clear of debt and that his additional equity contribution of cash be translated into materials in place before any of the proceeds of the mortgage are paid out. In the case of large structures, lenders require that the contractor secure a completion bond.

MORTGAGE RISK ANALYSIS

When an application for a mortgage loan is received by a financial institution, the loan officer or loan committee must decide upon its acceptability. It is usually assumed that the prospective borrower will pay the going rate of interest and that the mortgage loan will be repaid or amortized within some maximum term of years which represents the current policy of the lender. The loan officer is confronted with the problem of determining the acceptability of the mortgage investment under these conditions; or if it is not acceptable under the customary mortgage contract, he may propose modifications in the terms, such as a higher interest rate or faster amortization, which might make it a good investment. Of course, he may conclude that it does not meet minimum standards, even with adjustments in terms. The basic analytical problem of the lender is the evaluation of mortgage risk. This same problem confronts FHA and VA in deciding upon the acceptability of an application for mortgage insurance or mortgage guarantee.

The Nature of Mortgage Risk

The objectives of the mortgage lender are to make a loan which will produce a gross return sufficient to (1) cover the costs of making and servicing the loan, (2) provide a basic or pure interest return on the capital, and (3) yield a sufficient reward for risk taking. The costs can be estimated with reasonable accuracy; the basic interest rate is a product of current money market conditions; but the degree of risk inherent in the mortgage investment situation is dependent on a complex of financial and real estate factors. The problems of evaluating mortgage risk are the most critical as well as the most difficult which confront the lender in selecting mortgage loans for investment.

Mortgage risk is the danger of impairment of expected yield or of invested principal. It is the chance that the borrower will fail to meet the terms of the contract and that his failure to make debt service payments will reduce the yield on the investment, or that the principal of the debt will be impaired because the value of the collateral property is not sufficient to cover costs of foreclosure and the full amount of the unpaid balance of the loan.

The analysis of mortgage risk is mainly an evaluation of the defenses against loss. The borrower is the first defense. No lender wittingly makes a mortgage which he expects to have to foreclose; if he could accurately test and foresee the borrower's ability and inclination to meet his obligations, no mortgage loan would ever come to foreclosure. But there are many uncertainties in predicting the future financial behavior of the mortgagor and thus some chance that foreclosure will be necessary in every loan. For this reason, the lender must carefully judge the strength of the second line of defense against loss, the collateral real estate. The effectiveness of this protection will be measured by the relationship between the unpaid debt (and other accumulated obligations such as back interest) and the proceeds of the foreclosure sale when the collateral is liquidated.

Note that mortgage risk is not a circumstance which exists only at the moment the loan is made. To the contrary, risk is present at all times during the life of the loan until it is completely extinguished by repayment. From time to time while the mortgage is in force, the risk may change in degree as the financial fortunes of the borrower ebb and flow and as the value of the collateral property shifts with changes in the structure, environment, and market.

Mortgage risk is the product of a set of relationships among borrower, property, and loan elements. The loan elements are the amount of the debt, the interest rate, the repayment plan, and the term of the loan. In relationship to one pattern of loan elements, a certain borrower might be a high risk; with another pattern, he would be a low-risk borrower as for example if the amount of the debt were reduced, or the term extended so that the monthly payments would be smaller. We will give later consideration to the modification of mortgage risk through changing the relationships between the loan elements and the real estate elements represented by the collateral property.

Real Estate Elements in Mortgage Risk

Since this is a book on real estate, we shall only briefly recognize the mortgage credit risk elements in a loan situation before exploring in some detail the real estate elements of risk. The brevity of treatment here is no measure of the importance of mortgagor risk in analyzing the soundness of a mortgage loan, particularly a home loan. It is true that many income properties are owned by corporations with no other assets and that the mortgagee must rely primarily on the productivity of the real estate to meet mortgage payments on schedule. Even in this case, the credit standing of the stockholders enters into mortgage risk analysis for their financial status suggests the probability that the owners may dip into personal resources if necessary to protect their ownership interests should a temporary decline in the productivity of the property threaten default. The payment of debt service on a home mortgage depends on the personal income and assets of the borrower and his family; thus a home mortgage is akin to consumer credit extended in automobile and appliance financing where the credit rating of the borrower is all important.

Initial Property Value

One of the first steps in mortgage risk analysis is the appraisal of the property. Generally this value figure is presumed to represent the current market value, i.e., what the property would sell for within a reasonable time in a transaction involving prudent and informed parties acting under no compulsion or pressure. The purposes of an appraisal are twofold:

1. Most lending institutions are restricted by law or regulation to loans which are no more than a stated percentage of the value of the property at the time the loan is made. Thus national banks cannot exceed two-thirds, while savings and loan associations in New York State may go to 90 per cent. It is an interesting fact that this limitation is self-administered to the extent that each lender's own appraisal is usually accepted by the regulatory agency. However, the institutions are subject to periodic examination which includes spot checks or complete checks of the mortgage portfolio to see that the rules are being observed.

2. The value figure is related to the amount of the proposed loan as a test of mortgage risk. It is assumed that the lower the ratio of initial debt to present value, the safer the loan, *other things being equal*. The assump-

tion is sound but impractical, for other things are *not* equal. It is true that the wider the margin of value over debt, the greater the depreciation in the value of the collateral which can occur without danger; and the greater the owner's equity, the more his incentive to prevent default which might wipe out his ownership. But the initial relationship of debt to value is a temporary thing and will change over time in response to the unique set of forces which impinge on the property and the borrower. The original value figure is nevertheless an important datum in risk analysis since it is the point of origin of the pattern of future value. This pattern has great significance in determining risk when matched against the pattern of future outstanding debt.

The procedure of arriving at a capital value by appraisal methods has been discussed in the chapter on real estate investment analysis, Chapter VI.

Predicting the Pattern of Value

Figure VII-5, page 174, portrays the principle that mortgage risk is a changing thing over the life of the loan, and that for each property, the future pattern of the significant debt-value ratio will differ. The line M represents the reducing unpaid balance of a mortgage loan which began at $10,000 and is retired through the usual level monthly payments of interest and principal in twenty-five years. Line V^1 represents the hypothetical pattern in the decline in market value of an old house nearing the end of economic life starting from a present value of $12,000 and falling to $4,000 in thirty years. Line V^2 is the predicted value pattern for a newer $11,000 house with a long remaining useful life.

If the mortgage lender relied only on the initial debt-value ratio, he would conclude that the same mortgage loan amount would be better secured by the older but higher-value house; other things being equal, the lower initial debt-value ratio reflects a lower mortgage risk. But the future patterns of value are quite different in the two cases. The stable value and longer economic life of the $11,000 house results in an ever-increasing margin of safety between debt and value. The safety margin shrinks almost from the start for the $12,000 house, drops below the other margin about the sixth year, and disappears almost entirely by the fifteenth year.

The chart may be used to illustrate the suggestion made earlier that the terms of the loan can be adjusted to the estimated future pattern of values to minimize real estate risk. In the case of the $12,000 house, a smaller original loan with the same term would increase the initial margin of safety and maintain some margin for a longer time. A better adjustment would be to shorten the term by eight or ten years thus accelerating repayment and maintaining a margin of safety at all times.

The concern of the mortgage lender is with the ability of collateral real estate to resist all forces of value decline. He has little interest in the possibility that the property may increase in value save that it would widen the margin of safety. Unlike the owner-investor, the mortgage lender with his fixed claim cannot share in appreciation of value; thus he will not consider the possibility of capital gain as an offset to the chance of loss as does a speculator.

Mortgage risk is financial risk, for it is a function of the financing contract. The mortgagee must accept as a given factor the business risk

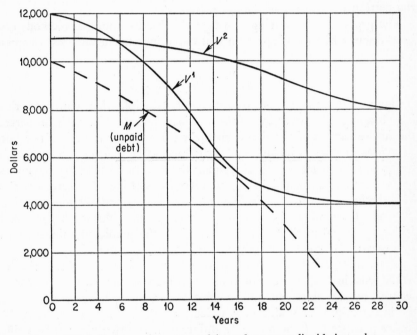

FIGURE VII-5. Patterns of mortgage debt and property liquidation values.

growing out of the productivity characteristics of the property. It has already been pointed out that he can control financial risk to some extent by modifying the mortgage terms. In the same sense that we have used the term in Chapter VI, risk is the uncertainty of prediction. If the lender were certain of the future pattern of value, he could manipulate the terms of repayment so that the liquidation value of the property would be in excess of the debt at all times. But because the prediction is necessarily uncertain, there is risk always present, and the more inadequate the basis of prediction, the higher the risk. And the higher the risk, the wider is the margin of safety which the prudent lender demands.

The real estate prediction which is primary for mortgage risk analysis on income property is productivity in terms of rental revenues. This problem of productivity analysis has been discussed in Chapter VI. The first application of the forecast of net income before depreciation is to relate it to debt service requirements. If there is an ample margin of safety the mortgage payments can be met even though revenues may suffer some drop. With a narrow margin, default may be threatened by even a small decline. Should foreclosure ensue, the liquidation of the property at foreclosure sale would be the last defense against loss.

The value of an income property, and hence its sale price at any time, will depend almost entirely upon the buyer's evaluation of its productivity in terms of net income. Thus both the first and second lines of defense are no stronger than the income-producing capacity of the property; and the degree of mortgage risk is almost entirely a reflection of the level and pattern of rental income and operating expenses.

When the present value of the real estate has been established the mortgage analyst has a point of departure for his prediction. As a practical matter, it is impossible to forecast year by year the changes which are to take place in the liquidation value of the collateral property. But it is not out of the question to attempt certain generalizations. We may conceive of the property value as a time series in the form of a secular trend which has a certain general pattern and arrives at the zero value at the end of an estimated time period. Thus, starting with the present market value of a modern, well-designed, and high-quality home in an excellent location, we might forecast a basic value trend like the trend line V^2 in Figure VII-5. But for an older home in a neighborhood where blight and decline seem to be accelerating, the value pattern might be like line V^1 in Figure VII-5.

Another form of generalization is the expression of the predicted value decrease as a rate of decline. This rate can be compared with the rate of decline of the debt as determined by the amortization schedule to measure the presumed change in the margin of safety.

One precaution is suggested which has special application when the real estate market is out of balance. In times of shortage in supply, current market prices are usually greatly inflated. It would be unreasonable to use such values as the point of origin for a forecast. A prior step is required to adjust the current inflated value to a lower figure which would more nearly represent conditions in a balanced market. This adjusted value could then be used as the origin of the predicted value trend. An upward adjustment would be indicated if current values were seriously deflated.

Whether or not the mortgage risk analyst attempts to predict the pattern of future values, he must at least judge the risk of the value falling below debt at some time during the life of the loan. We shall now consider the real estate risk factors which he evaluates.

Economic Background Analysis

The economic health of the community is of primary concern to the mortgage lender. In a city where job opportunities are declining, incomes falling, and population static or decreasing, all real estate values will suffer. Though some areas of the community and some types of property are harder hit than others, lending risk is generally high. In contrast, business expansion and city growth will sustain property values over most of the community. Lenders favor urban areas of economic stability and and steady growth over cities of explosive expansion but erratic economic behavior. Diversification in sources of employment is considered to be an asset for it imparts stability to the local economy.

The forecasting of community growth and prosperity begins with a study of the primary economic activities. The distinctions between primary and secondary employment were discussed in Chapter II. Because primary activities are city builders, real estate values depend ultimately on the purchasing power which such activities channel into the locality. When these activities have been identified and their relative importances established, each primary industry or employment source is studied to reveal trends in employment, factors which may influence the competitive position of the local establishments, and the general prospects for over-all national growth of these industries or employment sources. The attractions of the area for new industries should be studied as a basis for predicting future employment trends. Considerations which influence new industries include available land, tax rates, labor supply, living conditions and costs, community facilities for recreational and cultural pursuits, access to markets and materials, transportation facilities, local labor relations, wage rates, and climate.

A close look at the economic base may reveal prospects for change which will have special impact in certain areas of the community or on certain classes of property. For example, a new automobile assembly plant to be built on the west side of a city means more jobs for semi-skilled industrial workers and will stimulate real estate values in this part of the community. There will be need for additional housing and service facilities to meet the needs of new families entering the area to fill the jobs. The closing of a plant will have the opposite effect. A new establishment, such as the home office of an insurance company, to be located in the central area may have only indirect and long-term beneficial effects on property values. In such a case the required workers may be female clerks to be recruited from the existing labor pool and generating little in-migration. Some housing for executives and supervisors will be required in the better residential areas, and clerks recruited from nearby farms and villages will need rooms or apartments. In the long run, the added payroll of the new enterprise will benefit retail and service businesses and thus commercial property values.

Economic base analysis may expose long-term trends in local economic activity such as an increasing predominance of certain types of industry or employment. The area may develop as an automobile center as did Detroit, or a medical center like Rochester, Minnesota, or an insurance center like Hartford, Connecticut. Where there is a pool of labor with special skill and know-how, industries requiring such skills will be attracted. The existence of a major university may attract commercial research establishments or other firms engaged in highly technical work where contact with university faculty and facilities is of value. When such trends are detected their effects on the several classes of real estate can be interpreted together with the impact in different neighborhoods.

Although changes in primary or basic economic activities are the major factors in urban growth, other forces may act to influence real estate values and the structure of land use. For example, social change may modify local expenditure patterns with a consequent impact on land values. Technological change may have other similar effects. Changes in the export of purchasing power through external investment and the buying of goods and services outside of the community will lead to changes in the pattern of real estate values.

Local Market Characteristics

The prospective mortgage lender examines the local real estate market to discover its peculiarities and special characteristics as a guide to the future of real estate values. The home mortgage lender is concerned with attitudes toward homeownership and any changes in the proportion of owner families. Cities differ in the degree to which homeownership is the accepted pattern of living in reflection of local cultural back-grounds, customs, and the degree of economic stability. Tenancy may be a preferred way of life in cities having a mobile population which is a reflection of instable employment; or in a university town among the substantial floating population of married students, young instructors, and visiting professors. In the older Eastern cities tenancy is the accepted pattern among large segments of certain income groups.

In addition to an analysis of the quality of demand for the services of real estate, the mortgage lender looks to the competing supply in the form of the standing stock of real estate facilities. Its adequacy and its quality will have an influence on the pattern of future real estate values. In addition, the efficiency of the local home-building industry is of general interest, for if it is poorly organized and inefficient the situation may invite competition from outside which could affect all values in the housing market.

Structure

The value-generating attributes of the structure and site improvements must be evaluated as a part of mortgage risk analysis. Judgment must be made of the ability of the collateral structure to resist the forces of physical deterioration and obsolescence. The productivity characteristics of land improvements were presented in Chapter III.

Location

In Chapter IV we explained the highly significant relationships between productivity, value, and location. Unfavorable environmental change or prospects of change can impair the value of collateral property and thereby create or increase mortgage risk. Thus, locational analysis is a fundamental step in the process of appraising the collateral property and predicting the stability or pattern of its value.

SECONDARY MORTGAGE MARKET

It has long been a common practice among some of the primary lenders or originating mortgagees to sell mortgages to investors who hold them to maturity. The seller makes a profit on the sale and often continues to service the mortgage for a fee, i.e., to act as a collection agent. Typical of this kind of operator is the mortgage company which seeks a rapid turnover of its capital by making and selling mortgages, and at the same time builds up a profitable mortgage servicing business. Mortgage lending institutions may sell mortgages in order to secure free loan funds or to shift from mortgages to a type of investment which promises a higher yield. They buy mortgages to convert liquid funds to long-term investments or to shift from lower to higher yield securities.

Another method used by primary lending institutions to secure more loanable capital is to borrow from other financial agencies often pledging the mortgages held in their portfolios. In 1932 the FHLB System was established to give greater flexibility and expansion of lending power to member institutions, largely savings and loan associations. It is a credit reserve system made up of eleven regional banks from which member institutions may borrow to meet short-term needs by pledging their mortgage assets. In 1958 total loans to member institutions were over $1.3 billion, and at the year's end some 2,000 members owed $1.3 billion.

The extensive use of FHA insurance and later, VA guarantee, vastly extended trading in mortgages. With government guarantee the mortgage acquired a standardized form and an essentially uniform investment quality. Thus the shifting of mortgages among lenders was greatly facilitated without regard for the location of the mortgaged property. For example, during the year 1956 financial institutions purchased and sold some 371,000 FHA-insured obligations aggregating $1.8 billion in original face amount.

Another agency, the Federal National Mortgage Association, popularly known as Fannie Mae (FNMA), has been created to perform certain central mortgage banking functions. It buys and sells FHA and VA mortgages under terms which are modified as conditions change in the mortgage market. Funds for its operation are secured from the United States Treasury and from the sale of FNMA debentures. With the objective of converting FNMA to private ownership, sellers of mortgages are required to purchase stock in the agency. In addition to the function of manipulating the flow of secondary credit into and out of the mortgage market, the agency is called upon to implement government housing policy by providing credit for certain special programs such as housing for the aged, for cooperative projects, or for families displaced by urban redevelopment projects. This end is accomplished by standing ready to purchase FHA-insured mortgages used for such purposes. In effect, this process is direct lending, since the originating institution performs little more than a brokerage function.

The *warehousing* of mortgages is a practice which has evolved with the extension of the secondary market for government-guaranteed loans. The term refers to the temporary holding of a group of mortgages by an institution awaiting assignment to another institution for its investment portfolio. A bank, for example, may originate and warehouse a group of mortgages on a tract development on reliance of an agreement with a life insurance company to buy the entire group out of investment funds which will be available at a later date. A variation arrangement is a short-term bank loan to the insurance company or the purchase of mortgages from the insurance company under a repurchase agreement. In each case liquid capital is made available to the insurance company which permits it to take advantage of a favorable investment opportunity in advance of the accumulation of its own investment funds available for permanent commitment.

LOCAL MORTGAGE MARKETS

There is much variation among urban areas in the proportioning of mortgage lending activity by the several types of lending institutions. In part, these differences are traditional or historical and in part are related to the balance of supply and demand in the local mortgage market. Where local savings fail to meet the need, investment capital must be imported, usually through the agency of the mortgage banker, loan offices, and correspondents of life insurance companies and commercial banks. Where there is a sufficiency of local investment capital, savings and loan associations, mutual savings banks, commercial banks and trust companies, and individuals are the more important sources of mortgage money.

Data based on loans on new houses in 1949 illustrate the extreme local differences which may occur.[4] In the Boston metropolitan area banks, including mutual savings banks, provided funds for 88 per cent of new houses built, while in Dallas and Miami the percentage was 3. Savings and loan associations financed 41 per cent of the new homes in Los Angeles compared with a percentage of 2 in Philadelphia and 4 in Seattle. Mortgage companies originated 95 per cent of the loans in Miami, 65 per cent in Detroit, and less than 1 per cent in Boston. Insurance companies made 33 per cent of the mortgages on new homes in Seattle, 4 per cent in Chicago, and 1 per cent in Pittsburgh.

The importance of outside mortgage funds in the various Federal Reserve districts is illustrated by the ratio of the volume of loans serviced for others (representing imported capital) to the volume held for own account (local capital).[5] In the Boston district there was only $3 of outside capital for every $100 of local investment. In the Dallas district $125 was imported for every $100 of local funds invested in mortgages.

Differences in mortgage interest rates among the localities and regions of the country have been considerably reduced as the result of the various government programs. Through the medium of the FHLB System, FNMA, the VA direct loans, the Voluntary Mortgage Credit Program, and the secondary mortgage market activities in FHA and VA loans, real estate credit has attained a considerable geographical mobility. Funds from areas of surplus can now readily flow into deficit localities before local interest rates rise very far in response to the market imbalance. In the same manner, this mobility of investment funds acts to check a depression of rates when a local surplus develops.

There are certain localities where the risk of real estate investment is more than normal and these are shunned by mortgage lenders. Examples are depressed industrial areas which are losing population and locations where there are military establishments and defense activities of uncertain life. Special government programs involving the underwriting of mortgage risk have been used in an effort to induce a flow of mortgage money into such areas.

---

[4] SOURCE: U.S. Bureau of Labor Statistics, *Construction*, February, 1951, table 20, p. 28.

[5] *Federal Reserve Bulletin*, June, 1952, p. 634.

MORTGAGE INTEREST RATES

Because of the critical role which credit plays in the real estate market, a restriction in the supply of available loan funds tends to depress the market—to limit effective demand by eliminating the marginal buyers who are most in need of liberal credit and to cause a softening in prices and a reduction in market velocity because of narrowed demand. Building activity slows down because both builders and new home buyers find it more difficult to secure loan funds. An important concomitant of a restricted supply of credit is a rise in interest rates as the prospective users of credit bid up the price of money. Along with rising interest rates, and in many cases, preceding an increase in the level of rates charged by lending institutions, comes greater selectivity on the part of lenders and changes in other lending terms. Lenders can now pick the best risks among the various lending opportunities; they may shorten the term of repayment or eliminate such disadvantageous provisions as the prepayment privilege. Fees and services charges may be added or increased in amount. Of course, in the case of a surplus of mortgage money, competition among lenders to put investment funds to work leads to lower interest rates, more liberal lending terms, reductions in fees, and more liberal appraisals for lending purposes.

The real estate market must compete with the credit requirements which arise in many other sectors of our economy. Needs for large amounts of long-term loan funds are found among industrial corporations to finance expansion, state and local governments for highway and public works expenditures, and the Federal government in financing the deficits which are ever-present whether the nation is prosperous, depressed, or at war. The flow of investment funds through lending institutions tends to move in the direction of the most attractive investment opportunities, sometimes toward and sometimes away from the real estate market. Rising interest rates, other things being equal, tend to attract investment funds.

The general level of interest rates in the capital markets of the country is a reflection of the balance of over-all demand and supply factors. Mortgage interest rates tend to move with changes in the general level of rates; on the demand side particularly, conditions in the real estate market will have a special effect on mortgage rates. On the supply side, the rate of savings in such specialized mortgage institutions as savings and loan associations will be reflected in mortgage interest rates in those localities where such lenders supply a substantial share of the needs. Regional and local differences in mortgage interest rates will be found at all times though these differences are tending to be less marked as secondary mortgage market facilities become more effective in channeling interregional flows of loan funds. To some extent these local and regional differences are the result of differences in investment risk which is a by-product of the economic health of the area. In most cases, the higher rates are found where rapid growth with the attendant capital needs outstrips local savings as in the South and West. The lowest rates are found in such mature regions as the Northeast where local capital has accumulated and where growth is moderate.

While the general level of mortgage interest rates is controlled by demand and supply conditions in the mortgage market, the contract interest rate in each individual loan situation is generally adjusted to the risk characteristics of the borrower and the collateral property, and to the other terms of the loan. For example, a moderate loan value ratio may permit a lower rate than in the case of a more liberal advance. A mortgage on a property which is in a neighborhood with an uncertain future will justify a higher rate than where neighborhood stability is assured. A second mortgage is riskier than a first lien and carries a higher rate. A short-term loan may be made available at a rate lower than a long-term loan; the rapidity of amortization may be reflected in the interest rate. In actual practice mortgage lending institutions tend to cling to an established rate and to accommodate to differential risk largely by adjusting length of term, amortization schedule, and debt-value ratio or to adjust yield to risk through fees and discounts.

Governmental manipulation of the money market and direct Federal intervention in the mortgage market through selective credit controls are strong influences in determining the level of mortgage interest rates. Federal Reserve policies are directed to commercial banks but have an impact in the general capital market. Through variations in the rediscount rate and in reserve requirements, the volume of credit can be modulated to the extent that a somewhat delayed and dampened effect will be felt on the availability of mortgage money and, ultimately, on its price. The open market operations of the Reserve authorities in government securities will have an influence on the flow of investment funds. These devices may be used as a stimulant for a lagging economy, or at another time, restriction of credit and rising interest rates may be a part of government policy in combating inflation. In either case the real estate market will feel the effects.

The policies of the Treasury Department in the management of the public debt can affect the supply and price of credit. When government borrowing is primarily in short-term obligations the competition with mortgage money is indirect; but when long-term government securities are issued there is direct competition. At times the results can be drastic, as at the issue by the Treasury of the "Magic 5s" in 1959, an issue so attractive to private investors that millions of dollars were withdrawn from savings institutions and invested in these securities. The result was to reduce the funds available for mortgage credit.

Direct intervention by the Federal government in the mortgage market comes through FHA, VA, FNMA, and the FHLB System. The maximum rates permitted on FHA and VA mortgages have, in the past more than recently, strongly influenced the rates on conventional loans. When ample supplies of mortgage money were available, as in the immediate postwar period, rates on conventional mortgages could not move too far above the rates on government-underwritten mortgages. But more recently, with conditions of stringency appearing with greater frequency in the mortgage market, and with a continually rising level of property values and general prosperity, the appeal of the government protection has weakened. Rates on conventional mortgages have been pushed up well above the FHA and VA limits.

The effect on mortgage interest rates which is exercised by FNMA is through its secondary market operations. In times of credit shortage mortgages are purchased, and the new funds which infuse the market weaken the upward pressure on interest rates. When funds are seeking investment interest rates are supported by the purchase of mortgages. The FHLB provides a credit reserve which may be drawn upon by member institutions when money is tight. As a regulatory body, the FHLB Board can influence the supply of loanable funds in its member institutions by modifying the required liquidity ratio, i.e., the proportion of their assets which must be kept in cash or government securities.

The price of credit is not always expressed by the interest rate stated in the mortgage note. The price of credit should be properly measured by the effective rate of interest which may differ from the contract rate. Such differences occur when the lender levies a charge on the borrower, popularly known as "points," as a fee for making the loan and as a method of adjusting the contract rate so that the actual yield on the investment conforms to the market rate of interest. Regardless of the objective, the levy of one or more points, or percentage points, at the time the loan is made, has the effect of increasing the cost of money to the borrower and the return to the lender. On a $10,000 5 per cent twenty-year loan, a five-point discount means that the borrower receives a net proceeds of $9,500 but must repay the face value of the loan, or $10,000. The effective rate on the money which he actually receives, $9,500, is thus raised to 5.4 per cent. A ten-point charge would result in an effective rate of nearly 6 per cent.

Lenders resort to this device of points under various circumstances. In the case of conventional loans, it may be a first step toward raising contract interest rates early in a period of credit stringency. With borrowers bidding up the price of money by the pressure of their demands, lenders may be reluctant for a time to formally raise interest rates and prefer to use this discount device to secure the higher yield which money market conditions justify. Thus if the credit stringency is temporary, there will be no need to formally reduce interest rates from a higher level when money again becomes plentiful.

The practice of charging points in recent years has been popularized by the reluctance of the Federal government to increase maximum FHA and VA interest rates fast enough to keep pace with the general rise in rate in the capital market and the mortgage market in particular. The rigidity of FHA and VA rates has necessitated the widespread use of discounts and premiums to make adjustments to changing market conditions. Premiums appear when, in the face of a surplus of funds seeking investment, investors offer to purchase existing mortgages at more than par; in these cases a premium is paid above the unpaid balance of the loan which effects a reduction in the yield on the actual investment to that level below the contract interest rate which the investor is willing to accept in light of money market conditions. During the last few years credit stringency has been more characteristic of the market than credit ease so that discounts have been widespread and premiums few.

A borrower on an FHA-insured mortgage, which in 1960 was limited to $5\frac{1}{4}$ per cent interest plus $\frac{1}{2}$ per cent mortgage insurance premium, might have to pay several points in order to induce a lender to make the loan in face of going rates on conventional loans at 6 to $6\frac{1}{2}$ per cent. Federal regulations limit the number of points which a borrower is permitted to pay. Where this limit is unrealistic, the seller of the property is required to pay the excess over the limit but often manages to recapture this amount in a higher price for the property. In the extensive trading in FHA and VA mortgages in the secondary mortgage market, prices which are quoted and paid, as in the corporate bond market, tend to adjust the effective interest rate to the market rate. Thus in May, 1960, VA mortgages carrying $5\frac{1}{4}$ per cent contract interest rate were quoted at 92, or an 8 per cent discount.

A variation of this method of interest rate adjustment frequently occurs in connection with the use of land contracts and junior mortgages. Contract interest rates are higher on these instruments than on first mortgages, but the effective rates demanded by many investors in land contracts and second mortgage are very much higher than the typical contract interest rates. These investments are often quite risky, and the $6\frac{1}{2}$ to $7\frac{1}{2}$ per cent rates at which they are often written are not sufficiently attractive. However, instead of charging a fee or discounting the loan as in the case of the first mortgage, a common practice is to increase the purchase price of the property which is being acquired with the aid of this form of shoestring financing. The increase in the price has the same effect as charging a fee in so far as the additional burden which the borrower must bear. Builders who find it necessary, in order to effect the sale of a house, to take back a second mortgage or to sell on land contract, will increase the price of the house by the amount which they know will be necessary to discount the instrument when turning it into cash by selling it to an investor. This discount may be as much as 20 to 30 per cent. For example, a $2,000 7 per cent five-year second mortgage which is discounted at 20 per cent, or $400, will yield 18.7 per cent to the buyer of the security, and at the same time, represents a corresponding burden on the home buyer who probably paid about $400 extra for the house for the privilege of a low down payment.

VIII

PROBLEMS OF HOME
INVESTMENT

INTRODUCTION

There are some 30 million homeowners in the urban areas of this country representing about 60 per cent of all nonfarm families. Each year about 4 to 4½ million families invest in homes of their own, making home purchase the most frequent type of real estate investment transaction. In 1959, 80 per cent of all new urban dwellings were built for owner-occupancy. With the proportion of home ownership continuing at a high level and with the great prospective growth of our cities, home investment is steadily increasing in its social and economic impact.

This chapter deals with the decisions which the homeowner must make from the time he first seriously considers the possibility of moving from rented quarters into a home of his own. It carries through the real estate and financial problems encountered during his occupancy to the time when he liquidates the home investment by sale.

Homeownership in this country is characterized not only by its pervasiveness but also by its great relative importance as a repository for family savings. Some one-half of all urban homes are held free of debt, though few of them were originally acquired without the aid of credit. For most home-owning families home purchase is the greatest financial undertaking, and, in time, as the debt is retired it becomes the largest single asset and a very high proportion of total family assets. Except for a relatively small proportion of families, mainly in large metropolitan areas, homeownership is the common goal of all young couples; it represents a cherished way of life and is the expected living arrangement of those who value social status. Homeowners on the average live in better accommodations than tenants, in better locations, and have higher incomes.

Homeownership has become so common an experience on the American scene that the home purchase transaction has largely lost its terror. It

186

is far from uncommon for a family to occupy three or four owned homes during the family cycle; and the average duration of occupancy is said to be about ten years. The rising turnover rate is, in part, a reflection of employment mobility which leads to frequent job changes and locational shifts. Furthermore, there appears to be an increasing tendency for families to adjust to changes in family composition and income by a change in homes.

Though the mechanics of home purchase is widely understood, sound home investment decisions are by no means universal. There is need for a better understanding of the nature of the home investment in order that family objectives may be attained and that the maximum in satisfactions may be derived from each dollar invested.

TO OWN OR TO RENT?

In terms of long-run objectives this alternative has no meaning for most American families. Homeownership is the accepted way of life and the almost universal goal. True, there are families in large cities who prefer the convenience of location and the freedom of responsibility which rental quarters can provide. There are people who were raised in neighborhoods of flats, tenements, or apartments and for whom homeownership is so foreign from their own experience that it has no appeal. There are those among lower-income groups who assume that homeownership is beyond reach. And in every corner of the country and in every walk of life, there are those who simply do not want to be bothered with the homey jobs of maintenance and upkeep which so many homeowners truly enjoy. Finally, the aged and the physically handicapped may find rental dwellings less demanding on their limited strength and energy.

But at some time almost every family considers the pros and cons of homeownership. Though there are many variations, the general choice in living accommodations is between a free-standing single-family house with a yard, and a flat or apartment in a multifamily structure with little or no attached open space. The rental unit is typically located in the older, more central, and more congested part of town, while the house is in suburbs in a newly built neighborhood peopled with families of similar age, composition, and income level. Family circumstances, particularly family composition, will strongly influence the relative evaluation of these two ways of life. The family with growing children values suburban living above convenience; the old couple prefers to live close to downtown facilities and to be free from yard work and snow shoveling. In short, the choice of a way of life as conditioned by living quarters and their location is largely based on subjective considerations not to be judged by others.

For some time there has been a developing trend toward locating rental units in outlying locations. Attractive garden apartment developments of low density provide a living environment which reduces the differential advantage of a free-standing home. The convenience of a compact dwelling and freedom from maintenance responsibilities when coupled with open planning, "tot lots," and parklike areas, appeals to families with preschool children, working couples, and childless families.

The question of whether it is cheaper to own or to rent deserves short shrift. Few people actually seek the answer; the nearest issue is a matching of the satisfactions of tenancy related to its cost against the satisfactions of homeownership related to its cost. An attempt at direct comparison of tenants' and owners' costs is fruitless for these reasons:

1. In real life the comparison is not between equivalent dwellings and thus not between equal services received.

2. The costs of different dwelling types are not comparable.

3. One of the largest costs of homeownership (depreciation) is not determinable without knowing the cost of acquisition and the proceeds from the sale at disposition. But the selling price will be strongly influenced by market conditions at time of sale, which is indeterminate.

4. In a changing housing market there are times when ownership is a better bargain, and there are other times when market conditions favor tenancy.

The true financial issue of homeownership is whether the family can meet the financial obligations without sacrifice of other essentials. In many instances sacrifice is required; undertaking the purchase and maintenance of a house calls for reductions in other outlays, and the choice is open to each family. But in no event should the health and happiness of any member be endangered. Within this limit, if the family chooses to spend its income for a home instead of a vacation trip, a new car, or a fur coat, the only financial test is whether it can be accomplished without sacrifice of essentials or without the assumption of a burden so onerous as to destroy the peace and tranquility of home life.

Certain financial advantages of homeownership are frequently presented by its proponents:

1. It is an excellent and safe depository of savings; a hedge against inflation.

2. Payments on the mortgage represent enforced savings which might not be accumulated but for the contractual obligation.

3. Homeownership is an aid in establishing a favorable credit standing.

4. Income tax regulations permit the deduction of property taxes and interest on the mortgage debt.

5. When the homeowner sells his home at more than he paid for it, he is subject to no capital gains tax provided that he purchases another home of at least equal value within a year.

On the other hand, the tenant retains greater financial flexibility. At the end of his lease term he is free to adjust his housing expenditure to either a decreased or an increased income by moving to another dwelling.

INVESTMENT CONSIDERATIONS

Though the home investor buys primarily for use, he should and usually does attempt to evaluate the investment qualities of the property. It is true that the use-value of the structure will continue undiminished during his ownership so long as he maintains the property in good physical condition. However, obsolescence in design and equipment or changes in the environment may reduce the satisfactions of living for his family. From a financial standpoint he is concerned with the preservation of the capital which he commits to his home in his down payment and principal payments on the debt. The hazards to this investment are (1) a fall in market value as of the time when the homeowner may wish to or be forced to sell and (2) the chance that the fixed financial charges—taxes, insurance, and mortgage payments—may become so burdensome that foreclosure and loss of the property will ensue.

With respect to the market or liquidation value of the home, the typical home buyer is necessarily somewhat vague in his expectations. His aim is clear enough, to procure as high a price as possible when he sells. But he cannot predict when he will sell, whether he will be under compulsion to sell quickly, or whether he will be in a position to hold for the most favorable market conditions. Recent years of constantly rising real estate values have led him to hope to sell out at more than he paid. He typically fails to follow the usual business practice of periodically reducing the book value of his investment by a deduction for depreciation. He may not recognize in his calculations that with the passage of time and with continued use a house suffers physical deterioration and obsolescence which reduces its value. This fact is not changed even though pressures of market shortages and inflation may, as they have in recent years, more than counterbalance the value-reducing effects of age, wear and tear, obsolescence in design and equipment, and deteriorating neighborhood. But regardless of the homeowner's bookkeeping or lack of it, he aims to preserve as much of his capital as possible while still attaining his nonfinancial objective of a cherished way of life for his family. To assure the maximum dollar return when he sells, he should therefore choose a property with a view to its ability to resist the forces of deterioration and obsolescence. In this respect his objective precisely parallels that of the mortgage lender who helps him to finance the purchase, for the lender is partial to real estate collateral which promises to be relatively stable in value. But we should not forget that though the objective may be the same, the home buyer will be strongly influenced in his final decision to invest by non-financial considerations.

In a relatively small number of cases the home buyer plans to secure a capital gain by buying at a bargain price and reselling later at a profit. Or he may purchase in anticipation of a general rise in real estate prices, or in a neighborhood which he believes is developing favorably and where home values will probably increase. This kind of investor protects himself by investing in a capital object which he can use while awaiting the expected increase in value and which he can continue to use if the expected value fails to materialize. Investment for capital gain in general has been discussed in Chapter VI.

TYPES OF PROPERTY

The most common physical form of the capital investment of the home buyer is the familiar single-family free-standing house and lot. However, in many areas, particularly in the East, each separate unit of a two-family, side-by-side structure may be individually owned. Likewise, there is often individual ownership of each dwelling unit in a row house structure containing several self-contained living quarters separated by common walls. The cooperative form of organization provides for individual ownership in all but a strictly legal sense for each dwelling unit in an apartment structure. The cooperative development of a group of single-family homes is generally intended to eventuate in separate ownerships.

The home investor has the choice of buying an existing home or building one to suit his requirements. He may balance a newly completed house in a suburban neighborhood against an older home in a mature area. The advantages of an older house in an established neighborhood are that (1) the buyer can see exactly what he is getting in the house and does not have to try to visualize it from a set of blueprints; (2) the house has been physically shaken down; structural faults are evident or have been corrected; (3) there is probably more usable space per dollar of investment than would be secured in a new house though the home lacks the first blush of newness and may suffer from some obsolescence in design and equipment; and (4) the neighborhood is fully built up and its character established in contrast with a new, partly filled area where the desirability of later homes and neighbors may be in question. A carefully selected older home in a protected neighborhood, which can be acquired at a price which properly reflects accrued depreciation, can be a stable investment. The chances of a capital gain are not good, but an investment loss is more unlikely than in some new areas.

A home investment in a new and partially developed neighborhood is subject to certain hazards:

1. Unless protected by deed restrictions the character of future homes may be less desirable than those already completed. This change could come about as a result of changing economic conditions which produce declining levels of income, or changes in environmental conditions which reduce the desirability of the neighborhood.

2. Unless the open areas in the vicinity are protected by zoning or deed restrictions against undesirable uses their development for commercial or industrial use might be detrimental.

3. Changes in the highway system or in transport routes might make the neighborhood less convenient to places of employment or shopping.

4. Changes in market conditions or in the environmental situation might stop or delay the further development of the neighborhood.

5. There are many factors which might bring about long delays in the provision of the essential facilities and services such as school, sewerage, water, shopping areas, and public transportation. The lack of such facilities is costly in time, convenience, and money.

These investment hazards show the importance of a careful analysis of the location of the neighborhood within the structure of the urban area and a study of the dynamics of growth as a basis for forecasting changes in the environment. If the growth forces are favorable the future development of the neighborhood will probably sustain values. In any event, the existence of legal protective devices such as zoning and deed restrictions are of great importance. An effective local subdivision ordinance will guide the development of surrounding open spaces in a beneficial manner. Where a master plan or official map has been prepared by the local or regional planning authority the future of the area can be more dependably predicted.

Offsetting the investment hazards of a partially developed neighborhood, there are real potentials for value increase in a well-located adequately protected area. Land values typically increase during the time when a new subdivision is filling up with homes. As the street improvements are completed, the houses landscaped, and the park strips planted, the area becomes more attractive physically; as it fills up with families with children, it becomes more appealing to other families with children; as neighborhood facilities such as schools, churches, parks, and shops are installed it becomes a more convenient place to live. These changes lead later buyers to pay higher prices for building lots than did the pioneers, and tend to push up the prices of homes for sale. The tendency for values to rise diminishes as the area matures. Values then level off to a plateau for some time until the forces of depreciation and obsolescence begin to be reflected in slowly declining sales prices.

In acquiring a new and previously unoccupied house, a buyer makes a choice between a custom-built architect-designed home built on contract to suit his own tastes and needs, and the standard product of a speculative home builder already built and ready to move into or to be built on order from a model house or plan book. The custom-built home will no doubt provide the greatest satisfactions of use and possession but these values are gained at a higher price as suggested by the following points:

1. The owner will inevitably end up with a larger investment and thus a larger financial burden than he anticipated.

2. Through inexperience or ignorance he may make mistakes in design or structural quality which will add to costs or reduce resale value.

3. If the house departs too far in design from the conventional, its future salability will be hampered and the liquidation value diminished. Mortgage lenders are generally conservative, and there may be difficulty in securing the required credit.

4. For equal space and the same basic facilities the custom-built house will cost more than the more standard home offered by the operative builder.

5. The project will require a considerable investment in time, effort, and frustration on the part of the owner during the planning phase and construction operations.

6. The greater over-all period of time for planning and construction adds costs and delays occupancy.

Cooperative Home Investment

In the interests of economy prospective homeowners sometimes band together in a cooperative organization to provide housing for the members. The assumption is that by wholesale purchases of land, materials, and professional services, good housing can be produced at a lower cost. Where individual houses are built, each member usually takes title to the completed home with its own parcel of land. Where the project is in the form of multifamily housing the ownership is in a corporation of which the cooperators are the members. Each member is assigned an apartment which he may occupy as long as he pays his share of operating expenses and debt service.

The success of housing cooperatives depends to a considerable extent on the quality of management and upon the ability of the members to agree. Many such ventures have failed because of the inexperience of the leaders and the difficulties in arriving at agreements among the members on essential matters of planning or organization. The most successful housing cooperatives have been operations large enough to hire professional management and are composed of members of relatively homogeneous social and economic backgrounds so that differences of opinion are minimized. Where these conditions do not exist the expectations of cost savings are often unrealized; poor management and internal discord are not productive of economies. The prospective investor in a housing cooperative should assure himself on these points before committing his capital.

Another important concern of the investor should be the provisions for the withdrawal of a member. Some plans provide for buying out the interest of any member who wishes to withdraw. If the provisions for repurchase are too liberal this may be a potential source of danger to the whole cooperative should too many members elect to withdraw at the same time. If the repurchased shares cannot be promptly sold to new members, the remaining members may not be able to carry the full burden of operating expenses and debt service.

A sounder scheme is to make the withdrawing member responsible for finding a purchaser for his share, usually limited to someone acceptable to the co-op; the co-op reserves the privilege of purchase at its option. In this case the original cooperative investor takes the risk of selling at a loss. Many co-ops contain restrictions on selling at a profit.

HOW MUCH SHOULD WE PAY FOR A HOME?

The question of how much a family can afford to pay for a home is not answerable by a simple ratio. Yet, it is very common, and too often very misleading, for bankers or real estate brokers to use such crude rules of thumb as "two and one half times income." Another common recommendation is to spend no more than 25 per cent of income for housing. The facts are that sound and satisfying homeownership can and does exist over a very wide range of ratios between income and the financial measures of housing cost. The only satisfactory answer to this question requires as a first step, an evaluation of all family obligations other than housing and a determination of the residual resources in assets and income which are available for housing. With such an estimate it is possible to calculate how much of a debt can be supported and thus how much total capital, equity investment, and borrowed funds, can be assembled for home purchase.

The three fundamental dimensions of the home investor's financial situation which influence the financial arrangements which he can make for home purchase are:

1. Assets—the nature as well as the amount; the ease with which they can be converted into cash by sale or as collateral for a loan with a minimum of delay and cost; the present rate of return on invested assets; potential cash in form of a gift or loan from friendly sources. The amount of his assets will determine the upper limit of his down payment, and the nature of the assets and his obligations will affect his decision on how much of his assets he should convert into cash for home investment and what should be kept intact for other purposes.

2. Earning capacity—present rate of family earned income; stability, dependability, and trends of earnings. The present level of earnings will indicate the level of outlays on the home which can be supported but the prospective trends in earnings will help to determine an appropriate long-range pattern of payments.

3. Obligations—debts, contractual payments, and present and prospective family expenses. Present and prospective financial and family expense obligations will be factors in determining the amount of assets and income available for housing.

A first step in the evaluation of the home investor's financial position is a listing of assets which can be converted into cash for a down payment. This list should include assets which can be used as collateral for loans as well as sources of gifts or loans from friends and relatives. The following list suggests the usual items:

Checking account
Savings account
Bonds (market value less broker's fees)
Stock (market value less broker's fees)
Real estate (market value of equity less broker's commission)
Life insurance (loan value)
Potential gifts
Potential loans from relatives (interest rate, terms of repayment)

The analysis of earning capacity must cover both the present and the prospective levels of income. In occupations where earnings fluctuate, such as in selling on commission, the average income based on the last three to five years is a sounder basis for judgment than the income for any one year. The earnings of secondary workers, wives and children, should be judged in terms of how long they can be counted on. Income other than earned income—from investments, roomers, gifts—must also be evaluated in terms of reliability and duration.

It is true not only that the contributions of secondary earners will not always continue indefinitely at the same level, but also that the level of income of the primary earner may change. If a decrease is probable it would not be wise to undertake a long-term obligation which can be met only if the present level of income continues. For example, a buyer well along in years may expect a declining income in many kinds of occupation. On the other hand, his family living obligations will probably decline as an offset. The important point here is that both income and obligations must be forecast over the period of the proposed mortgage loan contract in order to judge the probabilities that payments can be met over its entire term.

Obligations must be deducted from income to determine the balance available for housing expense and home investment. The first deduction is the income tax and the deduction for retirement benefits and other regular withholdings. Figured on a weekly or monthly basis the balance is the equivalent of take-home pay. Other regular obligations include food and clothing, medical care, life insurance and savings, transportation (including car expense), and installment payments on appliances and furniture. The balance left at this point is that available for housing—mortgage interest and principal payments, taxes, insurance, maintenance, fuel, and utilities. Estimates for any given house covering taxes, insurance, maintenance, fuel, and utilities can be deducted to arrive at the maximum available for mortgage payments of principal and interest. This potential payment can be converted into the amount of mortgage debt which can be serviced. By subtracting the sum which can be borrowed from the price of the house the buyer can calculate the necessary equity contribution he will have to make. Or by adding the amount which can be borrowed to the sum of the liquid assets which the buyer has available for a down payment he can establish the maximum price he can afford.

The field offices of one of the government mortgage agencies employs a short-cut approach to estimating a borrower's ability to pay for a home. This method has the important virtue of recognizing the well-established fact that the percentage of income actually devoted to housing tends to be in inverse proportion to the level of income.

Percentage of Expense to Income

Net effective income	Typical to maximum housing expense	Ratio in percentage
$250	$ 93–$107	37–43
300	97– 115	32–38
350	101– 122	29–35
400	114– 128	28–32
450	120– 137	27–30
500	127– 143	25–29
550	135– 150	24–27
600	142– 157	24–26
650	148– 165	23–25
700	157– 172	22–24

The first step in this system is to determine *monthly net effective income*, or the family income from all sources which can be expected to continue less withholdings, or take-home pay. Then the *monthly prospective housing expense* is estimated including hazard insurance, taxes on the property, utilities and heat, maintenance, and debt service. This estimate requires the assumption of a specific property and a given mortgage debt and terms.

The ratio between housing expense and effective income is calculated and matched against the table on page 195 to determine whether it falls within the acceptable range. This range of acceptable relationships is based on a tabulation of actual mortgage situations modified by the judgment of informed and experienced practitioners in mortgage lending. In practice, it is used as a guide and not as an arbitrary and final test.

FINANCING PATTERNS

Among the determinants of the financial burden of homeownership are the terms of the mortgage contract. These terms are the major elements of the home-financing pattern which includes the following:

Amount of equity investment
Amount of the borrowed capital
Interest rate on borrowed capital
Schedule of repayment (amortization) of borrowed capital

In earlier chapters it has been made clear that by varying the elements to create different combinations we can adjust the debt burden in level and timing. As a basis for determining the financing pattern and adjusting it to the requirements of the borrower, the two significant financial variables are (1) the liquid assets which the borrower can use for the down payment or equity investment and (2) the level and prospective pattern of his income available for housing.

In the case where liquid assets are ample and income is high there is no difficulty in working out a mortgage pattern that will fit the borrower's needs. But in the typical case resources must be strained to permit the purchase of a home of the size and quality desired. To a considerable extent, in homes as in cars, American families find that their tastes outrun their pocketbooks. The following discussion aims to show to what extent it is possible to adapt the mortgage terms to the financial capacity of the home buyer that he may enjoy the best possible dwelling under the given circumstances. We shall consider the case of a family with adequate assets but a low income, a family with restricted assets but a good income, and a family with low financial capacity in both respects.

Adequate Assets—Low Income

The problem here is that the income available for housing is too low to meet the payments on a loan even after all available assets have been used to make up the down payment and reduce the loan to a minimum. A longer repayment period to reduce monthly payments might be justified if the borrower is young with a stable income and if the collateral property is new and well located. If the borrower has good prospects of an increased income, and if the property is relatively new, the lender might be willing to reduce principal payments during the early years. The FHA and VA plans offer longer repayment periods than most conventional loans. Savings and loan associations and life insurance companies will lend for longer terms than banks. It might be necessary to pay a somewhat higher interest rate for the privilege of slow amortization and a longer term.

The principle of consolidating debts to reduce the total burden is practiced at the instance of some lending institutions which require borrowers to pay up all special assessments for water, sewerage, and other improvements at the time of purchasing the home. Such assessments are usually spread over eight to ten years with an interest charge of 5 to 6 per cent. By the advance payment of these obligations the reduction of the debt to the municipality will increase the value of the property by an equal amount. This increase can then be covered by mortgage credit in the same proportion as the total mortgage bears to the total value. Thus in the case of an 80 per cent mortgage, the owner out of his own assets would reduce by 20 per cent the amount owed by reason of the assessments, and the balance would be paid out of mortgage proceeds and consolidated with the mortgage debt to be repaid on easier terms at a reduced burden.

Low Assets—Adequate Income

When the borrower cannot meet the minimum down payment requirements for a conventional loan, even after borrowing on life insurance and getting help from relatives, the VA and FHA plans offer the most promise, in that order. If eligible for veteran's benefits the borrower may have a loan guaranteed by VA with as little as nothing down, provided that he can find a willing lender. The FHA plan permits down payments as low as 3 per cent on homes in certain value classes.

If his income permits him to make large monthly payments the borrower will have a better chance to arrange for the seller of the property to finance the transaction by taking back a first or second purchase money mortgage or selling on land contract. In either case the large monthly payments will reduce the debt rapidly to a point where the buyer will be able to refinance with a savings and loan association or bank and pay off the seller. The ability to make large regular payments might also permit the use of a higher interest rate or a discount to attract a liberal loan from a private individual. Junior mortgage financing is a common solution in such cases.

The purchase of a new home is generally the occasion for acquiring expensive appliances and furnishings such as a stove, a refrigerator, and carpeting. Short-term credit for such purposes is expensive in interest rate and burdensome because of short terms of repayment. Some lenders will increase the mortgage loan to cover these items and thus give the borrower the advantage of lower interest rates and a long term for repayment. This "package mortgage" device is useful for all borrowers but particularly for the home buyer whose assets are insufficient both to cover the required down payment and to equip and furnish the new home properly. This method of financing reduces investment risk both for borrower and lender by reducing the total burden of all debts in relation to income.

Another plan, known as "lease-option," involves the leasing of the property with an option to the tenant to purchase the property at a stipulated price. A part of his rental payment is used to build up a down payment which is credited to him when he exercises the option.

Low Assets—Low Income

Where the buyer is low on both assets and income home purchase is probably financially unwise. Sometimes he may make homeownership possible by reducing his aspirations to the level of his pocketbook and accepting a more modest home.

Sellers in a slow market, or who are offering properties with less attractive qualities of design, condition, or location, may be willing to assist the buyer in financing his purchase. Sale with a low down payment and low monthly payments might be arranged under a land contract purchase or with a small down payment and a purchase-money first or second mortgage taken back by the seller. In the purchase of a new house, arrangements can sometimes be made for the buyer to receive credit toward building up an equity in return for his own labor in completing the structure or in the case of an older home, for work done in modernization and improvement. This form of capital contribution is popularly known as "sweat equity."

The lease-option plan might be used, but since rental payments will be low it will take a long time to build up an equity. However, this method will permit the buyer to live in the house and to get some credit for his rent on the purchase.

COSTS OF CREDIT

Among a borrower's objectives in working out a financing pattern for his home investment is to keep financing costs as well as financing burdens at a minimum. The burdens of financing are measured by the actual outlays of cash required at the time the loan is placed and the periodic outlays in the form of mortgage payments. For example, many monthly contractual mortgage payments include one-twelfth of estimated annual taxes and insurance. But these items are not financing costs. Further, a correct definition of cost does not include that portion of the payment which covers debt retirement. While all borrowers aim to keep costs at a minimum, most of them are equally concerned with minimizing the periodic outlay or burden. However, borrowers whose income is sufficient may have good reason to prefer larger payments or outlays in order to speed the repayment of the debt for the purpose of stopping interest costs.

Interest on borrowed funds is generally viewed as a burdensome cost of financing. Lower interest rates are certainly to be sought as a method of reducing this burden, and any reduction in the level of periodic interest payments is an advantage. However, the view that a large down payment or an accelerated schedule of amortization will reduce the total interest cost is misleading. True, fewer total dollars will be paid out to the lender in interest charges. But on the other hand, from an investment standpoint, there is an imputed interest charge on the capital which the owner invests; by investing in his own home, he deprives himself of a return which he might be receiving in cash were the capital invested in stocks or bonds or mortgages on the homes of others. While the charge for the use of his own capital is not a contractual cash outlay, it is nonetheless a real cost. The homeowner must recognize an interest cost on all capital invested in his home be it equity or debt. In summary, it may be said that it is sound personal finance to make a down payment of sufficient size to provide a safe equity and to reduce the monthly housing outlays to a safe level. It is sound to step up debt reduction payments until a safe equity has been created. But it is not a true argument in favor of either expedient to point to a reduction in total interest costs in the amount of interest payments stopped. There may be some saving in interest costs, it is true, provided that the borrower is able to earn less on the capital under his control than the rate he pays on the mortgage. Thus, if the option is to pay off a portion of mortgage principal on which 5 per cent interest is being paid or to invest in government bonds at 4 per cent, a saving in interest cost of 1 per cent will result from paying off the mortgage. But if the owner can secure a yield of 5½ per cent on his money when invested in a mutual fund there is no direct financial advantage in reducing the debt.

The initial costs of mortgage financing incident to the purchase of property may include both (a) charges for business services and (b) advance payment of interest by way of a mortgage discount. These items vary among lenders and among VA, FHA, and conventional types of loan. There is also variance over time with changing demand and supply relationships in the mortgage market.

The charges for business and professional services may cover some or all of the following:

1. Credit report: to assist the lender in judging mortgagor risk.

2. Appraisal report: to establish value for lending purposes and to aid in the evaluation of property and neighborhood risk.

3. Property survey: to establish the exact location of the property.

4. Title insurance and legal expense: to protect the lender against loss arising from title defects. Where title insurance is not required, the borrower may be required to have his abstract of title brought down to date and to pay the costs of examination of title by an attorney for the benefit of the lender.

5. Mortgage recording: to cover the costs of public recording of the mortgage instrument.

6. Closing costs: to cover clerical and administrative costs as incurred by the lender in making the loan. In the case of a construction loan the charge is higher because of the additional work required. This item would include escrow fees where this method of closing is used.

7. Brokerage: a finder's fee to compensate the mortgage broker for negotiating the loan where such a service was performed.

In times of a surplus of funds seeking investment lenders may reduce or absorb some of these charges through force of competition. In times of a shortage of loanable funds lenders are able to collect the full charges and, in addition, may charge a discount on mortgage loans, i.e., pay out to the borrower from 1 to 5 per cent less than the face value of the loan which is to be repaid. The financial result of discounting is to increase the effective rate of interest or yield to the lender on the loan; a 5 per cent discount on a $10,000 fifteen-year loan at 6 per cent interest rate would result in an effective rate of 6¼ per cent paid by the borrower and earned by the lender.

SHOPPING FOR A HOME

The first step in shopping for a home is to decide on certain basic specifications with the full knowledge that no one property will fulfill all of them. Acceptable locations and neighborhoods should be identified, the minimum size of house determined, and the general price range established in light of financial capacities. It is well to avoid exact specifications and a rigid and unyielding insistence on meeting them precisely. A common experience is for a shopper to end up purchasing a house which is quite unlike the dream home which he envisioned at the start.

Purposive and methodical shopping will save money and yield greater ultimate satisfactions. It will take time and energy but will develop in the shopper a perspective on market values and a sense of discrimination among design and quality characteristics. After a careful study of many homes offered for sale he is less likely to overlook important defects or to pay more than a justified market price for the home which he selects.

Where to Look

Shopping for a home usually starts with the classified ad section of the local newspaper. For-sale signs are a common indication of availability. Real estate brokers have their own listings of houses for sale, and where a multiple listing system is in use each broker has information on the listings of all other brokers. Builders advertise their products in newspapers in classified and display ads; they use radio and television as do many brokers. A valuable source of information is word-of mouth notice of intent to sell which passes among friends and acquaintances. Buyers who are determined to find a home in a certain neighborhood have been known to canvass the area house by house to inquire whether anyone knows of a house for sale now or which is soon to come onto the market.

It is a common belief, often misleading, that a house can be purchased at a lower price by going directly to the owner and short-circuiting the real estate broker, thus saving the commission. In some cases some saving may be the result, for brokers' commissions at 5 to 6 per cent amount to no inconsiderable sum on even a moderately priced home. Of course, where the owner has an exclusive listing with a broker, it usually includes an exclusive right to sell; the commission must be paid regardless of who sells the house. Another point is that many owners who eschew the broker's services and try to sell direct have no intention of passing on to the buyer the saving of the commission. Finally, the real estate broker argues with some truth that the owner normally overvalues his property with the result that his asking price is greatly inflated; and that when the broker accepts a listing it is at a lower price more nearly at the market. The broker also points out that he is an expert negotiator and is more effective than an amateur horse trader in bringing asking price and offering price together at a reasonable figure.

Trade-in

The practice of trading in a used car on a new one has its counterpart in home investment. A family which has built up an equity in their present home may wish either a larger or a smaller one, depending on their situation. The owner may, of course, convert the equity into cash by selling the house and apply the cash to the purchase of another property. With a little searching he may find another homeowner with a suitable house who is seeking a house such as the first owner occupies now. The two owners can arrange to trade equities measured by the difference between the market value of each property and the amount of indebtedness. If there is a difference in the two equity amounts, it can be adjusted by a cash payment or by the holder of the larger equity securing the difference by a purchase-money-second mortgage to be retired by regular payments.

Some builders will accept older homes in trade on new houses. The builder will have to sell the older house to get his down payment on the new home and, to cover this risk and expense, will expect to take in the older home at something less than its probable market value. One plan used by builders is to enter into a sales contract on a new house with the down payment to be made out of the sale of the trade-in house guaranteed by the builder to be not less than a stipulated amount. The guaranteed sales price is usually 80 to 85 per cent of the expected sales price. Thus where a house owned free and clear is expected to sell for $20,000, the builder guarantees a price of $16,000, or 80 per cent, and gives the buyer credit in advance in this amount on the purchase of a new home. The buyer retains title and attempts to sell within an agreed time limit at the best possible price. If he receives more than $16,000 he may apply the difference on the purchase of the new home. If he cannot sell for more the builder takes over the house and liquidates it as best he can.

Agreements to sell are sometimes made in the form of an option for a limited time which the buyer may exercise if he can sell his present home.

Inspection

The effectiveness of inspecting a home with a view to purchase depends on the skill and knowledge of the buyer. Certainly, he is in the best position to judge the adequacy of the home to fit the requirements and living habits of his family. No one else can substitute in evaluating the aesthetic appeal of the architecture features. But in the matters of the quality of construction, the physical condition of the structure beyond the obvious surface indications, the extent of deterioration of mechanical equipment, and the reasonableness of the price, most home buyers are ill equipped to judge. Even in the analysis of the neighborhood, though the buyer is competent to appraise its physical appearance and to forecast whether it will provide congenial environment, there are broader and more obscure forces which are molding the future character of the area and which he may well fail to understand. A trained and competent real estate salesman is informed on all these matters. But many salesmen are not competent and informed; and there are few salesmen, earning a commission only when a sale is made, who are able to give truly objective counsel to the prospect.

In light of the large investment which a home represents the prospective owner is well advised to hire competent and objective professional counsel to cover his own ignorance and inexperience. For a small fee relative to the price of the house a professional appraiser will inspect the property and the neighborhood and evaluate the physical and economic aspects of the house. He will point out all defects and indicate a reasonable market value. Should there be any legal or engineering problems beyond his ability to judge, he will so indicate. With such professional counsel the home buyer can avoid serious and costly mistakes.

Offer to Purchase

In addition to expert counsel on what price to offer, the amateur home buyer needs guidance on the form and content of the offer. It must be in writing to be enforceable; thus a verbal proposition will not be taken seriously by the seller. He cannot be expected to commit himself beyond reprieve unless the buyer does likewise. A written offer meeting the formalities of the law is irrevocable once it is accepted so that it is highly important that the writing be proper and complete. A competent realtor or a lawyer can provide counsel on this matter; many brokers are equipped with printed "offer to purchase" forms which meet the requirements of the state statutes when properly filled in and signed.

The most important part of the preparation of the offer is to assure its completeness; all aspects of the intended agreement must be covered in clear and unequivocal fashion so that no disputes will arise later because of omissions or misunderstandings. Some of the more important components of the offer are:

1. Exact description of the real estate
2. Listing of any items of personal property which are included in the sale and any fixtures which are to be excluded
3. Complete description of any encumbrances which are to be assumed by the buyer such as mortgages or unpaid special assessments
4. Statement of any conditions limiting the offer, such as a provision which voids the offer if the buyer is unable to arrange satisfactory financing
5. The purchase price, the amount of earnest money payment accompanying the offer, and the manner and timing of the payment of the balance
6. The kind of deed which the seller is to sign and the exact name or names of the grantee
7. The date for closing the sale and the date for giving over possession of the property
8. The provision for prorating taxes and insurance premiums
9. The names of the parties to the contract

The haggling in the real estate market place is traditional. The asking price is usually higher than the owner is willing to accept, and the original offer is typically lower than the buyer is willing to pay. As a result of the bargaining margin incorporated in the transaction by each party, a number of offers and counteroffers are usually made before an agreement is reached. Where a real estate broker is involved he serves as go-between, pursuading the buyer to raise his offer and encouraging the seller to lower his price until a figure mutually acceptable is attained. If he serves his principal well the real estate agent will not attempt to force the price below a fair market value. Thus, the buyer may expect no help from the broker in getting a bargain.

The prospective buyer of a home needs three different value figures in mind as he enters negotiation:

1. The price at which a property of substantially the same type and quality can be built or purchased in the current market
2. The price he will pay, if necessary, in order to acquire the home
3. The lowest price which the seller will accept

This last figure he will have no way of knowing at the outset. In fact, the seller does not know what he will do until he has a bona fide offer in hand. But as negotiations proceed, the buyer or the broker will begin to get a feel of the seller's attitude. The successful negotiators are those who can read this attitude correctly.

On his part, the buyer may not really know what he is willing to pay until threatened with losing the opportunity. It is probable that most buyers pay more than they intended to; and of most sellers it can be said that they rarely receive what they had originally set as a bottom price.

The current market value of the house is determinable within fairly close limits. The buyer will have a fair notion of it as a result of his shopping experience. But a much more dependable figure can be secured as small cost from a professional appraiser. Armed with such a figure the buyer can bargain with greater confidence and better results.

Before making a firm offer in writing, the amateur buyer is normally beset with misgivings that he might be able to buy at a lower price than he intends to propose. But if he is not offering more than he believes the home to be worth to himself and his family, or more than he need pay for another equally attractive home, he cannot be damaged. To buy at a lower price would be a windfall—nice, but hardly to be expected. He may find some consolation in the same answer to his hesitation to buy now in view of the possibility that real estate prices may be lower next month or next year. Furthermore, there is an equal chance that values will rise. He should not deprive himself of the satisfactions of homeownership in confidence that he can outguess the real estate market where experts have failed.

Closing the Deal

When an offer has been accepted the final step is closing the deal. The offer provides for a time period, from thirty to sixty days, during which each party prepares to carry out his part of the bargain. The seller has the abstract brought up to date and turns it over to the buyer. He arranges for title insurance or has the title examined by his attorney.

The seller's attorney prepares the deed and any other documents for which he is responsible. The buyer arranges for financing the purchase by assembling his cash down payment and negotiating a mortgage loan, if necessary. On the appointed day, all parties with their attorneys meet to culminate the sale by exchanging the purchase price for the deed which is immediately rushed to the register of deeds office for public recording.

In many cases, the closing process is placed in the hands of an escrow agent, a specialist in real estate transactions who operates under an escrow agreement to which both buyer and seller are parties and which instructs the agent to prepare the papers and to close the deal when both parties have carried out their parts of the purchase and sale contract.

SHOPPING FOR HOME CREDIT

The picture of the banker as a hard-eyed Shylock persists among unsophisticated borrowers and is even encouraged by some mortgage lenders. The fact is that the lender is a merchant of credit who must dispose of his inventory at favorable prices if he is to prosper. He is eager to find good loans to make, and the prospective borrower with good credit standing and good property collateral is in a favorable bargaining position. Borrowers will find that shopping for credit is a common practice and will pay off in more favorable terms. Shoppers will also discover that lenders, like retail merchants, differ in the type of merchandise offered for sale. Differences are found in the ratio of loan to value, the term of repayment, amortization provisions, the level of fees and discounts, prepayment privileges, package and open-end features, and contract interest rates. All lenders will modify the nature of their offerings and its price with changes in the balance of demand and supply of funds in the money market. There are differences among localities in terms on which loans are available to the borrower.

The differences among institutions in mortgage lending policy is a reflection first of the law and regulatory controls under which each type must operate, the sources of their investment funds, and finally, a matter of individual decision. In general, savings and loan associations are able to lend at higher loan to value ratios and longer terms of repayment (70 to 90 per cent and twenty to thirty years on conventional loans) than banks and life insurance companies. However, their interest rates tend to be a bit higher. Some life insurance companies come close to matching savings and loan mortgages, but, in general, they are more conservative. National banks are restricted to twenty-year terms and loans of two-thirds value. State banks are not so restricted in most states but tend to maintain policies about the same as national banks. Mutual savings banks in many communities are competitive with savings and loan associations. Individuals with mortgage money to lend have no restrictions but, in general, seek conservative loans of 50 per cent or less in loan to value ratio and with partial amortization or none at all; terms are rarely more than ten years. Mortgage banking companies serve as correspondents of life insurance companies and otherwise engage largely in making and selling FHA and VA mortgages.

In a competitive market interest rates are usually the same for all institutions. However, some institutions may accept a lower rate on a conservative loan of 50 per cent or less of value. In general, competition among lenders is not expressed so much in interest rate cutting as in reducing fees, extending terms of repayment, and most particularly, in liberal appraisals which permit loans of larger amounts at the maximum loan to value ratio. Borrowers will also find it easier to secure prepayment privileges and open-end features in a competitive market.

When there is a shortage of loanable funds interest rates may rise, appraisals will become more conservative, fees will be increased, discounts may appear, and the banker will be more selective in choosing among loan applicants.

All institutional lenders make some FHA and VA loans. Other things being equal, they prefer to make conventional loans under their own plans in order to reduce the paper work, speed up the transaction, and in preference to paying it over to FHA, collect for themselves the equivalent of the ½ per cent mortgage insurance premium. In general, the yield to the institution on conventional loans is higher than on government-guaranteed mortgages. Banks make FHA and VA loans in part because it puts them on a competitive level with the other lenders with respect to liberality of terms. All institutions are aware of the public relations aspects and the desirability of serving customers who prefer the government programs. All institutions find some advantage in the ease with which FHA and VA mortgages can be sold in the secondary mortgage market. Finally, there may be some truth to the assertion that lenders handle the choice loans on a conventional basis and try to get government protection on the more questionable cases.

From the standpoint of the borrower, the government-guaranteed loans offer high percentage long-term mortgages which may exceed in liberality the credit available under conventional plans. The interest rate on such loans will be as low or lower than on conventional loans. In the case of a mortgage on new construction, there is the advantage of inspection by the government agencies during construction and the enforcement of reasonable standards of construction quality. The acceptance of any property as collateral for a government-guaranteed loan is evidence of having stood close inspection and analysis and having met fairly high standards of investment quality.

The disadvantages of government-guaranteed loans from the standpoint of the borrower may be found in the paper work, delays, and higher initial costs and outlays. These objections appear to be more valid in their application to FHA loans than to VA mortgages. The regulations of both agencies exclude many cases and result in a more impersonal lending procedure than where the lender is not constrained by government red tape and fiat.

PROTECTING THE HOME INVESTMENT

The home investment is exposed to several types of hazard:
1. Financial loss or even loss of ownership through defective title
2. Destruction through fire, flood, or windstorm
3. Forces of deterioration and obsolescence of structure and of environment which can diminish the use-value of the home and reduce its market value
4. Financial disability of the owner which prevents him from meeting his obligations and which may end in foreclosure and loss of part or all of his equity

This section presents methods by which these types of investment risk can be minimized.

Prevention of loss through defective title can be prevented at time of acquisition. Title insurance represents a method of shifting the risk. A careful title examination by a competent title lawyer should reveal any clouds in the title of the grantor. By insisting that these clouds be removed before closing the deal the buyer can dissipate the risk; by insisting on a warranty deed he can secure an added protection which is as strong as the financial resources of the grantor. The risk of an error in description can be removed by an engineering survey of the boundary of the property before accepting delivery of the deed.

Preserving the Property

The risk of loss from fire or from the natural forces of wind and water can be shifted through casualty insurance of various kinds. Most homes are insured, but vast numbers of them carry inadequate protection. Owners may fail to carry comprehensive coverage against all types of hazards, or the amounts of coverage may not have been increased to reflect rising costs of repair and replacement.

There should be no question of the wisdom of proper maintenance and repair of the house. Given a sufficient protection of exterior and interior surfaces with paint and the prompt repair of damage or deterioration the structure will last indefinitely. The cost of adequate maintenance will more than be repaid in the added value and utility of the property.

Deferred maintenance results in both unattractive appearance and higher ultimate costs of repair.

Developments of new appliances and gadgets, changing tastes, new standards of comfort and convenience, many forms of social and economic change—all tend to make the older home less attractive and thus less valuable in comparison with new homes. We are all familiar with similar factors of obsolescence which rapidly depreciate a new car. Many families invest substantially in modernizing their homes in order that they may enjoy a higher level of service without having to move out of a familiar and cherished neighborhood. Whether a given expenditure for modernization is sound from an investment standpoint can be determined by a relationship which is simple to understand but difficult to measure— the relationship between the cost of the improvement and the added market value of the property.

If a kitchen remodeling job costs $2,000 but increases the market value of the house by only $1,000, then it is not sound from a purely financial standpoint. If such improvement should increase the price which a buyer might be expected to pay by $2,500, while at the same time increasing the number of potential buyers because the kitchen is now modern, the expenditure is clearly a wise one. Only an experienced realtor or appraiser can estimate the effect of an improvement on market value. When putting an older house on the market it is usually a good investment, as a minimum, to freshen it up with a coat of paint, point up the masonry, and redecorate any rooms which may give a prospective buyer the impression of shabbiness.

Substantial modernization or remodeling often requires borrowing by the owner. Banks and savings and loan associations are prepared to extend credit for such purposes for terms of two to five years on an unsecured note at rates comparable to those paid on car and appliance installment loans. Many institutions insure such loans with FHA under Title I. Title I loans are limited to $3,500, with repayment period up to about five years. The VA will guarantee loans for similar purposes.

In anticipation of the time when repair, modernization, or remodeling will require borrowing, home investors would be well advised to do their underlying financing on an open-end mortgage. A usual arrangement is for the mortgagee to agree to make future advances secured by the original mortgage lien when called for by the mortgagor up to the difference between the original face of the mortgage and the unpaid balance at the time. Thus, if the mortgage loan was originally $10,000 but had been paid down to $7,500 the mortgagor could borrow $2,500. The open-end mortgage is not available in all states nor at all lending institutions. However, its use is spreading, and it now has the blessing of VA and FHA.

Protecting the Neighborhood

In progressive communities subdivision regulations and zoning powers, in conjunction with a master plan for the metropolitan area, can effectively protect neighborhoods from the encroachment of inharmonious land uses. But many new areas are in unzoned jurisdictions with no over-all planning and little control over platting. Here dependence must be placed on deed restrictions and sound subdivision design by private developers. Property owners should push for zoning and for an effective platting law at the earliest possible time.

But zoning alone is not always sufficient. Much zoning was badly conceived when adopted and needs revision; even zoning originally sound becomes obsolete if conditions change. Property owners should study their environment and petition for rezoning to correct errors in the existing ordinance. And they must be ever vigilant to see that rezoning actions instituted by others are not potentially harmful to their investments.

The value-destroying forces that accompany the aging of a neighborhood are insidious and hard to combat. They are, in part, a result of structural obsolescence but arise largely from changes in the occupancy of the homes in the area. Most new neighborhoods are originally peopled by young families who are prideful homeowners. With the passage of time, parents age, children grow up and leave home, the proportion of rented homes tends to increase, the level of maintenance drops, and values fall as the neighborhood becomes less attractive and desirable in comparison with new districts. Organized neighborhood effort can slow down this decline by motivating each homeowner to keep his property up to a high standard of attractiveness.

Financial Adjustments

The direct financial risk of homeownership is the danger of losing the home investment by reason of inability to meet the mortgage payments and taxes. These obligations must be met out of the income of the homeowner. Thus, the primarily financial risk is in proportion to the margin of safety between obligations and income. A narrow margin can be extinguished by only a small decline in income or even by an increase in taxes. When the home investment is threatened by the financial disability of the owner, there are a number of possible counter measures:

1. It may be possible for the family to move into cheaper quarters and to rent the home for enough to carry the obligations until such time as the owner gets back on his feet.

2. In a normal or favorable market the property can be sold for enough to liquidate the investor's equity.

3. If the mortgagee can be convinced that the drop in the owner's income is only temporary, he may be willing to waive principal payments for a time and accept interest only. This relief may be enough to enable the owner to continue to carry the property.

4. The mortgagee may be willing to recast or rewrite the mortgage note to reduce monthly payments to a level which the borrower can meet.

5. If the mortgagee is unwilling to make the necessary adjustments, the borrower may be able to refinance the debt on more favorable terms with another lender. This possibility suggests a reason why the mortgagor should incorporate a prepayment privilege in the original mortgage.

Wise and frugal borrowers seek to accelerate the repayment of their debts when their incomes are high or when a financial windfall comes their way. Some mortgagees will agree to accept payments in advance of the contractual schedule and credit such advance payments against later payments which the borrower cannot meet because of financial difficulties. In any event, a prepayment privilege in the mortgage is necessary to assure that the mortgagee will accept advance payments.

Serious difficulties may arise when the income of the borrower is stopped by his death. To protect his widow and family against the untimely loss of their home a borrower may take out life insurance in favor of the lender. Should he die, the proceeds will pay off the mortgage and leave the home free and clear. Some life insurance companies offer favorable mortgage terms to borrowers who will buy from them such "mortgage insurance." The premiums are added to the mortgage payments. There is no special advantage in borrowing and subscribing to insurance from the same company. Any borrower can take out additional insurance at the time he undertakes a mortgage debt on his home if he wishes to pass on his home free of debt should he die before full repayment. But many borrowers are not able to carry the extra burden of premium payments, and some family heads prefer to allow their widows a choice in the disposition of insurance proceeds rather than to commit the money in advance to the full repayment of the mortgage debt.

Insurance salesmen often watch mortgage recordings to reveal prospects. They approach the borrower and point out that he has undertaken a large financial obligation and should protect his family by carrying additional life insurance. In fact, the home buyer's net worth is no different than before his purchase. He has incurred a large debt to be sure, but at the same time he has acquired a valuable asset in his home. The balance between assets and liabilities is unchanged, but the home purchase has raised the living standards of his family. The real justification for the additional insurance, therefore, would be to permit the family to continue to live at the new high level should the borrower die.

IX

MANAGING THE INVESTMENT

INTRODUCTION

The act of investing in real estate is only the first step toward the investment objectives which prompted the commitment of capital. To produce the expected net return, the real estate enterprise must be successfully and profitably operated as a business. Thus the investor is faced with the diverse problems of managing the enterprise until such time as he liquidates his investment. Our discussion of his problems and the approach to their solution will deal primarily with income properties which produce a dollar return. This limitation rules out vacant land and owner-occupied properties. Nor shall we attempt to cover all of the aspects of general business management which are encountered in operating a real estate enterprise. Those principles and techniques which are common to all business enterprises—organization, accounting, purchasing, and personnel management for example—we will touch on only as there may be some unique or critical application in real estate management. The emphasis will be on the real estate aspects of property management which affect productivity and the preservation of capital.

In Chapter VI the various investment objectives were presented. These objectives reduce, with variations and combinations, to those of receiving an income and securing a capital gain. We shall view the principles and methods of real estate investment management as devices for (1) maximizing the productivity level of the property, (2) extending the productive life period, and as a by-product of (1) and (2), (3) preserving and enhancing the capital value. For such purposes the management functions are:

1. Merchandising space to secure a maximum gross income
2. Reducing operating and maintenance costs to produce the maximum net income
3. Reducing the financing burden
4. Adapting the property to environmental and market changes through

changes in management policy, through investing additional capital in remodeling, modernization, or additions for the purpose of either increasing gross income or reducing expenses

The special characteristics of the real estate enterprise have been outlined at various points in previous chapters. In application to the problems of managing real estate investments, the physical fixity of real estate and its durability and long life have special significance. The long life gives rise to the need for long-range planning in order that productivity in later years may not be sacrificed for short-run advantages. The fixity in terms of location and the structural rigidity of the improvements limit the extent to which physical changes can be made to sustain or increase revenues under changing market conditions. Fixity signifies vulnerability to environmental factors of location which are beyond the control of the management and to fluctuations in the real estate market. The product of the real estate enterprise can be sold only for consumption on location; the services of shelter can be enjoyed only at the point of production and cannot be shipped to other more favorable markets. Services measured in time cannot be stockpiled for future sale and use. Thus the economic value of unoccupied space dissolves and vanishes as the clock ticks.

MERCHANDISING SPACE

The subject of merchandising is presented at this point in its relationship to investment objectives and certain other management policies. For example, under certain conditions, it is possible to reduce tenant turnover by pursuing a tenant selection policy which excludes certain classes of applicants. Under other conditions, a wise and profitable policy may be to charge top rents but to accept more instable tenants. The policy on providing facilities and services in addition to shelter, such as furnishing maid service, will affect the nature of promotional efforts. When the expected life of the structure is short by reason of its physical condition or impending demolition to make way for some public improvement, merchandising will be guided by short-run considerations. These are but a few examples of relationships between merchandising policies and the underlying management objectives which reflect the nature of the property and the intentions of the investor.

Market Analysis

It is fundamental that any merchandising program must start with market analysis. The commodity must be analyzed, the prospect groups identified and their characteristics evaluated, and market conditions studied with respect to current status and outlook.

The analysis of the property from the viewpoint of tenant-prospect groups is the first step in market analysis. The purpose is to evaluate the appeal which the accommodations, location, and services will make to the various types of potential tenants. Some residential tenants seek convenience of location as a prime requisite; others are attracted to neighborhoods which have an aura of social prestige; an attractive view and outlook appeals strongly to some; the availability of various services is a consideration for many; young couples may want efficiency apartments, while families with children seek ample space, nearby schools, and play areas. For retail tenants location and environment are all important. Industrial occupants usually have more flexible locational specifications but may be more concerned with the structural facilities, transportation facilities, and employee parking areas. Office tenants seek convenience for customer and employee and often cherish a prestige address. In short, the specifications of the commodity will dictate the kinds of tenant groups which are prospects. Of course, changes can be made in some of the commodity specifications to attract other groups. This subject will be discussed later.

When residential tenant-prospect groups have been identified, an analysis of their economic characteristics will suggest the level of rents which can be expected. Their social characteristics will suggest their probable stability as tenants and thus the rate of tenant turnover to be anticipated. Other social characteristics may give an indication of the effect of their tenancy on maintenance costs.

Market analysis also includes a study of the current balance of demand and supply of space of various kinds in the local real estate market. For example, the over-all situation with respect to both sale and rental housing is relevant because of the interactions of the several submarkets. In particular, the competitive situation which directly affects the property under consideration must be carefully analyzed to judge the alternatives in respect to quality and price which are open to the prospect groups.

A market forecast is the final step in market analysis. Management policies must look to the future. If a competitive oversupply of space is in prospect extra efforts to keep present tenants are called for. If a shortage is impending greater selectivity in tenant procurement is possible, and a decrease in the advertising and promotional budget can be anticipated.

The identification of prospect groups through market analysis is a guide to promotional efforts so that advertising can be directed to produce the best results at least cost. The analysis of the economic and social characteristics of the prospect groups leads to a more realistic rental schedule and the pursuit of management policies which are suited to the expected behavior of the prospective occupants. The study of current market conditions reveals the competitive position of the property and leads to the selection of policies suited to that situation. Finally, the market forecast allows the management to bolster the operation against expected shocks, or, as the case may be, to be prepared to take advantage of a favorable turn in the market.

Merchandising with a Purpose

In this context, the term *merchandising* comprehends advertising and promotion, pricing or rent setting, the selection of tenants to meet certain general specifications, and minor modification of the product through beautification or alteration in the services covered by the rent. Merchandising, then, is the marketing of the space-commodity. We have already suggested how merchandising policies may be manipulated to carry out management policies. We propose now to identify certain management policies and to suggest how merchandising can be used in their pursuit.

The common and basic objective of management is to maximize net income. But this may be approached either by raising rental revenues or by reducing operating and financial expenses. Which approach or combination of approaches is best will depend on the property, its location, and market conditions.

Rental income is a function of rental rates and occupancy ratios. High rents relative to competing properties may create tenant resistance, increase tenant turnover, and reduce occupancy. A four-flat building with rents at $100 per month will produce $400 per month when all dwelling units are occupied. A 10 per cent increase in the rental rate will add $40 per month to gross income. But if the increase is responsible for one month's vacancy, or a loss of $100, it will require two and one half months at full occupancy for the rent increase of $40 per month to offset the loss of $100. Furthermore, higher rents may lead to faster tenant turnover and, in consequence, more total time unoccupied during cleaning and redecorating between tenants, as well as higher total costs of redecorating. It is apparent, therefore, that rent increases will not always result in greater net income. For some properties under some market conditions and for all properties in time of housing shortage, rent increases are justified from a management standpoint. But a careful analysis of the elasticity of demand must be made before raising rents. Under some circumstances managers maintain a rent schedule just below the competitive level in order to assure full occupancy and to permit more careful selection of tenants. In other properties and locations the only group of potential tenants may be families who move frequently. When competitive conditions permit, rents are set high enough to offset the rental loss through greater vacancy.

Property managers find it easier to lower than to raise rents. When the rents are being raised incoming tenants are asked to pay the higher rent, and as the leases of the present tenants come up for renewal the higher figure is made effective. When rentals are to be adjusted downward, it is often advisable, in the interests of harmony and good will, to reduce all rents at the same time regardless of lease expiration dates. When the manager, on the basis of market analysis, concludes that the weakness in the rental market is only temporary, he will be reluctant to announce a lower rent schedule. Thus, in order to give the appearance of maintaining the same level of rents and to avoid the resistance to later restoring rents to their former levels after a reduction, the tenants may be asked to sign leases at the old monthly rates, but the contract will provide for twelve months' occupancy for eleven months' rent. This type of adjustment is known as a "concession."

Careful and directed tenant selection can be helpful in maximizing rental income. A thorough analysis of the character, financial circumstances, and credit rating of each applicant will increase the proportion of tenants who are stable long-term occupants who pay their rent promptly. There is sometimes an advantage in establishing a reputation for the property based on the nature of the occupants. Depending on the circumstances the manager may give preference to professional men, to families with children, to old couples and pensioners, to theatrical people, to military personnel, or to childless young couples. If the market demand is sufficiently broad this type of specialization may produce higher rents and lower vacancies. In all cases revenues will be higher if tenant selection can eliminate those occupants who will be offensive to other tenants and whose presence will result in more vacancies and lower rents.

Another device to increase revenue under certain conditions is to increase or decrease the services covered by the rent. For example, furnishing some or all of the apartments may reach a consumer group not interested in unfurnished dwellings. The provision of maid service may provide an effective appeal. Or, under other circumstances, a reduction in services with a corresponding reduction in rent may reach an untapped market.

In leasing commercial and office space there is some danger in specializing in one type of tenant business. Should this business suffer economic distress, the landlord might find a large portion of his building empty. Diversification of tenant types often promises greater stability.

Merchandising policies are subject to modification when market conditions change. When there is a surplus of competing space, particularly when a new attractive and modern building threatens to drain off the tenants from an older structure, the major merchandising efforts are directed at retaining the present occupants. When the economy is dormant commercial and office vacancies can be filled only by enticing tenants from other buildings, for few new enterprises are being formed, and contraction of space needs rather than expansion is the order of the day. During prosperity and growth in the locality potential tenants for office and industrial space are found among expanding local concerns, enterprises planning to move into the area, and new companies being formed. In such periods chain retail organizations are usually expanding and are interested in well-situated storerooms. New local retail merchants also appear in search of good locations.

Institutional and governmental office space users seem to require constantly increasing amounts of space; local governments outgrow their facilities; state governments establish branch offices outside of the capital city; the Federal space needs seem insatiable. Other types of institutional users which show a constant increase in space needs are trade associations and labor organizations. A study of the economy of the community, the distribution of employment by type and activity, and the characteristic response of each type of business or activity to the ups and downs of the business cycle, will serve to guide the adjustments in merchandising efforts as the economic climate changes.

REDUCING OPERATING EXPENSES

For purposes of this discussion operating expenses are defined as cash outlays which are necessary to maintain the productivity of the property. The problem of reducing debt service, which is also a cash outlay, will be considered in a later section. A high operating ratio is characteristic of many forms of real estate enterprise. When operating costs are high in proportion to revenues and when the regular cash obligations of interest and principal payments on the mortgage are added, the total typically leaves a relatively narrow margin.

The actual figures for a well-managed apartment project of seventy-eight dwelling units in 1956 reveal that operating expenses were 60 per cent of gross income expectancy. This ratio might run higher for office buildings and lower for retail store properties. The fixed burden of debt service will vary with the amount of the debt and the terms of its repayment.

Fixed costs are typically high relative to variable costs in real estate enterprises. In the apartment project just mentioned variable costs at full occupancy were about 40 per cent of total operating costs and would have been in a higher proportion in other forms of real estate enterprise. The fixed costs which run on though occupancy and revenues fall include property taxes; general structural maintenance; insurance; cleaning and maintenance of sidewalks, grounds, and public areas; advertising and promotion; management; and other costs depending on the type of property. Thus since costs do not fall as fast as revenues, the net income may be pinched off before vacancies and rent reductions have gone very far. If mortgage payments are added to the fixed costs the break-even point will be reached with only a moderate reduction in gross revenues. Were our apartment example to be financed by a two-thirds mortgage under a typical contract, with only a 10 per cent reduction, revenues would probably touch down to fixed obligations. It is the part of wise management, therefore, to minimize the burden of fixed obligations by shifting fixed costs to a variable basis wherever possible. For example, the management fee to a property management firm should follow the usual practice of calculation as a per cent of gross revenues, typically 5 per cent, rather than a fixed amount.

The forces and factors which drive revenues below the danger point are often short-term, and the manager's problem is to carry the enterprise through the storm without disaster. One policy is to set up reserves in time of prosperity which can be tapped during adversity. Another policy, less sound but more common, is to postpone maintenance and repairs where such delay will not immediately reduce the earning capacity of the structure and to lower standards of service to the point which competition will permit. For example, in an office building, lower occupancy may allow one or two elevators to be temporarily withdrawn from service. On the financing front a strategic retreat may be made if the mortgagee can be pursuaded to forego principal payments until normal productivity is restored.

Lease Terms

At times arrangements are made with tenants to undertake some of the operating responsibilities such as providing their own heat, redecorating, making repairs, and performing janitorial services. These arrangements reduce operating expenses, it is true, but corresponding adjustments are made in the rent paid. However, the assumptions of such operating costs by the tenant can be advantageous to the landlord. For example, in some kinds of properties, the reduction in rent is likely to be less than the costs to the landlord of providing the services which the tenant assumes. Furthermore, the landlord is relieved of the burden and annoyance of meeting minor emergencies, hiring and maintaining the necessary personnel, and maintaining an inventory of supplies. His working capital needs are reduced and less supervisory time is required.

Tenant Selection

Careful tenant selection can favorably influence operating costs. Well-behaved and responsible tenants usually mean lower costs for maintenance and redecorating. Some kinds of people demand unusually high standards of service, and others are satisfied with reasonable attention. A property which establishes a fine reputation or which can specialize in a certain type of tenant may be able to develop a waiting list and thus reduce advertising and promotional expenses.

The selection of tenants who will continue in occupancy for long periods will reduce the costs which accompany a change of tenants. Less advertising will be required; there will be a lesser burden on management and operating personnel in showing the space, interviewing and investigating applicants, and settling the new tenants in their accommodations.

Efficient Management

The advantages of sound business administration apply with equal force to all forms of business enterprise. In the management of real estate there are efficiencies and savings to be gained from the pursuit of well-recognized business principles in the following respects:

1. Selection of competent and experienced management, either an individual or a property management firm

2. Installation of an efficient operating organization

3. Employment of effective accounting and budgeting controls

4. Maintenance of favorable customer relations

5. Use of effective collection methods

6. Use of proper personnel policies in hiring and training, supervising and compensating employees

7. Application of intelligent and careful purchasing methods

Efficient management will not only reduce management costs as such but can effect savings at many points of expenditure for labor and materials. Good management will be reflected in many intangibles—the general appearance and orderliness of the property, the attitudes of employees, smoothness in building operation, and the prompt meeting of complaints and emergencies. Good management cannot only cut costs but can improve tenant relationships, establish a favorable reputation for the property, and thereby contribute to higher rent levels and lower vacancy rates.

The owner-investor who wishes to shift management responsibilities and duties to a professional manager may do so by contracting with a local property management organization. Many real estate brokers combine this function with selling, and in the larger cities, large management firms are found which specialize in handling other people's properties. This service is a boon to absentee owners who cannot very well attend to the frequent and numerous problems and transactions involved in operating an apartment or office building. The management fee is earned not only by carrying out the onerous duties of administration but also through the higher net income produced by skilled management.

Maintenance

There is flexibility in maintenance expenditures on those items which do not directly and immediately affect productivity. Repainting can often be postponed; the replacement of a failing roof or of decrepit stoves and refrigerators may not require immediate action; the life of rusted downspouts may be extended for a time. Whether or not the delay in some repair will affect revenues is often dependent on competitive conditions in the market except, of course, for those cases where deterioration or failure makes space literally unusable.

From a long-run viewpoint prompt repair and replacement are the best policies. The renewal of deteriorated structural parts and surfaces will prevent the spread of damage and minimize ultimate costs. In the the short run there may be situations which justify postponement of repairs and replacement. When vacancies in all competing buildings are high, demand nonexistent, and revenues too low to meet essential expenditures, it may be necessary to defer some of the less critical maintenance and replacement because of a lack of funds to make payment. When the market demand is so stagnant that modernization would have little influence on occupancy or rent levels, obsolete equipment such as refrigerators, stoves, or elevators can be continued in use as long as they are still serviceable.

Under some conditions certain maintenance operations are most economically handled by staff employees; under other conditions costs can be minimized by letting contracts for the work. For example, salaried full-time painters may be low cost when there is sufficient work to keep them steadily occupied. Where painting is intermittent, contracting is indicated.

The importance of repair and replacement on keeping and attracting tenants and on rent levels has already been strongly implied. A building which is shabby in appearance, suffering from structural defects which impair its efficiency, and obsolete in equipment will suffer by comparison with well-maintained modern competitors. And there is another basic investment policy to which adequate maintenance contributes. This policy is the extension of the productive life of the property. A shortsighted maintenance and replacement policy may shorten the economic life of the property as well as reduce the level of earnings.

Modernization of Equipment

Savings in operating costs can sometimes be accomplished by replacing obsolete and inefficient equipment with modern counterparts. Heating plants and elevators are the prime examples of such opportunities for saving. An efficient automatic heating plant may save enough in fuel cost and man-hours of an engineer or janitor to repay the additional capital expenditure and yield a net saving in costs of operation. For example, assume a building has a heating plant which would normally be expected to last for another five years. A new and more efficient plant will cost $7,500 and will save $1,000 per year. The new plant has an expected life of fifteen years; thus an annual deposit of $500 in a reserve for replacement is indicated, or a lesser amount on a sinking fund basis. Advancing the replacement by five years will add $2,500 to expenses for a reserve for replacement but will reduce costs by $5,000 through savings in fuel and labor. Savings in elevator operating expense arise when automatic self-operated equipment replaces the hand-controlled type which requires attendants.

Adjustments in Services

Reductions in services must usually be accompanied by offsetting reductions in rents. But there are situations where the rent reduction may be less than the reduction in costs. Such a service as garbage and trash collection may be greatly reduced in frequency and cost by the installation of garbage grinders. The convenience of the grinders would be sufficient to offset the less frequent trash collection, and no rental adjustment would probably be required. A central telephone switchboard and reception desk might be eliminated in some buildings with a net saving. Self-service elevators have already been pointed to as an economy. In general, with labor costs at such high levels, there are usually savings in substituting machines for employees and in shifting from employees to tenants the responsibility for service functions.

Taxes and Insurance

Alert management can often effect property tax reductions. Control of inventories so that their value is at the low point on the assessment date is one device of minor importance but not to be overlooked in jurisdictions where tax rates on personal property are high. Of greater potential is vigilance over the real property assessment and appeal for reduction when it appears to be out of line. Property owners should be willing to join with others in the eternal effort to shift some of the burden to other tax sources.

Savings in insurance premiums are often possible. The property manager should assure himself of competent and objective insurance counsel in order to effect the necessary coverage at the lowest cost. Certain types of commercial and industrial tenancies give rise to increased premiums because of the extra hazards inherent in their operations. Such tenants should be avoided or a clause inserted in the lease which requires the tenant to pay the increased insurance costs. Insurance premiums can sometimes be reduced by minor structural changes which decrease fire hazard or reduce risk of personal injury.

Insurance coverage should be frequently reviewed to take advantage of possible savings from changes in rates and coverage. Under conditions of rising construction costs and inflation coverage should be increased, for there is no economy in underinsurance.

REDUCING FINANCIAL CHARGES

Under some conditions an investor may wish to retire the indebtedness on a property as fast as possible. However, most investors prefer to keep mortgage payments at a minimum. Their purpose is to reduce financial risk by leaving the widest possible margin between gross revenues and the total of operating expenses plus contractual debt service. Another purpose is to free more cash for distribution to the owner or for plowing back into the property by way of capital improvements. Investors prefer to determine the use of revenues above operating expenses and interest rather than have most of it committed to contractual debt retirement.

Investors and property managers should be alert to the possibilities of reducing the debt burden in the form of regular contractual payments. As the mortgage market changes in complexion and as outstanding indebtedness is reduced, opportunities for refinancing on more favorable terms may arise. To prepare for such a possibility it is necessary to arrange the initial financing so that a prepayment privilege is included in the mortgage.

ADAPTATION TO CHANGE

Our discussions of managing the real estate investment have tacitly assumed that the property consists of buildings and improvements which are suited to the site and appropriate to the location. We have recognized that management policies require adjustment to changing market conditions; policies which suit a market at balance in demand and supply must be modified if a surplus develops or if a shortage ensues. The physical aging of a property may also bring changes in the type of tenants to whom it appeals and thus changes in merchandising and management policies. But the kind of adaptations which are the subject of this section are responses to changes which are outside of the property itself. These changes may be classified as (1) environmental, or changes in locational factors which influence the productivity of the property, and (2) social (in the broad sense of social, economic, and technological), or changes which contribute to obsolescence in the property. Both classes of change reduce productivity below that of the highest and best use of the site.

We will present examples of the two classes of change and some suggestions of how adaptations in policy and modifications in physical form can help to sustain productivity and preserve value.

Types of Maladjustment

It is possible, of course, that a building is obsolete in one or more respects from the time it is completed. The land may be under- or overimproved; the building type unsuited to the location; the interior planned inefficiently, the equipment outdated, or the architectural treatment out of style. Many of these defects may develop over time as results of external change in environment and in social and technological factors. Thus, with the passage of time in a dynamic society, a structure which at time of construction was modern, efficient, and stylish, can become obsolete and unproductive as a result of its vulnerability to external forces beyond the control of the owner.

Environmental change affecting productivity may take many forms, some beneficial, some detrimental. Accessibility may be modified by changes in traffic routing brought about by one-way street systems, by street closing, new freeways, changing bus routes or subways, and modifications in parking facilities. Services of importance to occupants of the property may be increased or reduced. For example, convenient restaurants to serve lunch to office workers are a valuable service, as are nearby convenience goods outlets such as supermarkets, drugstores, and dry cleaning and laundry establishments for the benefit of apartment dwellers. For commercial space, changes in adjacent occupancies may affect the attractiveness of an area for the kinds of activities which are functionally linked, for example, an area where women's shopping goods stores tend to cluster, or where financial and certain office activities are found in close physical proximity. Conversely, some kinds of land uses tend to repel other kinds; noisy, dirty industrial activities are undesirable neighbors for residential properties, office use, retail activities, and even other kinds of industry. Changes in land use can improve or detract from the physical attractiveness of a neighborhood, and with the passage of time, the aging of structures in an area tends to affect its appearance and atmosphere in spite of efforts to maintain the exterior of the buildings. Our earlier discussion of location has provided other examples of the dynamic nature of location and the effect of locational change on productivity. Note that some location changes affect an entire neighborhood; other changes are focused in their influence on one or two properties.

Social change as used here is a term which includes shifts in the attitudes, customs, and value systems of groups of people. Demographic change refers to the composition of the population; economic change to the supporting activities of the community, change in the general struc-

ture of the national economy, alterations in economic or business processes, and institutional change in governmental regulations and legal inter-
pretations. The examples of social change are numberless, but investors
are, of course, interested only in those changes which influence the productivity of a given property and particularly in those changes which
reduce its productivity. For example, changes in recreational habits of
Americans growing out of the five-day week, television, and the popularity of do-it-yourself activity have taken the bloom off the movie
theater property. The extension of homeownership to more than 60 per
cent of all nonfarm families reduces demand for apartments. On the
economic front the movement of textile plants from New England cities
has left vacant industrial properties and has reduced the need for space
for secondary service activity. Modifications in local zoning laws may
permit or prohibit, as the case may be, profitable operations in the properties affected. The decision by the United States Supreme Court which
outlawed discriminatory deed restrictions had its effect on property values
in certain cities of the country. Changes in public taste expressed in
preferences for architectural styles, furniture design and placement, and
decor may all have an effect on the appeal of a given property to prospective occupants to the detriment of structures which are judged to be
outmoded.

Another type of change which creates obsolescence in buildings is
technological change. Advances in heating and cooling equipment and
in structural methods and materials have a direct effect. Changes in
industrial technology influence factory design and location. General
advances such as the development and widespread ownership of the
automobile, television, and mechanical refrigerator have influenced almost
all phases of human existence and have rendered many properties obsolete
in varying degree. As these various changes take place the structure may
become maladjusted to its environment, or it may become more poorly
adapted to providing service in a changing society or under an advancing
technology. In the next section we will consider the kinds of adaptations
to change which the investor should consider making in the property.

Types of Adaptation

Adaptations to external forces which reduce productivity take the
form of (1) changes in management policy, (2) physical changes in the
property, or (3) a direct counterattack on the factors which are creating
the deleterious change. In each case the aim of the investor is to maintain
productivity at as high a level as possible. In some cases no remedies are
practicable, and the aim of management is to minimize operating losses
until the time is ripe for demolishing the structure and rebuilding for the
highest and best use under the new conditions.

Operational Adaptation. Some types of maladjustment, arising from either environmental or market changes, can best be met by changes in management policy. Without making a basic functional shift the type of operation can be modified to better fit the new conditions. For example, an apartment building which has been occupied by families in the upper-income groups may find itself losing business because of creeping blight in the neighborhood which makes it unattractive and diminishes its prestige value. It may prove profitable to alter management policies to appeal to a clientele in a somewhat lower-income group. Promotional efforts would be redirected, some types of services, such as a doorman and a central switchboard might be eliminated, and rents scaled down accordingly. The result would be to tap a broader market of families who are not willing to pay for a prestige location or for luxury services. Similar changes in policies are at times appropriate for office buildings, loft buildings, and industrial structures.

Modernization. Maladjustments arising from obsolescence can often be offset by a program of modernization. This remedy involves no basic change in management policies or property functions but rather is a matter of restoring the structure to maximum attractiveness and productivity. The modernization program may involve replacement of obsolete equipment, the installation of additional equipment such as for air cooling, changes in space arrangement, redecoration of interior areas, and modernization of the façade.

Conversion. This form of adaptation to change involves a shift in function to one which is better suited to the new situation. There are examples of unprofitable neighborhood theater buildings which have been converted for retail use. Apartment buildings have been converted to office buildings, warehouses to retail use, and factory buildings to warehouses. Both modernization and conversion may require substantial amounts of new capital. Whether or not the investment is justified can be tested by a before-and-after comparison. The additional net revenue before depreciation must be sufficient to retire the added investment during its economic life and to yield an attractive return from year to year on the unretired portion.

Controlling Change. Individually and collectively property owners can sometimes act to forestall, reverse, or modify changes which will detrimentally affect their properties. By the same token they can often induce and encourage favorable change. This kind of action is usually directed at the basic source of the environmental or institutional force. For example, cooperative action with other owners in the neighborhood, perhaps enforced by publicly sponsored renewal programs, may slow or reverse the forces of blight. In many of our cities today downtown businessmen's associations are successfully combating the competition of outlying shopping centers and preventing central business districts from becoming the deserted areas that some prophets have foreseen.

Changes in zoning can seriously affect the profitable operation of buildings. Property owners can intelligently and effectively fight detrimental changes in zoning, or they can sponsor zoning changes which will permit the conversion of their properties to a more profitable use. They can have a hand in modifications of traffic patterns and controls and in the provision of public parking facilities.

Each owner or manager must be alert to the impact of the property tax and should be prepared to defend his property against unfair assessment and to join with other property owners in movements to restrain unnecessary public expenditures and to shift the burden from the property tax to other sources of revenue.

Carrying the Property during Ripening. A building in a neighborhood which is being subjected to drastic environmental change may be so obsolete and so close to the end of its physical life that no form of renovation or modification can be economically justified. In some cases the wise policy is to operate the property with as small a loss as possible and to replace it with a new structure at the appropriate time. However, if the revenues are insufficient to pay operating costs and taxes, it may be cheaper to tear down the building, thus reducing taxes to the amount levied on the land, and to hold the land vacant. In other cases a parking-lot operation will help to carry the burden of taxes; or an inexpensive, one-story structure, referred to in the trade as a "taxpayer," may produce a return above operating expenses and taxes which will write off the building cost in a few years. A larger and permanent structure can then be erected.

The kind of situation which calls for carrying the property even at a temporary loss is encountered in the central areas of most of our larger cities. There are transitional zones surrounding central business districts which are blighted with obsolete structures, disrepair, and dingy appearance where marginal activities are conducted, turnover of occupancies high, and rents low and uncertain. In the portions of these zones of blight which are contiguous to the vital and active business district it is observable that many of the buildings have been wrecked and parking lots are operating. In many cases the parking business yields a higher net profit than did the building which was removed. It is the expectation of most of the owner-investors in the area that the ultimate expansion of the central business district will absorb their property and justify the erection of a permanent and profitable improvement. Each situation in each city is different, and even a careful analysis by experts will not always provide a certain forecast. Investments in these transitional areas are thus largely speculative for the speed and character of their redevelopment depends on a complex of many uncertain factors. However, the owner of property must act on probabilities, or, in baseball parlance, play the percentages; in any event he can often cut his loss by demolition of a structure which no longer can carry itself.

LIQUIDATING THE INVESTMENT

For one reason or another there may come a time when an owner seeks to liquidate his investment in a real estate enterprise. Most of the reasons for such action are included in one of the following:

1. *To Cut Losses.* The investor may be suffering continuing loss on the property and sees no prospect of improvement.

2. *To Shift Capital to a More Profitable Investment.* Other more attractive investment opportunities may lead the owner to convert his real estate equity into cash.

3. *To Meet Emergencies.* Some urgent need for cash may lead to liquidation.

4. *To Take a Profit.* The owner may seize the opportunity to sell under favorable conditions and capture a capital gain.

X

THE REAL ESTATE MARKET

INTRODUCTION

In one sense the real estate market is the sum of the transactions of buying and selling and renting real property. A broader connotation would include all the factors and forces of demand and supply which influence market price and which affect the rate or intensity of market activity. Thus, the market is not a particular place, nor would it be feasible to draw a geographical line around all of the market influences which come to focus on the market transactions. True, we recognize the local nature of real estate markets and we refer to them by the name of the locality in which the property is found and within which the most powerful of the many market factors are known to originate. But market factors may be regional or national; the price of a small house in a village may be largely the product of local factors, but the price of an office building in Chicago is set in a market where national factors play an important role.

Why is an understanding of the real estate market essential to sound real estate investment decisions?

In the first place, an investor needs to know how the market currently evaluates properties of the type which he plans to buy or to sell. Thus he proceeds to analyze recent transactions involving similar properties; and in order to evaluate these sales he must understand the nature and significance of the current market situation which conditions the transaction. In Chapter VI we described the market-comparison method of arriving at an upper limit to the investment value of a property. If the investor plans to sell his property he is concerned not only with price but also with the level of market activity as an idicator of its absorptive capacity, i.e., the speed with which a sale can be effected.

In the second place, a sound investment decision requires two kinds of forecasts based on predictions of real estate market conditions:

1. In forecasting the productivity of a given property, say an apart-

ment building or a retail store building, the analyst must predict the future pattern of the level of rents. Changes in the balance of demand and supply will affect rent levels as will certain institutional factors. An understanding of market reactions to various kinds of forces is therefore essential to predicting future rental returns.

2. The forecasting of trends in transaction prices is a necessary part of real estate investment analysis. Every buyer would prefer to buy at the lowest possible price; if he anticipates a drop in the market price of the kind of property he plans to purchase he will postpone his offer; if he believes prices will soon rise he will act promptly. The seller of real estate follows much the same lines of action though in reverse; his eagerness to sell and his asking price will be influenced by his forecast of market trends. Investors with a view to capital gain act only when they are able to foresee a rise in market price. No useful forecast of trends can be made by an investor without understanding the mechanism of the market and the nature of internal market interactions.

It is clear from the foregoing paragraphs that the focus of market analysis is the transaction. Either the analyst is evaluating actual sales prices and rental rates as the market facts of today and the near past, or he is attempting to predict the influence of future market forces and factors on the transaction prices of the future. Closely related to the forecast of price trends is the forecast of market activity, or the ease and speed with which a sale or purchase can be made. As in the stock market rising prices of real estate are generally accompanied by increased market activity as measured by the number of sales; a slow market means stable or falling prices. But again, like the stock market, a rising rate of activity can sometimes mean that owners are hastening to sell out in anticipation of falling values.

We think of the market in aggregative terms, as the totality of market transactions. By summing and analyzing a group of transactions it is possible to establish market price trends. But all types of real estate in all locations do not move together in price. There are submarkets on which impinge the special demand and supply forces affecting certain classes of real estate. For example, changes in the price of industrial real estate are determined by a largely different set of factors than those which influence apartment rents, though certainly there are some factors in common. We shall later present some of the special characteristics of the more recognizable submarkets.

Should we examine the special circumstances which surround each separate market transaction we would appreciate that no two transactions are the same. The differences originate from the following:

1. Each property is structurally and locationally different and thus subject to certain special influences.

2. The parties to each transaction are individuals with distinct personalities, objectives, motivations, business judgment, family, and financial circumstances. Given the same set of facts each individual may arrive at a somewhat different conclusion.

This second point leads naturally to a very fundamental economic principle—that voluntary transactions take place only when each party believes that he will benefit. Thus, each party to a purchase and sale, having considered the same long-run productivity factors and short-run market factors affecting the same property, satisfies himself that he will benefit by the exchange of the property for an agreed sum of money. The buyer prefers to have the house rather than the $20,000; the seller prefers the $20,000 over retaining the house. Since the house is the same and the factors affecting its value are the same the difference in the conclusions of buyer and seller must be largely subjective in origin—a reflection of knowledge, the completeness of the facts at hand, judgment, objectives, and to be sure, personal financial circumstances.

The fact that each transaction is unique does not make it impracticable to detect or predict market trends. We can arrive at useful conclusions by combining a sufficient number of similar, though not identical, transactions and measuring the aggregate behavior. And on the basis of past behavior patterns in the market we can do some forecasting of what changes in prices and market activity will result from changes in basic market factors.

MARKET FUNCTIONS

The basic function of any market mechanism dealing in whatever economic goods is to effect exchange. In a barter economy goods are exchanged for goods. In a money economy goods are exchanged for money and money for other goods. The result of exchange is a redistribution of goods and money; in other terms, this is the process of allocating economic resources. In the real estate market the process of exchange brings about the production and allocation of facilities in accordance with the preferences and desires of users and their financial abilities. Thus the basic exchange function results in price establishment, a distribution of existing space, an adjustment in the supply of space, and the determination of the use of each parcel.

Price Establishment

As the product of demand and supply forces the price of various types of property is established through market transactions. The underlying tendency is for similar properties to sell for the same price. But the lack of standardization among properties and the other imperfections of the real estate market make the law of single price only partially operative.

Herein lies a trap for the careless and the uninitiated. The fact that a certain house sells today for $17,500 whereas a similar dwelling sold for $16,000 last month does not establish a price trend. Each transaction needs to be examined to discover any special or unusual circumstances which may have resulted in a nonrepresentative transaction price. Some examples are a sale between members of the same family, a forced sale, uninformed parties, or unusually liberal financing. Useful conclusions can be drawn only when the facts on many transactions in similar property types and locations can be assembled and when they show consistency in direction of price change.

Distributing Existing Space

The price mechanisms of the market act to allocate the existing real estate resources among alternative types of use and to change the intensity of use. The real estate market is notoriously slow in making adjustments in total supply in response to changes in demand. The long life of structures and land improvements and the eternal life of space means that the supply of usable urban real estate declines at a very slow rate with the passage of time. The supply of existing housing, for example, is estimated to be diminished by about 130,000 dwelling units per year or about 0.25 per cent of the standing stock of housing. Not only are all types of urban facilities retired from use slowly as a result of deterioration, obsolescence, fire, succession, and other causes, but increases to the supply are sluggish and delayed in response to rising demand. The processes of the construction industry are complex and require time for planning and production. As a result of the slow adjustment of supply to changes in demand, the market mechanism acts to ration the existing supply among the bidders for it generally as determined by the amount bid. Thus, before supply can be adjusted to the new level of demand, occupancies may shift and the intensity of space use may be modified.

We might illustrate the results of a sudden increase in demand for housing as it might develop when a new and large industry moves into a community of moderate size. As an initial response, vacant dwelling will be quickly absorbed by incoming plant workers, and prices and rents will rise. Families of modest income will suffer from rent increases and will take in roomers to supplement their income or will move to smaller or less desirable quarters. The higher level of market prices will induce some homeowners to sell. Thus, the pressure on the existing supply will bring about shifts in occupancy and will increase the intensity of use of the housing stock.

The initial effects of a sudden decrease in demand are to reduce intensity of use. Increasing vacancies breed lower rents and prices and permit families to move upward in the quality scale of housing into more commodious dwellings or to get along without the income from roomers. Note, however, that both increases and decreases in demand give rise initially to a shifting about within the existing supply.

The allocation of existing housing resources can be influenced by general changes in family income levels. Changes which directly affect only certain segments of demand can produce a shift in occupancies which may carry repercussions through the entire market.

Adjusting the Supply of Space in Quantity and Quality

Demand pressures, if continued, will usually eventuate in new construction and an increase in supply. Falling vacancies, rising rents, and stiffening prices spell profit opportunities for investors and builders. Thus, through new construction or remodeling, the market mechanism effects a closer adjustment of supply to the needs of users.

Though increases in the supply of space are slow to materialize, decreases in supply are far slower. Long life is typically built into land improvements, and owners are slow to take them out of use. However, when the costs of carrying the property continue to exceed revenues year after year and the prospects for improved returns continue unfavorable owners finally raze the structures to reduce taxes, or they abandon the property altogether.

It is through the market mechanism that changes in the character or quality of demand bring forth corresponding changes in the quality or characteristics of the new supply added to the market. For example, immediately after the war the new and small families of veterans sought economical housing. Liberal credit made homeownership attainable with the result that builders produced millions of two-bedroom homes which were well suited to the immediate family needs of the veterans and to their financial capacities. Within a few years two-bedroom homes were a drug on the market in many communities. The increase in family size coupled with pervasive prosperity created strong demand for three- and four-bedroom homes. The builders of the nation quickly responded to this change in the quality of demand, and the two-bedroom speculatively built house became a rarity.

Determining Land Use

In Chapter XII we will examine in detail the market competition among land uses for urban sites. By a process of competitive market bidding among investors the ultimate utilization of each site is determined, and by this parcel by parcel determination the urban structure is formed. In general, the land use which can most efficiently and productively exploit a given site will be able to command its use by outbidding all competing uses.

ORGANIZATION OF THE MARKET

Up to this point we have been careful to avoid a narrow and localized concept of the real estate market. It has been defined in broad terms to emphasize the wide ranging forces which are brought to focus on each transaction. But to the extent to which there is a market structure or organization it is primarily local, and thus we can say that in this sense there is a market place. Of course, there is no single spot where sellers display their goods and buyers come to shop; there is no meeting room, as in the wheat market or the stock market, where trading is concentrated. But in each community the market place can be defined in terms of the real estate which is being offered for sale, the prospective buyers and sellers, the functionaries (lawyers and bankers) who facilitate the transactions, and the web of relationships among all of the participants. There is no open square or trading room where all participants assemble, but there is a definable organization and a consistent procedure which can be described as a useful generalization and with which all buyers and sellers should be familiar.

Participants

The majority of buyers and sellers in the real estate market are inexperienced in real estate matters; they are not professional traders and may participate in a real estate transaction but once or twice during a lifetime. There is a higher degree of sophistication among investors in income properties and in speculative ventures than in the home market.

Most real estate is locally owned, but absentee ownership is not uncommon. Income property is sometimes held under corporate ownership or owned by institutional investors. Multiple ownership is quite common and often results from the distribution of interests in a property among several heirs. Most homes are held in joint tenancy by husband and wife.

Because real estate investment decisions are made by people the personal characteristics of the participants in any real estate transaction are important in the decision-making process. Of primary significance is their knowledge and understanding of real estate values and the real estate market; also of great significance are the motivations of the participants.

The objectives which motivate investors are varied and diverse, but they do provide a basis for the broad grouping of investors which we identified in Chapter VI:

1. *Investor-Users.* This group includes individuals, business enterprises, and institutions which hold or seek to buy real estate for their own use as a home, as a place of business, or as a location for other activities of the owner.

2. *Investors for Income.* This group is made up of those who seek a regular return on invested capital.

3. *Investors for Capital Gain.* The objective of these investors is to hold real estate for resale at a profit or capital gain.

In addition to the buyers and sellers who are the primary activators of transactions in the market there are a number of types of functionaries who perform secondary or facilitating functions. This group includes real estate brokers, surveyors, lawyers, mortgage lenders, title companies, escrow agents, and others. For the most part they are all well informed in real estate matters related to their activities. Their motivations are purely financial—to earn a commission or a fee for services rendered. A little later we shall trace the steps in a typical sale and will show what role each of these actors plays in the consummation of a transaction as well as the interrelationship among them.

The real estate market is the locus not only of transfers of ownership through purchase and sale but also of transfers of possession and occupancy by renting or leasing of residential and commercial property. Thus, landlords and tenants are among the active participants in the market. The types of transaction in the rental market range from the common month-to-month tenancy in the residential market, which is a simple arrangement usually involving no written agreement, to a long-term lease in a purchase and lease-back deal which may be expressed in a very involved and complicated document requiring long negotiations.

Communication

Beyond word-of-mouth information there are three main methods of communication between prospective buyers and sellers in the real estate market—for-sale signs on the property, newspaper ads, and brokers' listings.

For-sale signs are widely used for announcing the offering of all kinds of property. They may be placed by the owner or by the real estate broker with whom the property is listed.

Newspaper ads in the classified section are perhaps the most important and widely used method for bringing buyer and seller together. The ad may be inserted over the name of either owner or broker. For industrial, commercial, and subdivision properties display ads are sometimes employed.

The owner may choose to contract with a real estate broker to endeavor to sell the property. The broker receives a commission if a sale is consummated. He usually places his sign on the property and advertises it in the newspaper. These methods attract the inquiries of interested buyers, and in addition, shoppers drop into the broker's office. In many cities brokers have organized an exchange of listings or multiple-listing systems. Under this plan participating brokers are informed of all properties listed for sale with any member of the group and may show and sell any listed property and share in the commission. Finally, the broker and his salesmen will call the offering to the attention of prospects whom they know to be on the lookout for this type of property. Some brokers specialize in industrial or commercial property, and some residential brokers specialize in certain sections of the city.

The real estate broker is a most important agent of communication in the market. It is his business to know what properties are for sale, their description, and their asking price. He endeavors to know who is in the market shopping for various kinds of properties. He is well informed on sales and the prices at which they were consummated. He canvasses for listings to fill the needs of prospective purchaser-clients and for prospects in trying to sell listed properties. His influence on market price is considerable, for he advises his client in setting the asking price, and in his functioning as negotiator, he influences both parties in arriving at a price agreement.

The rental market employs the same channels of communication except that the broker is less important in renting residential space where the newspaper ad is the main market notification. Signs are freely used. Brokers play a large part in commercial and industrial leasing.

REAL ESTATE BROKER

Because of the importance of the broker in the real estate market we will turn to a closer examination of his functions and *modus operandi*.

Broker's Functions

The real estate broker stands ready to assume the responsibility for the sale of other people's property. He may also be retained to purchase property for a client or to negotiate a loan on real estate security. Many brokers also handle the sale of business enterprises, usually small concerns, known in legal language as "business opportunities." In addition to the selling of real estate and small business enterprises many brokers sell casualty insurance, and some brokers engage in mortgage lending as loan correspondents for insurance companies or as loan brokers. Other related activities are appraising and property management. A minority of brokerage firms also engage in property development such as promoting apartment houses or shopping centers; the broker may perform the entrepreneurial function of assembling the elements of the enterprise on behalf of the real entrepreneur and risk taker. In such case he selects and acquires the site, arranges the financing, counsels with the architect in the planning phase, leases the space to tenants, and manages the going concern. Some brokers engage in such real estate developments as entrepreneurs; they also are found in subdivision development and in home building. The spread of prefabrication has brought many brokers into house building. Factory production of the shell of the house reduces the amount of field supervision required, speeds capital turnover, permits the erection and mechanical work to be done on a subcontract basis, and allows the broker to use his promotional and selling facilities and skills with a minimum of diversion to the production activities.

The primary function of the broker is to sell other people's property, and this activity engages most of his time and attention. His first service to a client is to give counsel on the pricing of the property. Some brokers refuse to accept overpriced properties which are thereby difficult to market. The ethical broker will recommend a price which, in light of current market conditions, will result in sale within a reasonable time and with reasonable promotional efforts. A broker who accepts a listing at the owner's price without a careful inspection and an estimate of the most probable market value is not serving his client and may well be inviting difficulties for himself. During the period of the listing the broker may review the price from time to time and recommend price adjustments as conditions may justify changes.

In seeking a buyer for his client's property, the broker, at his own expense under the usual listing contract, advertises in the classified section of the local newspapers and in radio and television announcements, places his sign on the property, and calls the offering to the attention of all of his prospects who are looking for this kind of property. In addition, in the case of a residence, he may hold an evening or week-end "open house" in the property, i.e., advertise that it will be open for inspection at certain hours, place a large open-house sign in the yard, and floodlight the home at night. Salesmen are present to conduct visitors through the house. He may prepare a descriptive brochure on the property, and in case of a home, canvass the area in search of prospects among friends of the neighbors.

Brokers often invite the aid of other brokers in selling listed properties. This may be on an informal basis with an understanding on how the commission is to be shared in case of a sale. In many cities the arrangement is formalized in a multiple-listing system, usually under the auspices of the local real estate board or trade association. Participating brokers agree to exchange listings and to split the commission in case of a sale. The selling broker receives the largest share, a small share goes to meet the expenses of the multiple-listing system, and the balance compensates the listing broker. Where this system is in operation the broker can assure his client that all other participating brokers will be informed that the property is for sale and may show the listing to their prospects. The market exposure is thereby greatly broadened, and the chance of sale at a good price is enhanced.

The conversion of a prospect to a buyer is a broker's function calling for both a full knowledge of the property and a broad understanding of human nature. Where the broker or his salesman shows to a prospect a property which suits his needs and his pocketbook an effort is made to procure a signed offer to purchase. This function involves not only the art of salesmanship, but more often than not, the working out of a plan for financing the purchase and the finding of the mortgage money which the prospect will require.

The strong horse-trading tradition surrounding real estate transactions quite normally results in offers which are lower than the asking or listing price on the property. In many cases the asking price is set deliberately high by the owner to allow for some bargaining room and in the hope of catching the unusual prospect who might unquestioningly offer the full price. The broker's task is to bring the parties to a compromise which will result in a sale. As negotiator he occupies an anomalous position. He is the agent of the seller and thus obligated to secure the best possible price; but the rules of ethical salesmanship should bar him from persuading the buyer to pay more than the property is worth; and his own immediate financial interest lies in securing such concessions from either buyer or seller as may be required to close the deal upon which his compensation is contingent. The highest of ethical standards, which no doubt produce the largest financial return to the broker in the long run, require that the broker lose a sale rather than to induce the buyer to pay more than the property is worth or to persuade the seller to let the property go at a lower price than can be justified by market conditions.

The conveyance and mortgaging of interests in real estate are transactions conducted in a complex of legal rules and technicalities. The broker does not provide legal counsel, but he is familiar with the conveyancing and mortgaging procedures and with the more common legal pitfalls and can advise his client when a lawyer is needed. The broker frequently prepares some or all of the documents required at the closing of the deal, prepares a financial statement showing the position of the parties, and is present at the closing conference to represent his client's interests.

Listing Contract

The relationship of property owner to real estate broker is that of principal and agent. The listing contract must be in writing to be enforceable in some states and certainly always should be in writing as a matter of sound business practice. The contract describes the property and authorizes the broker to offer it for sale at the price and terms specified in

the listing. The manner in which the property is to be conveyed is indicated. The basis of payment for the broker's services is made explicit,
usually as a percentage of the sales price. An expiration date for the listing contract is usually included. The commission rate on homes is usually
from 4 to 6 per cent of the sales price. It is frequently the practice to use
a higher rate for unimproved properties, and in some localities the commission rate is reduced as the sales price rises.

There are several forms of the listing contract which vary in the degree
of protection afforded the broker. The *open listing* is used when the
owner wishes to employ a number of brokers. Each broker is authorized
to offer the property and the first one who presents an acceptable offer is
to receive the commission. Thus no broker can expend time and effort in
seeking a buyer without the considerable risk that his efforts will be in
vain if another broker finds a buyer first. The owner can count on no
broker to work hard for a sale and fully represent his interests. Sometimes the open listing takes the simple form of a notice to all brokers that
a certain property is for sale at a stated price.

The *exclusive agency* gives the right to sell to only one broker and
obligates the owner to pay him a commission if the property is sold
during the term of the contract regardless of who negotiated the sale. The
one exception is the owner himself, but under the exclusive-right-to-sell
listing contract, even though the owner makes the sale, the broker may
collect the full commission. This last form of contract provides the broker
with the greatest incentive to risk expenditures for advertising and to
devote his time to finding a buyer. Sometimes this kind of contract is
modified by a clause reserving to the owner the right to sell to a limited
number of specified individuals who have shown an interest in the property prior to the listing contract.

The Brokerage Business

There are 275,000 licensed real estate brokers in the United States. A
substantial proportion of the licensed brokers are not engaged full-time
in the real estate business. Many of them are lawyers and businessmen
who only incidentally act in a broker's capacity. Other brokers are persons with full-time employment in other occupations who sell real estate
in the evenings and on week ends. Still others are retired people seeking
to supplement limited incomes or to keep occupied by an occasional deal.
Because of the ease with which one may enter the real estate brokerage
business many thousands of brokers are ill equipped to give professional
counsel to their clients. They have come from all manner of unrelated
backgrounds and are without education or training in real estate. It remains a business which requires little or no initial capital but which,
thanks to a gradual extension of state licensing laws and the raising of

standards in their administration, is becoming less and less open to the inexperienced and incompetent.

The typical real estate broker's office is a one- to three-man establishment—a single broker, two brokers as partners, or a broker with one or two salesmen. The salesman is responsible to the broker, and the broker is responsible for the acts of his salesman while acting as his agent. State license laws usually require that salesmen be licensed and that they cannot act except under a duly licensed broker. In the larger market areas there are large brokerage establishments with many salesmen and various combinations of related services such as insurance, mortgage lending, and property management. Some of the firms engage in property development, subdividing, and home building.

One of the broker's most troublesome problems is to find and hold competent salesmen. The usual basis of compensation is a straight commission on sales; some of the larger firms provide a drawing account, and a very few start a salesman on a salary. The turnover in salesmen is high in part because of the uncertain income, particularly for a newcomer, and in part because the ease of entry attracts many persons who are ill fitted to the work and ignorant of the field. Only in the larger offices is there an organized training program for new salesmen.

Trade association activity has done much to raise ethical and professional standards in the real estate business. The National Association of Real Estate Boards (NAREB) has some 70,000 members, but this number is only one-quarter of all licensed brokers. However, the influence of NAREB is not to be gauged by this ratio. Certainly the share of all real estate transactions handled by members is far larger than the percentage might indicate. In each community the leaders in real estate activities are almost always members of the constituent local real estate board. NAREB has fought long and hard for state license laws and for higher requirements for licensing. It has promulgated a code of ethics which local boards enforce among their members. It has encouraged the spread of curricula in real estate at institutions of higher learning and promoted in-service training for practitioners. Branching out from NAREB, there have developed specialized and professional groups such as the American Institute of Real Estate Appraisers, the Brokers Institute, the Institute of Real Estate Management, the Farm Brokers Institute, and the Society of Real Estate Counselors. NAREB has also made itself felt in the political arena.

NAREB is a confederation of local real estate boards whose individual members are required to belong to the national organization. This form of membership entitles them to use the designation of *realtor*, a copyright or registered appellation which nonmembers may not employ. In most states there exist state-wide brokers' organizations dedicated to vigilance over state legislation affecting the real estate business. Some state groups carry on educational activities and usually hold an annual state convention.

License Laws

There are now about 275,000 licensed real estate brokers and 325,000 licensed salesmen. The primary purpose of the real estate license laws now effective in almost all states is to protect the public from unscrupulous and incompetent brokers and salesmen. The test of competence varies widely among the states ranging from not much more than a simple demonstration of literacy to the passing of a stiff written examination, a minimum period of practical experience, and the completion of educational requirements. To bar the unscrupulous the state requires the applicant to secure endorsements from responsible citizens and to reveal any brushes with the law out of his past. Once licensed the broker or salesman may have his license suspended or revoked for improper, fraudulent, or dishonest dealing, misrepresentation, false promises, acting for more than one party in a transaction without the knowledge of all parties, demonstrated untrustworthiness, and incompetency to act in such a manner as to safeguard the interests of the public, and other offenses.

PURCHASE AND SALE TRANSACTION

One of the first choices which confronts the owner who decides to sell his property is between selling direct or listing the property with a broker. Under direct sale the owner seeks to locate a buyer through advertising and other means and to negotiate directly with all prospects. He may or may not hire a lawyer to advise him on legal aspects of any offer to purchase which is presented and to handle the closing of the deal. In a simple cash sale the owner often proceeds without legal counsel.

By listing the property with a broker the owner shifts to the broker all of the functions and burdens surrounding the sales transaction except the final responsibility for naming the asking price, for the decision to accept an offer, for the act of conveying title to the buyer, and for payment of certain costs including the broker's commission. The wide employment of brokers to handle property sales strongly suggests that there are many advantages to the owner in such arrangements.

The choice between selling direct and employing a broker will depend upon a balancing of the sales commission against the time, effort, and expense of the owner's selling efforts, the value of professional counsel by the broker based on his intimate knowledge of conditions in the local real estate market, the superior merchandising ability of the broker and his skill in negotiation which may result in a higher selling price, the advantage of the special knowledge of the broker in working out financing arrangements for the prospective buyer, the value of the broker's contacts in finding mortgage money, and the advantage of multiple listing where broker cooperation is in effect. In a seller's market the owner may feel that he can sell his property simply by advertising in the newspaper, but even in such case, because of ignorance of market conditions or inept negotiation, he may sell for less than a skilled broker might have secured for him, or he may stumble into some pitfall around which the broker might have guided him. When the market is dormant, the advantages of employing a broker are more easily recognized by sellers; and when the need for selling is urgent, owners are more inclined to employ an expert.

By outlining the steps in a typical purchase and sale transaction we can describe the procedure and view the parts played by the various market functionaries. We may start with the owner who decides to sell. He decides on an offering price and acceptable sale terms. He may contract with a broker to sell the property and, if so, the broker will advise him on asking price and terms. The property is now advertised for sale and the broker, if any, sets about to solicit likely prospects.

In the meantime a prospective buyer has entered the market to shop for a certain type and class of property. He learns of the offering through the advertising, the sign, or the broker's solicitation. Arrangements are made to inspect the property in company with the broker if the property has been listed. If the buyer is interested in the property after shopping through the market for other possibilities he may hire a professional appraiser to place a value on the property as a guide in negotiating its purchase; or the buyer may hire an engineer to examine the property for structural defects and deterioration which might call for later expenditures. Before making a firm offer the buyer may wish assurance of the exact physical description of the property and retain a professional surveyor to check the boundaries of the land. Unfortunately, the majority of buyers of small residential and commercial properties do not take the precautions to hire their own experts to check such important points as value, physical condition, and exact location.

Real estate is rarely sold at the asking price. It is traditional for the asking price to be set higher than the seller will take and for the buyer to offer less than the asking price and less than he will pay, if necessary. As a result there is often a series of offers and counteroffers with the final sale price ending up at some compromise figure. Our buyer, then, prepares a written and signed offer to purchase in which all the terms of the offer are fully stated. If the buyer plans to finance the purchase with a loan, he may make his offer conditional upon securing a loan of a stated amount and terms. The buyer may have assistance from a lawyer in drafting the offer, or he may depend on the broker to prepare a proper and sufficient offer. The offer is presented to the seller by the buyer, or if a broker is involved, he will present the offer and act as negotiator in effecting an agreement on price and terms of sale. When an agreement is reached the purchase offer is accepted and signed by the seller, and the buyer usually pays over a small amount of earnest money to bind the bargain and to be applied against the purchase price. Several weeks are allowed to prepare for the final closing of the deal and conveyance of title.

In preparation for the closing the seller provides the buyer with an abstract of title in order that the buyer's attorney may examine the chain of title for any defects which might threaten future possession of the property. Special abstract or title companies exist to prepare the abstracts. In many areas title insurance is used to protect against defects, and, in such cases, the title insurance company must examine the title. The seller arranges for the preparation of the deed which conveys title to the buyer. He also arranges for the insurance policies to be transferred to the buyer. If the buyer requires mortgage credit he must find a lender and have all arrangements worked out by the closing date. The closing of the deal on the appointed day takes place in the broker's office or in the office of the attorney for one of the parties in the presence of the parties, their attorneys, and the broker, if any. The purchase money changes hands, and the deed and mortgage are signed. Immediately the deed and the mortgage are rushed to the county recorder or register of deeds for entering upon the public record.

In many cases the closing of the transaction is handled, for a fee, by specialists known as "escrow agents," who operate under an escrow agreement with both buyer and seller. This agreement authorizes the agent to close the deal when all documents and payments are in order and on hand, to turn the money over to the seller, and to give the signed deed to the buyer.

SUBMARKETS

All types of real estate are subject to certain common market factors; they are all in potential competition for land in the community; many brokers deal in all classes of property; the same channels of communication are used to bring buyer and seller together and the same group of market functionaries are used in all real estate deals. Furthermore, all real estate is affected by common community-wide factors such as population changes and local business conditions and prospects. There is some interaction among all transactions; the price paid for land for one use-type will influence the price of land for other uses of higher and lower intensity. But within this pattern of common factors and interrelated transactions there are definable submarkets. These submarkets deal in fairly homogeneous property types; property values and market activity respond uniquely to the community-wide market forces, and each submarket is subject to important special and independent forces.

The housing submarket is fairly distinct from the markets for nonresidential properties. It is further subdivided between the rental and sales markets, though the two are closely interrelated. Families have the option of renting or purchasing a dwelling and typically compare the offerings in both groups. There is much shifting back and forth from one tenure status to the other. Offerings in the sales market are mainly single-family homes; the rental market also deals in large numbers of single-family homes, but the majority of rental units are in multifamily structures.

Two closely related submarkets are the market dealing in vacant land or acreage and the market dealing in prepared building sites or subdivision lots. The raw land market provides space for all kinds of urban land uses though predominantly for residential purposes. The subdivision lot market deals in processed or semiprocessed land in the nature of a producer's good which the builder combines with a structure to provide a home. The market price of acreage is closely tied to the market price of the finished lots.

The submarkets for residential space are sometimes split geographically in a large community. There may be effectively little competition among dwellings for sale in suburban developments far across town from one another. Both sales and rental markets may also be effectively split into quality or price subgroups. For example, there is little interaction between the rental market for high-rent Gold Coast apartments and tenement units in blighted areas.

Other submarkets include those for retail space, wholesale space, offices, and industrial property. These types of property are all particularly sensitive to changing business conditions. These markets are not otherwise importantly interrelated because, with the exception of loft buildings which can serve for either wholesale or light manufacturing activities, the properties are special purpose structures.

MARKET IMPERFECTIONS

The purpose in studying the structure and processes of the real estate market is to develop an understanding of its operations as a basis for predicting changes in price levels and rate of activity. If the cause-effect relationships among factors of demand and supply were simple and direct, prediction would be easier and more dependable. But unfortunately, the compounded effects of many market forces which are making themselves felt at the same time are complicated, and their indirect effects are hard to trace. Our understanding of the market is largely deductive, for we have no scientific measurements of the degree of change induced in one factor, such as price, by a given change in another factor, say, supply. We know the direction of the change, to be sure, which is quite useful knowledge, but there is no certainty as to timing and degree.

The perfect market concept or model which was employed by the classical economists in their descriptions of market mechanisms was a self-regulating market; prices were relatively uniform and stable and demand and supply were never far out of balance. The commodity traded was in the form of standardized units, quickly consumable, quickly supplied, and easily transported. Traders in the market were all-wise operators guided by enlightened self-interest and instantly informed on all bids, offers, and sales.

The basic economic laws which govern price and activity changes in the real estate market are essentially the same as in the theoretically perfect market of the classicists. But the market is far from perfect and its imperfections stifle, distort, and delay the reactions which in the perfect market would be prompt and untrammeled. Before we look at market reactions to the dynamic forces of demand and supply, and to the market effects of institutional change, we had best understand the limitations to this form of market analysis and forecasting. As we set forth the various market imperfections it will become clear why they result in delayed reactions whose timing is most difficult of prediction; and why a substantial change in basic market conditions, as it loses force amid the frictions of an imperfect market, may bring about only minor changes in price or production activity. Some of the primary market imperfections are:

1. The special and unique characteristics of each parcel of real estate makes it difficult to describe, grade, and compare. The lack of a sufficient number of transactions relating to properties which are even generally similar hampers the establishment of a market price.

2. Accurate information on sales prices and terms is hard to discover, and there is no central source of timely and complete information which can serve as a satisfactory guide for traders.

3. The long period required for planning and building new structures delays the response to pressures of demand.

4. The long useful life of buildings means that supply is not reduced substantially when demand falls off and new construction stops.

5. Lack of experience, understanding, and awareness of market trends on the part of the majority of the buyers and sellers of real property delays action in response to market trends.

PREDICTING MARKET CHANGES

At the outset of this chapter we explained that an understanding of the market mechanism and of market interactions was essential to market forecasting of price levels and activity rates; and that such prognostications are prerequisite to investment decisions. Investors for capital gain are largely guided by their anticipations of future real estate values; and all buyers and sellers are opportunists. When buyers foresee falling prices they will postpone action; on the other hand, sellers will be eager to sell before prices fall off. In the face of rising prices sellers are in no hurry, while buyers are impelled to act.

We are now ready to consider the factors which cause market prices to move up or down and the market indicators which suggest that price changes are in prospect. Common parlance recognizes the changing character of market conditions by the use of such terms as *sellers' market* and *buyers' market*. In a sellers' market the demand presses on supply, and sellers are in a favorable position to ask and get higher prices. In a buyers' market sellers compete for the few buyers in the market, and prices tend to fall. Though the market is rarely at the point of balance between demand and supply neither does it remain for long at the extreme stages of shortage or surplus. Thus by reason of the self-adjusting mechanism, market prices tend to be in almost constant motion. The art of market analysis is to predict the direction, terminal point, and velocity of that motion.

We can describe the real estate market only in terms of economic phenomena which we can measure. Market price and market activity, the dependent variables, are the end products of a variety of forces, the independent variables, which we call "market indicators." When a change occurs in the market indicators, a change in the levels of market price and activity is indicated. Investors are interested in demand and supply factors, not as finally significant guides to action, but only for their predictive value in anticipating movements in the dependent market variables of price and activity.

The following discussion of market interactions will deal with the housing market. We have more information on housing than on other types of property. The market is larger, the transactions more numerous, and the phenomena more subject to generalization. Most of the principles illustrated are transferable with minor adjustments to the other submarkets. However, this chapter includes consideration of the special characteristics of the major submarkets.

Housing Market

Prices and Activity. It is an unfortunate fact that accurate measurement of the most important and critical market fact, the level of prices, is almost nonexistent. The construction of a price index for real estate presents serious technical problems arising from the lack of homogeneity of the product and the relative infrequency of the sales of properties which are even relatively comparable. Wenzlick publishes a price index for single-family houses in the St. Louis market. In the San Francisco Bay area an effort has been made to periodically reprice representative houses in the several price classes for different geographical submarket areas. However, in most communities analysts must rely on conclusions drawn from practical familiarity with actual market transactions and from the exchange of informed generalizations among active participants in the market such as brokers, appraisers, mortgage lenders, and developers.

The fact that prices and real estate activity or turnover tend to move together is an aid in price analysis. A useful measure of activity is available in deeds-recorded series which are maintained in a number of communities and which are published on a national basis by the Wenzlick organization. The number of bona fide sales fairly measures the rate of market activity; and the number of deeds recorded at the county recorder's office, with the exceptions noted, is a measure of sales. Excluded from the series should be conveyances which are gifts or involuntary conveyances following mortgage or tax foreclosure; also quit claim deeds which are issued to clarify title. The use of land contracts creates a problem; they are often not recorded, and they usually mature into a deed at a date long after the sale was actually consummated. Because of the practical difficulties of sorting out the various types of property the deeds-recorded series is an aggregate which does not reflect differences in the rates of activity within the various submarkets. In spite of these imperfections deeds recorded do indicate changes in the level of market activity which is of value to the investor-analyst.

It is unusual for real estate prices to rise except in company with increased sales activity, or for increased sales to occur without a rise in prices. Thus the early intimations of change in the level of market activity are precursors of changing values save in unusual situations. However, it is possible for prices to be sustained in the face of falling market activity. For example, during late 1957 and early 1958 the Wenzlick index of real estate activity was falling to a point well below the normal or trend line, while at the same time, the Wenzlick price index for homes was well sustained.

Wenzlick and others have contended that there is a strong tendency for real estate activity to move with a cyclical regularity. Wenzlick has measured these cycles over a century or more and finds an average cycle of eighteen and one-quarter years. Others believe these cycles to be so strongly modified by irregular and unpredictable factors as to be of small predictive value.

In the housing market, as in much of the real estate market in general, an instable demand impinges on a relatively stable supply with the result that market prices are in constant flux. Demand factors change often, and the degree of change may be considerable. Reacting against a supply that can be increased only slowly and which rarely declines, fluctuating demand levers a fairly rapid response in prices. Slow though it may be an increase in supply finally does appear after prices rise, in consonance with classic economic theory, and the ultimate effect is to check further price increases. Thus in interpreting the effect of positive demand forces on prices we recognize the importance of the status of the responding construction activity. For example, the opening of a new industry and a flood of immigrant workers will generate substantial early effects on house prices. Later, however, when the local home builders have stepped up the rate of production a further immigration may have little price effect.

A large part of our discussion of the factors affecting prices in the market of homes for sale has application to any of the many possible subdivisions of the housing market. For example, the homes-for-sale market can be split into markets for homes of various price class and location. However, it is often possible to sort out special market factors influencing certain classes and locations—houses in the $20,000 to $30,000 price class or homes in the western suburbs of a metropolitan area.

In most communities the investor will find a discouragingly inadequate supply of market facts available on which to base his analysis of future price trends. To a considerable extent he must rely on informed opinions and general impressions. However, in a few areas, notably Los Angeles and San Francisco, there are effective cooperative efforts among realtors, builders, and lenders to collect and publish significant market data. The market information published by private services and governmental agencies on a national or regional basis is useful within limits, but the essentially local nature of the real estate market means that conditions in each market may be significantly different. In spite of this basic truth many of the real estate factors do appear to move together in many areas, but exceptions are so numerous as to indicate the need for local facts if conclusions are to be dependable.

Demand Factors. Because changes in the quantity and quality of demand are mainly accountable for changes in market prices during most of the cycle we will examine them first. The distinction between *quantity* and *quality* of demand is important to recognize. Sheer increase in the number of households to be sheltered will not change prices in all corners of the housing market. And in the presence of a constant demand, prices may rise for one type of housing and fall for another when shifts in tastes occur. The quality of demand, then, is expressed in the specifications of the dwelling units demanded.

Another distinction of importance is between *potential* demand and *effective* demand. The potential quantity and quality of demand becomes real or effective only when backed by purchasing power, or money in the hands of the consumer. There are families which need shelter and prefer an independent dwelling unit of given description but are not in the market because they cannot pay the price or rent. Unless housed at public expense they have to double up with relatives or break up the family. Such families represent potential, but not effective, demand. In times of prosperity the proportion of such cases is very small and of little market importance.

There is a chronically large potential demand among tenants for homes to purchase, but a lack of savings to provide a down payment or of sufficient income to meet monthly purchase payments prevents much of this demand from becoming effective. We have seen how a liberalizing of credit terms through FHA or VA can convert such potential demand to effective demand.

In the following discussion of demand factors in the housing market we will identify and discuss the various statistical measures which are available as market indicators and which the investor must seek out and analyze in his attempt to forecast price and activity movements. In addition, we will show the sequential relationship between changes in each factor and in other market phenomena, particularly prices.

Economic Base. In earlier chapters we have urged the thesis that urbanism is essentially an economic phenomenon. If cities are founded on economic considerations, it follows that their future growth will be vitally affected by what happens to the originating forces and by other economic factors which may appear from time to time. The demand for the services of urban real estate, then, has its beginnings in the economic base of the community—the unique combination of economic activities and resources which are the source of income for its inhabitants in the various forms of wages, salaries, dividends, royalties, pensions, rents, insurance or annuity payments, interest, or profits. We have already distinguished primary and secondary economic activities and identified the former as the more important early indicator of change in local demand factors. When local areas are viewed as separate economies in a balance-of-payments framework the importance of the basic or exporting activities is revealed by the fact that a persistent imbalance in payments may result in a falling local price level, reduced standard of living, and unemployment and emigration. The distinction between primary and secondary activities has further significance in that the growth or decline of the primary industries depend on factors external to the community, while the secondary industries and services are directly affected by changes in local income, and such changes are likely to originate in the primary industries.

It may be well to restate the fact that a first step in the real estate investment process is the measure and prediction of the pattern of productivity. Generally speaking, in a growing community the demand for the services of real estate and thus real estate productivity and value will be sustained or will rise. In a stagnant or a declining area the reverse tends to obtain. Thus real estate investment decisions are strongly influenced by the prospects for future growth or decline, and to a greater or lesser degree, every parcel of land in the community will be affected by such prospects. Of course, some types of land use and some areas of the community will be affected more than others; the expansion of heavy industry, for example, may bolster land values in the industrial section of the city and have only indirect effect elsewhere. The closing of a military post near a small city may depress rents and residential values in certain price ranges and reduce the productivity of tavern properties but only mildly influence values in the better residential districts and in the downtown retail center. Economic base analysis should be directed to the prediction of both the quantity and quality of change in an effort to foretell not only the degree of the impact on real estate but also the kinds of properties to be affected. The degree to which local economic activities are subject to cyclical fluctuations is also a matter of interest to the real estate investor, for an instable economic base will be reflected in fluctuating property income and value though long-term trends may be favorable. Such instability tends to increase the financial risk in real estate investment and call for more conservative financing where fixed charges can be minimized.

Local economic activities may be measured in terms of units produced or value of production, sales, or of services rendered. Perhaps the most commonly used measure is the number of persons employed. While this measure leaves much to be desired as an accurate reflection of the relative economic importance of the various activities and the several establishments, it is generally the most available information. Employment data have the further virtue of expressing growth or decline in terms of job opportunities. It is the expansion of such opportunities which leads to immigration and population growth; job reductions result in unemployment, emigration, declining local income, and falling property values.

Rate of Growth (or Decline). In general, predictions of community growth or decline call for predictions of the economic health of the primary industries. Expansion or shrinkage in the number of workers employed in primary activities is usually followed by similar changes in the secondary or service activities. It is possible for the secondary activities to prosper and expand without expansion in the primary activities but only slowly and in small measure. It is quite unlikely that secondary activities may expand in the face of a decline in primary industry or vice versa. To a major extent, therefore, though not exclusively, local real estate values in general will rise or fall in response to factors which are external to the community. Real estate values in Detroit are influenced by the degree to which general national prosperity adds to the number of two-car families; Miami hotel properties shift in value as business conditions change in New York and Chicago; farm incomes in Wisconsin influence university enrollment and thus the value of rooming houses near the campus in Madison. On the other hand, industrial migration has its effect both on land values in the city deserted and in the new location without reference to exogenous business conditions.

Quality of Growth. The point has already been made that the specific impact of economic growth or decline will reflect the specific industry which is involved. Of course, the decline of the major local industry will be felt by all property owners, though not all at the same time. It is hoped that the St. Lawrence Seaway will stimulate the entire Middle Western economy and, presumably, increase land values. But it is unlikely that all lake ports will share equally in its benefits; where business is affected, the impact will be on port facilities and activities related to shipping, and on those industries which can reduce shipping costs in either the importing of raw materials or the exporting of finished products. Again, one might contrast the effects on real estate values of a new heavy industry, such as a steel plant and a new institution such as a large VA hospital. The steel plant would call for a large site in the industrial district with rail or water facilities. There would be a large number of new job opportunities for semiskilled and unskilled workers and a smaller number of engineers and executives. The kinds of additional services demanded at the secondary level—housing, entertainment, medical care, or clothing—would reflect the income level and cultural backgrounds of new citizens brought in to fill the jobs. In contrast, the VA hospital facility would be located in quite a different part of the city, and the high proportion of doctors, technicians, and nurses required to man the hospital would result in quite a different pattern in the impact on real estate values.

Stability. The term stability has two different meanings in the context of economic base analysis. It is used to mean resistance to decline, and it is also used to mean a minimum of short-term or cyclical fluctuations. The real estate investor is interested in both of these aspects of employment in the industries which make up the local economic base. The long-term trend in the demand for its products is the best evidence of an industry's ability to resist secular decline; industries dependent upon natural resources such as minerals or forests are stable only so long as the resources are unexhausted. Highly competitive industries which are subject to technological or style obsolescence are not dependable components of the base while industries dealing in the necessities and staples of life are more likely to maintain present levels and even grow with general population increase.

In general, diversification in the economic activities which comprise the base lends stability to it. The larger the number of firms included in the base, the more stable it is. Single industry towns are vulnerable; if external economic conditions reduce the demand for its products there is no cushioning employment in other basic industries, and the effect on the community may be drastic. The stability of any industry is conditioned by the nature of its product; the demand for luxuries and for durable goods is less stable than for necessities and nondurables. The broader the scope of the market, the more stable the demand. The production of producers' goods is more volatile than the production of consumers' goods.

Demographic Factors. A healthy and expanding economic base is generally accompanied by an expanding population; increasing economic opportunity attracts individuals and families from outside and retains in the community most of those who come of age and enter the labor force. On the contrary, in stagnant and distressed areas, population stabilizes or declines; there is nothing to attract migrants and population loss occurs when the unemployed move out in search of jobs in other communities, and the young people, finding no opportunity at home, venture forth to seek their fortune elsewhere. In the long run the demand for the services of real estate rises and falls with changes in population; but an analysis of the economic base and its prospects will indicate how large a population can be supported in the area and thus will foretell future population trends.

Birth statistics have their special meanings in terms of the demand for real estate. The birth of a child often brings a change in the quality of the family's housing demand. It increases the space needs and may increase the value which is put on suburban living. But for some families, living near the level of subsistence, another mouth to feed may call for reducing the housing budget and seeking a smaller, cheaper, and less well-located dwelling. New babies mean more business for diaper services, children's wear shops, obstetricians, and pediatricians; and thus more space is needed for these services.

An increase in population in a community through natural increase, i.e., the excess of births over deaths does not create a proportionate increase in the need for housing. In fact, the number of units required by the larger population might actually decrease; death often results in the dissolution of a family and the release of a dwelling unit as the survivors move out of town, shift to a room, or share quarters with relatives. On the other side of the balance, a new baby does not call for an additional dwelling unit, though a larger one may be indicated. Babies do not rent or buy housing until they reach marriageable age; thus the babies of today will not add to the quantitative demand for another twenty years.

The net change in community population is the sum of births plus migration less deaths. Migration may flow in either direction depending upon local economic conditions or such special attractions as a warm climate. The immediate effect of migration upon real estate values depends on the social and economic characteristics of the migrants. Facts on migration in and out of the community are hard to secure. Information from moving companies is usually incomplete. The United States census gives some guide to the rate of movement in reporting on the place of previous residence for families which recently moved. Some estimates of migration are made by assuming that the difference between total population change and natural increase is explained by migration. Accurate annual figures on population change on a local basis are also rare. Such estimates are made by chambers of commerce or city planning officials and tend to be optimistic. Annual school censuses provide accurate counts of children by age groups in many cities. Intercensus population estimates, using the United States decennial count as a base, may be reasonably dependable for a few years immediately after the census but decline in accuracy as the years pass. The change in the number of utility meters is often used as an indicator of population change.

The age distribution of the community population is an important demand factor. Each age group differs to some extent in the services which it requires and the activities in which it engages. Thus the demand for park benches and shuffleboard courts is much stronger in St. Petersburg, Florida, than in Detroit, Michigan. Young families with children seek suburban homes with generous yard space. The housing needs of older persons reflect reduced family size after the departure of the children, the reduced mobility of the older couple, reduced income as the peak earning years are passed, and less physical vigor to meet the demands of maintaining house and yard. The number of persons who are to enter the 18 to 22 age group each year is a significant fact in evaluating housing demand. The average age at marriage is now about 20; the more families formed by marriage, the greater the demand for the kind of housing accommodations which young people require, mainly rental quarters of small size. Because of the common custom for both man and wife to hold jobs for a time after marriage, convenient and central locations are often sought; and because of the double income more than modest rents can be met.

It has been noted that the average age at time of home purchase is around thirty-five though it appears to be falling. Thus the demand for single-family homes will be influenced by the number of persons entering this age group. It is an interesting fact that on a national basis, calculated on the age distribution of persons now in the population, between 1960 and 1970, the number of persons reaching twenty years of age each year will be sharply increasing, while the number of people reaching thirty-five years of age each year will be declining. This latter figure will start to rise about the end of the decade. Of course, in each community, the situation will be different, depending upon the age distribution and the effects of migration. If the migrants are older folks, as in many areas in Florida and the Southwest, the effect on housing requirements as well as on other service activities which use real estate will be different than if the migrants are young people attracted by jobs in industry.

The basic unit of housing demand is the household; a surprisingly high proportion of households, about one-quarter, are not the natural families of married couples with or without children. There are many single-person households which occupy family-type dwelling units; and there are many groups of unrelated individuals which absorb dwellings in competition with natural families. Marriage data available from the county records are not a complete measure of household formation, for they do not include these other household situations. Furthermore, if they are to be used as an indicator of housing needs, a deduction should be made for family dissolution by death or divorce where a dwelling unit is released.

Income. Changes in family income have important effects on both quantity and quality of housing demand in the sales market. An early effect of an increase in income is the increase in total demand for housing by encouraging the separation of families sharing accommodations, stimulating the marriage rate thus stepping up the number of families formed, and making it possible for single individuals and nonfamily groups to occupy separate dwelling units. These incomplete families represent one of the most elastic elements of demand.

There are no useful measures of the income elasticity of housing except the ratios of income to housing expense. There is considerable evidence that the proportion of income devoted to housing tends to decrease as income rises. As the income moves up, it may be assumed that the family tends to adjust its dollar expenditures for housing upward somewhat in proportion to the ratio for the income group into which it moves, but that the proportion of income devoted to this purpose will decline. But there are many lags and delays to such adjustments, and only a portion of all families which enjoy an increase in income will react by increasing housing expenditures. With prices stable, an additional housing expenditure is accompanied by a move upward in the housing scale of quality. Renter families may find that they are able to embark on homeownership. Owner families are able to trade up into more commodious homes. Of course, if housing rents and prices are rising along with incomes, much of the upward movement will be inhibited. In fact, the bidding of these fortunate families against a static or only slowly increasing supply will cause prices to rise to a point where the increase in income is little more than enough to maintain present levels of housing quality, and there will be no more trading up.

Rising incomes are generally the product of business prosperity. Thus a forecast of expanding business activity is a forecast of rising incomes and increased housing demand. With new job opportunities in the community a rising immigration can be anticipated. But though the quantity of demand should remain static, the trading-up movement generated by rising incomes would create demand pressures for many, if not all, classes of homes for sale but might leave a vacuum among the less desirable categories of homes and rental units.

When business prosperity departs and incomes turn down, the trading-up movement stops but does not reverse direction until conditions reach distress levels. Some homeowners are forced to reduce expenses by selling out and moving to smaller quarters. But initially, at least, most owners manage to hang on. In any event, the readjustment downward, as the counterpart of trading up, rarely develops until the depression has continued for some time, and unemployment and reduced incomes have reached serious proportions.

It may be said that unfavorable business prospects, though incomes be little affected, are sufficient to reduce greatly the effective demand for homes to buy. Moderate unemployment, slackening business activity, and a bleak outlook act rapidly to convince prospective home buyers to maintain their assets in liquid form, to avoid increased obligations, and to put up with their present housing, though inadequate, until the future brightens. The opposite situation, when business prospects are encouraging and a mood of optimism prevails, is calculated to lead home buyers cheerfully and willingly to sign on the dotted line.

Indicators of local employment, earnings, expenditures, and general business activity give some light on income levels and prospects. In some areas average weekly earnings for certain classes of workers are reported, and employment data are available in various forms. The local chamber of commerce often publishes data reflecting local business activity such as bank debits, postal receipts, auto sales, department store sales, and other series.

Mortgage Credit. It has been made abundantly clear that home purchase is largely a credit transaction. True, some homes are paid for in cash, but total annual borrowings for home purchase are of the order of $20 billion. It is patent that the availability of credit and the terms on which mortgage money can be secured may have a powerful effect on the conversion of potential demand into effective demand. And need we repeat that only change in effective demand generates price adjustment in the market.

The sources of mortgage credit were discussed in Chapter VII, where it was made clear that the causative factors making for surplus or shortage of loanable funds are factors which are external to the housing market. But because of the importance of credit in the housing market, the real estate analyst must understand the operations of the mortgage market and must have knowledge of current developments if he is to foresee price trends in housing. Prediction is particularly difficult because of the active participation of the Federal government in the mortgage market and the uncertainties of the political factors which inevitably are operative.

As in any other market, a shortage of mortgage money leads to a higher price for credit. Accompanying this trend are less liberal terms and greater selectivity. Thus lenders may require larger down payments and will favor shorter repayment periods. The better collateral properties and the better credit risks will be favored. Interest rates will be raised, but the initial adjustment to the price of money to the borrower is often in the form of increased fees and "closing costs." As borrowing becomes more difficult and terms less liberal more and more potential home purchasers are frozen out; the reduced effective demand leads sellers to cut prices, and the general level of market prices tends to decline. As credit eases the reverse effects are observed; more potential buyers become effective units of demand and, pushing on supply, tend to force prices upward. When production does not respond to keep supply in near balance with the increased demand, the effect of the continued shortage of dwelling units is for more liberal credit terms to be absorbed in price advances rather than to allow buyers to enjoy improved housing standards for the same monthly mortgage payment. Fisher points out that in a seller's market, easier mortgage credit terms are translated into the amount which one can borrow at a constant debt service. The buyer is thereby able to carry a higher-priced house, and the seller is in a bargaining position which enables him to sell the same quality house at a higher price.[1]

[1]Ernest M. Fisher, *Urban Real Estate Markets*, National Bureau of Economic Research, New York, 1951.

The effect of liberal credit terms on the rate of market activity and the level of prices seems to vary somewhat with the particular financial situation of the majority of the potential buyers. Following a depression, when the liquid assets of families are at low ebb, the most effective form of credit easing is to lower the required down payment. In postdepression prosperity the buyers can meet the monthly payments but can produce only a modest down payment. Under other conditions, after a period of prosperity when savings have accumulated, the buyers may have a substantial down payment, but as a result of rising prices, the mortgage and its monthly payments may be too burdensome unless interest rates are lowered or the term of the loan extended, or both, so that the monthly payment may be reduced to a level within reach of the buyer's income. When this is done the effect of the increase of effective market demand may be felt on prices.

All mortgages are recorded at the office of the register of deeds or its equivalent. In some cities daily or weekly listings of mortgages are published and distributed on a subscription basis. Too often details such as interest rates and terms of repayment are not reported. However, inquiries at various lending institutions can establish trends in rates and terms. A rise or fall in interest rates is an indicator of a change in the availability of mortgage money. Because higher costs of money result in heavier monthly payments, higher rates tend to reduce effective demand for home purchase.

Foreclosures. Since the early thirties foreclosures have fallen to a long-sustained low level. During prosperity, and with rising real estate values, homeowners who overbuy or cannot meet payments for other reasons are able to unload at no loss and often at a profit. Thus the number of cases of delinquencies which actually reach foreclosure action is small indeed. However, in a buyer's market, and without the sustaining force of full employment, the rate of foreclosures may rise in reflection of a housing surplus and falling values. This indicator is not of the sensitive variety which foretells trouble and price decline. Foreclosures are trouble already arrived, and fall at the end of a chain of factors related to prices, for it is unlikely that foreclosures will increase substantially save after a price decline. For the past several years, on a national basis, foreclosure data have shown stability at a low level in foreclosures per 100,000 families.

Inventory Utilization (Vacancies). Changes in the utilization of the standing stock of real estate facilities in a community are important market indicators. Such change may be measured in the following two ways:

1. The proportion of spatial units which are occupied and in use. The number of vacant or unused units related to the total stock provides the familiar measure of the vacancy percentage.

2. The intensity of use. In the housing supply this relationship is expressed in terms of the number of cases of families doubled up or sharing a dwelling unit, or in the ratio of occupant persons to the size of the dwelling, e.g., persons per room.

The gross number of vacancies in the housing stock may be a misleading statistic. Not all vacant units are on the market; some are seasonal dwellings, some are boarded up, and others held off the market for various reasons, for example, houses which have been sold and are awaiting occupancy. In the census counts of vacancies in 1959 the total gross vacancy was around 10 per cent of all dwellings in nonfarm structures, but the proportion actually for sale or rent was only 3 per cent. Thus less than one-third of the vacancies were effectively on the market as factors which might influence rents and prices. This fact strongly suggests the importance of refining local vacancy counts to provide a true measure of the surplus hanging over the market.

Increasing vacancies foretell a weakening in prices and rents in accordance with classical market behavior, while a declining surplus of space suggests that rents and values will stiffen. Changes in the intensity of use are not only harder to detect and measure but are also of lesser significance. In times of severe housing shortage, families may be forced to double up or crowd into dwellings which are too small, but such a situation is rare and is concomitant with other more easily observed indicators of shortage. At other times, doubling up and overcrowding may be a reflection of a business recession, low family incomes, and unemployment accompanied by high vacancies and falling real estate values. When vacancy data are available for the several housing submarkets—by type of structure, by location, by tenure, or by price and rent class—the information on changing balances of demand and supply are particularly useful in investment analysis and in directing the activities of builders.

In using vacancy data to forecast price change, it is useful to know the critical point in the changing vacancy percentage at which price begins to be affected. For example, vacancies might increase up to x per cent before sellers find that price reductions are necessary to attract buyers. As vacancies decrease owners find that they can begin to raise prices after the x per cent level is reached. Actually this critical vacancy percentage will vary among classes of homes and among communities. Its effects are more clearly apparent in the rental market but also are evident in the sales market. Generalizations to the effect that a 4 or 5 per cent vacancy is normal should be viewed with skepticism. The analyst has little use for the concept of a normal vacancy but will be assisted in forecasting if he can discover the critical vacancy point for the class of property in the locality with which he is concerned.

SUPPLY FACTORS

Construction Costs. Costs of production of housing exert a basic influence on price. If costs including a profit cannot be covered by selling price, no new building will take place. When costs are rising, prices must rise correspondingly if new construction is to be profitable. Over the long run, prices of existing houses as well as new houses tend to follow construction costs. Another observable trend is that construction costs tend to rise as the volume of house production rises. With these two factors moving upward, market prices of new and older homes shift in the same direction, though there may be a time lag in the movement of prices on existing houses. If so, it will become evident to buyers that they can find a better bargain among the older homes. This increases demand for existing houses and tends to bring their prices into line with those of new homes.

As construction costs continue to rise, a point is reached where buyers can no longer follow. They must either be satisfied with a house of lower quality or buy no house at all. Enough potential buyers will decide to wait so that sales will fall off. The marginal or high-cost producers among the builders will suffer most as lower-cost producers are able to lower prices by 10 to 15 per cent without experiencing net or out-of-pocket loss.

Construction costs are slow to fall even after production has slumped. One of the large items is labor, and once wage rates have been raised, there is great resistance to reduction. As unemployment spreads, effective labor costs do decline some by reason of the greater productivity of workers and because some workers, even union members, may accept less than union scale. The prices of building materials and equipment eventually are adjusted downward, but even before this change occurs, major cost reductions result from closer bids by contractors and subcontractors. When faced with serious competition, contractors' bids will be figured more closely, profit margins reduced, and items to cover contingencies cut to a minimum.

Land costs are another major item in house building. An increasing share is accounted for by the improvements which are required to make the land usable—sanitary and storm sewer, water, sidewalk, curb and gutter, and streets and pavement. These items may contribute one-half to two-thirds of the finished land cost to the builder. But in a buyer's market, if there is an ample supply of subdivision lots ready for use, prices to builders will be substantially adjusted downward by subdividers who hesitate to face the costs of carrying unsold vacant land with its taxes, special assessments for improvements, and costs of sterile capital.

Local series on costs of construction in index form are available only in a few of the larger cities as published by commercial real estate and appraisal services. FHA field offices maintain detailed cost information and occasionally release summaries. The most useful form of a cost index for residential construction is based on periodic estimates of the cost of a standard house, reflecting changes in specific materials prices and labor cost in the proportions in which they contribute to the total. Information on changes in materials prices and wage rates will give an indication of the direction of cost changes. This kind of nonintegrated information, as well as the more refined standard house cost index, fails to reflect changes in the efficiency of labor and in the profit margins of contractors which occur with changes in pressures on the productive capacity of the building industry.

National indexes of construction costs are useful if applied to local situations with caution and with an effort to make adjustments where local cost factors are known to be moving at a different rate than is generally true in most other areas.

Building Activity. The rate of new construction of the various kinds of urban real estate facilities is an important market indicator for it represents more or less permanent additions to the supply. To arrive at a measure of the net addition, one should count as deductions the structures which are demolished for one reason or another. Actually, this is a relatively small figure for nonresidential buildings, in fact, so small that on a national basis it may be ignored for most purposes. The number of residential dwelling units destroyed by disaster, demolished, or lost through merger for various reasons is estimated at from 130,000 to 300,000 per year, which is 10 to 25 per cent of recent levels of house production.

Construction of all types tend to move forward together in response to basic forces of growth. Expanding communities need houses, apartments, shopping centers, churches, hospitals, sewage-disposal plants, and factories. Not all of these submarkets move at the same rate or with the same timing, for each is influenced by its special set of demand and supply factors. In each market construction activity increases after demand pressures have been exerted; vacancies decrease, and rents or prices start to rise among the existing facilities. Particularly in home building, activity responds to easy credit, which strengthens effective demand, and to prosperity, and rising family incomes. Thus, rising vacancies, falling rents and prices, tighter credit, and unfavorable business conditions are precursors of declining construction activity.

Construction activities are measured in the dollar value of contracts awarded or in work put in place. F. W. Dodge publishes estimates on the contracts figure, and the U.S Department of Commerce issues estimates of construction volume on a national basis. However, for local analysis, reliance must be placed on building permit data. It is customary for the contractor to give a cost estimate when the permit is issued. This figure may represent only a part of the total cost, depending on local regulations, for it may omit important cost elements covered by separate permits and inspections such as electrical work, heating, and plumbing. Furthermore, the cost figure is an estimate and usually conservatively low. Consideration should be given to the fact that there is often a time lag between the date of the issuance of the permit and the beginning of the actual construction and a further time interval of several months before the building is complete and becomes an effective part of the supply. Building permits for residential structures usually provide the information needed to measure the number of dwelling units which are being started and thus the prospective additions to the housing stock in terms of number of family accommodations. However, in the short run, the rate at which new houses are being started and the rate at which they are absorbed by the market may be significantly different. The difference will appear in an increase in the unsold inventory of new houses and in the interval of time between completion and sale.

Another measure of production in the housing market is subdividing activity. Since each new subdivision is always recorded, it is easy to count the number of new lots added to the supply of building sites. The recording of a plat usually means that the lots are ready for sale or for use.

RENTAL SUBMARKET

Several types of real estate investor are interested in future rent changes in the residential rental submarket. Home buyers considering the alternatives of renting and buying will be influenced by the relationship of rents to the costs of homeownership. Thus if rents move downward there will be some reduction in the effective demand for homes, a change which will contribute to a softening of home prices. Rising rents will increase the relative attractiveness of homeownership and will add to effective demand for houses. The prospective home buyer who foresees falling rents may expect that home prices will follow rents down and that he can buy more advantageously later. The prospective seller will hasten to act before prices begin their downward pursuit of rents. New investment in the construction of rental properties is strongly influenced by rental prospects.

Among the factors influencing the demand for housing certain aspects have special application to rental accommodations. For example, the initial impact of immigration into a community is on rental housing. New citizens prefer to rent for a time in order to become acquainted with the various neighborhoods and with property values before buying. If the immigrants are industrial workers in unskilled or semiskilled categories, many of them may not expect to become homeowners.

The age distribution of the existing population is a useful fact in evaluating the probable effect on rents of rising incomes. Where the proportion of people of marriageable age is large, rising incomes would stimulate more marriages than if the age distribution were skewed to the upper or lower age ranges. Since newly married couples typically seek rental units the pressure of effective demand would be greater. In general, any factor which increases the marriage rate is the precursor of rising demand pressure on rental housing. It is also true that old people resort to rental housing, but rising incomes have only a mild effect on their housing expenditures; as pensioners their incomes are relatively stable.

The effect of rising incomes in the rental market is to encourage an upward movement into higher quality units. However, where year leases are generally used, such adjustments are delayed. Another product of rising incomes is a move to homeownership on the part of many tenant families ripe for such a change. At the same time, an increment to rental demand appears in the form of families who stop sharing their living quarters and in households of one person or unrelated persons who move from rented rooms into fully equipped dwelling units. These demand changes are checked as rents rise under their pressure. They are reversed when incomes fall. It is probable that rents are more sensitive to reduced demand and that adjustments come more quickly than when incomes are rising.

A residential rent index on a national basis is maintained by the Bureau of Labor Statistics (BLS) and reflects general trends. Some local indexes are maintained by cooperative efforts of apartment house owners and managers. There are such substantial local differences that national figures can be misleading. Even in the same community the rents on different kinds of housing move to a different timing. A continuing study and recording of rentals for different types of units as advertised in the newspapers is a practical method of detecting major changes. However, as vacancies increase, some landlords conceal rent reductions by giving tenants concessions, such as a month's rent free out of a year in order to maintain the appearance of stable rents.

On the supply side of the rental market, we find that the single-family house is active in both the sale and rental market at the same time. Owners who face a slow sales market frequently rent houses until a more favorable time for sale arrives. Between 1940 and 1950 the number of rented one-family homes declined from 6.2 to 5.2 million under conditions of a housing shortage and high prices. Few houses are built originally for rental purposes, but a substantial proportion of older homes have been rented at one time or another.

Production of new rental units responds to the profit potential growing out of a favorable rent-cost relationship. But other factors, particularly favorable credit terms, appear to be of basic importance. It should be recognized that a large share of multifamily housing is originated by builders and contractors on their own account. The small two- to four-family structures are often built by home builders to keep busy in slack seasons and to "store" some of their profits from home-building operations. Under some conditions the builder can sell the apartment structure at a later time and pay tax on only the capital gain above his builder's profit. The buyers of small rental properties are not usually informed investors but rather persons of small means who may expect to occupy one of the units and to manage the property. They often appear to be satisfied with a low return on their investment and in some cases, no doubt, their ignorance of rental housing operation results in overestimating income and underestimating expenses. Because of the relatively small equity capital required, particularly where the builder may count his builder's profit as equity, construction of this kind of small rental structure does not depend so much on highly favorable credit terms as in the case of the major apartment development.

Except in the largest metropolitan areas the history of the last thirty-five years strongly suggests that there is more likely to be substantial construction of apartments when very liberal credit arrangements are available. Tax considerations also play an important part in investors' calculations. In recent years the policies and programs of the Federal government have strongly influenced the flow of capital into large-scale rental housing projects. The forecaster, then, should watch legislation and changing regulations for indications of credit terms and tax advantages which might stimulate activity in rental housing construction.

RETAIL PROPERTY

Market forecasts relating to retail space are based on an analysis of factors affecting rental rates and occupancy. The investment or market value of this type of real estate reflects current rent levels and rental expectations based on market trends. Because of the high ratio of tenancy in retail space the most common expression of productivity is rent per square foot per year. With few exceptions, commercial rental arrangements are expressed in a written lease signed by the parties to the transaction. Such leases are often long and complicated documents which cover many conditions of tenancy other than the basic items of rent and term of occupancy. The major terms and conditions of a commercial lease cover such items as:

1. Description of premises leased

2. Rent reserved and schedule of payments
3. Duration of tenancy, beginning and terminating dates
4. Services included in the rent—heat, water, hot water, air cooling, gas, electricity, cleaning of public areas, cleaning of tenants' quarters, etc.
5. Maintenance and repair
6. Insurance coverage
7. Payment of taxes
8. Subleasing
9. Limitations on the use of the building
10. Provisions in case building is rendered unusable
11. Procedure in case of default
12. Arbitration of disputes
13. Alterations and additions

The particular combination of provisions contained in a lease is an important aspect of the transaction. As in the case of residential accommodations, landlords provide more than space in many instances. Space in the larger buildings is usually heated, and janitor service may be provided. Air cooling is available in the more modern buildings. In office space over stores heat may be included in the rent, but more often than not the tenant is responsible. In all rental arrangements, the responsibility for repairs and structural maintenance should be clearly established. With few exceptions, landlords have responsibility for maintaining the shell of the building, the outside walls, and the roof. Repairs and maintenance of the interior are shared in various ways between landlords and tenants.

The leasing of property, unlike its outright sale, creates a continuing relationship between landlord and tenant, and the lease spells out the terms of this relationship. Both parties are concerned with such terms as well as with the amount of the rent reserved. To the extent that the lease provisions restrict the tenant or impose financial responsibilities or subject him to contingent liabilities, he will seek an offset in the form of reduced rental payments. The landlord will view terms which similarly affect him in just the same way. The duration of the tenancy is an important item for both parties. For certain lines of business, retail, for example, a long lease may be worth a higher rental rate than a short lease, for with occupancy assured for the longer period, the retailer can hope to familiarize customers with his location and can fully write off his initial investment in fixtures and front. Under certain conditions the landlord may be willing to accept a lower rental rate on a long lease if, for example, he anticipates a decline in rents in the area.

Another factor which the landlord weighs heavily, particularly on a long lease, is the tenant's credit rating. The general financial responsibility of the tenant is a bulwark behind the rental contract during a business decline when the tenant enterprise may be losing money.

Leases which run for five years or less generally call for a constant rental rate. For longer leases, the landlord may demand a step lease, for example, providing a higher rate during the last half of a ten-year term. Leases may have any number of steps or rate changes at various time intervals. The landlord employs this pattern to reflect, as nearly as he can accomplish in his negotiations with the tenant, his expectations of rent changes in the area and what he might secure from a new tenant if free to negotiate. On his part, the tenant seeks to restrict the rent increase to increments which he expects to be able to meet out of increased business volumes.

Today's most popular form of retail rental contract is the percentage lease. Under its terms the landlord receives as rent a share of the sales receipts of the tenant during a specified period, usually a month or a year. Landlords seek to include a provision that in no event shall the rent paid fall below a certain minimum. Or the lease may provide a stated rent with a percentage of gross sales in addition. The minimum rent provision is included in most retail percentage leases except in the cases of certain strong tenants whose records of effective merchandising assures a sufficient sales volume to yield an acceptable rental. Percentage leases may contain upper limits on rental to be paid and may be based on other measures of business success, such as profits.

It should be apparent to all that the percentage lease joins landlord and tenant in a species of partnership. As the tenant prospers, so does the landlord. Tenants feel some justice in sharing the benefits of a location which grows in productivity as the community expands. There is also justice in the percentage lease to protect the landlord in case of inflation. But tenants are not happy in the sharing of increased sales receipts which are the product of their own merchandising skill and exceptional industry.

The percentage of sales paid by various types of retail business varies according to the nature of the business operation. Low percentages are paid by operations which have a high volume and low markup, such as a supermarket, which may pay 1 to 2 per cent. At the other extreme is the specialty shop with a high unit price, high markup, and low turnover. Such stores may pay from 7 to 10 per cent. While leasing practice has established certain ranges in percentages for the several retail types, this provision of the lease is subject to negotiation in light of the other provisions. For example, the minimum guarantee of rent and the percentage tend to be complementary. If the landlord demands a high minimum he may have to accept a lower percentage provision. Or if he is willing to take his chances on the volume of business which his tenant will reach, he can negotiate a higher percentage in return for a lower minimum guarantee.

One of the considerations of the landlord in fixing a minimum guaranteed rent in a percentage lease is the total of the fixed financial obligations which he, the landlord, must meet with respect to the property. He will try to negotiate a minimum which will cover the taxes for which he is responsible, operating expenses, and debt service. In fact, to secure a favorable mortgage loan on the property, particularly in the case of new construction such as a shopping center, there must be leases from financially responsible tenants with guaranteed minimum rents which cover fixed obligations, including debt service. Thus the lender is, in effect, protected by the assets and earnings of the tenants.

Because real property taxes on commercial property are so heavy a burden the lease provisions on the payment of taxes are important. Even though the landlord is legally responsible for tax payment, he is dependent on rents received for the funds required. Increased taxes over the years are almost certain; lower taxes almost unknown. Taxes are raised either because of increased costs of government or because the location grows in productivity and the assessed value is raised. The landlord seeks to pass on to the tenant any increase in taxes by providing in the lease that the tenant pay all taxes or that the tenant pay any increase in taxes during the term of the lease.

The first principle for the landlord to apply in his effort to secure optimum rent is to choose a tenant whose business can best exploit the location. For most types of retail business, location is a prime determination of success. For all types of commercial tenant, a poor location not well suited to the needs of the business is to be avoided by both tenant and landlord. The tenant can afford to pay a higher rent for an appropriate location and will pay it more cheerfully and dependably. The landlord should be reluctant to accept a tenant business ill suited to the location regardless of the rent which it is willing to pay. In deciding on the suitability of a given type of business from a locational standpoint, the landlord will need to apply the principles of city growth and structure discussed in all earlier chapters. He can learn much by analyzing the locations where are now located successful enterprises of the various types. He may need to call upon the expert services of a real estate counselor or commercial lease broker who is well versed in matters of retail and commercial location.

Chain store organizations have developed techniques for estimating the volume of business to be expected in a given location. While the estimates are subject to considerable error, because of incommensurable factors, the chains base their rent offers on these forecasts. Also, out of considerable experience in locating stores and on the basis of locational analyses of both successful and unsuccessful units, the chains have developed general locational specifications which are employed in locating new stores or relocating existing units. One of the common tools of locational analysis is the pedestrian traffic count. A tally is made of the pedestrians passing a given location during the business hours of the day. To be meaningful, such a count must be analyzed qualitatively to determine how many of the passers-by are potential customers. For some purposes only women are counted. In other cases the analyst tallies only persons carrying packages on the grounds that such people are in the shopping mood.

Before striking a rent bargain the landlord should know what rents are being paid for other properties in the neighborhood and in comparable locations in the community. However, this information must be carefully interpreted lest it be more misleading than helpful. In some of the larger cities, and for some classes of commercial property, there is a sufficiently active market to provide useful evidence of the market value of commercial space. However, because of differences in time and circumstances of the relatively infrequent commercial lease transactions, it is often difficult to establish useful generalized measures of rental value. The percentage lease, which joins landlord and tenant in partnership, avoids the necessity for a refined measure of space value. If the parties can agree on the perimeters of the deal as expressed in the minimum rent and the percentage of gross sales, and if the tenant business is a proper use for the site, the total rent payment will reflect the basic productivity of the location within the limits of the merchandising skill and energy of the tenant.

In an active market rental contracts tend to reflect the expected productivity of the business enterprise in the location. Forecasts of rents or of real estate values in specific retail locations involve forecasts of expected gross sales. The factors influencing gross sales are:

1. *The Number of Potential Customers for the Product or Service.* In order to judge the probability and degree of increase or decrease in the number of persons or families, the tributary or trade area of the retail store must first be defined. For a neighborhood delicatessen this might be but a few blocks in radius; for a downtown department store it would include the entire metropolitan area. Whether the population in the tributary area decreases, increases, or remains stable will depend on the combined effect of a variety of urban growth factors.

2. *Purchasing Power.* The ability and propensity to spend for goods and services at retail depends upon the incomes and attitudes of the people in the trade area. Thus the level of future retail sales will be influenced by the general economic health of the community, and in particular, by the employment prospects and incomes of those persons in

the tributary area. If the area is in a transitional stage the changing character of residential occupancy will often bring with it changes in occupational characteristics, in income levels, and in buying habits which may affect both the volume and nature of retail purchases.

3. *Competition.* The aggregate of the retail purchases in each line is shared among many retail outlets. Thus the effectiveness of present competition and the prospects for future competition are matters for estimation in forecasting retail rents and values in a given location. The competition may be located at a considerable distance from the retail district under study. For example, outlying shopping centers in the suburbs offer a serious threat to central business district retailers; wholesale houses and furniture stores in suburban spots are in competition with other like stores all over the community.

Retail properties in central areas are often strongly held either by the business firms which occupy them or by investors who look to the long-term productivity of the real estate for a regular and safe return. Such properties are rarely offered for sale; many of them are held on long-term leases. As a result, central area values are stable and react slightly to short-run influences. To the extent that short-run market factors have an effect, some of the following changes may influence values in the central area:

1. Local business booms or slumps affect retail sales and wholesale activity and thus influence the demand for central business district space.

2. Opening of new outlying shopping centers will have an effect on central area business. Even though this be a temporary effect, it will be interpreted by some owners as a permanent disaster.

3. The ebb and flow of capital seeking this form of investment may influence price.

4. The short-run impetus of the opening of an expressway, additional parking facilities, or the encouragement engendered by a cooperative program of downtown promotion and rehabilitation may give a fillip to values.

In outlying areas the basic factor determining price of commercial land is the growth prospect. This is a long-run productivity factor rather than a short-run market factor. However, real estate prices are likely to exhibit speculative behavior as a result of rumor, overoptimistic interpretation of growth trends, and competition among investors for choice sites. A frequent result is the overbuilding of commercial facilities well in advance of need. Concomitant with this speculative expansion, and in part explaining it, is the competition among chain stores and among local merchants for representation in new commercial centers with the result that commercial rents are bid up to higher levels than current productivity would justify. There is some evidence that commercial facilities in out-lying areas are built in spurts of activity because of the highly competitive nature of retailing, particularly among chain organizations. Following an excess of new construction there often comes a period of quiescence while the new facilities are being digested by the market.

In the older outlying and neighborhood shopping districts, and along string-street retail developments, the long-term trends are often downward in the demand for space and in the rentals which landlords can command. The competition of the more modern and better organized shopping centers is difficult to meet. At the same time, the tributary areas of the older retail districts are becoming less productive of business as the residents age and the neighborhoods grow less desirable. Lower-income groups tend to move in, and the purchasing power in the tributary areas falls off.

SUBDIVISION LOTS

The current inventory in the building lot market has some influence on price. The significant number is the count of vacant lots provided with the basic utilities, primarily sewer and water. Convenient and adequate school facilities are also important. Platted lots without utilities or nearby schools have much less force in the housing market. A shortage of lots served with utilities leads to rising prices; a surplus leads to price competition, for it is costly to hold lots unsold. This price cutting may take the form of quantity discounts to builders and of sales to builders on easy land contract terms sometimes requiring payment only after the builder has sold the house which he constructs on the site.

The investor for capital gain or speculator in subdivision lots must look to the basic housing demand factors as indicators of future price trends. Current and prospective levels of home-building activity are measures of the rate of building lot absorption.

OFFICE SPACE

Rental rates for office space move with changes in vacancy. Thus favorable business prospects may be the precursor of rising rents, for a business expansion will bring with it additional firms requiring space and will create added space needs for existing occupant firms. A business decline reverses these results and leads to vacancies and rent reductions. Additions to the supply of office space through new construction may weaken the rent levels if the increment is a substantial proportion of the total supply.

INDUSTRIAL LAND

The price of industrial land is related to the amount on the market in locations served by transport facilities and available in tracts of sufficient size for modern one-story plants, employee parking, and expansion. Present-day trends toward outlying and even remote locations mean that the effective supply of industrial sites is ample in most areas and that short-run factors are of low potency in affecting price.

XI

CONSTRUCTION

INTRODUCTION

In the discussion of the real estate market up to this point we have concerned ourselves almost entirely with the demand side, though some consideration was given to the standing stock of usable real estate as a market factor. But there remains to be presented the important productive process popularly termed *construction*, through which additions are made to the supply of urban real estate facilities. These supply increments are a response to the interplay of market forces; as additions to the supply, they alter the market balance and create repercussions in rents, prices, and market activity. Construction includes the processing and improvement of land as well as the fabrication of building materials into structures; it is all part and parcel of the same productive operation, though the preparation of the land and the construction of buildings may be separated in time and conducted by different agencies and enterprises.

Land is not ordinarily usable for urban activities without the application of capital and labor. Land is but one of the raw materials which is combined with other raw materials, semiprocessed and finished products, in the creation of a productive real estate enterprise. The land, of itself, provides space and support, but unless land is combined with pipes to bring the services of sewer, water, and gas; with other pipes to drain it of storm waters; with wires to carry electricity; with streets and roads and walks to make it accessible; and, in most cases, with structures to enclose the essential activities, it is of small value for urban uses. True, there are useful open spaces such as parks, plazas, and parking lots; but even in these cases, some modification of the original gift of nature is required.

The kinds of processing of land, installation of land improvements, and fabrication of structures which are comprehended under the term

269

construction can be classified on the basis of the product of the construction activity. The categories with relevance to urban areas include: [1]

Residential
Manufacturing
Commercial
General business
Health
Religious
Protective and penal
Judicial, legislative,
  and governmental
Power and light—production
  and transmission
Gas—production, storage,
  and distribution
Telephone and telegraph
  exchange and lines
Radio and television
Light manufacturing
Hotels and dormitories

Recreational, amusement,
  and assembly
Educational
Transportation—
  structures and tracks
Waterfront facilities and
  harbor improvements
Water supply—plants
  and pipes
Sewers and treatment
  plants
Highways, streets, and
  bridges
Airfields
Flood control—canals,
  dams, levees, and storm
  sewers

The relative importance of the modifications made to raw land for urban use is well illustrated in the case of the new suburban single-family homes built on land newly absorbed from agricultural use. If three home sites per acre are created (allowing for streets, parks, and service areas), the agricultural use value of the land per home site might range from $100 to $200. The builder or subdivider might pay from $2,000 to $3,000 per acre for raw land at the edge of a small city like Madison, Wisconsin. Thus, his raw-land cost would run from $667 to $1,000 per home site. On such a site a home to sell for $25,000 might be built. Thus, the agricultural value of the land would represent less than 1 per cent of the final investment value, and raw-land cost to the developer would be but 3 to 4 per cent. In larger cities these ratios might run a little higher, but in any case, the difference between the inputs of raw land and the economic value of the end product is very large indeed. This difference represents the contributions of site planning; engineering; grading; street improvements; sewer, water, gas, and electric services; and walks, curbs, and gutters; in addition to these site improvements is the structure itself and large off-site investments which add value to the property such as

[1] Classification adapted from Miles L. Colean and Robinson Newcomb, *Stabilizing Construction*, McGraw-Hill Book Company, Inc., New York, 1952, Appendix A, p. 179.

highways, public transportation facilities, schools, parks, shopping centers, and churches.

The objectives of this chapter are twofold. In the first place, many investment decisions involve new construction and will be the sounder for an understanding of construction procedures and the industrial organization involved in the creation of urban real estate facilities. Secondly, the home-building industry is of great social and economic importance; its products, for better or for worse, are the materials of which cities are made and create the environment with which urban populations perforce live in intimate contact. This chapter may provide useful perspective on home-building operations.

GENERAL NATURE OF THE CONSTRUCTION INDUSTRY

The economic importance of the construction industry is too well recognized to require extensive documentation in this volume. It plays a major role as a factor in general business conditions. Construction accounts for 10 to 12 per cent of the gross national product; the industry employs 3 million directly and millions more in the related activities of suppliers. In an active year construction may involve an investment of $50 billion including $20 billion in residential construction.

The production of urban real estate facilities, like all other production in our economy, is a response to forces of demand. It is the demand for prepared land and structures necessary to the conduct of urban activities which generates activity in the construction industry. The pressures of manufacturers and distributors for more space for the conduct of their businesses, the needs for office space, the requirements of institutions and governmental agencies for land and buildings, and the needs of a growing urban population for housing, schools, churches, streets, and utility services are among the demand forces which result in land development and construction. In addition to the forces of urban growth, other factors which may stimulate production of real estate facilities include the growing complexity and diversity of urban activities, rising standards of living, and technological and social change which makes existing facilities obsolete. Other forces of deterioration and obsolescence call for repair, replacement, and modernization.

The special characteristics of the demands for construction have resulted in the evolution of a unique industrial organization. The great variety in the types of structures and facilities which are demanded has required specialized types of producing organizations with considerable internal functional flexibility. Another form of flexibility is called for by the variability in the volume of construction demand which requires the productive capacity of the industry to expand rapidly and to accom-

Table XI-1

Value of New Construction Put in Place
1957, 1958, and Estimate for 1959

Type of construction	Value, in millions of dollars		
	1959	1958	1957
Total new construction	52,300	48,800	47,200
Private construction	35,200	33,800	33,300
Residential buildings (nonfarm)	19,500	17,700	16,530
New dwelling units	15,000	13,300	12,125
Additions and alterations	3,880	3,780	3,915
Nonhousekeeping	620	620	490
Nonresidential buildings (nonfarm)	8,500	8,730	9,155
Industrial	2,080	2,460	3,170
Commercial	3,630	3,500	3,585
Office buildings and warehouses	1,900	1,980	1,870
Stores, restaurants, and garages	1,730	1,570	1,715
Other nonresidential buildings	2,790	2,720	2,400
Religious	950	865	870
Educational	600	565	525
Hospital and institutional	600	605	505
Social and recreational	420	425	300
Miscellaneous	220	260	200
Farm construction	1,600	1,600	1,600
Public utilities	5,400	5,575	5,825
Railroad	325	300	450
Telephone and telegraph	950	900	1,075
Electric light and power	2,100	2,250	2,100
Gas	1,625	1,750	1,800
Other public utilities	400	375	400
All other private	200	195	190
Public construction	17,100	15,000	13,900
Residential buildings	1,125	830	505
Nonresidential buildings	5,075	4,625	4,470
Industrial	375	370	455
Educational	3,000	2,880	2,830
Hospital and institutional	475	400	330
Administrative and service	750	530	430
Other nonresidential buildings	475	445	425
Military facilities	1,400	1,210	1,275
Highways	6,000	5,350	4,825
Sewer and water systems	1,520	1,390	1,345
Public service enterprises	690	450	395
Conservation and development	1,080	1,000	965
All other public	210	210	120

SOURCE: U.S. Departments of Labor and Commerce.

modate to low levels of demand without lasting disruption. The fact that construction must take place on the site creates special organizational, administrative, and technical problems to which construction companies must adapt. The local nature of construction demand and the immobility of the product call for mobility of industrial facilities among communities to serve unusual demands in various localities.[2]

The direct demand for new construction generally comes from one of the following:

1. User: the individual or organization which will occupy and use the facility

2. Public agency: the governmental unit responsible for providing the service or facility

3. Investor: a person or group with capital to invest in a real estate enterprise which is expected to yield a return or profit

The actual physical construction and processing in land preparation and building is done:

1. On a custom basis on land owned or purchased by the ultimate user and in accordance with plans and specifications provided by him

2. By a builder without an order for the product and in anticipation of a future sale at a profit

As an example of a user building on order would be a life insurance company constructing a home office building. In the case of single-family homes both custom building on order by the user and speculative building before sale are widely encountered. Public agencies providing courthouses or highways, water service, or public parking ramps carry out the construction on their own land by order in accord with their own plans and specifications. Real estate investors plan and contract for the construction of apartment buildings and shopping centers. At times, construction companies will build investment type properties with the expectation of selling them to investors at a profit. Or the construction company may play the parts of both investor and builder and retain ownership of the property for investment purposes.

It has been estimated that only one-sixth of all home construction is custom-built by a general contractor on order. With the exception of speculative home building and do-it-yourself home building, however, almost all other construction is on order. Thus, out of a total construction volume of $49 billion in 1958, speculative home building accounted for some $9 billion which means that nearly $40 billion was in the form of contract work based on the orderer's plans and specifications.

Except in the home-building field, construction is largely done by contracting organizations which undertake to build a bridge or construct an office building to specific plans and specifications for an agreed price.

[2] *Ibid.*, chap. 6, pp. 90ff.

A relatively small proportion of all construction is done on "force account," i.e., by workers hired directly by the owner and using materials purchased by him. In the home-building field the building organizations at various times engage in both custom building on contract and speculative building in advance of orders. In the larger markets the volume home builder may do no contract building except by way of taking orders to build standard models at an agreed price.

Only in the exceptional case does the contractor perform with his own employees and equipment all of the construction operations under the contract. He may employ a number of special trade or subcontractors to perform a variety of functions. In a typical house-building operation, the primary or general contractor may use subcontractors for heating, plumbing, excavating, masonry, tile, electrical work, painting, and roofing. Home builders who build in advance of sale also perform much of the work through subcontractors. The typical small home builder hires a few carpenters and laborers and does the rough and finish carpentry. Most of the rest of the building operations are done on subcontract with up to twenty specialty operations involved. For large buildings the diversity of subcontractors may be greater with forty to fifty specialty operations and nearly as many subcontracts. In some kinds of construction, road building, for example, the prime contractor may perform all operations with his own equipment and employees. Some buildings are built entirely by subcontractors with the prime contractor acting only as general superintendent and coordinator.

In the heavy construction field there are a number of giant firms which take jobs anywhere in the world. There are also many smaller organizations which operate on a local, state-wide, or regional basis. On many projects bids are taken and contracts let to a prime contractor and directly by the owner to specialty contractors for the major mechanical work such as plumbing, heating, and electricity. The prime contractor acts as coordinator. On the largest jobs two or more prime contractors may share the work and the risk.

Construction contracts with both prime and subcontractors are usually awarded to the lowest bidder. However, contracts may be negotiated with a single contractor and let at an agreed figure. A home builder often establishes continuing business relationships with certain subcontractors whom he comes to trust; the builder does not bother to ask for bids from others but accepts the one subcontractor's figure as reasonable and regularly employs him on all jobs. Another basis of contracting is cost plus or an agreement to pay the sum of all direct labor and material costs plus either a percentage or a lump sum to cover the contractor's overhead and profit.

Before a contractor can bid on a job or negotiate a price, he must estimate his expected costs on the basis of the plans and specifications for the work to be done. Such cost estimates are subject to considerable variation even among expert and experienced estimators. On a relatively small project, such as a dwelling, it is not uncommon for bids to vary by 20 per cent. In part such variation may be the result of different cost estimates, and in part it may reflect differences in allowances for contingencies and profit. Among the many hazards of the contracting business are the risks of loss from mistakes in estimating costs or from unforeseen situations which may increase costs during construction such as rising prices of materials, unexpected underground rock or water, work stoppages from strikes, material shortages, or wet weather, wage increases, and wasteful mistakes on the job.

Construction materials and building products which the general contractor puts in place with his own employees are purchased by him from suppliers. In house building the major items are lumber, millwork, sheathing, and insulation. Thus the lumber dealer is the home builder's chief supplier. The subcontractors procure their own building products and include the material costs in their contract figures. In many cases the subcontractor is also a local distributor of materials and equipment. Plumbers often operate a shop to stock and sell pipe and fixtures. Electricians may sell at retail and do contract work as well. Roofers, sheet metal contractors, tile contractors, and other subcontractors maintain stocks of material and may sell to other contractors.

The contractor has relatively few permanent employees. The builder of small homes may employ one or two carpenters and a laborer or two so long as he has work but maintains no organization between jobs. Larger contractors maintain office supervisory and professional personnel even through lean periods. In an active period both prime and subcontractors may employ large numbers of craftsmen and laborers on sizeable construction projects.

The amount of investment in equipment varies with the size of contractor and with the type of function which he performs. Small home builders may own nothing but a pickup truck and a few garden tools. It is the practice for some craftsmen, such as carpenters, to supply their own hand tools, but the contractor may provide large or special tools and power equipment. A road contractor requires a large investment in earthmoving machinery, trucks, rollers, and pavers. A general contractor in heavy construction work may own trucks, cranes, bulldozers, scaffolding, concrete forms, stationary engines, lifts, space heaters, tarpaulins, power saws, air compressors and hammers, and all manner of small hand tools. Some contractors are able to avoid the financial risks of a large and permanent capital investment in equipment by leasing equipment or, on a very large job, purchasing the needed machinery and writing off the cost against the contract.

LAND DEVELOPMENT

From a community standpoint, one of the most crucial phases in the productive process which creates usable space is the point at which land is taken out of agricultural use and prepared for urban use. It is here that the basic skeleton of the city is created and land use patterns are crystallized so that future changes are difficult and costly. In most jurisdictions considerable public control is exercised over the original land planning and development phases, and there is direct participation by public agencies in the provision of various utilities such as water and sanitary sewer and of public facilities such as schools and fire stations. These forms of public intervention have multiplied and intensified over recent years as an expression of the public interest in sound land development and the demand by suburban residents for the full complement of urban conveniences.

The outward spread of the city into the rural-urban fringe has proceeded at an irregular rate in response to changing forces of demand for more urban space. During the real estate boom of the twenties speculation in suburban lands led to the creation of a great oversupply of subdivision lots in most metropolitan areas which was not absorbed until after World War II. In recent years the conversion of agricultural lands to urban use has moved at a somewhat more rational pace, speculation in building lots has been less common, and the preparation of land has been geared more closely to demand from users. Nevertheless, the tracts of land which are converted are of all sizes usually unrelated to the optimum acreage for proper planning and efficient development. The pattern of development is scattered and the settled area does not expand in an orderly fashion. We shall see that the various public controls over land use do not include methods for forcing the landowner to proceed with development when the time is ripe. Thus development jumps about uneconomically from close-in to more remote locations through accidents of ownership and differences in owner's judgments on the proper timing of conversion to urban use.

Site preparation is often loosely referred to as "subdividing" or "platting." Much of the extensive growth of our cities begins with the platting of residential lots to be offered for sale by land developers. The lot buyers may be home building organizations who will build for sale or individuals who plan to build on contract for their own occupancy. The land developer may be a farm owner seeking to capitalize on the encroaching urban forces or at the other extreme, the entrepreneur may be a well-financed experienced real estate developer. The size of the plat may range from a few acres to several hundred and the number of lots from a dozen to a thousand. The larger subdivisions usually include parks, church sites, and commercial districts. They may also contain school sites and apartment areas. In most metropolitan markets some land development activities are conducted as a part of an integrated large-scale construction operation in which a single concern carries through the house building process from raw land to completed home. In other cases a number of small home builders combine for purposes of land purchase and development to assure the members of the group a supply of building sites at reasonable cost.

But the conversion of agricultural land to urban use is not restricted to the manufacturers of home sites. Investors may acquire substantial suburban acreage for garden-apartment developments such as embellish the countryside around Washington, D.C. The shopping centers which have sprung up in the penumbra of both large and small cities are typically built on land fresh from agricultural use. Modern industrial plants with single-story buildings and huge parking areas require acreage which can be found only in the rural-urban fringe. Office buildings, motels, restaurants, and warehouses are often the original urban use of erstwhile farm land, as may be hospitals, cemeteries, golf courses, and public works such as sewerage treatment plants, bypass highways, airports, and schools.

Land Procurement

The land developer or subdivider starts with raw land, usually unimproved agricultural land, at the edge of the city. The small operative home builder may buy his building lots from a land developer at any one of several stages of development ranging from lots served only with gravel streets to lots fully improved with water, sanitary sewer, curb and gutter, storm sewer, permanent paving, and sidewalk. The large tract builder buys raw land and performs the full range of functions through to the completed home with community facilities on hand. But whatever the circumstances of site purchase or development, the selection of the site and the amount of investment in land improvement should be direct functions of the intended utilization. The locational characteristics of the land in relation to the needs of those families which will be the ultimate users is its most important quality. The area of the parcel acquired should be related to the total demand for the intended services and to that part of the demand which the development can be expected to capture. The proportions of the parcel must be suited to the nature of the project. The geological characteristics of subsoil, contour, and drainage are of great practical importance, as is the orientation of the land. The financing of the land acquisition will be related to the financial positions of buyer and seller. The purchase price will reflect current market values, the urgencies of the seller, and the buyer's investment analysis.

Location. The earlier chapters of this book have made clear the primacy of location as the source of real estate value. For each use the locations of certain activities have great significance; others have none, and the rest are important in varying degree. Because the convenience of the ultimate user is primary, the land developer must consider the probable locational preferences of the class of buyers from which the ultimate occupants are to be drawn.

The importance of the environment of a home-building tract diminishes as the area increases and as more facilities are provided within its boundaries. A small subdivision is entirely vulnerable to adverse influences on its borders and provides no facilities but the home sites. Thus locational factors are of great importance. On the other hand, a large tract can be located with greater freedom because it is self-contained to a larger extent and can be so planned that the residential areas are insulated from detrimental influences outside the project.

For residential use in the form of freestanding homes, convenience to schools is perhaps the most important locational attribute. The explanation lies in the primary motivation toward home ownership—the welfare of the children. Families are led to suburban home developments so that children may enjoy space, light, air, and safety among juvenile companions from families of like social and economic characteristics. The facilities for primary education are of particular importance. If not close at hand the daily transportation problem may be onerous and costly. The only other journey with an equal frequency is the daily trip to work, but convenience to place of employment is generally rated by home buyers far below convenience to school. Parks, churches, and shopping facilities are important but becoming less so as the ubiquitous family car gives easy mobility. Shopping is only an occasional activity and can be done at night when the family car is available.

Physical Characteristics. In general, the location of a site will largely determine the class of residential development, but the physical and geological characteristics of the land are also conditioning factors. For example, the area of land in the parcel may be either too great or too small to be economically developed for a given class of buyers under the existing market conditions. The shape or proportions of the tract may be a limiting factor. If it is not possible either to purchase only a portion of the land or to acquire more land from contiguous ownerships, as the case may be, the parcel may not be economically usable for the intended purpose.

For high-grade residential use, forest cover and high elevations with views are considered choice. Trees add value for all classes of residential use, but the proportion of value added rises with the price level of the finished homes.

Geological characteristics of the land which have economic implication include the nature of the subsoil, drainage, orientation, and contours. Subsoil which is unstable or wet, solid rock, or heavy boulders place limitations on construction because of the substantial increase in costs which must be incurred to overcome such conditions. Subsoil conditions also determine the practicability of individual sewage disposal installations where public sewer mains are not available. The depth of the water table is important if individual wells are to be used.

The contours of the site have several implications. If the land is low lying there may be extra expense in disposing of storm water. A rugged terrain also adds to such costs and to the costs of installing streets and roads. For certain types of use, such as commercial, level land is essential, and heavy dirt-moving costs may be involved if an irregular site is selected. In residential development hilly land leads to higher costs of land development, house building, and lot improvement. Thus level land is sought for houses of modest price, while hillside sites are more appropriate for the upper price ranges. The orientation of the land is significant for some types of use. For example, for residential purposes, a southern slope is to be preferred to a northern exposure in the colder climates.

Utilities. The location of the site with reference to existing sewer mains and water supply is important for all uses. Residential developments must hook onto sewer and water mains, or if mains cannot be extended, they must locate where soil conditions permit the use of individual septic tank and disposal fields and where a sufficient supply of pure underground water can be tapped for individual or community wells.

Governmental Unit. The developer should give consideration to the political subdivision in which the property is located. His buyers must look to the local government for the provision of numerous and important public services. He is therefore concerned with the financial situation of the governmental entity, its debt, and its fiscal policies. He should be informed on the adequacy of the tax base, present and prospective, to provide essential public improvements. He must evaluate the present and prospective tax load and the honesty and efficiency of the governing body and its administration. Lower tax rates do not necessarily give one jurisdiction an advantage over another, for the tax rate is meaningful only when evaluated along with the ratio of assessed value to market value. Even taxes which are low on an equalized basis must be interpreted with reference to the public services which are available to the taxpayer and the additional costs of providing the missing services. For example, inadequate fire protection means higher insurance rates; lack of high school facilities may mean payment of tuition in another jurisdiction or in a private school; the added costs and inconveniences of poor snow removal, crowded school facilities, no waste and garbage collection, and lack of public water service and sewage disposal may not be offset in the minds of potential home buyers by the proportionately lower tax burden.

Land Use Controls. The value of a site selected for residential development is greatly influenced by the public and private land use controls to which it and its environment are subject. In peripheral areas of the city, lands in the several jurisdictions will be subject to different sets of zoning and subdivision controls which are differently administered. An analysis of any site must include the discovery of how zoning ordinances affect the subject property and how they control the pattern of growth in the vicinity. In some cases there will be master plans for the community which serve to guide the governmental bodies in decisions affecting land use. In addition to analyzing zoning ordinances, one should check for the existence of an official map which is used in many states to establish the location of future street systems in advance of development.

Private controls through deed restrictions or covenants both in the subject property and in the environs are important limiting factors.

Subdivision regulations have a great impact on new land development. The nature of the approvals required for each plat and the engineering standards established will affect the speed and cost of platting. The local requirements on the installation of street improvements and utilities determine the amount of capital which the land developer requires and must put at risk. In some localities the developer must install and pay for the full range of improvements—sewer, water, street and paving, curb and gutter, and sidewalk—before offering the land for sale or building on it. In other cases the developer installs some of the improvements, and the municipality provides the rest. The cost is usually charged against the land as special assessments spread over five to ten years or, less frequently, absorbed in the general fund.

Land Purchase. Small-volume home builders generally purchase developed building lots from subdividers. To avoid tying up their limited working capital the builders make as small down payments as possible or take options to secure building sites for future operations. Lots purchased on land contract can be paid for when needed as a building site and title conveyed at that time. Some subdividers will convey title without full payment while taking back an unsecured note for the balance to be paid off when the house is finished and sold. Credit extension by the seller is necessitated by the fact that it is very difficult for a builder to borrow on the security of vacant land.

The area of land to be purchased for development is determined by considerations of profit potential and available capital. The profit potential is closely related to the size and growth of market demand in the community. A builder in a dynamic market will relate his land purchase to his forecast of demand and his expectation of the share in the total sales which he can capture. He will be limited by the amount of capital which is available to him and by the managerial manpower which is free to be devoted to the project.

Capital requirements for land purchase and development are modified by the terms of the purchase and by the local subdivision regulations. Capital requirements will be minimized when land can be purchased with a small initial payment. The use of options to control the acquisition of successive installments of a large parcel also reduces capital needs. Capital which must be invested in land improvements by the developer is reduced to the extent that the municipality employs its credit to finance such improvements, for example, when the municipality installs sewer and water mains and charges the cost against the land as a special assessment, to be repaid over a period of years by whomsoever owns the land. In general, builders aim to develop at one time only as much land as can be built on and sold during the period required to prepare the next group of lots or tract for use as building sites. This scheduling keeps carrying costs and taxes at a minimum and maximizes capital turnover.

The upper limit to the price which a builder is justified in paying for land is set by the market price for other available land of equivalent qualities. Within this figure, for any given parcel, the buyer's calculation begins with estimates of the productivity of the completed enterprise; if an income property the forecast is in terms of a stream of income; if a land development or house-building project the prediction is in terms of end-product selling price. There are projects which combine income properties and house sales as in large community developments where shopping centers and apartments are involved. On a sales project the investor works backward from the estimates of gross sales by deducting all production and sales costs to determine the amount available to purchase the land and provide an entrepreneurial profit. In light of the risks of the project, he will decide on what profit is sufficient as compensation on the total investment. The residual will represent the upper limit for land purchase.

The builder should view the acquisition cost of raw land in its proper perspective against the total cost of the end product. For example, for a typical house selling for $20,000, raw-land cost to a tract builder may be from 3 to 5 per cent of this amount. A small premium in price paid for raw land in order to secure a superior location would make little difference in the total cost of production. At the same time, the superior location might be a valuable competitive advantage and greatly enhance the marketability of the home.

Land Planning

The variety in original urban land use types, the irregularity in the timing of suburban land development, the typically small size of the tracts prepared for urban use, and the wide geographical scatter in their location would create a disorganized and impossible urban pattern unless public control were exercised at several points. As we examine the steps in land development, we shall see how these new pieces in the jigsaw puzzle of urban facilities, streets, and pipes must be fitted into the existing pattern in order to avoid hopeless confusion in providing for the future needs of the growing community. And we shall see that when the short-term interests of a property owner run counter to the long-term interests of the community, public authority must step in. Thus, at an early stage, the developer must check his plan against the advance plans of the community as well as against existing land use, street, and utility patterns with which the new area must be integrated. These checks should include:

1. *Street and Highway Plan.* The city, county, and state usually have advance plans for the extension of the local street system, street and highway changes, and public improvements which may affect the property to be developed. In some jurisdictions such plans may be expressed in an official map which has the legal effect of putting all property owners on notice. Where an official map is put into effect, the cost of any structures thereafter erected in the intended rights of way cannot be recovered.

2. *Master Plan.* In many areas advance community planning is crystallized in a master plan which forecasts the land use pattern of the city or metropolitan area and includes the peripheral regions of new development. Such a plan has no legal standing as such but is a guide for public agencies in making decisions on street locations, school sites, and land use zoning.

3. *Zoning.* Under the police power, zoning ordinances adopted by local governments place limitations on the manner in which land may be used in the various zoning districts into which the municipality is divided. The ordinances may also establish minimum lot sizes, setbacks, side and rear yards, and building heights. If the intended utilization of a tract is in violation of the zoning ordinance, the only cure is to persuade the local legislative body to amend the law.

4. *Sanitary and Storm Sewer Plan.* The availability of sanitary sewer service may be a controlling factor in the profitable development of a new area. The problems of removing storm waters are also limiting factors.

The intended use of a parcel of land establishes the general land planning goals. The builder who has decided upon the class of home to be built in a tract property necessarily has outlined the general basis for land planning specifications. The investor who seeks a site for a predetermined type of development already has in mind a general land plan and needs an available tract for which such a plan is suitable in respect to size, location, and terrain.

The major features of a subdivision or community development plan are:

1. General pattern and allocation of land use for dwellings, parks, schools, commercial center, and churches

2. Street system

3. Plat of individual lots with dimensions, easements, and setbacks

4. Private deed restrictions to be imposed to assure development according to plan

Land planning applied to a single platted lot or to a small parcel for a single use produces what is termed a *plot plan*. This plan establishes the location and orientation of the structures, the ground and building elevations, the arrangement of drives, and points of access. It may be elaborated with a landscaping and planting scheme.

From the builder's standpoint, land planning is an important aspect of product design which has marked influence on salability. The land plan combines with the design of structures and improvements and the location to determine the net profit which the operation will produce. While the tract builder is restricted in land planning decisions by many forms of governmental control, he can determine or influence many aspects of the subdivision or community plan.

Surveys. Before a land use plan can be properly designed an accurate topographical map is required as well as a boundary survey of the tract. For large areas modern photogrammatic methods based on air photos will produce accurate and economical results. The topographical map permits the land planner to study the drainage problems and to lay out a street pattern which minimizes cut and fill. The boundary survey locates the tract with reference to the government survey, determines exact dimensions, and provides the reference lines for subdivision into lots. The topographical map also provides a basis for estimating the amount of dirt which may have to be moved by the developer in order to level off building sites by either cut or fill.

One other type of survey is usually required. When the street rights of way have been set a profile survey is run of each street showing natural elevations along each side of the right of way and along the center line of the street. With this information at hand city officials establish the final grade or elevation for each street. Thus the amount of cut and fill required to bring the streets to the established grade can be calculated. Calculations can also be made of the volume of ditching required to set sanitary and storm water sewers at depths required to permit flow by gravity.

Allocation of Land to Various Uses. The proportioning of land uses by area involves complex considerations which only can be suggested here. For example, land allocated to park use may yield a net return even though donated to the community. The presence of a convenient recreational area and its attractive appearance may increase the salability of residential lots and result in higher lot prices. On the other hand, in a plat of large lots for expensive homes, there is less need for park space. Church and school sites from which the return in sale price may be less than from alternative uses may contribute to the total income indirectly by more than this difference. Land allocated to commercial or to rental housing use may or may not be sound from a profit standpoint depending upon market demand, the strength of competition in the vicinity, and the strength of the depressing effect on the price and salability of contiguous single-family residential lots under the threat of an inharmonious land utilization. The decision on the distribution of the residential area among sites for homes in various price classes should be based on market analysis.

Internal Locational Relationships. The arrangement of the several types of land use within the subdivision is important to financial success. Facilities such as parks and schools, which serve the entire community, require locations which are accessible to all homes. Commercial facilities should be within easy reach of all home sites in the development but should also be in a prominent location accessible to a wider market area. Churches can occupy intersections of major streets, preferably on the periphery of the tract, to minimize the influence on nearby homes. Larger lots for higher valued homes can better occupy irregular terrain than smaller lots for more modest dwellings.

Street Pattern. A considerable variation in the conformation of the street system is usually possible within local governmental standards. Long blocks minimize street and utility costs and reduce the number of corner lots. Cutting the long blocks with pedestrian ways reduces the objection that long blocks force people to walk greater distances. The use of the cul-de-sac reduces utility and street costs, and creates protected neighborhoods. Street patterns characterized by curves and T-intersections contribute to aesthetic values and discourage through traffic. The loop-street device has its advantages, and streets which follow natural contours require a minimum of street cut and fill.

Lotting. The area, dimensions, and proportions of the individual building sites must be appropriate to the market intended to be served. For example, modern ranch homes require wider lots to avoid crowding than do the two-story homes which are reviving in popularity in some sections of the country. Lot depth beyond a certain point results in wasted land. The cost of utilities and street improvements which must be borne by each lot is roughly proportionate to its frontage; this burden places a practical limitation on lot widths.

Production Costs. Within local planning and engineering requirements the subdivider can exercise some control over development costs through land planning. For example, minimum lot sizes will hold street and utility costs per lot to the lowest level. Streets along natural contours will require little grading and minimize costs of preparing the building sites for use. Cul-de-sacs are economical, as are long blocks. Each economy must be balanced against its effect on the quality of the end product and the price reaction of the consumer.

The foregoing illustrations show how land planning can affect productivity. The developer's objectives are to create a plan which is functional, economical, and still attractive. He must fit the plan into the community pattern of land use, streets, and utilities. He must create a product which can meet competition. His plan should be calculated to preserve real estate values under the ever-changing conditions of the future. His plan must be acceptable to mortgage lenders and to governmental agencies, such as FHA, which influence the flow of mortgage money. In general, the investor's objectives are consistent with community objectives. A land plan which is economically sound is usually the best contribution to community development.

The importance of economic or market considerations in land planning is not always recognized in practice. The land developer frequently finds himself in conflict with the engineering approach to planning which gives primary weight to street grades, storm water drainage, and utility design at the expense of human values and preferences. Or the landscape architect may urge the creation of attractive vistas at the expense of convenience and economy for the inhabitants. And it is common for city officials to exert pressures on land developers to donate land for public purposes often at a cost well beyond that which might be a legitimate offset for benefits received. In the approach to land planning which is urged in this volume the consumer and his preferences are first in importance. It is the function of the developer in designing the product to interpret these preferences, involving as they do a complex balance of social, aesthetic, economic, and technical considerations. His analysis of the market is aimed at establishing the specifications of the product which the consumer is willing and able to pay for. Because the consumer is also the taxpayer, those public servants who administer land use controls should apply the same criteria.

286   REAL ESTATE ANALYSIS

Public Controls. The developer's freedom in land planning is limited by all manner of publicly administered regulations based upon the police power of the state. As it materializes in the form of a subdivision plat, the plan must have the approval of the planning commission or commissions having jurisdiction. Where such commissions have extraterritorial powers, typically 2 or 3 miles beyond their boundaries, a peripheral tract may fall within two or three planning jurisdictions. In some states all subdivision plats must be approved by the state planning board. The proposed land use must conform to sanitary and health codes. Major traffic ways are sometimes subject to special limitations of access. The streets must meet local standards of width and grade. The plan must provide for effective storm water drainage, and where it is to be served with sanitary sewer, it must allow for sewer design which minimizes the need for pumping stations and deep trenches.

Land planning must, of course, be consistent with zoning. However, for good reason, zoning can be modified by amendment by action of the appropriate legislative body. The procedure involves a public hearing to permit neighboring property owners to state their opinions; it calls for consideration and recommendation by the planning commission, and action by the local legislative body on the proposed amendment.

In general, land use controls benefit property owners, but in individual cases they may impose some hardship. Controls are justified as contributing to the general welfare of the community, the greatest good for the greatest number. Individual owners seeking relaxations or amendment to controls must be able to demonstrate that such change is consistent with the constitutional basis of the police power, and that after the change, the benefits to the community are undiminished. Zoning amendments often contribute to the general welfare when modifying an original zoning ordinance which was poorly drawn or where changes in community growth patterns call for revisions in the master plan.

Restrictive Covenants. To preserve the integrity of the land plan the land developer may need to impose private restrictive covenants or deed restrictions. Customarily such restrictions run with the land, but it is wise to provide for termination in twenty to thirty years unless perpetuated at the will of the then property owners. The restrictions supplement the local police power regulations and are intended to assure that the original land plan will be carried out. The covenants typically include the following items:

1. Restrictions on the type of structure and the use of the land. Such provisions are essential in the absence of zoning and may be more limiting than existing zoning restrictions.

2. Structural limitations. In residential areas minimum limitations on the

size or cost of the structure are often imposed to assure harmonious development. Minimum cost limitations are ineffective during inflation and unduly limiting during deflation. The most practical method is to limit the minimum ground-floor area of the main structure using a different basis for one- and two-story structures. Maximum limits can be placed on the heights of buildings.

3. Building placement. If zoning limitations fail to provide adequate setbacks, side and rear yards, such provisions can be included among the deed restrictions.

4. Architectural control. To secure the most attractive and harmonious neighborhood development, particularly where the building is to be done by a number of different builders and owners, provision can be made that all building plans must be approved before construction starts. Plans and specifications are submitted to an architectural control committee sometimes set up by the developer and sometimes chosen by the property owners in the subdivision.

Platting. When the land use of the tract has been decided by the developer and the surveys have been completed, the next step is to express the plan in a plat or subdivision map which can be submitted for approval by the appropriate public agencies and for recording. State laws controlling the platting of land are widely variant. Most states permit the sale of land by metes and bounds description, but many states place a limit on this method of uncontrolled disposition. For example, in Wisconsin, if an owner sells off more than three parcels per year, he must prepare a formal plat and conform to elaborate regulations. In order to assure proper land description and prevent subsequent disputes over ownership, the platting law calls for precision in laying out the lots and permanence in marking the lot corners. Engineering details such as street curves must be complete with all dimensions inscribed on the plat. In some jurisdictions it is required that the plat must have the approval of the local plan commission, the city council, all local authorities within 2 or 3 miles of the plat, the city engineer, traffic engineer, city attorney, health officer, park department, and the state director of planning. In addition the city and the county treasurers must certify that there are no unpaid taxes.

Only when the plat has met all of the statutory requirements is it acceptable for recording by the register of deeds. Since no lots can be sold until the plat is recorded, conformity to regulations can be effectively enforced.

Another form of public regulation of platting is the blue-sky laws by which the states act to prevent fraud and misrepresentation in the sale of subdivision lands by requiring full disclosure of all relevant facts and assurance that the seller can give clear title.

The Process of Land Development

The preparation of the raw land for community use, where the full array of modern standards are observed, includes the following steps:

1. Street grading
2. Street surfacing
3. Curbs and gutters
4. Site grading
5. Storm water facilities
6. Sanitary sewer mains and laterals
7. Water mains and laterals
8. Street and screen planting
9. Electric service
10. Gas service
11. Telephone service

It is almost universal in urban areas that electric and telephone service are required facilities and that they are readily available without initial cost on application to the local public-utility companies. Gas service is not always at hand in outlying areas, but usually it is extended as soon as is warranted by the density of development. The other items in the foregoing list are handled in various ways. In some jurisdictions the land developer is required to install and pay for all of the facilities; in other areas he does some of the work, and the municipality does the rest and charges the cost against the land served as a special assessment. In some areas storm water treatment, street surfacing, and street planting are charged to the general fund of the municipality.

The method of financing the improvements has an effect on the marketing of the end product. Where building lots or houses are sold with all improvements in and paid for, the price is increased to include the improvement costs thus creating more sales resistance; in part this resistance is psychological, and in part it derives from the fact that the initial cash requirement to be met by the purchaser is greater. Of course, in the long run, the buyer will pay for all of the improvements regardless of the agency which installs them. Furthermore, when the improvements are included in the price, they can be financed by the buyer out of the mortgage proceeds at a lower interest charge and a longer term of repayment than is typical of special assessment financing through the municipality.

Where public sewer and water service are not available the developer may choose to let each buyer provide his own well, or he may install a community water system. Only in very large tracts would a private community sewerage disposal plant be feasible. The usual procedure is for each householder to install a septic tank and disposal field.

The timing of installing the various land improvements may require decisions by the developer. There are those who immediately install the full complement of improvements on the grounds that the finished appearance of the neighborhood and the avoidance of a year or two of mud and dust will enhance the value of the product and speed its sale. Other developers find an advantage in the lower sales prices when improvement costs do not have to be included. Developers who are short of working capital may have no choice but to minimize the improvements for which they must advance the cost. Where a project is expected to sell off slowly the developer may be reluctant to tie up his capital in land improvements while he waits for buyers. The cost of carrying such an investment will result in a higher price to the buyer or a lower profit to the developer.

Each developer must judge in terms of marketing advantage and financial expediency such extra development costs as site grading of irregular lots, street and parkway planting, screen planting, the provision and preparation of parks, "tot lots," and playgrounds.

Developing Nonresidential Land

Subdivisions of land for resort purposes or for industrial districts call for about the same procedures as just outlined except that the complement of utilities and land improvements may not be so complete. Where the type of use does not require the division of the tract into smaller units for separate ownership, the platting procedure is not applicable. For example, an industry may require 20 acres for a new plant, or an investor may need 30 acres for a large shopping center. Such large unbroken tracts usually are sold by the owner without formal platting. However, the buyer may be subject to public limitations in the number and location of entrances onto public streets and highways. Of course, existing zoning restrictions would limit the types of land use and might affect the location and height of structures.

HOME BUILDING

Certainly home building is one of the most socially significant functions of the construction industry, judged either in direct satisfactions for consumers or as a productive economic activity. A million or more families are provided with the amenities of a new home each year. In recent years private home building has accounted for nearly 40 per cent of all private construction as measured by an expenditure of $13 billion per year. It employs 2½ million workers, of whom one-half work on-site.[3] Perhaps most importantly, new homes absorb most of the land in newly settled urban areas, thus setting the pattern, for better or for worse, for most of the new urban areal expansion.

[3] Burnham Kelly and Associates, *Design and the Production of Houses*, McGraw-Hill Book Company, Inc., New York, 1959, p. 9.

Table XI-2
Nonfarm Dwelling Units Started by Sales and Rental Type
1920–1959

Year	Total sales and rental	Sales type, 1-family	Rental type Total	Private Total	Private 2-family	Private 3- or more family	Public
1920	247	202	45	45	24	21	
1921	449	316	133	133	70	63	
1922	716	437	279	279	146	133	
1923	871	513	358	358	175	183	
1924	893	534	359	359	173	186	
1925	937	572	365	365	157	208	
1926	849	491	358	358	117	241	
1927	810	454	356	356	99	257	
1928	753	436	317	317	78	239	
1929	509	316	193	193	51	142	
1930	330	227	103	103	29	74	
1931	254	187	67	67	22	45	
1932	134	118	16	16	7	9	
1933	93	76	17	17	5	12	
1934	126	109	17	17	5	12	
1935	221	182	39	34	8	26	5
1936	319	239	80	65	13	52	15
1937	336	266	70	66	15	51	4
1938	406	316	90	83	18	65	7
1939	515	373	143	86	20	66	57
1940	603	448	155	82	26	56	73
1941	706	533	174	87	28	58	87
1942	356	252	104	49	18	31	55
1943	191	136	55	48	18	30	7
1944	142	115	27	24	11	14	3
1945	209	185	25	24	9	15	1
1946	671	590	80	72	24	48	8
1947	849	740	109	106	34	72	3
1948	932	763	168	150	46	104	18
1949	1,025	792	233	197	35	162	36
1950	1,396	1,151	245	201	42	159	44
1951	1,091	892	199	128	40	88	71
1952	1,127	939	188	130	46	84	58
1953	1,104	933	171	135	42	94	36
1954	1,220	1,077	143	124	34	90	19
1955	1,329	1,190	139	120	33	87	19
1956	1,118	981	137	113	31	82	24
1957	1,042	840	202	153	33	120	49
1958	1,209	932	277	209	39	170	68
1959	1,378	1,079	299	264	49	215	35

The data in Table XI-2 reflect the considerable fluctuations in residential building activity during the present century. The proportion of this activity which is accounted for by the housebuilders is shown to have fluctuated over a range from 56 to 90 per cent. The special factors affecting rental housing construction will be discussed later in this chapter, but we now might consider the factors which influence residential construction as a whole. The factors which appear to be of basic importance are the age distribution of the population, the rate of family formation, the level and prospects of prosperity, the availability of easy credit, and the rate of demolitions; these matters will be discussed in more detail below. There are many other influences to be considered such as war and rumors of war, special governmental controls such as rent control, and special stimulants such as the use of the FHA mortgage-insurance device to encourage cooperative housing and housing for the aging. There are general social attitudes which are in constant flux such as the value placed on homeownership, the attitude toward mortgage debt, and the importance given to household mechanical equipment and house design as it affects the rate of obsolescence. Somewhat strangely, available evidence suggests that the level of construction costs is not a primary factor in affecting the rate of residential construction. Costs and the rate of construction rise together, though no doubt the expected inhibiting effects of high costs do operate when costs rise too far out of line; and at the other end of the scale, low costs have some stimulating influence.

Age Distribution. The basic unit of housing demand is the family, or more accurately, the household. The average age at marriage is roughly 20; thus the number of persons in this age group in the total population strongly conditions the number of marriages. Another demographic factor of importance to housing is the number of families with parents falling in the age bracket from 30 to 35. This is the age when families buy homes; thus the more persons at this age level, the greater the potential demand for the product of the housebuilder.

Family Formation. It has already been suggested that the rate of family formation is influenced by the age distribution of the population. But other factors affect the marriage rate, particularly the level of prosperity and the economic outlook. Other longer-term changes in social attitudes have resulted in a lowering of the age at marriage, probably reflecting better earnings for younger people and a general acceptance of the practice of the wife holding a job at least until children start to arrive. Such a shift, coupled with a shifting age distribution, may bring about a change in the total need for housing accommodations.

Prosperity. Though basic housing need is a function of age distribution and family formation, effective market demand, which leads to the stimulation of construction, requires that households possess sufficient purchasing power to become active agents of demand. Thus the level of family income is an important conditioner of demand as well as the prospects for the future which may either encourage or discourage families from making new housing commitments. Another effect of prosperity is to generate additional units of housing demand in the form of single persons or groups of unrelated persons who, in less propitious circumstances, are wont to occupy furnished rooms. It may also be said that it is during prosperous times of expanding job opportunities in our urban areas that they grow most rapidly in population and thus in need for housing; and that conversely, in hard times, growth stops or even retreats. We have already pointed out the stimulating effect of prosperity on the marriage rate.

Credit. Easy credit is another method of translating need into effective demand and thus stimulating residential construction. Entrepreneurs, be they home builders or investors in apartment projects, depend on an ample supply of credit. The market for home purchase can be substantially extended in the presence of liberal mortgage terms and an adequate supply of mortgage money. The unremitting plaint of the otherwise ruggedly individualistic home builders for extended intervention of the Federal government in the mortgage market is accounted for by the dependence of the industry on a continuing flow of liberal credit as encouraged by the FHA and VA programs.

Demolitions. This factor is becoming more and more important as the number of existing dwellings which reach the end of their physical and economic life continues to increase with the passage of time and with the rising standards of housing which reflect an increasing concentration of family incomes in the middle brackets. Wenzlick estimates that in 1960 some 136,000 dwelling units will be demolished as a result of physical depreciation and that this number will increase to 201,000 per year by 1980.[4] In addition, there are many thousands of dwelling units which are lost to the supply as a result of public and private redevelopment activities, i.e., land use succession.

Attempts to interpret the past history of residential construction as a succession of cyclical swings of predictable regularity have not been successful. In any event, the important consideration for an investor is the local situation, for we have repeatedly pointed out that housing markets are local, and it is easy to demonstrate that the rate of building activity among local markets may vary markedly at any point in time. For example, during the year 1959 residential construction in San Diego, California, was increasing while in Orlando, Florida, it was falling off.

[4] Roy Wenzlick, *Real Estate in 1958*, Roy Wenzlick and Company, St. Louis, January, 1958.

Organization of Production

A surprisingly high proportion of all homes are turned out on a do-it-yourself basis; estimates run as high as one-sixth. There are all manner of variations in such arrangements from the prospective owner-occupant who puts the house together, piece by piece, with his own hands, to the owner who acts as his own general contractor and subcontracts all of the work. The usual division of labor finds the owner doing the portions of the work which require less skill and hiring the specialized skills. Do-it-yourself builders often work out an exchange of skills among a group of owners each of whom is relatively skilled at one of the specialized trades. One of the problems is to finance the do-it-yourself house; lenders are prone to assume that the quality of construction will be less than standard. However, under adequate controls and inspection, some lenders will advance mortgage credit and will recognize the owner's work as "sweat equity," i.e., as a contribution to the value of the property and as the equivalent of cash in calculating the owner's equity.

The proportion of new homes built on a custom basis under a general contract is estimated at 15 to 20 per cent. For the more expensive homes the typical procedure for the prospective owner-occupant is to hire an architect to design the house and to prepare a detailed set of plans and specifications. In the case of medium-sized houses it is more customary for the owner to select a plan from a magazine, newspaper, or lumber dealer's plan book, and to modify it to suit his preferences with the aid of a draftsman. General or outline specifications may be drawn up. On the basis of plans and specifications, from whatever source, a number of general contractors are asked to submit bids, and the job is awarded in most cases, but not always, to the lowest bidder. In this arrangement of custom or contract building, the contractor undertakes no risk except that he may have underestimated his costs in arriving at his bid figure. Some of his working capital is tied up temporarily during construction, but, if the owner is properly financed, the builder is assured of recovering this working capital when the house is completed, and the full contract amount has been paid. The contractor needs little fixed capital in the form of equipment since he subcontracts a large share of the work to special trade contractors who provide their own tools and equipment. The general contractor engages in no marketing activities save to seek the opportunity to bid. The small contractor maintains no separate office and keeps his pickup truck in the backyard of his home. He has no permanent employees, but as long as he is busy he gives steady employment to a few carpenters and laborers.

The real entrepreneur in the home-building industry is called variously operative builder, merchant builder, and speculative builder. His operation more nearly parallels the popular notion of a manufacturing enterprise than does the bid-contract system of production. Operative builders account for as much as 80 per cent of all new house building in some areas and the large housebuilders all fall in this category. The operative or merchant builder is a risk taker who produces in advance of orders. He plans the product according to his interpretation of market demand; he purchases and stockpiles building sites, stores materials, hires labor, enters into subcontracts, organizes and directs the processes of fabrication, and markets the product. He risks his own capital and relies on his own credit standing and the pledge of the project to secure working capital. Large operators, known as "tract builders," perform the additional function of land planning and development. The small builder usually acquires building lots ready-made, but the tract builder buys raw acreage and prepares the land for use by installing streets, utilities, and community services.

The distinction between the contract builder and the operative or speculative builder is by no means sharp. The speculative builder, particularly the smaller operator, may engage in both types of business at the same time. The large builder takes orders from model houses and contracts to produce a certain house on a given lot at an agreed price, just as does the contract builder. As market demand falls off the speculative builder resorts to more building on order and less speculative construction which involves the risk of carrying unsold inventory.

Because of the high value of its product, $16,000 to $20,000, and the long production period, three to six months, the industry is highly dependent on credit for working capital. The small builder typically has little capital, and even the large operator can supply only a fraction of the working capital which is tied up in goods-in-process. The consumer requires mortgage credit to cover a big proportion of the purchase price of a home. In the case of homes built on contract, the owner usually arranges in advance for permanent financing before construction begins. Using his own equity contribution and the proceeds of the permanent mortgage or of a temporary construction loan paid out in installments as construction proceeds, the owner supplies the builder with most of his working capital requirements. The speculative builder must borrow most of his working capital on a construction loan secured by a mortgage on the houses in process of construction. Where possible he arranges in advance for the permanent financing of the prospective, but unknown, purchaser.

It is a special characteristic of the home building industry that there is a minimum of bona fide risk-taking capital involved and that credit, which usually covers a high proportion of the builders' costs, is based on the product rather than the producing firm. His working capital is largely secured through mortgaging the building sites and houses under construction rather than on the basis of the credit standing of the firm.

There is evidence that since the war, an increasing share of all house building is being done by large builders. One per cent of all builders produce one-third of the privately built homes, and 10 per cent of the builders produce more than two-thirds.[5] Small builders, defined as producing between one and twenty-four houses per year, accounted for 46 per cent of the houses but constituted 96 per cent of all home-building organizations in 1949. The medium-size builder, from twenty-five to ninety-nine units, accounted for 22 per cent of total house production.[6] In the large metropolitan centers the builder with an annual volume of 500 to 1,000 or more houses is not uncommon. In the small cities a single builder with a volume of more than 100 units per year is rare.

Rationalization

The house-building industry, one of the nation's economic giants, has no doubt lagged behind other basic high-volume industries in the adoption of modern industrial techniques and organization. This lag is the result of a combination of factors.

1. The product is nonstandardized because the consumer insists on individuality in design and equipment.

2. Production takes place on the site.

3. The market is local, and only in large cities can there be volume production.

4. The historic organization of the industry is horizontal and resists vertical integration.

5. The introduction of laborsaving machinery and materials has been hampered by opposition from the powerful building-trades unions.

6. Materials producers and distributors have often resisted introduction of new materials and methods.

7. Archaic building codes, differing from city to city, discourage innovation and standardization.

8. The volume of demand is subject to considerable fluctuation which in part is a reflection of mortgage market conditions over which the industry has no control.

The slow advance of the home-building industry toward a better product at a lower cost since World War I has been disappointing to most observers. True, there has been an increase in the importance of large-scale builders and a higher level of managerial skill in some quarters. The

[5] *Ibid.*, p. 9.

[6] "Structure of the Residential Building Industry in 1949," U.S. Department of Labor Bulletin 1170, November, 1954, p. 21.

industry has organized in the National Association of Home Builders and is making haste to catch up with other more mature industries in supplying technical aid to its membership, raising standards of quality and ethics, and exerting political pressures. A start has been made toward rationalizing building codes and putting them on a performance basis. There is a movement to standardize dimensions of building materials and components and employ modular techniques in design. An increasing variety of building components are factory-processed and ready for installation, and some laborsaving methods are overcoming the resistance of labor unions. But basically, the house is fabricated much as it was in the twenties and by much the same industrial organization. The house-building revolution is still to come.

Prefabrication

Prefabrication has failed to revolutionize house building, but the business of factory fabrication of dwelling structures is growing. In 1958 some 250 firms produced about 100,000 dwelling units or about 10 per cent of the total house building. These producers operate through 10,000 local builder-dealers who buy the "package" of house parts from the factory, assemble and finish the house, and market the end product. The larger manufacturers have set up affiliate organizations to aid dealers in financing construction and in the permanent financing of the house purchaser where mortgage money is not readily available.

Today's prefab is indistinguishable from the conventionally built house in appearance and is composed of the same materials employed in the same structural system. For one reason or another most of the attempts to use other materials or to develop more efficient structural systems have not been successful. Recent developments in metal framing, plastics, the use of aluminum, and sandwich materials may lead to new and more economical methods.

The spreading consumer acceptance of the prefabricated house and the continuing breakdown of such obstacles as the inflexible building code and the resistance of trade unions has created a great potential market for the product. The economies of factory fabrication are sufficient to offset added transportation costs and to give some profit advantage to the local dealer in competition with conventionally built houses. The dealer benefits from the short construction time which permits rapid turnover of his capital. In addition, the manufacturers are increasingly passing on to the dealer more of the economies of large-scale purchasing and factory fabrication by including with the house package much of the mechanical equipment and finishing materials which the dealer typically adds to the prefabricated shell after assembly.

As long as the advantages of industrial methods apply only to the shell of the house, as is true of most of present-day prefabrication, there is a limit to the potential economies. In the typical case the cost of the house package is less than 40 per cent of the final price paid by the consumer. Thus to reduce manufacturing cost by 10 per cent means less than a 4 per cent reduction in cost to the buyer. Table XI-3 combines the house package and transportation cost in one item.

Table XI-3

Cost Breakdown of Prefabricated House, 1951

	Mean percentage *
House package and transportation	41
Preparation of site and basement	10
Erection and finishing	17
Plumbing installation	10
Heating installation	4
Wiring installation	2
Completing job and rough grading	4
Overhead and profits	12

* These percentages are based on reports of estimated cost breakdowns by seventy-two dealers.
SOURCE: Glenn H. Beyer and Theodore R. Yantis, *Practices and Precepts of Marketing Prefabricated Housing*, Government Printing Office, Washington, November, 1952, p. 3.

It is a reasonable expectation that prefabrication will continue to gain and that house building will be increasingly industrialized. New materials and new techniques will be developed and perfected, consumer insistence on individuality will decline in face of the economies of standardization, and the organization of the housing industry will move toward the degree of integration which has elevated productivity in other industries. And in turn, as higher numbers of houses are factory built, more of the economies of mass production can be realized.

A recent study of the house-building industry concludes with the hopeful prediction that a breakthrough is imminent and that a revolution in industrial organization and production methods is to follow the overcoming of the greatest block to rationalization, localism. The forces of change which are to generate this new day in housing include the increase in demand to a point when 1½ million homes a year will be built. This volume will be sufficient to require large-scale operations and new methods and materials. The recent increases in the size of building organizations is a precursor of the breakthrough as is the increased importance of off-site production. Another straw in the wind is the growing concern of the large producers of materials and equipment, particularly the appliance manufacturers, with respect to the end product in which their products are incorporated.[7] It is a hopeful sign that these large and well-managed firms are giving attention to house design, builder financing, the industrial organization and procedures of house building, and to the marketing problems of the home builder.

Governmental Intervention

Much of the impact of public controls over house building is at the land development stage. We have already discussed zoning, planning, and subdivision controls and their effect on the location of housing and the quality of the sites for new homes. Building codes represent a further control. These regulations are an expression of the police power and govern the materials, structural design, and method of installation to protect the health and safety of the occupants. There are usually separate codes covering plumbing, heating, and electrical installations. Modern codes are expressed to some extent in terms of performance standards, though few, if any, codes go all the way. Almost all codes express minimum requirements primarily in terms of specifications. The distinction between a specification and a performance standard may be illustrated by a code provision which requires that a wood-frame wall be constructed of 2 by 4 inch studs 16 inches apart from center to center. A performance code would not mention type of material, size, or structural dimensions but would simply require that the wall, however built, must be able to carry a vertical load of so many pounds per square inch and to withstand a horizontal thrust of so many pounds per square inch.

Government programs in the home mortgage market, such as under FHA and VA, have had a profound effect on the home-building industry. By manipulating the flow of credit into the housing market the government can encourage or inhibit new building. By instituting special programs resulting in liberal credit for selected consumer groups the government can stimulate building for such groups. The development of a secondary mortgage market and the advance commitment device have encouraged the emergence of large-scale builders. FHA and VA enforcement of quality controls for land planning, house design, and construction has raised building standards throughout the entire industry. On the other hand, there are those who feel that FHA and VA rigidity in accepting new designs, materials, and methods have stifled progress in the industry. Maximum interest rates on FHA- and VA-guaranteed mortgages are praised by some for the benefit to the borrower, while others allege that failure to adjust these rates promptly to changes in the mortgage market has induced an unhealthy industrial instability.

[7] Kelly, op. cit., chap. 10.

CONSTRUCTION COSTS

It is a common objective in all construction operations to minimize costs. The investor or the prospective owner-user who initiates the construction process seeks the lowest capital investment consistent with his investment objectives. The operative home builder strives to reduce costs so that he may meet competition and maximize the profit margin. The contractor who is a successful bidder must resist the squeeze between the contract price and his actual costs. In each case the goal is the optimum cost—as low as possible without endangering the attainment of other objectives.

Certain of the cost elements in a construction project are under the investor-owner's control, within limits, and other elements can be manipulated in some degree by the builder-contractor. The investor, the prospective owner-occupant, and the operative home builder can influence costs in the following respects.

Site Selection. Costs can be strongly affected by the physical characteristics of the site. Rugged and uneven terrain may require much dirt moving, terracing, and retaining-wall construction. A hillside site may create difficulties in materials delivery and in moving equipment and machinery. Underlying rock or bog will add to foundation costs.

Design. The architectural design of a structure, its dimensions, and aesthetic qualities are major determinants of cost which are largely controlled by the owner-investor. The architect or designer looks to him to decide upon the general character of the improvement, the size, the functional plan, and the extent to which architectural embellishments are to be employed.

Specifications. The materials and equipment called for in the specifications can vary widely in cost depending on their quality and aesthetic appeal.

In his decisions on site, design, and specifications, the owner-investor balances the virtues of reduced costs against the effect of economies on (1) productivity, and (2) operating costs. He considers the consequence of each cost saving on the prospective consumer—on the level of rents which a furnished apartment building will command, the sale price of a house, or the reactions of taxpayers in the case of public works. He considers the effect on the durability of the improvement and the length of its useful or economic life. He balances savings in original cost against operating economies which would result from installing sturdier but more costly building products.

Timing. Costs vary with changes in general business conditions and particularly with changes in the real estate market. By picking the right

Table XI-4

Builder's Cost Breakdown, 1960
One Story Single-family Brick Veneer Residence
Middle Western Location

Item	Cost	Per cent of total
Permits	$ 20.00	0.10
Excavating	187.00	1.10
Surveying	55.00	0.30
Mason work	2,493.00	14.50
Cement work	1,047.00	6.05
Lumber	1,780.00	10.50
Millwork	1,624.00	9.40
Shingles	137.00	0.70
Carpenter labor	1,757.00	10.21
Heating and tinning	675.00	3.92
Plastering	885.00	5.14
Plumbing	1,490.00	8.60
Painting	870.00	5.14
Insulation	150.00	0.90
Wiring	576.00	3.34
Light fixtures	75.00	0.40
Vanity mirror	40.00	0.24
Medicine cabinet	18.00	0.10
Tile work	321.00	1.86
Linoleum and sink top	256.00	1.50
Shades	87.00	0.50
Floor Sanding	37.00	0.20
Caulking	25.00	0.15
Rough hardware	82.00	0.45
Finish hardware	150.00	0.90
Built-ins	189.00	1.10
Weatherstripping	37.00	0.20
Grading	150.00	0.90
Plans and specs	55.00	0.30
Ornamental iron	73.00	0.40
Overhead	506.00	2.95
Profit and sales	1,364.00	7.95
	$17,211.00 *	100.00

* 1,129 square foot floor space @ $15.25 per square foot. 21,451 cubic feet at $.805 per cubic foot.

time the investor-owner may benefit from a number of cost savings such as the following:

1. When building activity declines land prices for vacant sites tend to fall.

2. With lower rates of construction materials prices soften, and dealers in building products are more liberal in offering discounts.

3. Delays in the delivery of materials are costly and occur most frequently during a building boom. Deliveries are prompt during a slump.

4. Union wage rates strongly resist reduction even when unemployment in the building trades is high; however, nonunion workers often accept reductions, and some union members may surreptitiously take a wage cut.

5. Even a low level of unemployment has the effect of increasing the productivity of workers in the building trades.

6. When construction jobs are scarce, contractors and subcontractors may reduce their usual profit margins, sometimes taking a job at no profit in order to keep their organizations together. In the face of an unfavorable market the contractor sharpens his pencil and "figures close" on his bids. This means, in effect, that he narrows his customary margin of safety in calculating expected costs or reduces the reserve for contingencies which is ordinarily included in his bid figure.

7. When building activity is down and there is an ample supply of building materials and labor, when the efficiency of labor is higher, and when the contractor can give full attention to supervising the few jobs which he has, the over-all construction time may be reduced with consequent savings in interest and taxes during construction and an advance in the time when the enterprise becomes productive.

8. Reduced building means reduced demand for construction loans and for mortgage money in general. Thus interest rates on both the temporary construction advances and the permanent debt might be lower.

9. Following a protracted slack period in construction, a rapid rise in demand will result in a rapid rise in construction costs; costs are likely to go up higher and stay up longer than would be the case for nondurable goods.[8] The explanation for this price behavior is (a) the relatively long time required for reorganizing construction enterprises, training skilled labor, restoring the flow of building products through the channels of distribution, planning and completing new structures, and (b) the pressures on the capacity of the construction industry to expand beyond past levels of normal production.

The elements of cost which are under the control of the contractor or builder are primarily costs which are a reflection of managerial skill and efficiency and the cost represented by the builder's profit. Efficient man-

[8] Colean and Newcomb, op. cit., p. 74.

agement can cut costs and reduce construction time. Some large contractors and builders can purchase materials at more favorable prices than can small operators. The large contractor may operate his own lumber yard and concrete plant. He can afford to hire the best superintendents and engineers and provide the most efficient construction machinery. To offset these advantages the large contractor or builder must carry a large fixed or overhead expense which the small builder avoids.

All contractors may influence construction costs by the margin of profit which they are willing to accept. It was earlier pointed out that this margin varies with the level of construction activity.

Among the cost factors which are beyond the control of either investor or contractor are police-power regulations such as state and local building codes, safety and sanitary codes, and zoning ordinances. The use of costly fireproof materials may be required in certain structures and areas. Safety features such as two stairways or fire escapes will add to costs. Codes may make impractical the use of prefabrication or may prevent the use of new and more economical materials.

In making his entrepreneurial calculations for the prospective investment, the owner-investor requires an estimate of the cost of construction of the proposed improvement. The only certain figure for such purpose is a firm bid from a responsible contractor based on complete plans and specifications. Such a bid would apply only to a limited time period, for changing materials prices, wages, and market conditions could rapidly outdate any figure. The difficulties of estimating costs even for a relatively simple structure such as a dwelling can be demonstrated at almost any bid opening where bids may vary by 20 to 30 per cent. Where it is not practical for the investor to wait for an actual bid he will be well advised to use a liberal figure in his calculations with a careful check to assure that all costs have been included. With few exceptions the investor will find that his actual expenditures for construction exceed the original estimates.

MULTIFAMILY AND COMMERCIAL STRUCTURES

In 1959 about 300,000 rental-type dwelling units were added to the supply at an estimated construction cost of $2¼ billion. The inventory of rental housing accommodations in 1956 was estimated at $72 billion in value and accounted for some 41 per cent of all urban housing accommodations.[9] It has been the history of apartment construction that the peaks of activity have been associated with the availability of liberal credit, and over the past twenty-five years investment in apartment house building

[9] Louis Winnick, *Rental Housing*, McGraw-Hill Book Company, Inc., New York, 1958, p. 84.

has been characterized by a rise in the ratio of debt to equity.[10] During the mid-twenties the apartment boom was financed by mortgage bonds which were issued so generously that many projects were mortgaged out. The bulge in activity in the late thirties reflected the availability of FHA mortgage insurance on loans which, in many cases, were complemented by only nominal equity contributions. The postwar "608" FHA program produced a substantial volume of apartments with an inconsequential volume of real risk capital. The downturn in activity in the early 1950s may have reflected a long-term trend toward homeownership considerably accentuated by the very liberal mortgage terms of the FHA and VA programs which enabled young families to acquire homes at an earlier stage with monthly outlays less than rent. The rise in rental construction in recent years to 22 per cent of all residential construction in 1959 is in part a response to a population age distribution which is shifting to increased proportions in age groups where family formation is most active and where older couples are giving up houses for apartment living. Other factors listed by Winnick suggest that the long-term prospect for rental housing is brightening: [11]

1. Vacancy rates are favorable.
2. Earnings are improving in existing apartments.
3. New equity capital is being tapped through syndicate arrangements.
4. The FHA rental-housing program has been made more attractive.
5. The number of single-person households will increase.
6. A back-to-the-city movement supported by the increase in the number of mature couples and working wives may get under way.

Large apartment buildings and commercial structures are generally built on a bid and contract basis. There are many cases, however, in which the contractor is also the entrepreneur and investor. In such cases a separate corporation is generally chartered to hold title to the real estate. The contractor holds part or all of the stock in the corporation and, of course, is awarded the construction contract. By taking equity stock to cover his profit on the construction work he reduces the amount of his cash equity contribution.

Small apartment buildings and small commercial structures are typically built by small contractors who are also engaged in home building on con- tract. They are local concerns who rarely bid on jobs in other cities. The large apartments, office buildings, and industrial plants attract bids from large general contractors who operate both within and outside of their home community. Some of the firms take jobs only when close enough to their headquarters to permit supervision from the home office. At the other extreme some large concerns will work anywhere in the

[10] *Ibid.*, p. 237.
[11] *Ibid.*, pp. 239–241.

world. These contractors rarely engage in house building except for very large community projects.

PUBLIC WORKS

Included in this category are new public investments in highways, bridges, city halls, fire stations, schools, waterworks, and a wide variety of other types of construction all required for proper operation of the urban mechanism. Such projects are initiated by governmental agencies in response to the demands and needs of the community as interpreted by the representatives of the people. Almost all of such construction is done under contract following closely regulated open bidding.

The assurance that public improvements will be constructed and the timing of such improvements may strongly influence the decisions of private investors because of the effect which such facilities have on the productivity of real estate. In many cases it is difficult to predict the time when public improvements will eventuate. It is well to understand that public, i.e., governmental, decisions involving construction are typically slow to crystallize into action. In many cases the problems of financing the improvements create delays, as when state or Federal aids are to be received or a local referendum on a bond issue is required. Because of the large size of the expenditure which often is involved, the local governing body may be reluctant to proceed and may postpone action until public demand is strong and unequivocal.

In progressive communities, where planning is practiced in government, public works expenditures are budgeted from five to ten years in advance in order that the new facilities may be in place to serve the growing and shifting urban structure. This form of advance planning, or capital budgeting, establishes time priorities among the needed improvements, helps to keep expenditures within the financial capacity of the city, and gives time to arrange for financing.

MODERNIZATION AND REPAIR

The repair, remodeling, and modernization of structures is a large business in the aggregate. In 1958 the dollar volume was estimated at about $4 billion on residences alone and may run as much as 10 per cent of all construction work. Except for major projects on large buildings, this kind of work falls to small contractors or is performed by regular employees of the owner or on force account by craftsmen hired for the particular job. For example, a large office building or apartment structure may maintain a full-time permanent crew of painters and building mechanics who take care of redecorating, maintenance, and repair. For pointing up the masonry the manager may hire a mason on an hourly basis, and for a new roof he will ask for bids from roofing contractors.

Much contract repair and remodeling work is done on a cost-plus basis because the uncertainties of the work make a firm bid hazardous. Contractors are reluctant to bid on some kinds of jobs, particularly remodeling, because of the frequency with which unforeseen costs arise as the work progresses.

Many homeowners have been bilked by unprincipled operators who solicit work through a house-to-house canvass by salesmen; secure contracts for new roofs or siding, for example, by high-pressure tactics and promises of easy financing; and then fail to carry out the contract as understood by the homeowner. In spite of efforts to stamp it out this racket reappears from time to time. Homeowners will be well advised to deal only with responsible firms when contemplating this kind of work.

XII

URBAN DYNAMICS

INTRODUCTION

In the preceding chapters of this book we have presented a progression of related descriptions and concepts forming all but the last segment of a closed circle which is the basic model of urban growth and structure. It is this theory which gives the whole complex pattern of activities in the real estate market a sense of order and purpose and explains the arrangement of urban land uses. This is a dynamic theory, for it is fully consonant with the observed dynamics of the city, the constant and eternal shifting of the urban landscape and the pattern of activities which give it vitality. This is the *investment theory* of city growth and structure which recognizes the economic motivations which have led to the numberless land investment decisions and capital commitments on the part of private individuals and corporate entities without which, in our modern society of free enterprise, no cities would grace the countryside.

But we have not completed the rounding out of this model; and before doing so, it will be well to recapitulate the steps formed by the preceding chapters in leading up to the integrated and complete explanation which we refer to as a theory. We first presented an overview of the urban scene as background for the discussion which was to come. We then explored the origins of real estate productivity and value with recognition that real estate is useful to man by reason of important physical characteristics, but that location, a quality peculiar to real estate, is a primary consideration. We defined the varied and devious legal forms which express interests or ownership in land and which circumscribe its economic benefits; and we learned of the pervasive effects of institutional controls regulating the use and development of urban land. We stood with the individual investor as he sought to predict the future productivity of a given parcel of real estate and as he attempted to quantify his forecast in a dollar figure. We gave recognition to the almost universal joining of equity investment and borrowed capital in the purchase

306

or development of real estate. We studied the mechanism of the real estate market in which the investor must operate and where the forces of demand and supply impinge on each individual transaction. And finally, in the immediately preceding chapter, we became acquainted with the procedures whereby the supply of usable urban real estate is originally produced or physically altered. Broadly speaking, we have presented the social, economic, and institutional environment in which real estate investment decisions are made, and we have described the process by which individuals arrive at specific investment decisions, i.e., the entrepreneurial calculation. We are now ready, in this chapter, to reveal the interactions among individual investment decisions within the framework of the real estate market, for it is these interactions, in the form of competition for individual parcels of real estate, which serve as a selective process in determining how each parcel is to be used. It is this parcel-by-parcel determination and the attendant investment of capital by the successful competitor which creates and molds our cities.

In the first two sections of this chapter we shall discuss this process of land use competition with full recognition that it is not the perfect competition of classical economics, and the land use pattern which emerges is therefore not predictable with exactitude. Despite these reservations, however, we can discern underlying trends, and without an understanding of the nature and effect of land use competition the forecasting of real estate productivity in the urban scene would be without foundation.

The second part of the chapter continues the discussion of urban dynamics from the standpoint of those changes which are taking place in our society which affect the functions of cities and the pattern of urban land uses. There are at work powerful forces of change—demographic, social, economic, political, and technological—which may bend and warp the market structure which we have described, and which may so alter the forces of demand for the services of urban real estate that there will emerge an urban form far different from the product of land use competition within the presently existing framework. We can only suggest some of the changes which are discernible and alert the analyst to the need for a constant sensitivity to any form of change which may have its impact in the real estate market.

COMPETITION OF USES

At the beginning of this book we painted a picture of the urban setting in which real estate investment and real estate use have their habitat. We warned the reader that it would require the rest of the book to explain how the arrangement or pattern of land use in the city was crystallized as the product of the forces of the real estate market. Of course, the market operates within an institutional framework of law, regulation, and governmental intervention which strongly influences each transaction and which we have frequently recognized throughout the foregoing chapters. Furthermore, while the pattern of land uses may be momentarily crystallized at any point in time, the city is actually a constantly changing mosaic of productivity and utilization. It is the ability to predict such change which is the essence of sound real estate decisions.

At the beginning of the chapter on the real estate market (Chapter X) the major functions of the market were listed; among these was the function of land use determination. Earlier chapters had described how the investor evaluated the productivity of the investment and translated his prediction into a value figure representing the worth of the real estate to him. Armed with this value conclusion, he was prepared to enter the market to buy or sell, as the case might be. But in the typical case there are other sellers or other buyers, and it is rare that transactions occur without both parties having first considered alternative opportunities. Thus there is ever-present competition in the market, and that transaction tends to be consummated which gives to each party the maximum returns available under present market conditions; the buyer gets the most property for his money, and the seller gets the most money for his property. Competing buyers quite often have in mind different programs of utilization for the property; in such event, we can say that the market interactions which brought off a transaction have determined the way the land will be used, and the competition was not so much between individual bidders as between alternative uses. For example, if a gasoline distributor outbids a food chain for a strategically located site on the basis of their respective calculations of productivity, we can say that a filling station outbid a supermarket because such a use can better exploit the location.

Now land use determination implies a change in use; and there are two major types of such change:

1. *From No Urban Use to a Productive Urban Use.* Examples are the conversion of agricultural land to urban land through sale and subsequent improvement with a house or factory, or the development of a vacant lot in a built-up area.

2. *Land Use Succession.* This involves a change in the nature of an existing urban use in one of the following ways:

a. Change in the *type* of activity, usually with a new occupant, and possibly accompanied by the replacement of the original improvement with a new structure, or the conversion of the original structure to accommodate the new type of activity.

b. Change in the *intensity* of the use without a change in the type of activity. This usually involves physical change in the structure such as converting big apartments into small ones, or adding a story to a building.

c. Change in the *quality* of the use without a change in the type of activity. Gradual deterioration of a residential area may lead to lower productivity as lower-income groups move in.

It is notable that land use changes can take place without the impetus of a transaction which involves a change in ownership. The owner of vacant land can himself build houses on it; or an apartment owner may remodel his building; or residential property in a blighted area may be allowed by the owners to deteriorate in consonance with environmental forces. But the fact remains that a high, though indeterminate, proportion of land use change follows closely upon a transaction which involves a change in ownership; in commercial property the instigating transaction may be a lease.

It will be well to illustrate and further explain the fundamental principle that all land use change, of whatever nature, involves either direct or indirect competition of alternative uses. Perhaps the best approach is to consider, one at a time, the types of land use change which we identified in the preceding paragraphs. The first type was the change from non-urban use or no use to productive urban utilization. Farm land at the edge of the city is constantly being absorbed into urban use, by far the greatest share for homes through the agency of the subdivider and tract builder. But some of this peripheral land is converted to shopping centers, highways, parks, and factory sites. Real estate developers, public agencies, plant managers, and investors are constantly prospecting for likely locations for their several activities. While some farmers may have no more than one firm bid for their land, there is no doubt but that every farm absorbed into urban use has been considered for many alternative types of development, inspected and studied, and perhaps rejected for most of them. Where more than one use type enters the competition it is because the parcel of land is suitable for more than one use; that use for which it is most suitable is most likely to win the competition by outbidding the others.

Vacant sites in the settled portions of the community are absorbed into use in much the same fashion as the peripheral farm land. Various potential users consider the sites for various potential uses and make their bids accordingly. We recognize that either the owner of the farm or the owner of the vacant lot may develop the land himself without sale to another. But, in effect, he is a bidder in the competition for he rejects the bids of others only when he has determined that the land is worth more for his own development than the offered prices from others.

Consider now the second type of land use change. The most easily recognized form of land use succession is a change in the type of activity occupying a given parcel of urban land, for example, the replacement of a group of old dwellings with a new apartment building. In this case the competition was between the existing dwellings and the proposed apartment, though it is possible that some other potential uses, perhaps a small store building, was also bidding for the land. This type of succession can also occur through the alteration or conversion of the original structure to accommodate a different utilization. During the wartime shortage of office space in Washington, with very little physical change, conveniently located apartment houses were converted to office use. Even where succession takes place without a change in ownership, the alternative uses effectively compete as the owner considers which alternative is to his best financial advantage.

We have pointed out that land use succession may involve a change in the *intensity* of a given use, and finally a change in the *quality* of a given use. Intensity involves a higher density, for example, in the case of residential use, by making two efficiency apartments out of one larger dwelling unit; or, in the case of commercial property, by increasing the ratio of usable floor space to ground area by adding a story on top of an existing building. Such changes as these do not alter the essential nature of the activity, but to some degree, they influence the character of the neighborhood in which they are located. Also, a change in the *quality* of the use does not introduce a new type of activity, but it may contribute to neighborhood transition. The shift in the occupancy of apartments and tenements in a blighted area to families of lower income or to migrants from the rural South is a change in the quality of use which may have significant locational implications. In a retail district the replacement of a women's shoe store by a restaurant will affect the locational values of neighboring retail outlets though it only substitutes one commercial use for another. These changes in the quality of use are as much the product of use competition as any other variety of land use succession. Even in a blighted area, where rents and values are declining, and except for the very lowest grade of housing, there is always competition for a given quality of housing between the income group already there and the next lowest income group.

It is clear that cities grow by a process of irregular accretion at the outer edges, by a filling in of interstitial areas between nodes of growth and by land use succession. The forces of growth, operating through the mechanism of the real estate market, bring new areas into urban use, cause vacant lots to be improved, and stimulate the redevelopment of parcels or larger areas to meet new demands. We have shown in earlier chapters how these growth forces are started in motion by the expanding economic opportunity in the primary or basic activities which support the community. But we must also recognize the fact that a decline in the demand for the services of urban real estate can generate change. In the face of economic distress and declining job opportunities in an area, real estate expansion and development ceases; taverns close, stand vacant, or are converted to another use; the less desirable houses and apartments suffer a high vacancy rate, are boarded up, or are torn down to save on taxes. The central business district shrinks as some merchants fail, and there is a reduction in luxury lines. Thus, market forces moving in either direction, expansion or contraction, will generate land use change.

Land use change breeds land use change. Whatever the causes which lead to land development or to land use succession in any of its several forms, the alteration of the urban landscape which results will, of itself, generate other changes. This principle was explained in the earlier chapter on location (Chapter IV) when we showed how any change in the activities to which a given land use is linked will modify the locational productivity of that site for that use. If the modification is drastic it may alter productivity to a point where some competing land use can displace the existing use. For example, if several old and obsolete structures in a retail area are demolished to make room for a large modern building to be occupied by a department store, the drawing power of the new department store may attract other women's shopping goods outlets and result in replacing an adjacent restaurant with a dress shop.

The competition among land uses which determines the uses to which urban sites are put is basically a matching of alternatives. Presumably, each owner is constantly studying his property with a view to max-imizing his return. Other investors and users are constantly in search for locations for certain activities or are seeking opportunities to acquire sites which are not presently being used to the best advantage in order to exploit them to the full and reap an honest profit. For each site there is a "highest and best" use, which means in appraisal terminology, that utilization which will extract the greatest productivity from the site, i.e., generate the highest economic rent or value. It is a highly significant characteristic of urban land that, for any given site, there are many alternative uses based on considerations of location and the physical nature of the parcel. But in reflection of the unique character of every urban location we shall see certain uses are more appropriate than others on a given site. Thus for each site there is a hierarchy of alternative uses ranked on the basis of the productivity of that site for each use. This hierarchy is said to be based on the rent-paying capacities of the several alternative uses.

Ideally, the over-all result of market competition among land uses and the choice by owners of the best use for their lands among the alterna-tives would be a city in which each site was occupied by that use which was most productive in that location. Why this end result is never realized will be discussed later; but though it is never entirely realized, it is approached. The land use pattern of our cities, with many exceptions, does tend to put each type of activity in its most appropriate spot, *considering the nature and the strength of competing uses*. It may be noted that it is neither a necessary nor a likely accompaniment that each use is in its own most productive spot; some uses will be able to command their own optimum locations, but others will be forced to take lesser spots by reason of competing bids which they cannot match.

IMPERFECT COMPETITION

The foregoing description of urban land use competition has assumed idealized market conditions not attained in real life. The market behavior has been presented, therefore, as representing tendencies and probabilities of varying degree rather than as immutable principles. Perhaps there is no need to remind our now-sophisticated reader of this fact, for after wading through this volume, he has had ample warning that the real estate market is far from the perfect market of the classical economist. In the chapter on the market (Chapter X) we specified some of the more important market imperfections. At this point, it might be well to review this matter with special application to the use competition which we have been discussing. Because of market imperfections and rigidities, and as a result of the impact of public regulation and governmental intervention, the self-regulating mechanism of the market frequently fails to bring off the expected reactions to the various market impulses, market predictability is seriously hampered, the pattern of land use is distorted, and the timing of land development and land use succession is modified and disturbed.

The ignorance and inexperience of many real estate owners and investors results in many serious investment errors. Where an understanding of the economics of real estate is lacking, predictions of productivity are likely to be off the mark, usually on the optimistic side. Such error leads to the wrong use of the land, or the right use, but at the wrong time. Developers subdivide land which is not ripe for urban absorption; owners build commercial buildings on land which should be reserved for an apartment house; and speculators develop shopping centers at locations which would have been revealed as second rate by market analysis. Such misuse of the land is the product of competition in which some or all of the competitors are misled and derive their bids from incompetent analyses of misinformation. Even the most competent of bidders or investors are hampered by lack of dependable and sufficient information. Measures of local market activity and price behavior are rare and unreliable. Our earlier discussion of market indicators revealed the dearth of recorded facts on real estate transactions.

The long life and physical immobility of structural improvements seriously hamper the adjustment of the urban land use structure to changes in demand and to changes in locational factors. An expensive building with many years of useful life remaining will perpetuate the existing use until such time as the value of the land alone, with the building removed, is greater than the value of the original land and building combined. Thus land use succession which involves structural replacement or the extensive remodeling or conversion of buildings is sluggish and delayed. The city responds slowly to changing conditions, and the past errors of investors which resulted in the misuse of land are perpetuated. The use of long-term leases contributes to this structural rigidity.

The free interaction of the locational and market factors which determine land use is further hampered by public intervention of multifarious and devious kinds. We have already made the acquaintance of local police power controls: zoning ordinances which limit the use which may be made of lands in the various zoning districts; building, safety, and sanitary codes which control building design, materials, and equipment and hence affect construction costs to a point which may inhibit or direct the nature of land improvement; subdivision ordinances which influence land planning and affect the costs of land development; the official map which reserves specified areas for future public use. Taxation is an instrumentality which is capable of influencing the use of land and the timing of its development. In some states the classified property tax permits special tax benefits to homeowners and has been used to encourage the improvement of vacant land. Many communities have attempted to lure new industry by the bait of tax exemption; and private urban redevelopment projects, such as Stuyvesant Town in Manhattan, are benefiting from a tax freeze. Another form of public intervention at the local level is the public use of land. By governmental fiat, and without the benefit of market competition, a substantial proportion of every community is dedicated to a wide variety of public uses ranging from streets to golf courses.

Urban renewal is a public device involving local initiative and management and Federal subsidy and control. It is used to generate massive land use succession through the clearing and redevelopment of blighted areas or rehabilitation and modernization of districts which are subject to renewal short of clearance. The land is acquired by the public agency and redeveloped by private investors or for public use in accordance with the master plan for the community. This program will be discussed more in detail later in this chapter. The point here is that land use succession in renewal districts is determined by the sponsoring public agencies, local and Federal, and is not the direct product of real estate market competition. To be sure, in so far as private investors are involved, market forces act as a limiting factor; if the public agencies restrict the land to a reuse for private investment which is not economically sound, no investor will appear, and the land will remain vacant.

It has long been a point of argument among economists as to whether rent is a monopoly return; relevant to this discussion is the question of whether the owners of urban sites enjoy a monopoly because of the unique locational nature of each parcel of land and whether such limitation on competition distorts the process of land use determination. Actually, there are very few land uses which can operate profitably on only one specific site. It is true that there may be an optimum location for each type of activity for which the highest rent would be paid. But a less desirable site at a lower rent might yield almost as much net profit for the business enterprise. Thus, in seeking a business location, the proprietor may consider a number of sites, and no one site can be said to hold a monopoly position. Of course, neither does pure site competition exist, for this condition would imply an unlimited number of potential sites. As a matter of fact, the effect of the degree of locational monopoly on land use determination is of small consequence. Here the competition with which we are concerned is among alternative uses for a given site. For almost any urban site there are many potential users. Even though for a given use the site be unique to the extent of pure monopoly, it will tend to be used by whatever activity which can most successfully exploit the location and thus make the highest bid.

DYNAMICS OF COMPETITION

An underlying thesis of this book has been that the city is an adaptation to the needs of man. It follows that if the needs of man are to change, so will the form of the city; this change may be in extent or area as man's needs expand, or the change may be in the structural arrangement of land utilization. If it were not for the fact that man's needs, demands, and institutions are constantly shifting, we could write "finis" to this book here and now! But our explanation of how cities grow and how land values are determined has been based on an urban society as we find it today, in 1961. To be sure, basic changes will not take place so rapidly as to outdate this explanation for many years to come; but in the application of the principles which we have developed, it is important for the analyst and investor to recognize the important trends which are affecting real estate productivity and value, trends which are discernible now and which will have increasing impact on city growth and structure during the next decade. It would be misleading indeed to assume a static society, for there are continual modifications in technology which affect land values; important shifts in social attitudes and in the urban way of life; significant demographic trends; and frequent adjustments in social, economic, and legal institutions which affect real estate productivity and the operations of the real estate market.

A backward look at conditions a generation or two ago will reveal examples of the kinds of change which we must consider in respect to future applications. The most trite, but perhaps the most significant, example is the coming of virtually universal automobile ownership, a development which has changed the face of our cities and shifted the patterns of land use and land value. The shorter work week and workday now permit more leisure time, have influenced home design and lot size, and have led to the expansion of many recreational land uses. Changes in methods of retail distribution have encouraged outlying shopping centers and have resulted in larger-sized retail outlets. Advances in manufacturing methods have pushed plants into suburban areas in search of space for one-level operations. Such changes as these examples are continuing and may be expected in ever-increasing number and complexity.

The interpretation of the shifting milieu of city growth is an important part of the real estate investment process. The prediction of productivity must be extended well into the future in most cases, and it would be quite unrealistic for the investor to assume a static environment. For example, the income from an apartment building is influenced by the age distribution of the population; if the age distribution in the community is shifting, this is a matter of concern to the investor. Because each parcel of real estate is vulnerable, in varying degree, to the long-run trends of social and technological change, each owner or prospective investor had best analyze their impacts on the property in which he has a present or prospective interest. And the investor or speculator who is looking for a promising opportunity with, perchance, a capital gains potential may be guided to a location or a type of property of promise through his interpretation of coming change and its impact. For example, the investor who discovers that on the basis of the present age distribution of the local population, the number of persons over sixty-five is increasing rapidly may well decide to invest in a residential development designed to meet the needs of retired couples. The real estate broker, the mortgage lender, the home builder and the city planner must all be aware of the basic trends in the real estate market if they are to be realistic in their forecasting and if they are to take advantage of the opportunities for profit and service which are coming around the corner of time.

It will do no harm to repeat the notion that our discussion of trends in the productivity factors of the real estate market is directed to the problem of forecasting the impact of these trends on (1) the demand for space and facilities for the various urban activities and (2) the locational structure of the city. In respect to the locational structure the investor is concerned with the effect of these trends on linkages among urban establishments so that he may forecast the land use succession which may result from the changing quality of such linkages.

DEMOGRAPHIC CHANGE

Demography deals with people; and because people are the active components of cities and the origin of the demand for the services of urban real estate, changes in the size, composition, and location of population have great significance in the analysis of real estate productivity. A great deal has been written about the vast prospective growth in population in this country which will eventuate in 1975 in a total of well over 200 million, an increase of 50 to 60 million in twenty-five years, or over one-third from the level of 1950. Already, in 1961, with a population of about 180 million, we are at the halfway point in this predicted twenty-five-year increase. But a word of caution is in point; population forecasters have been known to be far off in their prognostications. Before World War II various demographers had convincingly predicted that the maximum population of the United States would be 165 million, a level to be reached about the turn of the century, and that thereafter population would tend to decline. An unforeseen war, a baby boom, postwar prosperity, and changing social attitudes toward large families combined to embarrass the experts. The point is that predictions of vast growth which are so widely accepted today as sound and dependable may prove to be far from reality.

In considering growth prospects in urban areas we will discuss three basic aspects: (1) the extent or volume of growth, (2) the location of growth, and (3) the changes in population composition which will accompany growth.

Volume

The upper limit of the range of the United States census projections of population for the year 1975 is 228 million, an increase of 78 million from the 1950 level of 150 million and an increase of 48 million from the 1960 figure of 180 million. If these forecasts are realistic we will add to our population in twenty-five years about the same number of people who inhabited the whole of the United States in 1900. In the next fifteen years we will add as many people as now inhabit the United Kingdom.

Location

Since 1950 all of the population increase in this country has occurred in urban and rural nonfarm areas, and two-thirds of it has occurred in the

168 standard statistical metropolitan areas as designated by the United States census. The rural farm population continued its historic decline during this same period with a loss of 3.3 million, or 13.3 per cent. There is no reason to believe that this pattern of population change will shift in the coming decades. We may therefore expect that all additions to our national population will be in or near cities and that most of it will be in or near the larger urban agglomerations. In 1959 only 22 million people, or 13 per cent of the estimated total population of 174 million, lived on farms.

Another growth characteristic of recent decades that we may expect to continue is the more rapid rate of increase in the suburban areas around central cities than in the central cities themselves. From 1950 to 1959 the central cities in the standard metropolitan areas increased by only 1.5 per cent in population; in the area outside the central cities the increase was 44.3 per cent. Rural nonfarm population rose by 117.1 per cent within these metropolitan districts. Professor Hauser estimates that, out of a total metropolitan area increase of 60 million persons from 1950 to 1975, some 50 million will locate in the growth rings outside of the central cities and that one-half of this increase will occur in the unincorporated suburban areas.[1] This growth characteristic is not to be interpreted as simply a draining of the central cities by the suburbs. Central cities are fully built up, and of necessity, the increasing urban population pressures result in growth at the edge of the settled areas, for only this location can provide the needed space for homes and other added urban facilities. Some central cities have lost population as a result of a reduction in available dwelling units by reason of the process of land use succession.

For many purposes of real estate analysis the increase in the number of households has more significance than population increase. The net change in households is the difference between the number of new families formed by marriage and the number of families dissolved by death or divorce plus the net change in nonfamily households, such as single individuals who occupy separate dwelling units. Thus the age distribution of the population is a factor, for it determines the number of persons of marriageable age and affects the death rate. Immediately following demobilization the annual increase in households was at a peak, some 1.5 million. Between 1950 and 1954 this number dropped to an average of 818,000, reflecting the increase in the number of persons reaching marriageable age which, in turn, reflected the low birth rates of the 1930s. This postwar decline in net increase in households will continue until the early sixties when, bolstered by the products of the postwar baby boom, the corner will be

[1] Philip M. Hauser, *Proceedings of the Thirteenth Annual Conference for Senior Executives in Mortgage Banking,* New York University Business Series, no. 33, 1958, p. 46.

turned; by 1970, the net increase will reach 900,000 or more, and by 1975, about 1 million. It may be expected that the number of households will increase geographically in the same areas where the population is found and somewhat in the same proportion to population increase. Thus the added households, like the added people, will appear in the coming decades entirely in urban areas and largely in the metropolitan complexes. Farm households will decrease.

Population Composition

The increasing proportion of our population which is composed of older folks, 65 years of age and over, is a well-publicized phenomenon. From 1950 to 1959 the increase in this age bracket numbered 3.1 million. During the decade of the sixties this group will increase by another 4.5 million to about 19.5 million persons. The greatest numerical and percentage increases will come in the younger age groups; the number of persons 5 to 19 years of age has grown by about 17 million in 1960, and the people 20 to 24 increased by 12 million. The number of persons who reach the age of 35 each year during this decade will decline steadily until 1970. Thus we are facing a period when the number of young and old people are increasing and the number of persons in the most productive age groups is becoming proportionately smaller.

It is a significant fact that much of the growth of urban areas is accounted for by migration. Between 1940 and 1950 the standard metropolitan areas of the United States increased by 6.3 million persons through net migration, i.e., the difference between in- and out-migration. This figure is 43 per cent of the total growth.[2] A measure of the rate of migration between 1953 and 1956 showed that the South exported people to other parts of the country at the net rate of about 280,000 per year; the Northeast exported about 20,000 per year net. In-migration exceeded out-migration in the West by about 170,000 and in the North Central states by about 126,000. One significant aspect of this migratory flow is the migration of Negroes from the rural South to the urban North and West and to the cities of the South. This movement began during World War I and greatly increased as a result of the demands for manpower in industrial areas during World War II. In 1910 only 27 per cent of all Negroes lived in urban places, but by 1950, in the North and West, 90 per cent lived in cities, and in the South, almost 50 per cent.[3] In summary, during the coming years, we may expect about the same pattern of migratory flow as in the recent past:

1. A general movement from farms and villages to metropolitan areas
2. A small net loss through migration in the Northeast

[2] *Ibid.*, p. 50.
[3] *Ibid.*, p. 50.

3. Substantial net flows to the Southwest, the West, and Florida
4. Moderate net flows to the Middle West
5. Continued migration of rural Negroes to the North and West

The nature of the future demands for the services of urban real estate is a function not only of population size, age distribution, and migratory behavior, but also, to a very important extent, of the level and distribution of family income. The median income of nonfarm families is now about $6,000 and is rising at 2 per cent per year; by 1970 it will reach an estimated $7,000. But more important than the rise in the level of family purchasing power is the marked tendency toward a more even distribution of its benefits. Both the number and proportion of poor people is decreasing, and there is continuing to develop a large middle class of well-to-do families with incomes in the $5,000 to $10,000 range who can command a high standard of living. The number of families with incomes of less than $5,000 per year is expected to be smaller by 1970, and the number with incomes of more than this amount will increase from 25 to 38 million or more. In 1950 incomes of $10,000 or more accounted for only one in eight; by 1970 this proportion may reach one in four. It must be recognized that the upward shift in the income distribution, particularly in the $5,000 to $10,000 range, is in part explained by the large proportion of families with secondary workers—working wives and sons and daughters—whose contribution brings total family receipts into the higher and more comfortable brackets.

A more refined description of urban trends might lead to a discussion of the expenditure patterns of urban families and the changes in such patterns. One fact in this connection seems clear: there is an increasing tendency toward uniformity in expenditure patterns. It is also true that there are shifts which are measurable and which have some significance in their effects on the structure of cities. For example, there has been a shift toward greater expenditures for food as a result of an upgrading of the American diet to include more nutritious meats and vegetables, more processed foods, and more eating out. On the other hand, the share of family income going to clothing has tended to decrease. Since before World War I the proportion of family income spent on housing has steadily declined, though in recent years it has tended to stabilize. Certainly, the general upgrading in incomes has meant that more families have more purchasing power above subsistence needs which is available for recreation, education, and the luxuries of life. And among the middle class, the propensity to save has been institutionalized and weakened by social security, pension plans, unemployment benefits, hospitalization insurance, and a greater sense of economic security nourished by fifteen years of postwar prosperity. But buying habits, expenditure patterns, and attitudes can change, and by such change, they can affect the productivity of real estate facilities which serve the needs of the population and which are therefore vulnerable to changes in consumer demands.

ADVANCING TECHNOLOGY

In this age of rapid scientific and technological advancement there is no predicting what amazing new developments are just around the corner. Within the lifetimes of millions of those now living, there have come into widespread use such inventions and discoveries as the automobile, the telephone, radio, television, the airplane, the helicopter, atomic power, and electronic applications in business and industry which are revolutionary in their impact. Who knows what awaits us in the coming years, and who is to say that the developments to come will not be even more dramatic and disturbing to the present way of life than the discoveries so far revealed in the twentieth century? There are many ways in which advancing technology has affected our cities and the productivity of urban real estate. Perhaps the effect of the automobile is obvious, but its impact is not at an end. At present there are as many cars as families; this ratio is expected to rise until there is one car for every two persons. Without the freedom of movement which universal car ownership provides, our commerce, industry, and residential areas would have remained tied to public transportation routes, and the dispersion of industry and trade into suburban areas would not have been practicable. The motor truck has released many industrial and distributive activities from the railroad and tied it to the much more flexible highway system. As a result of this vastly increased mobility of goods and persons, our cities are growing after a different pattern and may be moving toward a cellular form in which most of the activities which are associated with urban settlements will be found outside the congested central cities. We may look forward to a tendency to mix industrial centers of employment, commercial and service centers, and various types of residential accommodations in the spatially convenient mixtures which are characteristic of European communities.

Developments in air transport have brought many changes to the urban landscape. Fifty years ago there were no airports; today every city and town boasts of one or more. Jet power has led to larger planes, faster landing speeds, and bigger land areas devoted to long runways, though the helicopter is moving people into congested districts without the need for vast open landing fields, and vertical take-off fixed-wing aircraft are on the way. The speed with which businessmen may now travel to all corners of the country is removing one of the reasons for the establishment of branch offices by large corporations and thus decreasing the demand for land for such purposes in many of the smaller metropolitan areas. The automobile, the airplane, and the truck have combined to take away many of the railroad's historic functions and have led to the abandonment of railroad right of way and the closing of terminals and passenger stations. Streetcars have almost disappeared, and what new means of transport may appear is a matter for speculation. The overhead monorail is under trial, and the implications of the experiments with vehicles which float on a cushion of air are exciting but uncertain. It is apparent that any changes in the mode of transport and in its cost may substantially affect the nature of linkages among urban establishments, the utilization of urban land, and the pattern of land values.

Evolutionary developments in the technology of production are of vast import in the changing pattern of urban settlement. The general use of electric power and truck transportation, combined with the fluidity of the labor force through the use of the private car, has imparted great locational flexibility to industry. Plants can be and are extensively being located in suburban and rural locations where the availability of large tracts of open land at low cost allows one-story plant layout and the production efficiencies which flow from such arrangements. Corollary advantages are room for expansion, lower property taxes, and plenty of parking space for employees. With increasing automation of productive processes there is an accompanying increase in capital investment per employee and in productivity per employee. The proportion of unskilled workers is decreasing, and the proportions of semiskilled and skilled workers and technicians is increasing. Accompaniments are higher earnings and shorter working hours. These developments have important real estate implication, with respect both to industrial location and land requirements and to the needs and demands of the employees for the services of urban real estate for consumption purposes.

There are stirring, in this modern world of rapid change, any number of technological evolutions and revolutions which are sure to have marked effect on the pattern of human settlement. The direction and impact in most cases are at present uncertain. Who can say what may be the developments in the peaceful uses of atomic energy which might bring shifts in the location of industry and in the residential pattern; for example, a cheap source of house power in the form of a small residential power pack might make the home completely independent of all public services and utilities so that it might be located with complete freedom at any point in the metropolitan area. Developments in facsimile transmission and other forms of communication combined with fast air transport of executives and with electronic office equipment are changing the land use requirements of many of our large commercial concerns. Certain types of functions can be centralized to a greater degree, branches can be reduced or eliminated and less floor space is needed for clerks, though more is needed for machines. Air conditioning and improvements in artificial lighting have already imparted greater locational flexibility to many kinds of industrial and commercial activities. We are on the verge of an economical method for desalinizing sea water; with unlimited water supplies, new urban areas will spring up in desert spots, and older cities may be affected by their competition.

In Chapter XI we suggested the possibility of a revolution in the construction industry, particularly in home building. Such a revolution would probably involve both new techniques and materials as well as modifications in industrial organization. A drastic improvement in the efficiency of house construction would no doubt have a number of locational implications. It would probably entail more large-scale building operations with a better quality of community and land planning. The need for large tracts of land might contribute to urban dispersion. A substantial reduction in construction costs might result in a compensating increase in expenditures on related amenities such as more mechanical equipment and more enclosed space, yielding larger structures and more land area per structure.

There is no doubt that many another technological change which may remodel urban America is in the offing. The sample which we have presented in the foregoing paragraphs is by way of warning to the real estate analyst and investor that the pace of technological change is advancing, and that there are in prospect many and various shifts in the patterns of real estate productivity as a result of technical advance. The successful investor will be he who can best anticipate and evaluate these transformations.

PATTERNS OF DISTRIBUTION

With an increasing proportion of total employment in retail and service activities have come concomitant changes in patterns of distribution. For a time there was a tendency for the specialized wholesaler to decline in importance and for the traditional wholesaling functions to be absorbed by producer and retailer; this tendency now appears to have been reversed. For some time retail store units have tended to become larger in floor area. Many types of retailing are turning to self-service operations in whole or in part. There is a tendency to carry an increasing number of lines of merchandise. Branded products marketed with the backing of the manufacturer's national advertising are invading new lines and increasing in importance. However, the most publicized development in retailing, the suburban shopping center, represents more of an evolution than a revolution. It is the history of growing cities that an ever-increasing proportion of total retail sales is made outside the central business district.

However, the modern shopping center does represent certain important departures from the older forms of outlying retail facilities:

1. The shopping center is a planned and integrated grouping of retail and service facilities which is designed for the motor age. It is attractive and convenient for the shopper and thus has more pulling power than the older forms of string-street retail developments or the nucleations around transfer corners which grew without central planning and architectural control.

2. Shopping centers have brought a greater offering of shopping goods and specialty goods to the suburbs. While choices are not as great as in the downtown retail district the shopper can supply a wide range of her needs. The spread of branded merchandise has reduced the need for competitive comparison shopping. More service facilities, such as banks, are going to the suburbs.

There may be changes in retailing which are on the horizon with even greater locational implications than the foregoing examples. It has been suggested that television can be adapted to permit shopping by the housewife without leaving her home. Whether or not this method will be acceptable is not so important as the surety that changes in retail selling are inevitable and that they will modify the quantity and quality of the demand for urban land.

INSTITUTIONAL CHANGE

The term "institutional" encompasses a broad range of social, economic, and legal arrangements which are man-made and which have evolved through the centuries as devices to make life more worth living. Marriage and the family are social institutions which we take for granted in modern life but which do not exist in the same form in some parts of the world today and which, down through history, have been subjected to constant modification. Homeownership is in the nature of an institution which is related to the institution of the family and which, together with the family, has much to do with the form and pattern of the modern city. Were homeownership to decline in incidence, the land use structure might be substantially modified if the single-family house were to be supplanted by a different structural form. Our economic system is an institutional construct, and as business relationships are modified and as our industrial organization and financial institutions are adapted to fit the changing times, so may there be new and different forces of demand for urban land.

The framework of law and regulation within which the forces of the real estate market now operate is the product of a long evolution as recounted in Chapter V. As this evolutionary process continues, the framework changes to impose new limitations on the freedom of individual action in the use of land or to remove or alter the older existing limitations in adaptation to man's changing needs and preferences. For example, during the past thirty years, there has been a significant broadening of the powers accorded public agencies to take private land for public purposes. It is through the courts' interpretation of what is a proper public purpose that the power of eminent domain has been extended to the taking of land for public housing and for urban renewal projects. Certainly we may expect new and as yet unforeseen public functions to require the acquisition of land, and we may anticipate that as such activities gain public acceptance as proper public activities, the courts will reflect the changing attitude in their decisions. Somewhat the same kind of evolution is taking place in respect to the police power controls of land use. The courts are according to municipalities an ever-widening control of land through zoning by including more and more aspects of land improvement as properly subject to regulation. Only in recent years have some state courts permitted the control of the architectural features of structures as in the public interest. More extensive and intensive regulation of subdividing and land developing has characterized the postwar years. In some areas land developers are required to donate land for such public uses as parks and schools, and in other cases cash contributions for such purposes at so many dollars per lot are mandatory.

Police power regulation must be supported by effective enforcement if it is to be a real force in determining the nature of land utilization. For example, we have long had sufficient regulations on the books in most cities to outlaw much of the unsafe and insanitary housing which continues to be occupied in slum areas. But lack of effective enforcement machinery and, in too many instances, lack of purposeful enforcement activity by public officials, has permitted these blighted areas to survive and spread. Thus a change in official attitudes and in the actual enforcement of present regulations could change the face of much of our urban area. Another important area of public control is that of transportation and traffic. Traffic regulations have great influence on land values, and to a marked extent, the productivity of much urban real estate is dependent on the manner in which traffic is channeled and regulated and the provisions made for parking. The installation of a one-way street system can destroy land values in some sections and create new values in other affected districts. The influence of local governments and state regulatory bodies on intra-urban public transportation systems can also create or destroy land values.

Some of the effects of legal change are indirect, but nonetheless important, in their impact on land values. For example, a recent amendment to the statute regulating mortgage foreclosure in Wisconsin permits a shortening of the period of redemption and thus accords added security to the mortgagee. The president of an Eastern lending institution stated that he believed this change would make mortgage lending more attractive in Wisconsin and would increase the flow of mortgage money into the state from outside sources. Clearly, an increase in the supply of credit could have a noticeable effect on new real estate development. Somewhat along this same line is the effect of changes which occur from time to time in the regulation of the investment outlets of financial institutions. Statutory changes which have permitted Eastern mutual savings banks to lend in other parts of the country have affected the rate and nature of land development and construction in those areas.

Sufficient attention has been given in this book to governmental intervention in the field of real estate finance so that it need be no more than mentioned in this context. FHA and VA mortgage programs have had a tremendous impact on the growth of urban areas. Changes in these programs, in the liberality of the credit terms, in aspects of the secondary mortgage market, in regulatory policies, and in many other phases of the programs are felt in the rate and pattern of growth in every urban area. Many other forms of Federal aids and controls affect city growth: highway aids, assistance to small business, grants and loans for public works, advance planning and construction, and numberless others. Income tax laws, Federal and state, can influence the flow of funds into various forms of real estate investment. For example, the treatment of depreciation for tax purposes favors investment in income properties; homeownership and thus home construction is encouraged by the allowance of deductions for tax purposes of property taxes and mortgage interest. Changes in tax laws should be watched carefully by the real estate investor to discover what effects there might be on the net returns after taxes from various kinds of property.

The political organization of the community can influence urban development in many ways. In the typical metropolitan area the Balkanization of governmental units results in scattered and unplanned urban expansion, and because many of the minor political subdivisions are hard pressed financially, growth may occur in settlements which may be inadequately served with essential utilities and community facilities. Any move toward rationalizing the political and financial structure of urban regions would bring a sounder and more satisfactory form of urban growth and a higher level of land values.

URBAN RENEWAL

It has been the purpose of this chapter to describe the processes of land use determination through a competition of uses in the real estate market; and to disclose how such processes are affected by the constantly changing milieu in which this competition takes place. We have demonstrated how pervasive is the influence of the public interest in the real estate market, expressed through government in law and regulation; and how the value pattern of urban land is intimately conditioned by the direct public use of land in streets, parks, and sites for all manner of public facilities. We now come to another variant in public intervention in land use in which private investment is facilitated by public action with financial aid as the catalyst with a view to accelerating and directing the processes of land use succession and hastening the adaptation of the urban structure to changing conditions. This program of city rebuilding has been made possible by heavy Federal subsidy with the action initiated by local government and the rebuilding largely the responsibility of private investors. The earlier label "urban redevelopment" has lately been replaced by the more inclusive term "urban renewal."

Earlier in this chapter the process of land use succession was described as a city growth process and as the product of land use competition. Later, the imperfections of the real estate market were outlined in explanation of why succession failed to produce the ideal urban pattern. In addition to the market imperfections discussed there, there are certain special factors which delay and impede the natural processes of land use adaptation in the blighted areas of our cities:

1. There is no encouragement for the individual owner in a blighted district to replace or modernize his structure, for it would then be surrounded by blight and would soon fall back to the level of its surroundings.

2. In many cases, the overcrowding of structures and the lack of adequate maintenance and repair are policies which are highly profitable to owners and which inhibit replacement and modernization. It has been argued that the present treatment of depreciation for income tax purposes encourages exploitation and discourages redevelopment.[4]

3. Slum properties are widely held by persons of small means who would have difficulty in financing replacement or renewal.

In view of all of the obstacles to natural replacement and adaptation the structure of cities has been slow to adjust. Blighted areas have spread and the antisocial conditions which are found there have become matters of great public concern. It has become clear that only wholesale action can effect any substantial amelioration; piecemeal renewal has been ineffective. The only practicable method for assembling tracts of sufficient size for proper planning and control is through the use of public powers which permit the compulsory acquisition by the municipality of neighborhood

---

[4] Arthur D. Sporn, "Some Contributions of the Income Tax Law to the Growth and Prevalence of Slums," *Columbia Law Review*, vol. 59, p. 1026, November, 1959.

tracts of sufficient size to permit clearance and disposal under adequate controls for redevelopment for both public and private purposes.

In the postwar period a number of states passed redevelopment laws, but outside of New York little action resulted. The Federal legislation of 1949, as modified by the 1954 act, has produced substantial though slow results, mainly through the important subsidy device which provides for contribution by the Federal government of two-thirds of the cost of the redevelopment project. This cost is largely measured by the difference between the cost of acquiring the land for clearance and the proceeds from its sale for redevelopment. The law also provides for financial assistance for the rehabilitation and conservation of neighborhoods which can be saved from blight by organized action short of clearance and rebuilding. The program also recognizes that open and partly developed areas can be blighted where their natural development has been arrested by problems of land title and by other factors. It is a basic premise of the program that the renewal of any blighted areas must be in accord with a long-range land use plan for the entire community.

It is most probable that public programs of urban renewal are here to stay and that they will expand rather than contract. It is a politically popular program and will continue to receive large infusions of public funds, mainly Federal. The real estate investor should be aware of the purposes of the program and its potential for accomplishing drastic changes in the urban landscape, particularly in central areas. Urban renewal may succeed in remaking the central city as an attractive place of residence for many households, particularly younger and older families without children of school age. With this impetus the back flow of intraurban migration from suburbs to central city may reach substantial proportions and offer attractive investment opportunities. In fact, urban renewal in general generates opportunity for the alert investor. In the project areas are tracts of land offered to private developers, and it has been the demonstrated experience that lands adjacent to redevelopment projects tend to share in their benefits.

CITY PLANNING

Organized attempts through governmental machinery to control the private development of land is fairly recent in the history of civilization, though city planning as the basis for public works is an ancient art. The difference lies in the manner in which the city plan is effectuated. The monarchs and governments of former times planned monumental public squares flanked by impressive public buildings, or systems of boulevards and highways, either for beautification of the city or for military purposes, and carried out the plans as public works with public funds. Today's city planning involves public works planning, to be sure, but also encompasses the entire community and all the uses of land, public and private; and the development of land in private ownership is dependent upon private investors who act only when profit possibilities are present. It is a corollary that planning, with the controls to effectuate the plan, carries the potential of destroying profit opportunities in land development and thus stifling the development of privately owned areas.

Local planning activities, for better or for worse, are real estate market facts which must be recognized and evaluated by the real estate investor. The efforts of local government to encourage the orderly development of the community through planning and the various activities and controls which aim to effectuate the plans are bound to have a marked effect on the pattern of growth, the arrangement of land uses, the productivity of real estate, and the level of values. Forecasts of the productivity of given parcels of land cannot ignore the public intention with respect to the city's future even though there is no assurance that plans will be realized exactly as laid out nor with the specified timing. The analyst must take into account not only the presently existing land use controls which are an expression of the city plan—zoning, official map, or street plan—but also the plans which involve future public works and future controls over private development which may affect the property under consideration. He will also need a judgment on the probability that the plans will be realized as laid out and an estimate of their most probable timing, particularly when their effectuation is dependent on a major public works program.

Objectives

The objectives of city planning which are to be expressed here stem from our explanation of the growth processes of urban areas and may not be entirely consistent with the pronouncements found in much of planning literature. We start with the premise that the arrangement of community land uses should be the product of social preferences; and that, but for the imperfections of the real estate market, the market interactions of demand and supply would create a city so organized. Thus we view city planning as a device for releasing the basic forces of demand rather than inhibiting them. We see the city planner as the interpreter of the market-expressed preferences of consumers, not as a mystic who knows better than the consumer what is good for him.

In general, sound city planning and sound real estate investment are consistent and not in conflict. The tract builder who locates his development on a site which provides optimum satisfactions for his buyers will make the highest profits in the long run. The city planner who realistically analyzes consumer preferences will approve the location as consistent with the public interest. Any alternative use of the same site should be tested in terms of the effect of such use on the aggregate of community consumer satisfactions. A land use pattern for the city which maximizes this aggregate of satisfactions also maximizes land values and investors' returns. The only objective test of consumer satisfactions is the economic test, i.e., what consumers will pay for locational returns. This line of reasoning is not inconsistent with the argument of city planners who contend that the consumer is not competent to interpret locational factors and thus to know what is good for himself. This is a matter of degree, for certainly, even the planner is not all-wise. But it is a proper function of the planner to educate the consumer and to reveal to him considerations and possibilities with which he may not be familiar. It is not the function of the planner, however, to decide for the consumer what he wants.

Sound city planning, which is based upon consumer preferences, with its attendant land use controls, can do much to release basic market forces and to create an urban structure which comes closer to a market-determined pattern than in the absence of planning. There can be controls over the owner who would exploit his property for quick gain at the expense of his neighbors; or over the speculator who feeds on uncertainty and may take advantage of the ignorance of others to exploit his own special knowledge. Planning controls can prevent the misuse of land through the ignorance and poor judgment of the owner. The existence of a long-range plan, though it be short of a guaranteed future prospect, greatly reduces the uncertainties of things to come and permits predictions of productivity for real estate which encourage sound investment and development. Thus by abating the imperfections of the real estate market, intelligent city planning, based on an evaluation of market-expressed consumer preferences, can serve to release the underlying forces of demand and to adjust more closely the supply and arrangement of urban real estate facilities to the desires of the people who live and work in the community and to the needs of the business operations which provide the economic lifeblood.

Process

City planning involves planning both in space and in time. As a derivative it involves planning in dollars for the public expenditures which will be required in carrying out the plan. Land use planning usually finds expression in a master plan which, to be of greatest value, should cover the entire metropolitan area which comprises the natural social and economic organism of the community. This plan is a generalized outline of the major land use areas of the present and future based on predictions which may run ten to twenty-five years into the future. The locations of all manner of public facilities—schools, parks, streets and highways, bridges, sewage disposal plants—are indicated. The land use districts—commercial, industrial, residential of various classes, recreational, and public—are mapped. This generalized plan serves as a guide for all public agencies in programs which involve the use of land. It is also the basis of land use zoning and the official map. Estimates of the timing of urban growth in the several segments of the community provide a basis for a scheduling of future public works and this, in turn, permits the development of a capital budget which is a schedule of future requirements for funds for public capital expenditures. As a practical matter the timing of the public works is likely to be controlled by the limitations of fund raising, even though the capital budget is a more or less exact reflection of needs for public facilities to meet an expected growth schedule. The master plan is never complete; as the dynamic forces of city growth impinge upon the community the plan must be continually revised to meet the changing conditions.

Limitations

Planning is an imperfect instrument with which to carry out community objectives. All things considered, the results are better than in the case of unplanned uncontrolled urban development; but when thought is given to the many and serious limitations of the planning process it is the inevitable conclusion that planning is neither a cure-all nor an adequate preventive for urban ills. In the first instance, the quality of city planning leaves much to be desired. There are too few people well trained in this highly complex process and too many persons in responsible planning positions who lack an understanding of basic city growth principles and who give major weight to engineering considerations or to aesthetic values or who view urban design as an esoteric art incapable of understanding save by the elect. Poor planning results not only from this kind of misunderstanding and lack of broad training in the social science of urbanism, but also from the lack of sufficient collected and analyzed facts as a basis for the plan. Planning information is hard and expensive to come by, but some planners attempt to proceed without having expended the requisite time and money for basic fact collection. Unfortunately, there are political influences which invade the planning process at various points and warp the plan out of venal considerations.

If the city plan is to aid in the attainment of community objectives and to express consumer preferences, there must be constant communication with community groups and individual consumers. Too often the planning is done in a vacuum or with expressions of community opinion ignored. This deficiency is to some extent curable, but one major limitation to long-range planning will never be completely overcome, namely, the rapid and unpredictable change in the social, economic, political, and technological milieu of the city. The perfect plan of today may be totally obsolete tomorrow. Another limitation which is being gradually overcome is the limited and artificial planning area which has characterized most planning activities. Cities may too often limit the planning area to their own political boundaries when the natural urban organism extends well beyond these limits and encompasses a broad metropolitan area including many suburban towns, villages, and unincorporated areas. This defect is widely recognized, and there are many successful examples of planning activities which cover broad urban regions and counties. However, there remains in many cases the continuing limitation that, while the planning efforts may be well coordinated throughout the metropolitan district, the effectuation of the plan remains the responsibility of the individual political subdivisions which may or may not carry out the letter and intent of the over-all plan.

Finally, it may be said of urban planning that the instruments of effectuation are crude and imperfect. For example, area land use zoning is usually limited to broad classes of land use when more refined specifications may be required. And since the development of private lands depends on the initiative of investors, zoning of itself is no assurance that such land will be brought into use in synchronization with related urban development and in an orderly manner; in fact, zoning is no assurance that the land will be developed at all. The difficulties and delays in financing major public improvements is another type of limitation; urban growth in a logical direction may depend on a new and costly bridge, but if the bridge cannot be financed, the master plan is a futile thing. Finally, plans and planning instruments are subject to change, but such changes are often slow and may lag far behind the needs of the community.

The foregoing account of the limitations of city planning is not to be interpreted as a thorough indictment, for the benefits of planning are many and obvious. The vast increase in serious urban problems has stimulated a wide interest in city planning and a greatly increased activity in planning. More and more communities are adding planners and planning staffs; more universities are undertaking the training of planners; more funds are available from city, state, and Federal sources for planning functions; and, we trust, more and better city planning will flow from these expanded facilities. Because we live in a dynamic society, the need for planning will never terminate.

INDEX

Dykstra, Gerald O., 86
Dykstra, Lillian G., 86
Dynamics of land use competition, 314
　advancing technology, 320
　demographic change, 316
　institutional change, 323
　patterns of distribution, 322

Easement, 90
Economic background, mortgage risk
　analysis, 176
Economic base, 25, 247
　demographic factors, 250
　diversification, 250
　family income, 252
　mortgage risk analysis, 176
　prediction of productivity, 248
　quality of growth, 249
　rate of growth, 248
　stability, 249
Economic organization of cities, 25
Effective gross revenue in productivity
　analysis, 108
Ely, Richard T., 82, 84
Eminent domain, 101
Entirety, tenancy by estate of, 89
Entry and possession, mortgage remedies,
　149
Equitable mortgage, 146
Equity of redemption, mortgage, 147
Equity capital, 143
Equity investment, 104
Establishment, definition, 64
　linked, classification, 67
　packet of functions, 65
Estate, in severalty, 89
　for years, leasehold estate of, 88
Estates in land, community property, 88
　conventional life, 87
　co-ownership, 89
　curtesy, 87
　dower, 87
　executory interest, 90
　in expectancy, 89
　fee simple, 87
　freehold, 86
　future interests, 89
　homestead, 88
　joint tenancy, 89
　leasehold, 87, 88
　legal life, 87
　in possession, 89
　qualified fee simple, 87
　remainder, 90
　reversion, 90
　tenancy, in common, 89
　　by entirety, 89

Escrow, agent, 241
　agreement, 100
Exclusive agency, 237
Exclusive right to sell, 237
Executory interest, estate of, 90
Expectancy, estates in, 89

Family income, economic base, 252
Fannie Mae, 179
Favorable exposure, 69
Federal Home Loan Bank (FHLB) Board
　(see FHLB System)
Federal Housing Administration (see
　FHA)
Federal National Mortgage Association
　(FNMA), 179, 180, 183
Federal Savings and Loan Insurance Cor-
　poration, 154
Fee-simple estates, 87
FHA, advantages, to borrowers, 162
　to lending institutions, 162
　disadvantages to lending institutions,
　　162
　maximum interest rate, 162
　mortgage insurance premium, 162
　mutual mortgage insurance, 161
　origins, 160
　Section 207, rental housing, 163
　Section 213, cooperative housing, 163
　Sections 220 and 221, urban renewal, 163
　Section 231, housing for elderly, 163
　Title I, modernization and repair, 163
　Title VII, yield insurance, 163
FHLB System, 154, 178, 180, 183
Financial capacity of owner, 116
Financial management, costs, 117
Financial risk analysis, 115
Financing, construction, 169
　home, 166
　income property, 169
Financing patterns, 116, 166
Fisher, Ernest M., 46, 55, 254
Fisher, Robert M., 46, 55
Fixtures, 85
Foreclosure, deficiency judgment, 149
　by judicial sale, 148
　strict, 149
Freehold estates, 86
Friction, costs of, 65, 68
　of space, 68
Functional efficiency, structure, 56
　(See also Structure)
Functionalism, urban, 18
Future interests, estates, 89

Government survey, land description,
　47